£17.50

REGIONAL POLICY
A EUROPEAN APPROACH

This book is one of a series of Studies in Spatial Analysis stimulated by the theoretical and applied research conducted within the Netherlands Economic Institute, Rotterdam published by Saxon House. Titles in the series are:

J.H.P. Paelinck and P. Nijkamp, *Operational Theory and Method in Regional Economics*
L.H. Klaassen, J.H.P. Paelinck and Sj. Wagenaar, *Spatial Systems*
J.H.P. Paelinck and L.H. Klaassen, *Spatial Econometrics*
Willem Molle, *Regional Disparity and Economic Development in the European Community*
N. Vanhove and L.H. Klaassen, *Regional Policy: A European Approach*

To Liesbeth and Annemarie

The nuns weren't alone in their wish
to help the distressed.

Bruce Marshall,
Vespers in Vienna

Regional Policy

A European Approach

NORBERT VANHOVE
College of Europe, Bruges

LEO H. KLAASSEN
*Netherlands Economic Institute,
Rotterdam*

SAXON HOUSE

058100

© Norbert Vanhove and Leo H. Klaassen 1980

Published by
Saxon House, Teakfield Limited,
Westmead, Farnborough, Hants., England

Printed in Great Britain by
Biddles Ltd., Guildford, Surrey

British Library Cataloguing in Publication Data

Vanhove, Norbert
    Regional policy — (Studies in spatial analysis)
    1. Regional planning — European Economic
    Community countries
    2. European Economic Community countries —
    Economic policy
    I. Title   II. Klaassen, Leo Hendrik
    III. Series
    338.91'4   HC241.2

    ISBN 0-566-00286-8

HT
391
.V36
1980

Contents

Foreword

Scanning the field of regional and urban economics — especially in its policy aspects — more often than not one comes up against a series of non pre-tested assertions about how to solve some partial problem.

The fundamental reason for that state of affairs is a serious misunderstanding of how economic and social phenomena project on geographical space. The temptation is great to stick to the map-drawer's view, and to try and discover in some problem region the causal factors that are supposed to explain the unsatisfactory state of affairs observed there. The result has been a depressing mess, both in regional analysis and in practical policy.

The volume we have pleasure in presenting is the antithesis of this easy-going approach; it integrates in a rigorous fashion spatial analysis and policy issues, adding moreover the special humanistic flavour of the European way of life. As the reader proceeds, he encounters such unexpected topics as Lösch equilibria, potential formulas, and migrational equations, not to speak of attraction models, relevant regions, and urban dynamics.

The very synthesis of it all is presented when it comes to European policy issues. We will not go into the details of the issues presented, but simply linger with an equation taken from the FLEUR-model:

$$\underline{q} = A\underline{d} + B\underline{s} + C\underline{l} + D\underline{g} + E\underline{p} + \underline{f}$$

which explains *multiregional multisectoral* growth as a function of multiregional demand and supply factors, $\underline{d}$ and $\underline{s}$ (the attraction idea, a brilliant analytical device due to the second author), labour markets and migration, $\underline{l}$, the urban structure and physical planning of the system of regions, $\underline{g}$, the measures of economic policy, $\underline{p}$ (on the measurement of the efficiency of which the first author is a renowned expert), and a series of more or less random factors, $\underline{f}$. The testing of equations like the one presented here is being done by expert econometricians of the Netherlands Economic Institute, having conceived of and developed the idea of *spatial econometrics* to implement such models as the above. It is the mighty synthesis of spatial economics and social analysis, measurement of relevant variables, careful specification of model forms, and adequate estimation and testing of their equations.

As such, the present book is bound to become a classic, not only for the interested student of an entirely new field of economic and social analysis, but also for the decision maker who, faced with urgent problems, wishes to familiarise himself with the fundamentals of what he has to decide about. *Timeo hominem unius libri*: this will be said all the more of *that* man who has worked through and mastered *this* book.

J.H.P. Paelinck

June 1979

Preface

Since the Second World War much more attention than before has been paid to the element 'space' in economic theory. Originally, economists became interested in space as they grew conscious of disparities between regions, and a regional economic policy began to develop. Only in a second phase was that policy in turn inspired by the theory of regional development.

Numerous books, reports, papers, and articles have been published on the subject during the last three decades. Meanwhile regional economics, in a wide sense, has become a vested branch of economic science, and figures on the programme of the economic faculties of several universities.

Although the Treaty of Rome does not contain any special chapter 'Regional Economic Policy', the idea has not been completely ignored in the EEC. Since 1958 regional economic policy on the Community level has taken shape, its relations with other common policies being gradually better understood. The College of Europe at Bruges was among the first to respond to the new scientific evolution by introducing, in the late 1960s, the subject of 'Regional Economic Policy, into the programme of the 'Economics Dominante', entrusting the course to the first author. The syllabus that was elaborated for the course, and revised every year, grew into an impressive pile of documents, forming a synthesis of regional economic theory and regional economic policy.

As far as we know, not a single book has so far attempted such a synthesis for all the EEC countries or the Community as a whole; that was what inspired the first author to prepare a volume on regional economic policy in the EEC. Cooperation with the second author enlarged the original concept, and the result is the present volume, intended as a handbook on regional policy.

With the publication of this book, a long-cherished dream of both authors has come true.

In the first chapter a review of the background and motivation of regional policies pursued on the national level is given. They aim at diminishing regional disparities within countries. In chapter 2, these disparities as well as those appearing on the level of the EEC are analysed in an attempt to make the reader understand how regions and nations within the EEC differ in their economic development. The same matter is treated in a much wider setting, and relevant basic data are presented, in Molle, W.T.M., Van Holst, B., and Smith, H., *Regional*

Disparity and Economic Development in the European Community, Farnborough 1979, a book that will be brought out by the same publisher as the present volume and from which, indeed, many data included in this chapter have been borrowed. Some analytical approaches to the explanation of regional differences make up the rest of the chapter.

From chapter 2 it will have become clear that the size of disparities depends on the regional division chosen; disparities tend to increase as the regional division becomes finer. In chapter 3 some theoretical concepts regarding regional division are presented. It becomes apparent that every kind of analysis requires its own regional division, the ideal regional division being the one that enables a researcher to make up the regions that suit his purpose best.

Chapters 4 and 5, treating the micro and macro aspects of, respectively, the location of firms, and of urban developments and the costs related to urban growth, are of an analytical nature. Theoretical concepts and models are presented as well as results of quantitative research in both fields, fields that are essential to proper regional planning. The growth pole concept is the element that binds the two chapters together. A point that emerges clearly from them is that regions (including urban areas) develop, not in isolation, but as a system of closely interrelated elements. In chapter 4 the theoretical framework of an interregional attraction model is drawn up; in chapter 5 an analysis of urban growth and urban decline in several European countries is given.

Chapter 6, on the Regional Impact of the Integration Process, marks a first attempt at analysing how integration has affected developments in the nations and regions belonging to the EEC. The explicit regional policy of the EEC does not yet enter the picture in this chapter, but it is tried to assess how the decision of some countries gradually to integrate their economies has affected the regions within these countries.

The Objectives and Strategies of Regional Economic Policy in the individual EEC countries are treated in chapter 7; the instruments used are presented and discussed in chapter 8 and their effectiveness in certain countries measured by various kinds of analysis.

In chapter 9, on Mobility and Migration Policy, the major links of that policy with regional policy are discussed, and various studies of migration introduced. In the light of the results of these studies, the links between regional policy and migration policy in France, Great Britain, the Netherlands and Sweden are reviewed.

Finally, in chapter 10 we arrive at the discussion of the regional economic policy pursued on the level of the Community. This chapter is of a descriptive nature, explaining the general philosophy behind EEC regional policy and mentioning the agencies involved and the funds made available for the purpose.

Chapter 11 bears the title: A New Basis for Regional Policy on the Community Level; it contains a plea for the use of analytical tools — in particular the FLEUR approach — as well as new instruments to promote a uniform, balanced, regional policy in the EEC as a whole.

We are indebted to Rector J. Lukaszewski, Professor R. Regul, former director, Professor G. Denton, director, and Professor J.P. Abraham, colleague at the College of Europe for their confidence in us, and for the opportunity they gave us to develop the course and their stimulus to publish. We thank also Prof. Dr. O. Vanneste, director-general of the Regional Development Authority of West-Flanders for interesting discussions on regional matters and the facilities provided.

We owe thanks to Professor J. van Ginderachter and Dr. P. Wäldchen, both of the Directorate General for Regional Policy of the Commission of the European Communities, for the documentation they provided, and for their stimulating comments and critical remarks on some chapters; of course, none of them are responsible for the arguments and opinions expressed in this book. We also thank Mr W.T.M. Molle of the Netherlands Economic Institute for the basic material he made available to us for the second chapter.

We wish to express our warm gratitude to Mrs A.C.A. Elderson and Mr J. Cooper for polishing the English with much care, and to Mrs S. Kleyngeld and Mrs F. Pille, who typed drafts and revisions as well as the final version with commendable patience and skill. Mr F. Tack assisted us by drawing a large number of maps and graphs.

N. Vanhove and L.H. Klaassen

February 1979

1 The background and motivation of regional economic policy at a national level

Introduction

Interest in regional problems is not very old. Before the world economic crisis of the 1930s it was believed that the geographical distribution of economic development was determined by natural circumstances and that it was vain to try and change that distribution. From the theoretical viewpoint regional disequilibrium was thought to be only a temporary problem in a general automatic system of economic equilibrium. All this led P. Samuelson to write: 'Spatial problems have been so neglected in economic theory that the field is of interest for its own sake'.

The basic assumptions of the neoclassical theory were: (a) free competition, (b) full employment of factors of production, and (c) full mobility of labour and capital.[1]

Let us start with an economy where three sorts of individuals exist: workers, suppliers of capital, and entrepreneurs. The objective of the entrepreneurs is to combine labour and capital in such a way that the total profits of the firm are maximised. This implicitly means that the entrepreneurs' demand for labour and capital has to be defined not only in terms of total quantity but also in terms of the region or regions in which the entrepreneur will exert his demand.[2]

In general he will be inclined to shift to regions where his chances of getting the maximum profit are highest. Assuming for the moment that differences in production costs determine differences in profits, we may start from the simplified assumption that the location of demand for labour and capital, which means the location of industries, is regulated by the level of total costs, composed of wages, the remuneration of capital, and the cost of raw materials and semi-finished products.[3]

Let us start from an equilibrium situation — which, in fact, never obtains — in which all regional incomes are equal and there is no unemployment in any region. In other words the assumption of the classical theory is fulfilled. Now suppose that some exogenous factor changes, for instance that foreign demand for products produced in region A increases. As a result the demand for labour and capital increases too, the remuneration of both factors of production increases,

1

and labour and capital flow from other regions to region A. The flow
will continue until a new equilibrium is reached. This equilibrium will
be at a higher level of income. In this new situation there is again no
reason for anybody, worker or supplier of capital, to shift his actual
supply from one region to another; neither is there any incentive for
the entrepreneur to change the regional distribution of his demand for
the factors of production. If such a mechanism worked in the real
world, there would be no reason to worry about regional problems: the
equilibrium would be restored automatically.

Causes of regional disequilibrium

Several factors are responsible for regional inequalities in a country or
in a group of countries such as the European Community. In this
section we shall mention many of them, but it is our intention to pay
particular attention to a number of phenomena which have been more
or less neglected or insufficiently acknowledged. We shall start with
two factors which are directly related to the classical theory outlined in
the first section.

Relatively low mobility of labour

In the classical theory a very important rigidity was neglected: workers
do not react immediately to differences in wages. Their reaction is slow
and lags behind demand. Many factors are at work here. It is therefore
not unlikely that a situation might arise in which, to take up the foregoing example, as a result of the increased foreign demand for products
in region A the demand for labour there increases more rapidly than the
working population, even including migration to region A. The
response of workers elsewhere is too slow for the necessary additional
labour to come available in good time. Wages will then rise more in
region A than in other regions and regional differences in income will
result. The discrepancy between industrial and agricultural regions can
often be explained from such developments. Because income
elasticity is much higher for industrial than for agricultural products,
the demand for workers in industry also tends to increase faster than
that in agriculture. The reasoning can be extended to the comparison
of industrial sectors or to the unequal income elasticity of demand for
industrial products and services. In combination with the relative
immobility of labour these differences in demand may cause substantial
and permanent differences in regional income.

In many economic textbooks the production factor capital is considered to be very mobile. If this were the case in the real world one could expect that as soon as the wage difference between region A and other regions is such that production outside region A can take place at lower costs than inside region A, entrepreneurs would immediately shift their demand for labour and capital to other regions where the price of production factors is lower. But, as in the case of labour, there is in fact a strong rigidity in the reaction of capital to differences in production costs; moreover, the mobility of capital (of the demand for capital by entrepreneurs) is relatively low.

The low mobility of capital can be illustrated with the following example.[4] Let us suppose an investment rate (investment to GNP) of 25 per cent, which is rather high. Let us further assume an average depreciation rate of the capital stock equal to 5 per cent, which is reinvested in the economy, and a gross capital coefficient of 3. On these three assumptions we find the following:

1   About 60 per cent of annual investment is reinvestment. Indeed, if the reinvestments amount to 5 per cent of the total capital stock annually, with a gross capital coefficient of 3.0, about 15 per cent of the GNP would be needed for replacement. This replacement of private and public investment is normally realised on the spot, only a minor portion being allocated to other regions.

2   It would be too optimistic to believe that the other 40 per cent of the annual investment is available for investments in problem regions. A large part of the net investment will be realised in the strong regions (for example to improve public transport) or utilised for the extension of existing firms. In other words, only a small percentage of the total national investment can be used for regional-policy purposes.

3   The mobility of capital and the amount of capital available for allocation to problem regions are in turn functions of the rate of expansion of the national economy. This leads to the thesis that a regional policy can only be successful in a period of rather high growth rates.

One general conclusion can be drawn from this and the previous section. The relatively low mobility of labour (i.e. the weak response of workers to changes in the regional distribution of demand for labour) and the low mobility of capital are two important causes of regional differences in income and employment.

In this context a few remarks must be made. In the first place it must not be inferred that the factor labour is completely immobile. The millions of Italians working in the EEC countries and Switzerland are proving the contrary. Nevertheless mobility is insufficient, and what is true on an international level is also true within each country.

Secondly, inflation and unemployment go hand in hand as a result of insufficient mobility of labour and capital. The demand for labour exceeds supply in the expanding regions, causing inflationary pressures there, and the supply of labour exceeds demand in the less expanding areas, causing unemployment in these regions.

Thirdly, it should be stressed that a high growth rate does not only lead to a higher mobility of capital but also to a lower average rate of unemployment. In such a situation, profit expectations in the different regions are determined not only by the level of costs, wages, and prices per region, but also by the availability of labour as such. The mobility of capital is then influenced by the availability of workers in a given region. That factor has played an important role in the decentralisation of industry in the Netherlands.[5] Availability of labour was also considered by Flemish entrepreneurs to be the most important factor in the choice of a new location at the end of the 1960s and the beginning of the 1970s.[6]

Fourthly, a number of factors counteract the classical theory and the market mechanism. In other words, not all the conditions for free competition are fulfilled. Two examples can be mentioned. The first is the institutional obstacle of trade barriers (tariffs and quotas) as existed between the two world wars. Another example is the creation of certain transport facilities; we refer to the radial railway networks in Belgium and in France, and the cheap railway tickets for workers in Belgium. It is also evident that national wage bargaining by sector imposes rigidities between regions that do not exist between nations.

Fifthly, the fast development of the tertiary sector and its high level of concentration pose a real danger of increasing disparities. Indeed, the income elasticity of demand for the services procured by the tertiary sector (financial, insurance, legal, and advertising services, universities, tour operators) is in many cases quite high.

The geographical factors

The most common explanation of regional disparities lies, of course, in the geographical situation in the broad sense. We think first of all of the geographical isolation of certain regions in respect of the economic centre of the country. It is not surprising that practically all the peripheral regions of EEC countries were problem regions in the 1950s, most of them still are. Another geographical factor is the poor natural endowment that certain regions have for economic development; mountainous areas and regions with a poor soil come under that heading.

On the other hand certain regions have been or are now able to benefit from an underground rich in coal, iron ore, crude oil, natural gas, or other raw materials.

The economic structure

In the foregoing points we have already implicitly referred to the economic structure of regions. Every region has a typical economic structure as far as the sectoral composition of its economy is concerned. The fact that certain regions are economically oriented to stagnating or declining sectors leads to grave employment problems. Other regions have the good fortune to have an economy based on growing sectors such as machine construction, chemicals, electronics, banking, etc.; in normal circumstances demand for labour in these regions increases fairly rapidly. However, in many European countries a number of regions owed their prosperity to their specialisation in a few industries, such as coal, iron and steel, shipbuilding, traditional branches of textiles (cotton spinning, linen, etc.). Owing to their one-sided economy and lack of ability to adjust to changing circumstances, many of these erstwhile prosperous regions are now depressed. A fall in the demand for the products of these regions together with a rise in regional demand for imports from abroad and from other regions (a lot of services are concentrated in a few strong regions of a country) causes these regions to run into employment and balance-of-payments problems. [7]

Is it possible to forecast which areas are likely to become depressed by examining regional economic structure? To a certain extent it is. But economic life is dynamic. Sectors that were prosperous in the past are stagnating today. The same will undoubtedly happen in the future to the growing sectors of today. To have an idea which regions are potentially depressed or likely to have more general problems, an index of structural growth potential can be calculated for each region. The starting point is a breakdown of the employment per sector and the potential employment growth rate per sector on a national or even international level, say the level of the EEC. The index of structural growth potential of region j (I_s^j) is calculated with the following formula:

$$I_s^j = \frac{\sum\limits_{i=1}^{n} g_i^{EEC} p_i^j}{\sum\limits_{i=1}^{n} g_i^{EEC} p_i^n} \cdot 100$$

in which

I_s^j : index of structural growth potential;

g_i^{EEC} : growth rate of employment (income) of sector i in the EEC;

p_i^j : share of sector i in the employment (income) in region j;

p_i^n : share of sector i in the employment (income) on the national (possibly European) level.

An index higher than 100 indicates that the growth potential of region j is better than that of the nation as a whole; an index lower than 100 is an indication that the sectorial structure will not, *ceteris paribus,* favour future employment or income.

Two remarks must be made. Firstly, it is advisable to set up the analysis with a fairly large number of detailed sectors. A sector such as textiles or metals is too heterogeneous and using it in such an analysis may lead to wrong conclusions. Secondly, the calculation of the structural index makes sense only if it is limited to expected growth rates over a maximum of ten years.

Other primary factors

Many other primary factors, about which we cannot enter into detail, are responsible for regional disequilibria.

Institutional factors may influence job opportunities or income generation per region. The centralisation of governmental institutions in France is a wellknown example. The centralising influence of French institutions is partially responsible for 'Paris et le désert français'. [8]

Political decisions may have regional consequences. The best known examples are the unification of Italy with its impact on Southern Italy, and, though the result of a political decision on the international level, the division of Germany into the Federal Republic of Germany and the GDR. This division made an abrupt end to the traditional trade relationships of the eastern regions of the FRG with the western regions of the GDR.

In certain cases we must pay attention to psychological factors such as attachment to traditions. This was clearly stressed by J. Milhau: 'It is in people and their work the real obstacles to the economic development of a region should be looked for'.[9]

Secondary factors

Besides the above mentioned primary factors, a number of secondary factors contribute to unequal regional development. They are called secondary not because they are less important than the first group but for the simple reason that they result from primary factors, or accelerate the process of regional growth or decline.

The most wellknown secondary factors are external economies. They can take many forms, and can be divided into three major groups: (a) technical external economies, (b) infrastructural external economies, and (c) pecuniary external economies. Once a region is developing owing to one or more factors, external economies are created. The region of Paris possesses an excellent communication and transport system, contact with government agencies is easy, the labour market large and labour well qualified, the number of supplying firms is large etc. All these external economies have a tremendous impact on the location of new firms. Certain regions benefit from external economies absent in other regions and the gap between regions is often considerable; the point will become clearer when we deal with the theory of growth poles.

The demographic situation is also frequently a cause of income disparities, a point that will be developed in the next section, where we refer to the backwash effects defined by G. Myrdal. Here we limit ourselves to two considerations. The first is the lack of education of the rural masses, which is not incorporated in the idea of backwash effects. The example mentioned by N. Hansen is more an illustration of a primary than a secondary factor. He partially attributes it to the education factor that migration from agriculture in relatively well-off areas, such as the Parisian region and the North-East of France, has been greater than that in areas such as Brittanny and Limousin, where real living standards are relatively low. In the middle of the nineteenth century the illiteracy rate in the North-East was 11.6 per cent against 62.9 per cent in Brittanny and 68.3 per cent in Limousin. Hansen concludes: 'Thus regions with poor education facilities were in a sense forced back on themselves at a time when the structures of agriculture in other regions were being altered by mass outmigration'.[10]

A high relative natural increase of the labour supply due to high fertility rates creates a deficit in the employment balance precisely in those regions whose economic structure does not generate a rapid increase in job opportunities.[11]

Cost and price rigidities are another secondary factor. E.V. Morgan raised the question: 'Why do regions stay depressed?' His answer is: 'There are also important rigidities that impede the normal ways in which a market economy adjusts to changes in supply and demand'.[12] Morgan takes the example of South Wales, which suffered a severe decline in the demand for one of its major products, coal. The decline in the demand for coal should have led to a fall in its price, but did not. Price reductions were limited by the rigidity of costs or checked by monopolistic arrangements among producers. The excess supply of labour in the mining district did not lead to a fall in the price of coal either. The relative position on the pay scale is an important element in union bargaining. In making comparisons, the Welsh miners take into account the earnings of British motor industry workers, but not those of German miners. Nevertheless, the fall in the demand for coal in South Wales has a negative impact on the spending power of the local population. A reduction in the demand for domestic products and for imports from outside cannot be avoided. What happens between countries should also happen between regions: the prices in the deficit regions should fall in relation to prices elsewhere. Prices of final-product markets can be adjusted only if there is a response in the factor markets. But there are a number of constraints in price flexibility between regions that do not operate between nations. E.V. Morgan gives a few examples. Multiplant organisations charge a uniform price throughout the country regardless of where the product is made. For the plants which produce components for products assembled outside the region, only a 'transfer price' is involved. The relative fall in factor costs in the afflicted region that seems likely after a general fall in demand for goods does not come about because the relative wages are rigid. The prevalence of national bargaining imposes rigidities between regions that do not exist between nations. That brings us to the point of rigidities in relative wages not between one sector and another but between one region and another. Morgan illustrates his thesis with the results of the October 1972 earnings' survey of the Department of Employment. He compares the average hourly earnings of adult male manual workers of the North, the North-West, Wales, and Scotland with the national average, taking into account eight industries that are widely distributed within the regions and outside them. In ten out of the thirty-two cases (4 regions and 8 industries) the regional earnings are higher than the national average; of the remaining twenty-two there are only seven where the level is more than 5 per cent below the average and only four where it is more than 10 per cent below. G.C. Cameron shares Morgan's ideas:

With regard to labour the major constraint is the broad degree of regional uniformity of wages for given skills achieved by nationally organized trade unions. Thus, regardless of differences in productivity, cost of living, or demand and supply conditions, wage rates within the lagging regions tend to follow the pattern set by bargains made in national negotiations or in the core regions. This effectively restrains the outflow of labour from the lagging regions and removes an obvious inducement which could attract large flows of capital to such regions.[13]

But even in the case of inter-regional differences in earnings, we are not sure about the reaction of firms to the resulting cost differences. The demand for components is a function of the demand for the end product. A reduction in the cost of a component may have only a minor influence on the final price. And when a firm has plants in two different regions producing the same product, the production capacity must be taken into account.

We are aware that not all factors that could be responsible for regional disparities have been mentioned. Our purpose is to stress the main factors and to introduce a way of thinking. The classification itself, with the distinction between primary and secondary factors, can be modified or extended. In the next section we shall examine an extension of the secondary factors in dealing with the backwash and spread effects identified by G. Myrdal.

Backwash and spread effects

Backwash effects are the detrimental effects suffered by poor regions as a result of their interaction with rich regions; spread effects are the beneficial effects enjoyed in poor regions of the same. G. Myrdal applied that notion to the relationship between nations as well.

Backwash effects

The main idea G. Myrdal wants to convey is that the play of market forces normally tends to increase rather than decrease the inequalities between regions.

Economic expansion in one region may have a negative influence on the neighbouring regions in different ways. Movements of labour, capital, goods, and services do not by themselves counteract the national tendency to regional inequality. Migration, capital movements, and trade are the media through which a cumulative process evolves upwards in the lucky regions and downwards in the unlucky ones.[14]

If region A is expanding very fast it can be expected to attract labour from other parts of the country, in the first place from its neighbouring regions. This does not counteract our statement in the preceding section. From a purely economic viewpoint such labour mobility is to be deplored; in a regional context there may be certain negative effects for the region with outmigration, at any rate if the movement of labour is considerable. Indeed, migration is always selective; for who are the people who will migrate to region A? In general terms the migrants can be said to have the following characteristics: they belong to the most dynamic groups, viz. the age groups between 20 and 35 years (with their children), and the skilled are relatively more represented than the unskilled. The consequences for the regions of outmigration may be severe; they lose the most talented and vigorous sections of their labour force, the persons with initiative and capacity for entrepreneurship. In the long run, and under certain conditions, the age distribution might, moreover, become unfavourable. A number of agricultural and depressed regions in Europe have by this influence of migration come in a situation of discrepancy between the working population and the regional resources.

A second backwash effect concerns capital movements. In strong regions investment is very important and savings tend to lag behind. In the problem areas we are confronted with the opposite situation. When there are no extensions of existing firms or new projects to invest in, savings will exceed the demand for capital. G. Myrdal states that studies in many countries have shown how the banking system tends to become an instrument for siphoning off savings from the poorer regions to the richer and more progressive ones where returns on capital are high and secure.

E.V. Morgan sees the capital exports of some problem regions in the United Kingdom as one of the major causes of regional disequilibria. The effect of the centralisation of the capital market in London is very important. That is illustrated by the developments of three sections of the capital market: banks, life insurance and pension funds and the stock exchange. E.V. Morgan's conclusion is not optimistic:

> . . . a lending region, like a lending country, must have a surplus on its current account payments in order to finance its lending. If outside demand for a region's exports is weak, while internal demand for imports is strong, how can a surplus be generated? The generation of a surplus is essentially the same as the curing of a deficit and the same conclusions follow. If it cannot be done either by cost and price adjustments or by exchange devaluation, there will be a depressing effect on demand that is likely to inhibit growth and accentuate unemployment.[15]

A third backwash effect is concerned with trade; it will be analysed in depth in the chapter dealing with the impact of integration on the regions. A few general remarks will be sufficient here. Widening of the markets will often give a competitive advantage to the industries of the core regions, which usually work with increasing returns, and firms in the problem regions may have difficulties. A historical example of this backwash effect is the domination of Northern Italy over Southern Italy after the unification of that country.

In the context of backwash effects G. Myrdal blames economic theory for disregarding so-called non-economic factors. We believe that this is unfair. The non-economic factors he is referring to are in fact partially economic (e.g. road systems), or are incorporated in the notion of external economies (medical care, schools). It is true that the populations of the traditional poor regions are, on an average, believers in the more primitive variants of religion and in less rational thinking. They are less susceptible than their rich neighbours to the experimental and ambitious aspirations of a developing society. But is all this not a consequence rather than a cause of poverty?

The spread effects

The above mentioned backwash effects do not cover all the economic relations between developed and less developed regions, nor do we claim completeness for the spread effects to be treated now.

The economic development in a core region is not without positive impact on its less developed neighbour regions. G. Myrdal identified three spread effects. In the first place there are the increasing outlets for agricultural products, referred to in Von Thünen's Theory. We must not forget, however, that the income elasticity for agricultural products is rather low. A second spread effect may have more impact: the regions in the neighbourhood of a core region will be stimulated to technical change. There is, according to G. Myrdal, a third type of centrifugal effects spread to localities further away, where conditions are favourable for the production of raw materials for the growing industries in the centres. We doubt that these effects need be given much emphasis in present day Western Europe. Rather should we pay attention to a new kind of spread effects which have been manifest in the past decade and will go on in the next. During the 1960s industry shifted to regions in the neighbourhood of strong ones which benefited from external economies and where labour was still available. Awareness of the social cost of concentrating economic activity in the big centres of Europe may in the near future have an impact on the location of new plants and tertiary activities. We will come back to this point when we discuss the issues, the objectives, and the instruments of regional economic policy. Firms in prosperous regions may also be forced to look elsewhere for space, supplies of unpolluted water, or harbour facilities.

In the past backwash effects have in most cases been much stronger than spread effects, and that will probably remain so in the future.

International trade theory applied to regions

G. McCrone was not the first to compare inter-regional and international trade. B. Ohlin did it before him, but McCrone has in any case the merit of paying particular attention in discussing regional disparities to inter-regional patterns.[16] Indeed the inter-regional development can be analysed by applying the theory of international trade to regions.[17]

The basic assumption of this theory is that regions will specialise in the products and services to which they are best suited by the principle of comparative advantages. The same as for nations, there are two fundamental conditions. The first is that the remuneration of production factors must reflect inter-regional differences in productivity level. The second is that the prices of the regional products, when translated into the (fictitious) currencies of other regions, should enable each region to sell the product in which it has a comparative advantage. Even between nations the fulfilment of these conditions does not guarantee a trade balance; the demand and supply elasticities of the exports have to be considered as well, and it is there that underdeveloped countries face a real problem.

If the principle of comparative advantage cannot always bring equilibrium to nations trading with each other, the problems are even greater in inter-regional trade. The basic conditions mentioned above are never fulfilled. Exchange rate adjustments between regions of the same country are impossible. Furthermore, the prices and the earnings of the production factors in each region do not reflect the different levels of productivity. The rigidity of the price and cost level was underlined in the preceding section; the regional differences in demand elasticity for exports and supply elasticity of exports give also reason for concern.

B. Ohlin assumed a much greater factor mobility between regions than between nations. With complete factor mobility we are back at the neoclassical theory mentioned in the introduction to this chapter. Equality of factor earnings between the regions would be the result.[18] Under the assumption of complete mobility of production factors, international trade is no longer based on the principles of comparative

12

advantage but on those of absolute advantage. If trade is based on absolute advantages and one region is less efficient than all other regions for all kinds of production, that region will be unable to sell at competitive prices to the others. The result is a concentration of its earnings. Thanks to factor mobility there is in the long run no unemployment and no income disparity.

The assumption of complete factor mobility is of course unrealistic. Labour is not perfectly mobile and neither is capital. Unemployment must therefore be taken into consideration and income disparities may persist. We agree that in most EEC countries national collective bargaining and social resistance to regional differences in wages for identical jobs, prevent wide disparities in income levels. Agriculture and self-employed activities may be exceptions to this general rule.

This brings G. McCrone to a fundamental conclusion:

> As a result regions neither have the advantage of factor immobility, which enables nations to trade on the basis of comparative advantage, nor do they enjoy complete factor mobility, which would make persistent unemployment impossible. It is therefore possible for a region to find that there is no product it can produce which other regions cannot produce more efficiently. Moreover, there is nothing to prevent a region from remaining in an adverse balance of payments relationship with the rest of the country for an indefinite period of time . . . an adverse balance of payments has a depressing effect on an economy in the same way as an excess of savings over investment, and will tend through the multiplier to produce regional depression and unemployment . . . Once a region gets into this position, the situation may well become self-perpetuating. [19]

The region not being attractive for investment, it will tend to enjoy less technical progress and benefit less from economies of scale than other regions. The vicious circle tends to persist and will only be broken by the application of a regional economic policy. Spread effects and autonomous factors are in many cases insufficient to reverse the contraction process in backward regions.

Two other conclusions of G. McCrone are also fundamental. Firstly, the fact that the principle of comparative advantage does not apply regionally makes it more likely that development concentrates in some regions while other regions are confronted with stagnation and unemployment. Secondly, the vicious circle — success breeds success and failure breeds failure — will accentuate any disparity which appears.

In the context of this theory G. McCrone has raised another very important question. In view of the disadvantages of inter-regional trade for certain regions, does it follow that some of the problem regions would fare better as sovereign states? According to G. McCrone in such a case a lower standard of living is likely but not inevitable. The lesson he suggests is to be learnt from his analysis for state intervention and regional policy in particular is important:

> If the processes of inter-regional trade produce some depressed regions where redevelopment is considered as an important objective of policy, this might be achieved by trying to emulate some of the policies which independent States would pursue in the same circumstances. Devaluation is, of course, out of the question, so is a drop in general real wage levels, but the purpose of these measures is to reduce home production costs so that import demand is reduced and exports increased. These effects may also be achieved by fiscal and budgetary means. Differential regional taxes or subsidies may be raised as a quasi-devaluation to stimulate production and at the same time restore something of the comparative advantage principle to inter-regional trade.[20]

Besides the classical doctrine of comparative costs which stems from Ricardo, the so-called Heckscher-Ohlin Theorem can be applied to regions. A country (region) tends to specialise in the production of and to export commodities using in their production large amounts of production factors in relatively abundant supply in that country (region), and to import from abroad commodities using in their production large amounts of factors in relatively scarce supply at home. The Heckscher-Ohlin theory of comparative advantage depends upon different production factor endowments among countries (regions) and different factor intensities of production processes for different goods.

J.R. Moroney and J.M. Walker have applied the Heckscher-Ohlin theorem to regional manufacturing in the United States.[21] [22] They distinguished two regions, South and non-South, a framework they thought preferable to most tests conducted with international data on the grounds, among others, that the production coefficients are fixed and identical in the two trading areas, and that it avoids the problem that international trade is obstructed by tariffs. They assume that the theory of trade depending on imperfect factor mobility among nations is equally applicable to regions in the United States because productive factors have never been fully mobile among regions. If full factor mobility among regions prevailed, factor price equalisation would result.

According to the theory, the South will specialise in the production of goods requiring relatively much labour because such goods can be produced at lower money cost in the South than in the non-South. The hypothesis implies that industries with a relatively low capital-labour ratio are concentrated more heavily in the South than industries with a relatively high capital-labour ratio.

Moroney and Walker first tested the null hypothesis that there is no correlation between relative regional factor endowments and regional location of manufacturing in the southern and non-southern regions of the United States. The model tested was limited to two factors of production, labour and material capital. Their second test concerned regional factor endowments and relative regional growth of manufacturing. The idea is that those industries in which the South has the greater comparative advantage should be developing relatively more rapidly in that region. The basic data for the test were the location quotients in 1949 and 1957 and the capital-labour ratios per industry (1957). The Kendall's ranking correlation coefficient was not convincing for the first test.[23] The reason is that a number of the most capital intensive industries (e.g. petroleum and coal) are highly concentrated in the South, and they are, of course, not attracted by the traditional factor endowments labour and capital, but by the availability of natural resources. Their second test — is there an inverse rank ordering between capital-labour ratios and percentage changes in location quotients? — is more convincing for the theory. For the period 1949—57 there was some evidence that the South tended to attract more strongly the relatively labour-intensive industries. The rank correlation coefficient $r = -0.322$ is significantly different from zero at $p \leqslant 0.06$.

V.R. Fuchs came to the same conclusion for the period 1929—54: the South attracted comparatively low-wage industries in which the wage bill was a significant part of value-added.[24] The test of J.R. Moroney and J.M. Walker, they agree in the final conclusions of their study, is largely influenced by the fact that the analysis is limited to two factors, while natural resources (including climate) represent an important determinant of comparative advantage. Their conclusion is 'Once the basic structure of comparative advantage is determined in view of climate and availability of natural resources, as well as in view of capital and labour endowments, a corollary of the Heckscher-Ohlin Theorem seems to be supported'.[25] This conclusion is not without significance for the economic integration process in the EEC. From the very beginning it was expected that the creation of a customs union and later an economic union would lead to specialisation among the regions. This would bring about a decrease in the disparities in the EEC. Climate, natural resources, labour and capital are indeed somewhat unequally distributed among European regions.

A few remarks should be made about the application of international trade theory to regions.

The first is that there seems to be contradiction between the two international trade theories. The one based on the classical doctrine of comparative costs cannot be applied to regions and makes it more likely that economic development will tend to concentrate in a few regions. But free moving labour and capital between the regions of a nation should in principle lead to the equalisation of factor prices. The Heckscher-Ohlin Theorem suggests a certain specialisation between regions. The essential difference between the theorems is in their assumptions about factor mobility.

The second remark concerns the Heckscher-Ohlin Theorem. Even within the EEC some basic assumptions are not fulfilled: transportation costs are not equal to zero, production functions are not identical in the different regions, there are economies and diseconomies of scale, and competition is not perfect.

G. Myrdal criticises the neoclassical theory of international trade. He does not believe that static general equilibrium analysis can explain what happens when barriers to interaction between regions with different incomes are removed. Such a removal will start a development process and the effect will probably be that the rich regions will become richer while the poor become poorer. Here we refer to the idea of backwash and spread effects.

International trade theorists were of the opinion that within the Common Market backwash effects (especially those due to the removal of barriers to trade) could be avoided by removing the barriers gradually during a long transition period.

A final remark concerns a comparison made by E. Olsen between the approach of an international trade theorist and that of a regional scientist.[26] Although the regional scientist can accept the conclusion that strong forces are at work to narrow down income differences, E. Olsen maintains that there are three important differences in approach: (a) regional science analysis is much more detailed than analysis using international trade theory (for example, it takes into account differences in activity rates, different skills in the labour force and, consequently, differences in stock of human capital); (b) the regional scientist has more tools than the international trade theorist and may therefore carry his analysis further (e.g. the economies of production make it possible for producers in metropolitan areas to pay labour a higher wage, which can compensate for the agglomeration diseconomies in consumption; rich regions spend more on research and development and this may widen regional income differences); (c) the international trade theorist usually excludes non-economic factors from his analysis: the regional scientist does not and considers for instance also non-economic barriers.

For our purpose E. Olsen's conclusion is important:

> The conclusion of the regional scientist seems to be that the establishment of a Common Market does not by itself lead to a

narrowing down of the differences in per capita incomes between the member countries. The forces working for a widening of the differences may be even stronger than the forces working for an equalisation of factor prices.[27]

Economic motives for regional economic policy

Regional economic policy implies a differential treatment of the economic regions of a country in order to realise its objectives. Advantages are provided to the problem regions while, possibly, disadvantages or physical controls are imposed on others. Such a policy needs justification. Nationally, the motives for a regional economic policy can be seen on four levels. Beside the purely economic arguments, we distinguish social, political, and environmental factors. The economic motives are usually considered the most important ones and are rather many in number. Their relative importance varies, however, from country to country; they are a function of local circumstances. The order in which the factors are mentioned below has, therefore, no significance.

The full utilisation of all factors of production

Problem areas are confronted with high unemployment rates. Spare resources mean a reduction of the gross national production of the country. In assessing the size of the labour reserve, not only the number of registered unemployed persons but also the number of underemployed people (working on a low level of productivity in agriculture, construction, or trade) and of potential female workers (reflected in the low activity rate of the female population) should be taken into account.

In the early 1950s many economists were in favour of moving the worker to the work. Later on an opposite strategy was defended: to move the work to the workers. More migration of unemployed persons to the core regions would indeed not solve the problem; increased mobility has its limitations. For one thing, migration becomes important when the level of unemployment in a region is already very high, well above the national rate. In that case, migration will not activate the two other components of the labour reserve. It is very difficult to increase low female activity rates through increased labour mobility. When the husband is employed in a region, there may be many non-economic factors which keep him from moving. The chances that an underemployed person from a low productivity occupation will move are also limited. Social linkages to the region are strong and very often the people involved are not aware of their low productivity.

For another thing, even if mobility could effectively reduce the labour reserve in the problem areas, there are still a number of disadvantages associated with migration. In the section 'Backwash and spread effects' of this chapter we have seen that it is the most enterprising, the most skilled, and the most employable people who tend to migrate. Their departure only makes it more difficult to employ the remainder. Furthermore the local market of goods becomes depressed. We agree that the negative multiplier effects of outmigration in the population losing regions have probably been overstressed. In this context A.J. Brown makes a distinction between primary and secondary effects.

> Changes in migration also carry some immediate effects through the income multiplier. These will be the least in conditions of generally slack demand when movements not directly affect employment. Unemployed outgoers obviously do not do so, while employed outgoers bequeath their jobs, in effect, to local unemployed. Incomers either stay unemployed or, more probably, get jobs that would otherwise have gone to local people. In the conditions the primary effect of migration is simply that the number of unemployed is reduced by the number of migrants in the region of origin, increased equally in that of destination. There are no primary effects on production in either region. There are, however, secondary effects, because some expenditure of unemployed people (financed by unemployment benefit, supplementary benefit and savings) is transferred with the migrants. At a guess the average expenditure of an unemployed person might be equal to something between 40 and 60 per cent of the average marginal net product of an employee in employment, and round about 40 per cent of such expenditure might go directly into factor incomes in the person's region of residence. With the help of the further operation of the regional income multiplier, the direct or indirect transfer of one unemployed person between regions might therefore mean the transfer of demand for local factors including the equivalent of anything between (say) 18 to 30 per cent of an average job. In other words a hundred occupied persons moving in these conditions of slack demand, might carry between eighteen and thirty jobs with them.[28]

It is also often argued that the migrants are going to congested centres and are increasing the unwanted externalities and congestion costs. Although that is true, it would be incorrect to state that outmigration is always towards congested areas. The British population analysis given by G.C. Cameron sustains this.[29] Movement to intermediate areas should indeed not be disapproved. It can be a solution for the problem areas and a good instrument in a real decentralisation policy; it is strongly defended in many contributions of N. Hansen.

According to L. Needleman, attracting industry to the areas where labour is available may be a good investment with a high rate of return not only in the form of growth but of increased government revenue. [30] He compares the costs and the benefits for the government. The cost item comprises the non-returnable costs per additional job. On the benefit side we have: (a) a reduction in expenditure since less unemployment relief and national assistance has to be paid; (b) an increase in revenue due to the national insurance contributions and taxes paid by the newly employed workers (additional indirect taxes included). Employment, once created, lasts for several years. The gain to the exchequer is therefore the present value of the benefits discounted for the time that the employment lasts. For the year 1965 Needleman estimated a net gain to the exchequer of almost £900 per workless man employed for £340 non-returnable cost. The approach is not, of course, a real cost-benefit approach;[31] an important cost item, viz. the infrastructure costs, is neglected. Nevertheless it is indicative.

Before dealing with the second economic argument in favour of regional economic policy, we should make three remarks. The first is that the above reasoning must be seen in a situation where full employment can be realised. A few years ago that was taken for granted; at this moment many economists are doubtful. The changed position in the labour market reduces the validity of the argument. The second remark relates to the factors of production. The whole argument has been restricted so far to the factor labour. The same argumentation is of course valid for the factor land. There are countries where the natural factor (soil, climate, etc.) is not fully exploited. It is also often argued that outmigration results in the underutilisation of social capital in the problem regions. This brings us to a third remark. We have to be very careful when we speak about underutilisation of social capital, for two reasons. The first is the actual situation of the social capital (schools, roads, housing, etc.). Very often this capital is depreciated or out of date. The second is that during the 1950s and the 1960s there were not so many economic regions with an absolute decrease of population. In that respect, the situation has changed and will change again in the future. We agree, however, that the stagnation of the population is coupled with a change in the population structure; this may lead to the underutilisation of certain forms of social capital (e.g. school infrastructure).

The economic growth argument

Although the relationship between the utilisation of production factors and economic growth is very close — the same is true for other arguments — we have another idea in mind. Even in a situation of full employment regional economic policy is a necessity. Every region has its own economic structure. Taken into account that certain sectors will always be stagnating, each country will at any time be confronted with depressed areas or potentially underdeveloped regions. The take-off of many developing countries and the further internationalisation of trade will only aggravate the situation. This implies that each country must be prepared for a continuous reallocation of productive factors.

Furthermore, the underdevelopment of certain regions in a country means a limitation of the market possibilities of the stronger regions. The theory of the regional multiplier proves this thesis. Nor must we forget that the core regions are obliged to assume fiscal obligations on behalf of the underdeveloped regions.

Optimum location of the firm

A location that is optimum from an entrepreneur's micro-economic point of view does not necessarily coincide with the location that is optimum from a macro-economic or socio-economic point of view. It is often said that entrepreneurs are the best judges of a location, and indeed they are in a good position. They have studied the project and they have a financial responsibility. Nevertheless there are also many cases where a number of location factors are wrongly evaluated or where there exist prejudices. In that connection G. McCrone has underlined the danger of the purely micro-economic approach. 'Business, it is held, will naturally choose the location where it will operate most effectively and, if this is upset, efficiency will be lost. This view ignores the interdependent nature of business decisions and the existence of externalities.'[32] Indeed not all locational advantages are directly translated into monetary terms. They can take different forms such as the presence of suppliers and of maintenance firms, the availability of sufficient and qualified labour, the presence of a socio-economic infrastructure.

But there are also cost items which are not translated into monetary terms or, in any case, not charged to private firms. An individual firm incurs two kinds of costs: private economic costs, which figure in the private cost calculation, and socio-economic costs, which result from the location and are paid by the community.

The consequences of the external cost advantages and cost disadvantages are twofold: (a) even if from a strictly private point of view region A may be less attractive as a location than region B, priority may be given to region A because region B offers no external economies; (b) as we stated above, the optimum micro-economic choice is not necessarily also the optimum macro location. It is that consideration that offers a weighty argument for shifting certain projects to or away from certain regions and/or for making certain regions more attractive.

A compromise between public requirements and the needs of firms is called for; governments should control to a degree the distribution of economic activity.

To conclude this section, it should be pointed out that business prejudices and lack of information often influence location choices. Concerning the less developed regions we agree with G.C. Cameron when he states in the context of Great Britain:

> ... every major surplus region is urbanized, industrialized and accessible to every region, has a labour force of broadly equal productivity (after training) for any given skill and is open to the flow of general technological information ... Accordingly, since the heart of the regional problem is how to adjust out-dated industrial structures, each problem region possesses the necessary attributed to make this reconstruction possible and successful. This means that over the long run the bulk of British manufacturing capacity can operate just as profitably within the labour-surplus regions as in the core regions.[33]

The cost of congestion

The cost of congestion argument is of course closely related to the optimum location argument. The high congestion costs in certain regions are increasingly considered an important argument in favour of an efficient regional economic policy. In many countries it is recognised that concentration of economic activities in a few areas brings about very high congestion costs *per capita*. Control of location or measures in favour of decentralisation in many European countries (e.g. Great Britain, the Netherlands, France, Italy) are indicative in that respect.

The costs *per capita* in a town or rather an agglomeration are not independent of the number of inhabitants. Initially the costs *per capita* decrease with size, but above a certain level they increase progressively. The reason is aptly expressed by G. McCrone:

> This problem arises because those who have to decide on the location of economic activity do so in the light only of those private costs which fall on them as entrepreneurs; it is not their

business to consider all the costs which may fall on the community as a result of their decisions. These comprise not simply the social costs, such as lack of amenity and air pollution which were referred to earlier; they also include the public investment required in housing, schools and transport facilities for an increased population.[34]

In that connection we call the high infrastructure costs in the big agglomerations and the high investment costs and socio-economic costs caused by the daily flows of commuters. The socio-economic costs of commuting consist in the opportunity costs of the travelling time in terms of potential production or free time.

One author has illustrated the development of congestion costs in a graph;[35] his argument runs as follows. The areas that are developed now, normally show very high population densities. They comprise agglomerations and population increases there exceed those in the smaller nuclei. (We admit that this is not always true and that it sometimes stops being true.) The larger agglomerations show a tendency to get bigger and bigger with all the attending disadvantages and, in fact, very few advantages, and there is reason to stop or at least to slow down the growth of these large agglomerations in favour of smaller ones in the intermediate regions or in the less developed areas.

The whole argument could also be treated differently, and run as follows. A growing city profits from many economies of large scale production which are non-existent in the smaller cities and towns. That holds not only for the economy but also for culture and education; there too, services can be produced because of the large demand exerted by the population of the city and its immediate surroundings. Such large scale production of services and goods will generally lead to a high nominal total urban income *per capita,* and it will be higher as the city is larger (see Graph 1.1).

However, as growth proceeds, the rate of increase in income is likely to fall. The additional advantages still gained are relatively small compared to those acquired on a lower level of population. Still, the nominal income *per capita* will go on to grow even when the agglomeration becomes very large.

On the other hand, the operating costs of the community increase, too, in particular the costs of transportation for the producer, and also for the worker, who finds his journey to work getting longer, not only in distance, but, proportionally even more, in time. Congestion in the central area leads to very expensive road construction. If we call these costs the operating costs of a city, there clearly must be a point where the difference between total income *per capita* and operating costs, that is the disposable income, is at a maximum. It is the point at which the

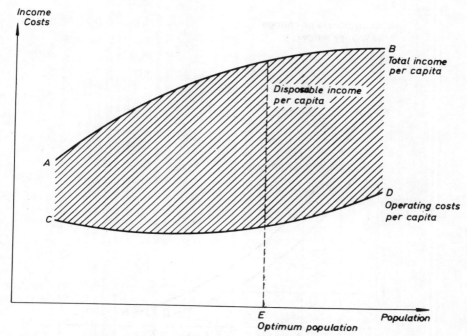

Graph 1.1 Income and costs as a function of population size of an
            agglomeration

city reaches its optimum size (point E in the graph). From this point
onwards disposable income per head will shrink, (although nominal
income will still be increasing), because operating costs grow more than
nominal income.

It is, of course, out of the question to demolish parts of London or
Paris. But cities should be built with the financial consequences in
mind: to make the contribution of all cities together to the total
national income as large as possible, the population should be spread
over the existing nuclei such as to ensure equal marginal disposable
incomes in all nuclei. Now each nucleus has its own geographical and
economic characteristics leading to specific total cost and operating
cost functions. If left alone, by the criteria stated above, cities with
low operating costs and high income levels will tend to grow larger than
cities with a reverse pattern. But the argument developed above makes
it clear that governments should not indiscriminately support migration
from less developed to developed areas; in fact, they should not allow
cities to grow beyond their 'optimum size'.

In chapter 5 of this study more attention is paid to the problem of
urban development. The regional policy of any country, and, of course,

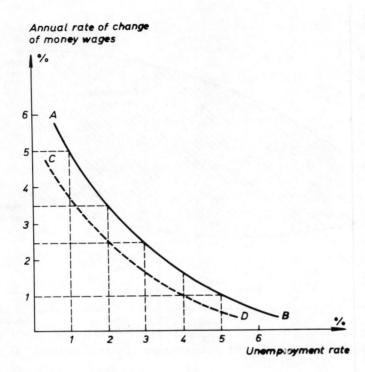

Annual rate of change
of money wages

Graph 1.2 Phillips curves

of the European Community, cannot be developed without taking heed
of new findings on that score.

Regional disequilibria and inflation

A very important economic argument in favour of a regional economic
policy is the relationship that may exist between regional disequilibria
and inflation rates. British authors (e.g. L. Needleman, G. McCrone, R.
Thomas and P. Storey, A.J. Brown, P. Sadler, B. Archer and Ch. Owen)
were the first to draw attention to this relationship. [36]
    The relation between changes of money wages and unemployment
was first analysed by A.W. Phillips. [37] The corresponding diagram is
known as the Phillips curve; it is based on hypothetical figures.
    At an unemployment level of 1 per cent, wages will increase by 5 per
cent per annum. If GNP increases by only 3.5 per cent per annum, the
excess of the wage increases over the growth rate will constitute an
inflationary pressure. An unemployment rate of 2 per cent is associated
with a change in money wages of 3.5 per cent. If the economy grows at

24

the same rate as the money wages, the increased output is matched by increased income and there should be no change in prices. The relationship depends, however, on the distribution of economic activity in comparison with that of labour. When the demand for goods increases in regions where the employment balance is in equilibrium or where there is a labour shortage, the pressure on the wage level will be very great, and a rise in wages can be expected. The overall level of unemployment in the country will not change unless there is a migration flow to these regions, but the mobility of labour being, as we have seen, far from complete, it is unlikely that inflation can be avoided. The situation is completely different when economic activities are more evenly distributed over a country. In that case a decrease of unemployment can be realised before there is movement in the direction of higher wages and, therefore, before inflationary tendencies set in. It is the aim of regional economic policy to shift the Phillips curve to the left, from AB to CD, so that with the same unemployment rate there is less pressure on money wages.

Inflation caused by regional disequilibria is not easy to keep under control. If general fiscal policy is applied to keep the inflationary pressure in check, unemployment will rise to unacceptable levels. Moreover, general measures to combat inflationary movements, while affecting to some degree all regions, will hit the backward regions, with their low productivity, most.

Profit margins of economic activities, already narrow in these regions, will be narrowed even further by the increasing costs due to restrictive measures. Regional policy measures may be regarded as attempts to put aggregate demand on a more selective basis (e.g. regional differentiated credit restrictions, grants or interest rebates to assisted regions, etc.).

In the case of deflation, the result is again detrimental to less developed regions. Indeed, when credit controls are slackened it is the developed regions that are the first to benefit, for they are well structured and hence most fit to translate credit facilities into economic activities.

The relationship between regional disequilibrium and inflation is in practice more complicated than is described above. It is the merit of the Commission of the European Communities to have analysed this relationship in more depth. An unpublished report, prepared by J. van Ginderachter, makes a distinction between cost-push inflation in the concentration areas and demand-pull inflation in the underdeveloped regions.[38]

Cost-push inflation in the concentration areas. Let us start from the hypothesis of full employment in a core region and external demand for the products of its fast growing sectors. The concentration area will

25

attract production factors at high prices. Such behaviour is not inflationary in itself, insofar as the pressure of competition keeps the rise of factor prices within the limits of the growth in productivity achieved. Nevertheless even then inflation is not excluded. We may be confronted with a triple indirect impact. On the one hand, other sectors within the region may be obliged to follow wage increases without benefiting from the same possibilities of increasing productivity. On the other hand, the export of the products of these less dynamic sectors to other regions and the possibly changed position on the labour market in the regions of outmigration will have some effect on costs outside the concentration area; the effect will be marginal, however, the more so as the outmigration fails to reduce the excess of labour supply in the less developed regions. Thirdly, wages tend to become uniform at the occupational level. Sometimes, however, inflationary tendencies are automatically corrected by the immigration of workers, that was what happened in West Germany and in Italy during the 1960s. The German and Italian economies may not have grown so rapidly in that decade, and they would sooner have encountered bottlenecks, if there had not been a substantial immigration of labour.[39] Insofar as foreign workers are sufficiently qualified to perform the work, and insofar, therefore, as they contribute to the production to an extent at least proportional to their wage, they do check the inflationary trend of wages in the concentration centres.

However, the essential question is whether the inflow of labour to the concentration areas adds more to demand than it does to supply. This will depend on how much has to be invested in social capital (housing, schools, hospitals, cultural centres, etc.) to accommodate the additional population and whether this is offset by increased savings in the short run. Indeed any extra social capital must be realised in a very short period since the existing social capital in the concentration areas is already utilised to capacity. Inflation is often the result. In any event it seems clear that if investments in social capital have to be made, it could be done with less risk of inflationary consequences in the depressed regions, where there are spare labour resources, than in the prosperous regions where they are lacking. The danger of inflation in the concentration area due to the need for social infrastructure in the short run has been admirably demonstrated in a contribution of G.C. Archibald.[40] This author states that the multiplier effects of a migrant's wage are probably far less important than the induced investment his presence leads to. Let us suppose:

ΔZ = annual earnings of the immigrant;

ΔI = annual induced investment in the first two or three years after the move of the immigrant;

26

$$\Delta I \quad = \quad i \, \Delta Z$$

$\Delta Y \quad =$ additional regional income;

$k \quad =$ regional income multiplier.

Then we have: [41]

$$\Delta Y = k \, (1 + i) \quad \Delta Z \qquad\qquad (1.1)$$

With $i = 2$ and at the minimum estimate of Archibald's multiplier, $k = 1.25$, $\Delta Y / \Delta Z = 3.75$. When $i = 1$, $\Delta Y / \Delta Z = 2.5$. Whatever the value of i, the net effect of immigration on the region in the period of induced investment is clearly inflationary.

Besides the inflationary pressure of additions to social infrastructure, we must remember the high cost of economic infrastructure in the concentration area. The economic growth of the core region and the existence of great political power in that area will lead the public authorities to carry out substantial infrastructural work (industrial sites, roads, etc.). The financing of these works is often very expensive owing to the price of land, the complexity of the civil engineering involved, and the high interest rates of the borrowed capital (in their longing to execute the works, authorities are prepared to pay very high interest rates). It seems clear that the budgetary charges imposed by these works are not met entirely by those who benefit from them, as the taxation system is not regionalised. It is not possible to rely on transfers from other regions of the country; they are generally less well-off regions which cannot afford to subsidise an increase of fiscal expenditure in the core regions. Under such conditions, the financing of these infrastructures has in whole or in part an inflationary character, which may be expressed immediately in prices or be temporarily contained.

The conclusions of the above mentioned EEC report are relevant:

> Thus, the concentration zones constitute a source of declared or potential inflation, both from the point of view of cost of infrastructures and that of cost of production factors, with a diffusion effect towards the less developed regions. If this analysis is correct, the conclusion to be drawn from it must be that the countries with most zones of concentration of economic activity show a greater propensity to develop inflation than those where economic activity is more evenly distributed over the whole of the territory. [42]

Demand-pull inflation in the less developed regions. The reasoning that leads to the conclusion that inflation in the less developed regions is of the demand-pull variety is reached as follows. With the improved information systems in all Western European countries, every region is daily informed about the way of life in the capitals and in the core regions in general. The inhabitants of the less developed regions have woken up to the attractive variety and the high level of consumption in the concentration areas, and it is only to be expected that they wish to participate in this way of life. The consequence is evident: a soaring demand which, failing a sufficient production level, may be financed by inflation. That cannot go on for a long time. The desired consumption pattern becomes one of the grounds to claim higher remuneration. Of course, that alone is no reason to fear inflation. However, the productivity level in many sectors in the less developed regions being rather low, the original demand-pull inflation is converted into a cost-push inflation. We have empirical evidence of such an evolution. In most countries the system of wage zones, which allowed setting different minimum wages in different regions has practically disappeared; the gap between the extreme values has become small or in any case smaller than the corresponding productivity gap.

One important remark should be made here. The situation of the labour market is not the same in all less developed regions. In a region with a large population and a high rate of unemployment, the inflationary tendencies of raised wages may be attenuated.

The general conclusion, surely still oversimplified, can be summarised as follows. The greater the regional disparities within a country (concentration areas versus much less developed regions), the greater the propensity to inflation. Regional disequilibria create inflation or amplify the inflationary movements originating elsewhere.

The environmental argument for
regional economic policy

A new argument in favour of regional economic policy finds its origin in the population's general preoccupation with the environment. This argument is, of course, related to the economic congestion argument and that concerning the optimum size of a city (see chapter 5). In the late 1960s regional economic policy in many European countries became more and more linked to physical planning objectives.

The environmental argument was put forward as one of the main motives for regional economic policy in the wellknown Thomson report.[43] The essential point is that regional economic policy is not only in the interests of those living in less developed regions; it is equally in the interests of those who live in the great conurbations with their increasing congestion. The financial poverty of the underprivileged

28

regions is matched only by the mounting environmental poverty of the areas of concentration. The pressure on housing, the miseries of commuting on overloaded roads, the pollution of air and water, all these phenomena mean that the environmental case for closing the geographical gaps is a strong one for those living in the so-called prosperous areas.

There is little doubt that certain agglomerations in Europe suffer from over-concentration of population and economic activity. The undesirable consequences of congested conditions are clearly reflected in revealed public preferences. At the end of the 1950s — long before people became generally aware of the environmental problems — A. Girard and H. Bastide organised a national inquiry about demographic problems in France. One of the questions put was: 'In the case of absolute freedom and under condition of equal income, would you prefer to live and work in the countryside, a small town, a large provincial town, or Paris'. The response is summarised in Table 1.1. [44]

Table 1.1
Dwelling place of preference according to actual
dwelling place, 1959—60

Actual dwelling place	Population size class (number of inhabitants)					
Dwelling place of preference	Less than 2,000	2,000 to 5,000	5,000 to 100,000	More than 100,000	Paris and suburbs	Total
Countryside	64	48	14	14	18	38
Small town	24	31	37	15	23	33
Large provincial town	8	14	20	60	14	18
Paris	3	5	7	8	44	9
No answer	1	2	2	3	1	2
	100	100	100	100	100	100

A number of conclusions can be derived from this table. First, about 70 per cent prefer the countryside or a small town as a place to live. Second, about 40 per cent of the population of Paris prefer a small town or the countryside. Third, the non-Paris population prefer to live where they are or in a place of similar size. Only a small part of the non-Paris population is interested in Paris. Locational preferences contain non-economic factors, but that does not mean that they are irrational. The physical income related to living in a particular place cannot always be translated into money terms but might be extremely relevant from the point of view of the emotional household. It is also important to note that the locational preferences of labour and capital have opposite effects on the spatial distribution of production. As W.H. Richardson says, the locational preferences of households tend to encourage dispersion by maintaining a higher level of population in lagging regions than would be expected according to income differentials. Locational preferences of firms, on the other hand, tend to perpetuate concentration and agglomerations. Many firms refuse to move away from centres of agglomeration even when more profitable sites are available elsewhere. [45]

The social motives for regional economic policy

Originally regional economic policy in most, if not all, European countries was largely motivated by purely social arguments. Only in the late 1950s and the beginning of the 1960s did the economic issues become dominant. The social arguments can be summarised under three headings.

The full employment argument

Before and after the Second World War a number of regions in every country were confronted with a very high rate of unemployment. The social need to give everyone an opportunity to work was the main reason to initiate a regional economic policy. Especially in France and in the Netherlands the officially designated problem regions that could profit from the aid system, were also the areas with high unemployment. Behind that purely social reasoning there was also the recognition that regional imbalances made it impossible to achieve full employment by means of monetary and fiscal policy on the national level. At that time the question whether the designated regions were worth developing or able, with help, to take advantage of favourable location factors was not given sufficient consideration. In the late 1950s, when the first results of regional policy were discernable, other criteria were used to identify problem areas.

Regional income distribution

Regional income distribution is a special case of general income distribution. The figures in chapter 2 show that there are important regional income differences within each country. They are very pronounced in Italy and France, less so in the Benelux countries and Great Britain.

Disparities of 1 to 3 are the rule in Italy. At the European level we get disparities from 1 to 5 or even worse, dependent on the definition (size) of the regions.

Income distribution can be explained, as we have mentioned above, by many factors, such as the employment balance in the last two or three decades, the expected evolution of the employment balance (supply and demand for labour), the economic structure etc., but the explanation does not justify these inequalities between regions from the point of view of social justice. However, in the regions with the gravest problems the relatively low income level per head is coupled with high rates of unemployment and underemployment.

Welfare considerations

It is very difficult to define welfare, and we do not aim to do so, but we would like to stress certain aspects that must be taken in consideration. Full employment, more even income distribution, and environmental considerations are related to welfare, but there is much more to it. From a purely economic point of view we can compare the different methods of solving the problem of unemployment in certain regions. Government actions can take the form of promoting the mobility of labour or of influencing the mobility of capital; both types of actions may be combined. We agree with G. McCrone when he states:

> Nevertheless, even if economic analysis could prove that full employment could be achieved more efficiently or at lower cost by moving labour than by encouraging industry to move, it still does not necessarily follow that this is the right thing to do. For a variety of reasons the population is likely to prefer to be employed in its own region and this preference may be particularly strong if there is some feeling of regional consciousness based on cultural or linguistic differences. [46]

Diversity in culture, custom, way of life are benefits which cannot be measured. But they should not be overlooked just because they are intangible.

The political issues

H. Schneider is one of the very few authors who underline the political argument in favour of regional economic policy on the national level. It is not always easy to distinguish between social factors and political issues in arguments about regional economic policy. According to H.

Schneider the injustice of large differences in the average real income *per capita* has important political consequences.[47] The results of national elections in many European countries in the 1960s and later proved that the people in less developed regions are more conscious of their situation than the people in the core regions. Great disparities are considered unjust by the population of the less developed regions; they give rise to tensions inimical to both community and national policies. The higher the disparities, the more difficult it is to take certain national measures with a socio-economic impact. Sometimes it becomes impossible to take the indicated measure because the regional economic consequences might be too serious.

Political issues are not only a matter of the self-interest of a government or a political party, nor are they only a matter of the cohesion of the state: they are above all human and moral issues. How true that is can be borne out, for instance, by the fact that the origin of present day regional and spatial planning in the Federal Republic of Germany can be traced to its constitution (The Basic Law), where it is explicitly stated that equality in living conditions has to be created and maintained in all parts of the country.[48] Moreover, the political issues of regional economic policy are very often mentioned in EEC documents. Indeed the problem of cohesion within the EEC is even greater than within a nation. Monetary, economic, agricultural, commercial, transport, energy and other measures may have negative effects on the most undeveloped regions of the community. The Commission is very conscious of this problem.

In the preceding four sections we have tried to justify regional economic policy on the national level. The motivation for any country can be found in economic, environmental, social, and political arguments. These same arguments are, of course, also valid on the EEC level. But from a purely economic point of view other very important factors justify a European regional economic policy; we shall deal with these factors in chapter 10.

The regional multiplier

On page 26 of this chapter we referred to the 'regional multiplier', a concept of more than purely theoretical value. It can help to get a precise and dynamic understanding of the potential economic growth or decline of a region. Furthermore, it may be used to prove that interregional migration flows are not as stabilising as might be expected; indeed, they are often highly destabilising.

The content of the regional multiplier is often misunderstood; that is quite natural in view of the fact that there are different kinds of regional multipliers. From the theoretical point of view much interest has been paid to the regional income multiplier and estimates have been made of its magnitude.[49] For all these reasons it is worth while clarifying the situation.

The regional income multiplier

The regional income multiplier can be used to answer such questions as: what happens to local income if the central government spends a certain amount of money on improvements in regional infrastructure?; what happens to local income if unemployed persons leave the region to seek work elsewhere?; what are the multiplier consequences of migration into the region? G. Archibald tried to answer such questions. In fact he tried to estimate a range of possible values of regional multipliers.

The Archibald approach [50] Suppose we write for a region (exactly as for a country):

$$Y = C + I + G + X - M \qquad (1.2)$$

Let G, I and X be autonomous and contain no import content. Let induced expenditure be given by:

$$C = a + cY^d \qquad (1.3)$$
$$M = b + mY^d, \qquad (1.4)$$

where Y^d stands for disposable income.

If the marginal rate of tax is t (we ignore the problem of undistributed profits) and the regional income multiplier k, then:

$$k = \frac{1}{1 - c + m + t\,(c-m)} \qquad (1.5)$$

from which follows

$$k = \frac{1}{1 - (c-m)\,(1-t)} \qquad (1.6)$$

If $(c-m) = \beta$, the propensity to add value locally,

$$k_m = \frac{1}{1 - \beta\,(1-t)} \qquad (1.7)$$

With t = 0.2 and a reasonable range for β , being assumed, say 0.2 — 0.5, the values of k vary as follows:

β	k
0.2	1.19
0.3	1.30
0.4	1.47
0.5	1.67

Archibald tries to narrow the plausible range, fixing a minimum value (β_m) below which the value of β for any region must not fall. The calculation of β_m makes it possible to estimate the minimum consequences of emigration. Introducing marginal rates of personal tax as estimated by A.R. Prest he arrives at the respective values of k_m:

β_m values	t—values					
	0.185	0.200	0.235	0.250	0.285	0.300
0.14	1.13	1.13	1.12	1.12	1.11	1.11
0.23	1.23	1.23	1.21	1.21	1.20	1.19
0.31	1.34	1.33	1.31	1.30	1.28	1.28

Source: G.C. Archibald, op.cit., p.32.

Although the range is still large, Archibald states that one might reasonably take 1.25 as a best guess at the level below which it is extremely improbable for the multiplier for any region to lie. Furthermore, the sensivity of k_m to t is not very high.

P.S. Adler, B. Archer and Ch. Owen reason that for two reasons no single income multiplier can be adequate. Firstly, on the production side, changes in the output of different industries will have markedly different effects on the local economy depending on the linkages between the various industrial activities. Secondly, differing effects on a regional economy may arise from changes in different forms and levels of income. For any one industry there will be a spectrum of employment that is different from those in other industries. Differing types of employment and differing levels of income imply differing patterns of spending by the members of each type and income level.

With the elements used in Archibald's approach it is possible to answer a number of questions. The first is that after the effect of regional migration. The migration of an unemployed person has a secondary depressing effect because of the loss of spending out of his unemployment benefit and its multiplier consequences. Here we have to pay attention to β_m. There are two reasons to believe that β_m for an unemployed person is higher than for the population as a whole. For one thing, it is unlikely that an unemployed person will save at all (higher c value). For another, the consumption pattern of an unemployed person is different from that of an employed worker. Such considerations suggest that β_m could hardly be less than 0.3, which leads to an income multiplier of approximately 1.3.

Having determined values of k, they may be used to estimate how many emigrants cause one more person to lose his job. More symbols are needed:

h	=	unemployment benefit;
a	=	local expenditure coefficient of an unemployed person;
Y_w	=	average weekly earnings.

Let
$$Y_w = k\,a\,hr \qquad (1.8)$$

where r is the number of payments of h (unemployment benefit) that satisfies the equation. In other words r is equal to the number of men whose emigration, by reducing unemployment benefit payments, will reduce regional income by Y_w.

Then:
$$r = \frac{Y_w}{ka\,h} \qquad (1.9)$$

If $s = \dfrac{h}{Y}$ (ratio of unemployment benefit to average weekly earnings)

$$r = \frac{1}{ska} \quad [51] \qquad (1.10)$$

If s is taken equal to 0.4, the range of r, or the alternative values of r, can be derived from the following table.

Estimated value of a	Estimated value of k					
	1.2	1.3	1.4	1.5	1.6	1.7
0.3	6.9	6.4	6.0	5.6	5.2	4.9
0.4	5.2	4.8	4.5	4.2	3.9	3.7
0.5	4.2	3.8	3.6	3.3	3.1	2.9
0.6	3.5	3.2	3.0	2.8	2.6	2.5

Source: G.C. Archibald, op.cit., p.37.

With a = 0.3 and k = 1.2, r is equal to 6.9. This implies that it is sufficient for seven men to leave their region to make one more man lose his job. This is an absolute minimum value. The larger s, a and/or k are the smaller r becomes.[52] If s = 0.6, a = 0.4, and k = 1.3, r becomes 3.2. The conclusion is evident: the secondary depressing effects of migration may become very serious. A very important remark must be made in this context. It does not matter whether migrants are employed or not, provided that the autonomous expenditure remains constant, so that any job vacancies caused by migration are filled by those previously unemployed.

Another use of the income multiplier is related to incoming migration. What are the consequences of immigration to a strong region? Let us suppose a job vacancy occurs in an agglomeration area. A person is attracted into the area to fill the vacancy. Does this person entirely meet the excess demand for labour? The process is not that simple. The immigrant provokes a secondary effect by spending his wages. Assume that the earnings of the immigrant in the region with excess demand are equal to the regional average; the net reduction in excess demand for labour caused by the migration can then be calculated. The induced income is equal to (k−1) times the migrant's wage; therefore the excess demand for labour falls from 1 to k−1, a net reduction of 2−k.

In the region of migration there is also a multiplier effect of induced investment due to immigration. In the section 'Regional disequilibria and inflation' we already dealt with this aspect of the migration process.

Another question that may be raised is 'What are the regional effects of public works and private investment?' The effect is of course largely influenced by the import content of any investment project. As imports here include imports from other regions, we may expect a rather high import content. Let u be the fraction of imports in the injection Δ I.

$$\Delta Y = k \Delta I (1-u) \qquad (1.11)$$

But public works that relieve local unemployment also reduce unemployment benefit. We assume that the transfers originated outside the region. If we make the extreme assumption that all local expenditure is devoted to hiring at the average weekly wage men who were previously unemployed, then: [53]

$$\Delta Y = k \Delta I (1-u)(1-s) \qquad (1.12)$$

where s is the above mentioned ratio of unemployment benefit to average weekly earnings. Let us now apply a bit of pure theory. We have an injection of 1 billion DM, a k value of 1.25, and u and s take the value of 0.3 and 0.5, respectively. Insertion of these values in the formula indicates an increase of local income of not more than 437.5 million DM, or only about 44 per cent of the injection. This approach is different from the one mentioned on page 39.

The Steele approach [54] In D.B. Steele's approach the difference between personal income and expenditure figures is an estimate of savings and direct taxation (S). He makes the assumption that average savings and marginal savings differ in the same relation as do average and marginal direct taxes.

$$k = \frac{1}{a S} \qquad (1.13)$$

where S is the amalgamated saving figure and a the marginal/average relation. Indirect taxes t are a function of consumption $(1 - a S)$; t is the proportion of regional consumption paid out in indirect taxes.

$$k = \frac{1}{a S + t (1 - a S)} \qquad (1.14)$$

or

$$k = \frac{1}{1 - (t - a S)(1 - t)} \qquad (1.15)$$

One important leakage, regional and international imports, is now introduced. D.B. Steele relates imports to income net of all taxes and savings. The argument is that there cannot be a leak of the same quantity of income twice and the coefficients of income must perforce add up to unity. That leads to the following formula, where m stands for the marginal propensity to import out of personal consumption net of indirect taxes:

$$k = \frac{1}{[1 - (1 - aS)(1 - t)(1 - m)]} \qquad (1.16)$$

The great merit of D.B. Steele's contribution is his application of this formula to the regions of Great Britain. He arrives at the following k values per region.

North	1.37	[55] [56]
Yorkshire and Humberside	1.19	
East Midland	1.37	
East Anglia	1.22	
South-East	1.41	
South-West	1.37	
Wales	1.33	
West-Midland	1.20	
North-West	1.27	
Scotland	1.89 or 1.70	

The differences in regional income multipliers are undeniable. The very high figure for Scotland is due to low relative savings and import coefficients. The strength of the multiplier in Scotland, North, and South-East supports the argument that net inter-regional migration can be highly destabilising. The most severe destabilising effects occur where the region of origin and destination both have high multiplier and induced investment effects. Knowledge of regional-income multipliers is also important to determine whether regional policy should be differential.

The regional investment multiplier and
the regional export multiplier [57]

In the Archibald approach we were already dealing indirectly with the regional investment multiplier. We are interested to know what change in regional income is likely to follow a unit change in regional capital formation or in regional exports. A.J. Brown takes the example of the exportation of motor vehicles to the value of say, £1 million. First of all we need to know the extra income that owners of primary factors of production in the region will draw from their direct contribution to the extra vehicles produced for export. The value calculated amounts to £0.25 − £0.28 million. This is only one part of the extra income created. The export of cars effects the intermediate inputs for the motor industry (and the extra inputs for the industry providing those inputs, etc.). To measure the effect, we need the input multiplier (activity multiplier), which varies from region to region as a function of the availability of component and subcontracting industries. In Brown's example the input multiplier varies from 1.2 to 2.0, which brings the extra income to £0.30 − £0.56 million. The income multiplier operating through consumers' expenditure will raise these figures by anything from a seventh to a quarter (k = 1.14 or 1.25), leaving us with a final extreme range of values for our 'motorcar export multiplier' of about 0.35 to 0.70, which is much less than unity; in other words an export of £1.0 million creates an income between £0.35 to £0.70 million for the residents of the region.

The same reasoning can be followed for the regional investment multiplier. The calculation must be executed in three phases: (a) determination of the local income elements in the investment, (b) application of the input multiplier to them, and lastly (c) multiplying the result by the income multiplier. Brown's example, based on a mixed bag of construction projects, leads to an investment multiplier of 0.6 to 0.75. Note that this approach is quite different from that of Archibald. There is a difference in the basic assumption about regional transfers and in the treatment of regional linkages $[\Delta Y = k\Delta I\,(1{-}u)(1{-}s)]$.

Regional employment multiplier

Regional employment multipliers provide a rough but useful means of assessing the total employment impact of gains and losses in a region's export activity. The regional employment multiplier is related to economic base analysis; this explains why the term economic base multiplier[58] [59] is also used.

Economic base analysis makes a distinction between basic or export industries and non-basic or non-export (service or local) activities.[60] A non-basic activity is defined as an activity that, for economic reasons, needs to be performed within the area considered, while an export industry is one that, although performed within the boundaries of the region, need not be located there. It follows from this definition that there is no inter-regional trade of services and goods produced by non-basic industries.

On the other hand, a basic activity is not necessarily an exporting industry. It might export its products, which implies that other regions import them. Thus it is basic industry that generates initial income in the area. This income will be spent partly in the area, partly somewhere else. If the non-basic activities are defined well, their products and services will be bought exclusively in the region. From the (repeated) spending of income on local products and services, a multiplier effect results. Each job created in basic industries induces an increase in employment in non-basic activities.

Economic base theory asserts that there is a stable relation between basic and service employment in a given region so that change in basic jobs will lead to predictable changes in service jobs and in total employment. As basic activities expand, requirements for non-basic activities increase and total employment will grow by some multiple of the initial increase in basic jobs.

$$k_e = \frac{T}{X} \tag{1.17}$$

where k_e = regional employment multiplier;

T = total employment;

X = basic employment.

S.J. Weiss and E.C. Gooding in their publication and A.J. Brown in his book, developed a method of estimating the regional employment multiplier. It is a linear regression method based on time series or on a cross-section analysis. [61] [62] T = a + bX (b = employment multiplier estimate). It must be remembered that the regional employment multiplier is influenced by the definition of the region X or, in other words, the size of the area considered. The same holds for the other forms of regional multipliers.

Some remarks should be made. First, it seems justified to contemplate whether non-basic activities comprise only those that result from the spending of consumer's income earned in basic activities, or also those which result from spending by the basic activities themselves. When, for example, basic industries purchase transportation services, part of these services might have to be performed within the region, but they would not be non-basic in the sense used so far. These services are rendered there only because the basic industry happens to be located in and producing within the area. It is induced or secondary production. Once these secondary activities are taken into account, the distinction between basic and non-basic becomes vaguer. The only thing that is clear is that secondary effects should be called 'non-basic' insofar as they necessarily have to be produced within the region, and 'basic' insofar as they do not. To what extent that will be the case depends on the nature of the basic industry. One industry might require considerably more non-basic services than another. The consequence is evident: the regional employment multiplier will be different from sector to sector.

Secondly, from the theoretical point of view, there should not be a large difference between the income multiplier and the employment multiplier. In practice, however, the employment multiplier is larger. The most important reason is that the income multiplier is calculated ex ante for the short run from changes in money flows. The employment multiplier is calculated ex post from changes in employment over long periods of ten to twenty years. This is very important. Indeed, a process of regional growth over a long period, involves different assumptions from those relevant in short term considerations, for example that of long term unchanged public relief expenditure due to unemployment and poverty. It should also be noted that employment multipliers fail to account for inter-industry differences in wages and productivity, while income multipliers do reflect these differences.

Thirdly, employment in the non-basic sector may increase independently of any change in the basic sector, perhaps owing to an increase in local income levels (transfer incomes included).

Fourthly, as we shall see later on, a diversified service sector plays a vital role in the attraction of basic activities to a region.

Compatibility between regional economic policy and general economic policy on the national and European Community levels

Compatibility on the national level

One of the essential targets of regional economic policy is harmonious growth, which must be manifest in a decrease of the income disparities between the rich and the poor regions. It is to be considered a specific result of the improvement in income distribution which is an objective of all general economic policy, the other objectives being economic growth, full employment, price stability, balance of payments equilibrium, and optimum use of production factors.

The growth objective can be defined as the highest possible (overall) growth rate. The objective of harmonised growth requires a differentiated growth rate: higher in the less developed regions, lower in the core regions. To what extent are these objectives compatible?

We must distinguish three cases. The first case is that of complete compatibility. It is possible that a policy of harmonised growth leads to the highest growth rate. Page 17 and following of this chapter contain a number of arguments in favour of that possibility. A policy which aims at (a) the use of all factors of productions by integrating the labour reserve in the production process, (b) a reduction of economic costs such as congestion costs, or (c) a higher sectorial mobility, is not in conflict with the

41

target of achieving the highest growth rate. On the other hand, and this was shown on page 3 of this chapter, a high growth rate is a necessary condition for harmonised growth. The higher the net investment rate, the larger the amount of capital able to make a new choice about the location of investment. The mobility of capital is therefore itself a function of the rate of expansion of the economy.

The second case is that of neutral compatibility or, in other words, the absence of any relation between the two objectives. We can even imagine a situation where the objective of the highest growth rate can be achieved by different policies, one of them being that of harmonised growth.

A third case is that of incompatibility. A situation of full competition is supposed to bring about an economic optimum. Any regional economic policy is an intervention in the market mechanism. Two remarks must be made. First, the optimum location of firms may be different from the micro and the macro-economic point of view. Secondly, we must make a distinction between the short term and the long term growth rate.

Sometimes the question is also raised to what extent a harmonised growth rate has a negative effect on savings and investment. We should certainly not overestimate such considerations. Later on we shall have the opportunity to discuss and evaluate the instruments of regional economic policy. It will be shown that the famous IDC's (industrial development certificates) do not have a real detrimental effect.

If there is a real difference between the growth rate with and without regional economic policy, it must be looked upon as the cost of harmonised growth. In practice we do not believe that the comparison can be made; it is feasible, however, to apply cost benefit analysis to a particular case. All costs and all benefits occurring through time must be compared to make a final judgement about a particular case.

Compatibility on the
European Community level

It is not our intention to anticipate the discussion of motives for regional economic policy on the European Community level which follows in chapter 10. The aim here is just to indicate how far the aims of European integration and of regional economic policy are compatible. Both aim at harmonised growth and an increase in welfare. What has been said about compatibility on the national level is also true on the Community level. Furthermore, certain Community policies cannot be realised without a regional policy. The most striking examples are to be found in the fields of monetary and economic union, agricultural policy, and industrial policy.

There is, however, a contradiction, or an incompatibility, when we take into account the instruments of regional economic policy. Economic integration means suppression of all hindrances to trade in favour of a free circulation of commodities, while regional economic policy implies a correction of the market mechanism. However, we should not overestimate that kind of incompatibility. The Treaty of Rome implicitly and explicitly approves of interventions on the regional level, as long as interventions such as financial aids remain within reasonable limits. Moreover, the financial advantages given openly to certain firms in less developed regions should be compared with the unknown advantages accruing to existing firms in the core regions. Public intervention in favour of the core regions means an indirect grant to the firms located there. Such indirect subsidies are often very important. And finally, regional disparities may actually impede the integration process.

Definition of regional
economic policy

Regional economic policy or regional planning includes all public intervention intended to ameliorate the geographical distribution of economic activities; in reality regional policy tries to correct certain spatial consequences of the free market economy in order to achieve two interrelated objectives: economic growth and improved social distribution.[63]

Five phases are to be distinguished: (a) definition of regional problems and their origins, (b) definition of objectives, if possible in a quantitative way, (c) definition of the strategy to be followed, (d) indication of the instruments to be used, and (e) evaluation of the policy. Each of these phases will be dealt with intensively in the following chapters.

It is important to distinguish regional economic policy from what the French call 'Aménagement du territoire'. 'Aménagement du territoire' comprises much more than regional policy or regional planning; it includes what the English call 'town and country planning'. R.P. Lebret defines 'Aménagement du territoire' as follows: 'The objective of "aménagement du territoire" is to create by rational organization of space and the implantation of appropriate equipment, optimal conditions for the valorization of the soil, and those conditions best adapted to the human development of the inhabitants'.[64]

Indeed, we must make a distinction between physical planning (town and country planning) and the introduction of the spatial element into economic policy. It is evident that physical planning can be a helpful instrument for the regional policy. Vice versa, regional economic policy is not without impact on physical planning. In this study the emphasis is on regional economic policy.

Notes

[1] Roger, Ch., 'La politique de développement régional et de l'aménagement de l'espace', Brussels, 1962, p.19.

[2] Klaassen, L.H., 'Regional policy in the Benelux countries', in Meyers, F. (ed.), *Area Development Policies in Britain and the Countries of the Common Market,* Washington, 1965.

[3] In small countries like Denmark and the Benelux countries price differences from region to region are very unimportant and therefore in these countries the two policies, maximisation of profits and minimisation of production and marketing costs, may be considered identical or very similar.

[4] One clearly should distinguish between the mobility of capital already invested, which, as a result of extremely high costs of relocation is almost zero, and the mobility of new capital, of current investments.

[5] Vanhove, N., *De doelmatigheid van het regionaal-ekonomisch beleid in Nederland,* Hilversum, 1962.

[6] Vanhove, N., 'The development of Flemish economy in the international perspective', *EEC, Regional Policy Series,* no.1, 1973.

[7] Morgan, E.V. 'Regional problems and common currencies', *Lloyds Bank Review,* October 1973, p.20.

[8] Gravier, J.F., *Paris et le désert français,* Paris, 1958.

[9] Milhau, J., *Etude sur une politique des économies régionales,* PUF, 1957, p.17.

[10] Hansen, N., 'Human resources and regional development: some lessons from French experience', *The Southern Economic Journal,* July 1967, p.126.

[11] Cameron, G.C. 'Regional economic policy in the United Kingdom', in Sant, M. (ed.), *Regional Policy and Planning for Europe,* 1974, p.2.

[12] Morgan, E.V. op.cit., p.22.

[13] Cameron, G.C., op.cit., p.3.

[14] Myrdal, G., *Economic Theory and Underdeveloped Regions,* London, 1957, pp.26—9.

[15] Morgan, E.V. op.cit., p.22.

[16] Ohlin, B., *Inter-regional and International Trade,* Cambridge, 1933.

[17] McCrone, G., *Regional Policy in Britain,* London, 1966, pp.77—86.

[18] We assume the same degree of skill in each region.

[19] McCrone, G. op.cit., p.80.

[20] McCrone, G., op.cit., p.85.

[21] Moroney, J.R. and Walker, J.M., 'A regional test of the Heckscher-

Ohlin Hypothesis', *Journal of Political Economy*, 1966.

[22] See also Dixon, R.J. and Thirlwall, A.P., *Regional Growth and Unemployment in the United Kingdom*, London, 1975, chapter 2.

[23] See also Dixon, R.J. and Thirlwall, A.P., op.cit., pp.24–7. Overall, however, the evidence for the regions of the United Kingdom is slightly more inclined towards the Heckscher-Ohlin hypothesis than are Moroney and Walker's results for the US. These authors refer also to a recent study of B. Smith using value added per employee as a measure of capital intensity. This study is more favourable to the neoclassical hypothesis. See Smith, B., 'Regional specialization and trade in the United Kingdom', *Scottish Journal of Political Economy*, February 1975.

[24] Fuchs, V.R., *Changes in the Location of Manufacturing in the United States since 1929*, New Haven, 1962, pp.165–75.

[25] Moroney, J.R. and Walker, J.M., op.cit., p.269.

[26] Olsen, E., 'Regional income differences within a Common Market', in Richardson, H. (ed.), *Regional Economics: A Reader*, 1970, chapter 8.

[27] Olsen, E., op.cit., p.113.

[28] Brown, A.J., *The Framework of Regional Economics in the United Kingdom*, Cambridge, 1972, p.275.

[29] Cameron, G.C., 'Regional economic policy in the United Kingdom', in Sant, M. (ed.), *Regional Policy and Planning for Europe*, op.cit.

[30] Needleman, L., 'What are we to do about the regional problems', *Lloyds Bank Review*, no.75, 1965, p.55.

[31] For a real cost-benefit approach see Blake, C., 'The gains from regional policy', in Wolfe, J.N. (ed.), *Cost-benefit and Cost Effectiveness*, Oxford, 1973, chapter 10.

[32] McCrone, G., op.cit., p.31.

[33] Cameron, G.C., op.cit., p.5.

[34] McCrone, G. op.cit., p.42.

[35] Klaassen, L.H., op.cit., p.8.

[36] Needleman, L., op.cit., p.47. McCrone, G., op.cit., p.38. Thomas, R.L. and Storey, P.J.M., 'Unemployment dispersal as a determinant of wage inflation in the United Kingdom 1925–66', *Manchester School of Social and Economic Studies*, no.39, 1971. Brown, A.J., op.cit., p.331. Sadler, P., Archer, B., and Owen, Ch., 'Regional income multipliers', *Bangor Occasional Papers in Economics*, University of Wales Press, 1973.

[37] Phillips, A.W., 'The relationship between unemployment and the rate of change in money wages in the United Kingdom, 1861–1957', *Economica*, 1958.

[38] EEC, 'Regional policy and economic and monetary union — Geographical disequilibria in the light of the implementation of funda-

mental economic equilibria', Directorate-General of Regional Policy, Brussels, 1971.

[39] Between 1960 and 1968 Germany's positive net migration balance reached 2,1 million persons (migration from Eastern Germany and later Italy). In Italy, between 1960 and 1969, the migration balance from the Mezzogiorno to the rest of Italy reached 1,5 million.

[40] Archibald, G.C., 'Regional multiplier effects in the United Kingdom', *Oxford Economic Papers*, vol.19, 1967, p.37.

[41] Archibald, G.C. arrives at the same formula in a different way:

$$\Delta = \beta(1-t)\,\Delta Y + (1+i)\,\Delta Z$$
$$\Delta Y - \beta(1-t)\,\Delta Y = (1+i)\,\Delta Z$$
$$\Delta Y[1 - \beta(1-t)] = (1+i)\Delta Z$$
$$\Delta Y = k\,(1+i)\,\Delta Z$$

in which β is the propensity to add value locally (value added locally; $L = c - m$, t is the marginal rate of tax.

$$k = \frac{1}{1 - \beta(1-t)}$$

We can also derive ΔY by the following approach:

$$\Delta Y = \frac{\Delta Z}{1 - \beta(1-t)} + \frac{i\,\Delta Z}{1 - \beta(1-t)}$$

$$\Delta Y = \frac{(1+i)\,\Delta Z}{1 - \beta(1-t)} \quad \text{or} \quad \Delta Y = k\,(1+i)\,\Delta Z$$

[42] EEC, op.cit., p.17.

[43] EEC, 'Report on the regional problems in the enlarged community', Brussels, 1973.

[44] Girard, A. and Bastide, H., 'Les problèmes démographiques devant l'opinion', *Population*, April — May 1960, p.271.

[45] Richardson, H.W., *Regional Growth Theory*, p.196.

[46] McCrone, G., op.cit., p.28.

[47] Schneider, H.K., 'Uber die Notwendigkeit regionaler Wirtschafts-politik', in Schneider, H.K. (ed.), *Beiträge zur Regionalpolitik*, p.5.

[48] See Krumme, G., 'Regional policies in West-Germany', in Hansen, N.M. (ed.), *Public Policy and Regional Economy Development*, 1974, chapter 4.

[49] Archibald, G., 'Regional multiplier effects in the United Kingdom', *Oxford Economic Papers*, vol.19, 1967. Steele, D.B., 'Regional multi-

pliers in Great Britain', *Oxford Economic Papers,* March 1969. Wilson, Th., 'The regional multiplier — a critique', *Oxford Economic Papers,* March 1968. Greig, M.A., 'Regional multiplier effects in the United Kingdom, a comment', *Oxford Economic Papers,* no.2, 1971. Weiss, S. and Gooding, E., 'Estimation of differential employment multipliers in a small regional economy', *Land Economics,* vol.43, 1968 (see also Richardson, H. (ed.), *Regional Economics: A Reader,* chapter 3.) Brown, A.J., op.cit., chapters 6 and 8. Brown A.J. and Associates, 'Regional multiplier', in Richardson, H. (ed.), op.cit. Sadler, P., Archer, B. and Owen, C., 'Regional income multipliers — the Anglesey study', *Bangor Occassional Papers in Economics,* 1973. Archer, B., 'The anatomy of a multiplier', *Regional Studies,* vol.10, 1976.

[50] Archibald, G.C., op.cit.

[51] We agree that r is much more an employment multiplier than an income multiplier. We follow here the reasoning of G.C. Archibald.

[52] In most European countries the s value is higher in practice.

[53] The assumption that all the men hired were previously unemployed is not necessary. The condition is that all other autonomous expenditure in the region be constant. A worker from another firm could be employed or the vacancy could be filled by a previously unemployed worker.

[54] Steele, D.B., 'Regional multipliers in Great Britain', op.cit.

[55] The k value of 1.37 for the region North is the result of the application of the formula:

$$a\,S + t\,(1 - a\,S) + m\,[(1 - a\,S) - t(1 - a\,S)]$$

or

$$0.15 + 0.17 + 0.61 \cdot 0.68 = 0.73$$

$$k = \frac{1}{\beta} \text{ or } 1.37$$

[56] D.B. Steele has also calculated the income multiplier with feedback effect. The leakage through imports to a particular region stimulates, via income, the imports of the rest of the country and, hence, the income of the original region.

[57] Brown, A.J., op.cit., p.188.

[58] Brown, A.J., op.cit., chapter 6.

[59] See also Weiss, S.J. and Gooding, E.C., op.cit.

[60] See also Klaassen, L.H. and Van Wickeren, A.C., 'Interindustry relations; an attraction model', in Bos, H.C. (ed.), *Towards Balanced International Growth,* Amsterdam, 1969.

[61] In the approach used by S.J. Weiss and E.C. Gooding the structural relations are expressed in regression equations and can be revealed in a simple linear model:

$$T = S + X \ (1) \quad (S = \text{non-basic employment})$$
$$S = a + hT \ (2)$$
$$S = a + hS + hX \ (3)$$

Solving equation (1) and (2) for T and S in terms of X yields the reduced forms:

$$T = a + hT + X \ (4)$$
$$T - hT = a + X$$
$$T(1 - h) = a + X$$

$$T = \frac{a}{1-h} + \frac{X}{1-h} \ (5)$$

$$S - hS = a + hX$$

$$S = \frac{a}{1-h} \quad \frac{h}{1-h} X \ (6)$$

Fitting these equations by the least squares method, yields a multiplier estimate of $\frac{1}{1-h}$ in equation (5); this multiplier is equal to one plus the coefficient $\frac{h}{1-h}$ in equation (6).

[62] Weiss, S.J. and Gooding, E.C., empirical study of the Portsmouth region based on three export activities (X_1 = private export employment; X_2 urban employment at the Naval Shipyard and X_3 total employment at the Air Force Base) reveals employment multipliers of $k_1 = 1.78$; $k_2 = 1.55$ and $k_3 = 1.35$ ($S = a + b_1X_1 + b_2X_2 + b_3X_3$). The underlying assumptions are: (a) inexistence of inter-industry linkages and (b) workers of any export sector divide their local spending among the service activities in a similar manner.

[63] Roger, C., *La politique de développement régional et de l'améngement de l'espace*, Brussels, 1962, p.49. 'L'objectif proprement économique de la politique régionale est d'assurer au niveau de l'espace géographique l'utilisation la meilleure des ressources disponibles, en réalisant un rapport optimal entre les coûts globaux (privés et collectifs) et les profits globaux'.

[64] Lebret, R.P., 'Esquisse d'une charte à l'aménagement', *L'enquête en vue de l'aménagement régional*, PUF, 1958, p.235.

2 The regional disparities in the European Economic Community

Introduction

The regional disparities in the European Economic Community can be expressed in many forms. We can consider disparities in population density, in employment possibilities, and in income level; or we can consider migration balance, economic structure, the consumption pattern, etc. All these indicators emphasise one aspect of the regional disparities, but are not necessarily an indicator of an unequal welfare situation.

In this chapter we limit ourselves to a general picture of the regional disparities based on several sources. For a more systematic analysis we refer to the recently published study of W.T.M. Molle, B. van Holst and H. Smit, 'Regional economic development in the European Community'. We shall focus first of all on the distribution of population and employment in the EEC, paying particular attention to industrial employment. Income disparities are our second field of interest. Both employment and income disparities are closely related to the different aspects of disparities dealt with in chapter 1.

This chapter is not only concerned with description, but also tries to measure the disparities. Measurement of the disparities makes it possible to study their evolution on the national and EEC levels. In many respects it is worth while to compare the EEC situation with that in the United States.

Particular attention is also given in this chapter to the structural aspects of the disparities and especially to the evolution of the disparities. In this context we shall present a regional comparative model and discuss the applicability of shift-share analysis.

Before continuing, it is worth noting that regional scientists in the EEC are confronted with one basic problem: the lack of comparable regional statistics, which often makes comparison very difficult. One of the most striking examples concerns unemployment: the content of unemployment statistics varies from country to country in the EEC. Therefore we must use unemployment ratios by region published in the Eurostat Labour Force Sample Survey of 1975 with caution.

Notwithstanding all the difficulties it is necessary to have an idea of the regional inequalities in the EEC; the available data make it possible. The best illustration is the abovementioned study made by W.T.M.

Molle with the collaboration of B. van Holst and H. Smit.

The geographical distribution
of the population

To illustrate the geographical distribution of the population we shall
make use of three sources. The first is the recent publication of W.T.M.
Molle, B. van Holst and H. Smit, 'Regional economic development in the
European Community', already mentioned. It is based in part on a
recent report of the Netherlands Economic Institute, 'Population by
region and employment by region and industry in the European
Community', prepared in the framework of the FLEUR study (Factors
of location in Europe) in order to determine the factors of regional
growth in Europe. A prerequisite of the FLEUR study was the availability of internationally and intertemporally comparable statistics on
total population by region and on the employment by sector and
region for the whole of the EEC. The report gives population and
employment by region for the years 1950, 1960, and 1970; moreover,
regional product and sectoral structure of employment by region are
also dealt with. Table 2.1, which gives the geographical distribution of
the population, the population density, and the evolution of the population by region, is based on the abovementioned two sources. The
third source is the EEC report on the regional problems in the enlarged
Community.[1] [2]

From Table 2.1 and Map 2.1 we can derive the regional composition
of the EEC as regards population (Map 2.1 is taken from the EEC
report because that gives a more detailed regional breakdown). A number of concentration areas and sparsely populated areas can be distin-
guished. The largest concentration area, occupying a central position
and consisting of adjacent regions, includes the English regions North-
West, Yorkshire-Humberside, East-Midlands, West-Midlands, and South-
East, and on the continent the French region 'Nord', Belgium, the
Dutch regions West, South and East, the six 'Regierungsbezirke' of
Nordrhein-Westfalen, Saarland and the Regierungsbezirke Darmstadt,
Rheinhessen-Pfalz, Nord-Württemberg and Nord-Baden in the South-
West of the Federal Republic of Germany. This whole area has a popu-
lation density of about 450 inhabitants per square km and accommoda-
ted (in 1970) 91,965,000 inhabitants, representing 36.5 per cent of the
total population, on 14 per cent of the total area of the EEC. It is
generally known as 'The North Western European Megalopolis'.

Map 2.1 shows three other, smaller, concentration areas, where the
population density is not only high but also several times higher than
that of neighbouring regions. They are the Paris region, the zone

50

Table 2.1
Distribution, evolution of population, and population density within the EEC by region, 1950, 1960, 1970 (x 1,000)

Region	1950	1960	1970	Share within EEC 1970	Index 1970 (1950= 100)	Population density 1970 (pers/km^2)
EEC	216,287	232,573	251,919	100.0	116.5	165
Germany (FR)	50,810	55,785	61,002	(24,2)	120.0	245
Schleswig-Holstein	2,595	2,304	2,511	1.0	96.8	160
Hamburg	1,606	1,829	1,794	0,7	111,7	2382
Niedersachsen	6,798	6,613	7,122	2.8	104.8	150
Bremen	559	702	735	0.3	131.5	1819
Nordrhein-Westfalen	13,208	15,799	17,005	6.8	128.8	499
Hessen	4,324	4,771	5,425	2.1	125.0	256
Rheinland-Pfalz	3,005	3,398	3,659	1.5	121.8	184
Baden-Württemberg	6,430	7,664	8,954	3.5	139.2	250
Bayern	9,184	9,448	10,561	4.2	114.9	149
Saarland	955	1,061	1,121	0.4	117.4	434
Berlin (West)	2,147	2,197	2,115	0.8	98.5	4406
United Kingdom	50,226	52,708	55,521	(22.0)	110.6	227
England	41,175	43,464	46,029	(18.3)	111.8	353
North	3,133	3,255	3,298	1.3	105.3	170
Yorkshire-Humberside	4,494	4,607	4,807	1.9	107.0	338
East-Midlands	2,909	3,136	3,389	1.3	116.5	278
East-Anglia	1,381	1,461	1,662	0.7	120.3	132
South-East	15,174	16,274	17,237	6.8	113.6	628
South-West	3,238	3,392	3,761	1.5	116.1	158
West-Midlands	4,422	4,762	5,116	2.0	115.7	393
North-West	6,424	6,577	6,759	2.7	105.2	845
Wales	2,584	2,640	2,725	1.1	105.4	131
Scotland	5,096	5,197	5,229	2.1	102.6	66
Northern Ireland	1,371	1,425	1,538	0.6	112.2	108
Italy	46,882	49,630	53,361	(21.2)	113.9	177
Piemonte	3,504	3,909	4,402	1.7	125.6	173

Table 2.1 continued:

Valle d'Aoste	95	101	110	0.0	115.8	33
Liguria	1,555	1,739	1,857	0.7	119.4	343
Lombardia	6,433	7,286	8,384	3.3	130.3	351
Trentino-Alto Adige	735	779	841	0.3	114.4	61
Veneto	3,841	3,780	4,100	1.6	106.7	223
Friuli-Venezia Giulia	1,200	1,170	1,237	0.5	103.1	157
Emilia-Romagna	3,509	3,617	3,830	1.5	109.1	173
Marche	1,352	1,316	1,347	0.5	99.6	138
Toscane	3,152	3,280	3,482	1.4	110.5	151
Umbria	806	782	774	0.3	96.0	91
Lazio	3,322	3,938	4,688	1.9	141.1	272
Campania	4,276	4,632	4,953	2.0	115.8	364
Abruzzi	1,238	1,138	1,122	0.4	90.6	103
Molise	398	339	303	0.1	76.1	68
Puglia	3,181	3,301	3,480	1.4	109.4	179
Basilicata	617	605	564	0.2	91.4	56
Calabria	1,987	1,941	1,869	0.7	94.1	123
Sicilia	4,422	4,614	4,581	1.8	103.6	178
Sardegna	1,259	1,363	1,435	0.6	114.0	59
France	42,010	45,997	51,013 (	20.2)	121.4	93
Région Parisienne	7,009	8,297	9,633	3.8	137.4	802
Champagne	1,110	1,197	1,315	0.5	118.5	51
Picardie	1,355	1,471	1,623	0.6	119.8	83
Haute Normandie	1,232	1,377	1,547	0.6	125.6	126
Centre	1,758	1,846	2.056	0.8	117.0	52
Basse Normandie	1,145	1,202	1,285	0.5	112.2	73
Bourgogne	1,376	1,433	1,534	0.6	111.5	48
Nord	3,309	3,610	3,864	1.5	116.7	312
Lorraine	1,874	2,170	2,323	0.9	124.0	98
Alsace	1,196	1,300	1,454	0.6	121.6	174
France-Comté	841	920	1,026	0.4	122.0	63
Pays de la Loire	2,293	2,438	2,637	1.0	115.0	82
Bretagne	2,358	2,386	2,503	1.0	106.1	92
Poitou-Charentes	1,379	1,448	1,496	0.6	108.5	58
Aquitaine	2,206	2,315	2,492	1.0	113.0	60
Midi-Pyrénées	1,982	2,055	2,206	0.9	111.3	48
Limousin	760	737	740	0.3	97.4	43
Rhône-Alpes	3,580	3,991	4,592	1.8	128.2	105
Auvergne	1,261	1,276	1,329	0.5	105.4	51
Languedoc-Roussillon	1,453	1,547	1,742	0.7	120.0	63
Provence-Côte d'Azur	2,351	2,805	3,400	1.3	144.6	108

Corse	182	176	216	0.1	118.7	24
Netherlands	10,165	11,550	13,116 (	5.2)	129.0	354
North	1,215	1,272	1,422	0.6	117.0	157
East	1,788	2,101	2,484	1.0	139.0	243
West	5,155	5,770	6,378	2.5	123.7	614
South	2,007	2,407	2,832	1.1	141.1	387
Belgium	8,653	9,197	9,650 (	3.8)	115.5	316
Vlaanderen	3,963	4,265	4,550	1.8	114.8	399
Wallonie	2,841	2,923	2,924	1.2	103.0	185
Brabant	1,849	1,991	2,176	0.9	117.7	645
Denmark	4,282	4,591	4,936 (	2.0)	115.3	114
Sjealland-Lolland-Falster	1,984	2,148	2,310	0.9	116.5	235
Fyn	396	415	433	0.2	109.3	124
Jylland	1,902	2.028	2.193	0.9	115.3	73
Ireland	2,962	2,818	2,980 (	1.2)	100.6	42
Donegal	132	114	108	0.0	81.8	22
North-West	102	87	79	0.0	77.4	23
West	302	273	259	0.1	85.7	23
Midlands	258	239	233	0.1	90.3	26
South-West	468	447	466	0.2	99.6	38
South-East	341	320	329	0.1	96.5	35
North-East	191	171	174	0.1	91.0	44
East	888	906	1,062	0.4	119.6	152
Mid-West	280	261	270	0.1	96.4	34
Luxemburg	297	315	340	0.1	114.5	131

Source: W.T.M. Molle with the collaboration of B. van Holst and H. Smit, op.cit., Appendix 3
Population by region and employment by region and industry in the European Community, 1950, 1960, 1970, Rotterdam, 1975 (see FLEUR study).

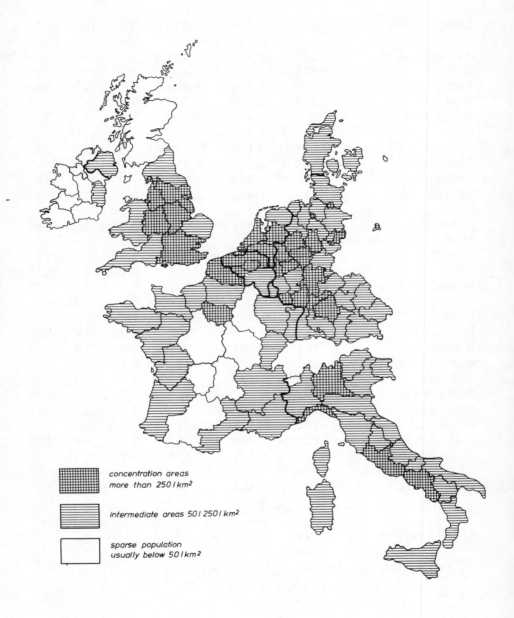

Map 2.1: The population density in the EEC by region, 1970.
Source: EEC Report on the regional problems in the enlarged
Community, op.cit.

Legend:
- concentration areas more than 250 l/km²
- intermediate areas 50 l/250 l/km²
- sparse population usually below 50 l/km²

Lombardia-Liguria in Northern Italy and the zone Lazio-Campania in Central Italy. Each of the three zones has a population of about 10 million.

On the other hand, Map 2.1 reveals three sparsely populated areas. There is first the strip of territory which runs obliquely across France and consists of regions with a population density of about fifty. It includes the regions Champagne, Bourgogne, Centre, Auvergne, Limousin and Midi-Pyrénées. In the second place there is Scotland with a density of about sixty-six, followed by practically the whole of Ireland, with a density below fifty. W.T.M. Molle comes to the conclusion that 25 per cent of the people who live in the most scarcely populated regions of the Community are spread across 55 per cent of the Community's total area.

Table 2.1 and Map 2.2 (based on Table 2.1) reveal a number of interesting points with respect to the evolution of the population in the period 1950–70.

During the post-war period, the EEC population grew from 216,3 million in 1950 to 251,9 million in 1970, an increase of 16.5 per cent or 0.8 per cent per year. Growth rates differed considerably from country to country and even more from region to region. The unequal development per country was due to many factors, which we shall not analyse in this study. Of course the general evolution was not without impact on the evolution of regional population.

A comparison of Map 2.1 with Map 2.2 indicates a certain relationship between the low density regions and the areas of population decrease or regions with a low population growth rate. Striking examples are Ireland, Scotland, Schleswig-Holstein, Limousin, Bretagne, Auvergne, and to a certain extent the regions of South Italy.

On the other hand, there are many high density regions with a high population growth, for example the Rimcity in the Netherlands, the Länder Nordrhein-Westfalen, Bremen, Hessen, and Baden-Württemberg in West Germany, the regions Paris and Provence-Côte d'Azur in France and Lombardia and Lazio in Italy. W.T.M. Molle also observed a slight increase in the disparity of population density. With the help of the coefficient of Theil (see further) W.T.M. Molle et al. studied the inequalities both within and between sets of regions. He comes to the conclusion that the disparities between countries (the between-sets inequality) accounts for only 30 per cent of total inequality in population concentration in the EEC. This means that the lion's share of total inequality is caused by the differences between the regions of the individual countries (the within-set inequality).

Most striking is the existence of several regions with a population decrease:

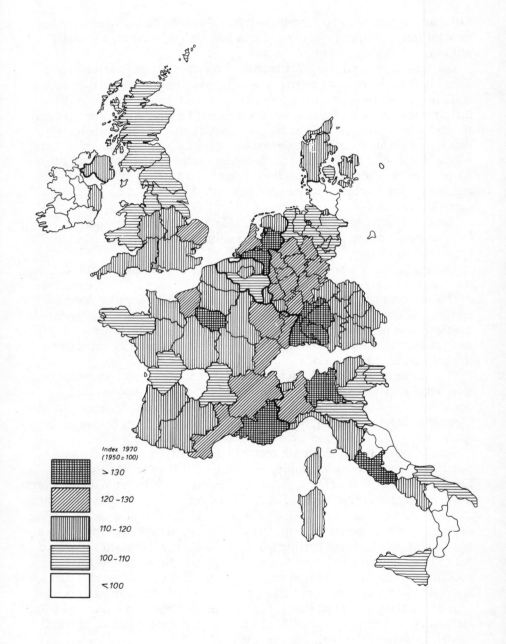

Index 1970
(1950 = 100)

> 130

120 –130

110 – 120

100 – 110

< 100

Map 2.2: The evolution of the population in the EEC by region, 1950—70.

all Irish regions (East excepted);
Limousin in France;
Schleswig-Holstein and West Berlin in West Germany;
the regions Marche and Umbria in Central Italy;
the regions Abruzzi, Molise, Basilicata, and Calabria in Southern Italy.

As we shall see later on, the European problem regions correspond to a large extent to the areas with a population decrease or a stagnating population. We can expect that the decrease or stagnation results from a fundamental regional economic problem. Ireland, Scotland, North-England, Wales, Schleswig-Holstein, Wallonie, Bretagne, Limousin, Auvergne, Southern Italy are all well-known problem regions. Population development is an exponent of the local economic situation.

The geographical distribution of employment

Total employment

The analysis of the geographical distribution of employment is entirely based on the abovementioned study of W.T.M. Molle et al. Employment is defined as including those who are usually occupied for payment or profit, in cash or in kind, in civil work in production units. Those who help in a family business are included. Part time workers are included only as far as the time spent on their occupation is a significant part of normal total working hours in their branch. Occupations in intergovernmental international organisations, defence, and domestic work are excluded. Those who are usually unemployed are excluded too.

In 1970, out of a total population of 251,9 million inhabitants, 99,3 million were employed. That means an employment rate of 39 per cent. This employment rate does not quite correspond with the activity rate. W.T.M. Molle uses the term participation rate. We mentioned above that occupations in defence and unemployed persons were not taken in consideration. Nevertheless the employment rate is a proxy of the activity rate. (The Eurostat publication 'Labour Force Sample Survey' gives for 1975 ratios of active population by regions; the regional breakdown is smaller and the labour force is given as a proportion of the total population, aged 14 years and over.) The average employment rate is not characteristic of all regions. A great variety can be distinguished: very high employment rates are noticed in the City Länder Hamburg (54.2 per cent) and Bremen (51 per cent), and in the economic regions Baden-Württemberg (47.1 per cent), Hessen (45 per cent), and Bayern (44.7 per cent) in West Germany; the West-Midlands (45.1 per cent) and South-East (47.7 per cent) in the United Kingdom; the Région Parisienne (47.7 per cent) in France, and Sjaelland (47 per cent) in Denmark.

Very low employment rates (lower than 35 per cent) are noticed in many regions of Italy (Liguria, Veneto, Friuli-Venezia Giulia, Lazio, Campania, Abruzzi, Puglia, Basilicata, Calabria, Sicilia, and Sardegna), two regions of France (Languedoc-Roussillon and Corse), three regions of the Netherlands (North, East and South), the Belgian regions of Vlaanderen and Wallonie, and finally four regions of Ireland (Donegal, West, South-West, and Mid-West).

From Table 2.2 we can derive that the differences are typical not only by regions but also of nations, West Germany, Denmark, and the United Kingdom have high employment rates. On the other hand the employment rates are rather low in Belgium, Italy, the Netherlands, and Ireland. The French rate is upgraded by the Paris region.

The evolution of total employment

During the period 1950—70 total employment in the EEC increased from 88.2 million to 99.3 million, a relative change of 12.6 per cent. This relative change varied for the different countries and for the different sectors.

The evolution ranged from an increase of 29 per cent in the Netherlands and 24 per cent in Germany (FR) to a decrease of 11 per cent in Ireland. In three other countries, Italy, Belgium and Luxemburg, total employment did not change very much. The annual growth rates are, however, unequal in the two decades considered.

	1950/60	1960/70	1950/70	Index 1970 1950 = 100
Germany (FR)	2.3	−0.1	1.1	124
United Kingdom	0.7	0.2	0.5	109
Italy	0.7	−0.2	0.2	104
France	−0.1	1.1	0.5	110
Netherlands	1.1	1.5	1.3	129
Belgium	−0.2	0.5	0.2	103
Denmark	0.8	1.1	0.9	121
Ireland	−1.3	0.2	−0.6	89
Luxemburg	−0.2	0.6	0.2	103
EEC	0.9	0.3	0.6	113

The total employment change is very unequal by region (see Table 2.2

Table 2.2

Distribution and evolution of employment within the EEC, 1950–70 (x 1,000)

Region	1950 Indus-try(a) (1)	Total (2)	Agricul-ture(b) (3)	1970 Indus-try (4)	Total (5)	Share within the EEC 1970 Indus-try (6)	Total (7)	Index 1970 (1950=100) Indus-try (8)	Total (9)	Orien. to agri-culture (10)= $\frac{(3)}{(5)}$x100	Orien. to in-dustry (11)= $\frac{(4)}{(5)}$x100	Employ-ment rate (12)= $\frac{(5)}{pop.}$x100
EEC	36,634	88,185	9,627	45,492	99,332	100.0	100.0	124	113	9	45	39
Germany (FR)	9,438	21,186	1,813	12,953	26,284	28.5	26.5	137	124	7	49	43
Schleswig-Holstein	273	812	90	365	903	0.8	0.9	134	111	10	40	36
Hamburg	293	700	10	343	973	0.8	1.0	117	139	1	35	54
Niedersachsen	899	2,584	298	1,311	2,901	2.9	2.9	146	112	10	45	41
Bremen	114	246	5	158	375	0.4	0.4	139	152	1	42	51
Nordrhein-Westfalen	3,083	5,414	217	3,684	6,919	8.1	7.0	119	128	3	53	41
Hessen	771	1,766	134	1,171	2,440	2.6	2.6	152	138	5	47	45
Rheinland-Pfalz	470	1,373	143	655	1,451	1.4	1.5	139	106	10	45	40
Baden-Wurttemberg	1,433	3,096	298	2,331	4,221	5.1	4.2	163	136	7	55	47
Bayern	1,538	4,063	606	2,299	4,721	5.1	4.8	149	116	13	48	45
Saarland	223	400	7	226	430	0.5	0.4	101	108	2	52	38
Berlin (West)	341	732	5	410	950	0.9	1.0	120	130	1	43	45
United Kingdom	11,129	21,585	680	11,315	23,616	24.9	23.8	102	109	3	47	43
England	9,305	17,925	498	9,558	19,897	21.0	20.0	103	111	3	48	43

Table 2.2 continued:

	(1)	(2)	(3)	(4)	(5)	(6)	(7)	(8)	(9)	(10)	(11)	(12)
North	702	1,264	43	673	1,328	1.5	1.3	96	105	3	50	40
Yorkshire-Humberside	1,179	1,998	52	1,100	2,044	2.4	2.1	93	102	3	53	43
East Midlands	773	1,285	47	839	1,463	1.8	1.5	109	114	3	57	43
East-Anglia	199	530	62	295	672	0.7	0.7	148	127	9	43	40
South-East	2,928	6,599	121	3,147	7,698	6.9	7.8	107	117	2	40	45
South-West	506	1,227	87	624	1,473	1.4	1.5	123	120	6	42	39
West Midlands	1,302	2,045	52	1,365	2,306	3.0	2.3	105	113	2	59	45
North-West	1,716	2,976	35	1,515	2,914	3.3	2.9	88	98	1	51	43
Wales	506	1,002	49	524	1,058	1.2	1.1	103	106	5	49	39
Scotland	1,070	2,117	88	981	2,112	2.2	2.1	92	100	4	46	40
Northern Ireland	248	541	45	252	550	0.6	0.6	101	102	8	45	36
Italy	5,621	17,517	3,412	8,001	18,294	17.6	18.4	142	104	18	43	34
Piemonte	679	1,569	224	959	1,725	2.1	1.7	141	110	12	55	39
Valle d'Aoste	18	42	6	20	42	0.0	0.0	111	100	14	47	38
Liguria	254	608	53	239	648	0.5	0.7	94	107	8	36	34
Lombardia	1,432	2,653	194	1,975	3,245	4.3	3.3	138	122	5	60	38
Trentino-Alto Adige	81	279	52	113	298	0.3	0.3	140	107	17	37	35
Veneto	426	1,417	232	659	1,420	1.5	1.4	155	100	16	46	34
Friuli-Venezia Giulia	161	435	54	192	430	0.4	0.4	119	99	12	44	34
Emilia-Romagna	363	1,481	332	649	1,534	1.4	1.5	179	104	21	42	40
Marche	127	612	159	193	516	0.4	0.5	152	84	30	37	38
Toscane	412	1,219	173	595	1,249	1.3	1.3	144	102	13	47	35
Umbria	80	325	68	112	274	0.3	0.3	140	84	24	40	35
Lazio	333	1,219	167	458	1,392	1.0	1.4	138	114	11	32	29

Table 2.2 continued:

	(1)	(2)	(3)	(4)	(5)	(6)	(7)	(8)	(9)	(10)	(11)	(12)
Campania	358	1,395	397	525	1,489	1.2	1.5	147	107	26	35	30
Abruzzi	77	451	120	121	371	0.3	0.4	157	82	32	32	33
Molise	20	184	52	30	112	0.1	0.1	150	61	46	26	36
Puglia	221	1,049	377	339	1,058	0.8	1.1	153	101	35	32	30
Basilicata	37	236	78	61	193	0.1	0.2	165	82	40	31	34
Calabria	131	673	194	174	561	0.4	0.6	133	83	34	31	30
Sicilia	318	1,288	373	460	1,341	1.0	1.4	144	104	27	34	29
Sardegna	93	382	106	127	395	0.3	0.4	137	103	26	32	27
France	6,409	18,070	2,721	8,460	19,914	18.6	20.0	132	110	14	42	39
Région Parisienne	1,441	3,091	50	2,039	4,599	4.5	4.6	141	149	1	44	48
Champagne	171	454	75	232	499	0.5	0.5	136	110	15	46	38
Picardie	199	528	87	276	584	0.6	0.6	139	111	15	47	36
Haute Normandie	201	512	69	276	605	0.6	0.6	137	118	11	45	39
Centre	212	756	145	334	781	0.7	0.8	158	103	19	42	38
Basse Normandie	126	520	158	166	506	0.4	0.5	132	97	31	32	38
Bourgogne	166	579	105	239	572	0.5	0.6	144	99	18	41	39
Nord	739	1,298	99	715	1,342	1.6	1.4	97	103	7	53	37
Lorraine	375	734	66	434	828	1.0	0.8	116	113	8	52	35
Alsace	219	517	54	265	561	0.6	0.6	121	109	10	47	36
Franche-Comté	145	363	51	215	399	0.5	0.4	148	110	13	53	39
Pays de la Loire	268	1,035	266	389	1,020	0.9	1.0	145	99	26	38	39
Bretagne	206	1,055	304	272	923	0.6	0.9	132	87	33	29	39
Poitou-Charentes	128	593	150	179	534	0.4	0.5	140	90	28	33	37
Aquitaine	236	1,016	210	308	905	0.7	0.9	130	89	23	34	36

Table 2.2 continued

	(1)	(2)	(3)	(4)	(5)	(6)	(7)	(8)	(9)	(10)	(11)	(12)
Midi-Pyrénées	220	910	195	278	788	0.6	0.8	126	87	25	35	36
Limousin	83	376	88	97	286	0.2	0.3	117	76	31	33	39
Rhône-Alpes	679	1,630	189	934	1,881	2.1	1.9	138	115	10	49	41
Auvergne	154	577	121	203	513	0.5	0.5	132	89	24	39	39
Languedoc-Roussillon	137	566	118	172	551	0.4	0.6	126	97	21	31	32
Provence-Côte d'Azur	294	897	104	424	1,185	0.9	1.2	144	143	8	35	38
Corse	10	63	14	13	52	0.0	0.1	130	83	27	25	24
Netherlands	1,440	3,540	311	1,956	4,575	4.3	4.6	136	129	6	42	34
North	137	416	56	205	467	0.5	4.7	150	112	11	43	32
East	273	644	86	391	845	0.9	0.9	143	131	10	46	34
West	695	1,789	108	844	2,287	1.9	2.3	121	128	4	36	35
South	335	688	61	516	976	1.1	1.0	154	142	6	52	34
Belgium	1,619	3,194	162	1,561	3,302	3.4	3.3	96	103	5	47	34
Vlaanderen	667	1,349	84	784	1,516	1.7	1.5	118	112	6	51	33
Wallonie	592	1,042	54	438	907	1.0	0.9	74	87	6	48	31
Brabant	360	802	24	339	880	0.8	0.9	94	110	3	38	40
Denmark	635	1,813	244	839	2,185	1.8	2.2	132	121	11	38	44
Sjaelland-Lolland-Falster	348	871	57	405	1,075	0.9	1.1	116	123	5	37	47
Fyn	59	168	27	78	189	0.2	0.2	132	113	14	41	44
Jylland	228	774	160	356	921	0.8	0.9	166	119	17	38	42

Table 2.2 continued:

Ireland	(1)	(2)	(3)	(4)	(5)	(6)	(7)	(8)	(9)	(10)	(11)	(12)
	288	1,148	273	343	1,025	0.8	1.0	119	89	26	33	34
Donegal	—	51	15	—	34	—	0.0	—	67	44	—	32
North-West	—	43	14	—	28	—	0.0	—	66	49	—	36
West	—	123	47	—	89	—	0.1	—	73	53	—	34
Midlands	—	104	35	—	78	—	0.1	—	75	45	—	35
South-West	—	177	47	—	156	—	0.2	—	88	30	—	35
South-East	—	126	37	—	109	—	0.1	—	86	34	—	33
North-East	—	79	24	—	63	—	0.1	—	80	33	—	36
East	—	338	24	—	376	—	0.4	—	111	6	—	35
Mid-West	—	106	32	—	91	—	0.1	—	86	35	—	34
Luxemburg	55	128	10	64	133	0.1	0.1	116	103	8	48	36

Source: NEI, Population by region and employment per region and industry in the European Community, 1950, 1960, 1970, Rotterdam, 1975 (see FLEUR study).

(a) Industry represents: mining and quarrying, manufacturing and repair, electricity, gas and water and construction.

(b) Agriculture represents: agriculture, hunting, forestry and fishing.

See also: W.T.M. Molle et al., op.cit., Appendix 3.

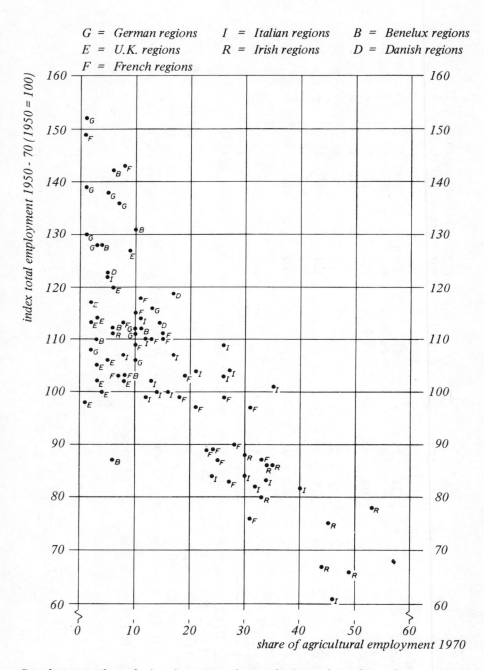

Graph 2.1: The relation between the evolution of total employment (1950—70) and the orientation to agricultural employment by regions.

and Graph 2.1). Regions with more than 20 per cent increase of employment during the period 1950–70 were those of Hamburg, Bremen, West Berlin (all city regions), Nordrhein-Westfalen, Hessen, and Baden-Württemberg in Germany, East-Anglia in the United Kingdom, Lombardia in Italy, Région Parisienne and Provence-Côte d'Azur in France, the regions East, West and South in the Netherlands, and Sjaelland in Denmark.

In many regions there was a decrease of employment during the period 1950–70, this was the case in:

United Kingdom	North-West (— 2 per cent)
	Scotland (— 0.5)
Italy	Friuli-Venezia Giulia (— 1)
	Marche (— 16)
	Umbria (— 16)
	Abruzzi (— 18)
	Molise (— 39)
	Basilicata (— 18)
	Calabria (— 17)
France	Basse-Normandie (— 3)
	Bourgogne (— 1)
	Pays de la Loire (— 1)
	Bretagne (— 13)
	Poitou-Charentes (— 10)
	Aquitaine (— 11)
	Midi-Pyrénées (— 13)
	Auvergne (— 11)
	Languedoc-Roussillon (— 3)
	Corse (— 17)
Belgium	Wallonie (— 13)
Ireland	All but East-region

Most of these declining or stagnating regions belong to the peripheral regions of France, the British Isles, and Italy.

The sectoral growth rates varied even more widely. In agriculture, employment decreased from 22.1 million in 1950 to 9.6 million in 1970, that is — 56.5 per cent; in industry the number of jobs increased from 36.6 million to 45.4 million, showing a growth index of 124. The greatest increase was realised in the services sector: from 29.4 million to 44.2 million, a growth index of 250. All this changed the economic structure of the EEC to a large extent:

	1950	1960	1970
Agriculture	25%	16%	9%
Industry	41%	45%	46%
Services	33%	38%	45%
Total	100%	100%	100%

Sectoral evolution mostly went in the same direction in all countries with two exceptions (United Kingdom and Belgium) as far as industry is concerned. This is illustrated by the following yearly growth rates by sector and by country (1950–70).

	Agriculture	Industry	Services	Total
Germany (FR)	−5.1	1.6	2.8	1.1
United Kingdom	−2.9	0.1	1.2	0.5
Italy	−3.9	1.8	2.4	0.2
France	−3.9	1.4	2.2	0:5
Netherlands	−3.5	1.5	2.3	1.3
Belgium	−4.2	−0.2	1.4	0.2
Denmark	−3.6	1.4	2.5	0.9
Ireland	−2.9	0.9	0.6	−0.6
Luxemburg	−5.5	0.8	1.7	0.2
EEC	−4.1	1.1	2.1	0.6

It should be noted that the decrease of employment in agriculture and the increase in the services sector is revealed in all regions mentioned in Table 2.2. The growth of the number of jobs in industry is also typical of all regions except four in the United Kingdom (North, Yorkshire-Humberside, North-West, and Scotland), one in Italy (Liguria), one in France (Nord), and two in Belgium (Wallonie and Brabant).

The growth rate in industry was particularly high (more than 2 per cent per annum) in the German regions of Hessen, Baden-Württemberg, and Bayern, in East Anglia in the United Kingdom, in Veneto, Emilia-Romagna, Marche, Abruzzi, Molise, Puglia, and Basilicata in Italy, and in Franche-Comté in France, in the regions North and South of the Netherlands, and finally, Jylland in Denmark. For further details about the development of employment by sector and region see the study of W.T.M. Molle et al.

The above figures already indicate how an orientation towards agriculture affects total employment changes; we will pay particular attention to this impact below.

Graph 2.1 shows the relationship between the evolution of total employment in the period 1950–70 and the orientation to agriculture. The general trend that can be derived from this graph is quite clear. The higher the share of agricultural employment in total employment, the lower the index of total employment for the period considered. All but five of the regions strongly oriented to agriculture (share of agricultural employment higher than 20 per cent) show a decrease in total employment.

Yet this graph reveals a rather heterogeneous composition: the relationship is not so close for all the countries[4] involved:

West Germany: medium relationship	R = − 0.62
United Kingdom: poor relationship	R = + 0.39
Italy: good relationship	R = − 0.80
France: good relationship	R = − 0.85
Benelux: poor relationship	R = + 0.03
Denmark: too limited a number of regions	
Ireland: good relationship	R = − 0.92
EEC: medium to good relationship (84 observations)	
linear relationship	R = − 0.36
log-linear relationship	R = − 0.72

The poor relationship in the United Kingdom and the Benelux countries can be explained by two factors: both were confronted with stagnating sectors in industry and most of their agricultural areas had a large labour reserve. Labour availability was, especially for the centre of the EEC, a very important location factor during the 1960s, as was evident in the Benelux countries and for West Germany.

A final remark seems in order. According to W.T.M. Molle et al. national factors seem to govern the participation ratios and the growth of total employment by region. It means that most of the total degree of inequality in participation ratios and growth of employment by region is due to differences between countries, and only a minor part to differences between regions of the individual countries (the within-set inequality).

Income disparities

The European Commission has published two interesting studies about income disparities in Europe[5] or, more precisely, disparity in gross domestic product. In these studies an effort was made to illustrate the income disparities within each country and on the level of the

Community as a whole. Although the figures relate to the 1960s and the beginning of the 1970s, and in spite of the difficulties of comparison, the publication shows us the magnitude of the regional income disparities in the Community. Most helpful, however, is the 1976 Eurostat publication 'regional accounts — economic aggregates 1970'. For the first time Eurostat published the harmonised results of regional accounts compiled by the Member States in accordance with the European system of Integrated Economic Accounts (ESA) on the level of the Community's basic administrative units. The figures in Table 2.3 are based on this Eurostat publication, except those for Denmark and Ireland.

Another very valuable source is to be found in the study of W.T.M. Molle et al. These authors have calculated gross domestic product (but at factor cost) by regions for the years 1950, 1960, and 1970. The figures are based on national resources; the very interesting harmonised results are summarised in Table 2.4.

In every country of the Community the income disparities (in fact GDP per head of population) are quite large, but the ratio between the extreme values varies considerably. For an exact interpretation of the disparities, it is necessary to emphasise how much the disparities are influenced by the size of the economic or administrative regions. The higher the number of regions in one country, the greater the disparities.

The disparities on the national level (see Table 2.3) vary between 1 to 1.3 and 1 to 2.6. If we take the Community as a whole, disregarding for a while the Land-city Hamburg, the ratio of the income *per capita* in the regions with the highest level (Sjaelland and the Paris region) to the region with the lowest level (Calabria) is about 4.6. Whatever remarks can be made about the comparability of the regional income levels, the ratio of 4.6 indicates a very high inequality within the Community. Taking into account that Table 2.3 and Table 2.4 are not entirely comparable, W.T.M. Molle et al. get slightly different results.

Another view of disparities in the Community can be found in Graph 2.3 which shows the population distribution in the Community of Nine according to the gross domestic product per head in 1970. This graph is based on the Eurostat publications 'Regional accounts, economic aggregates, 1970' and 'Report on the regional problems in the enlarged Community'. (Taking into account the results of Table 2.4, derived from the study of W.T.M. Molle et al., we shifted Wales and Scotland from the income class 80—100 to that of 60—80.) About 59 per cent of the population of the EEC has an income level within 20 per cent either side of the Community level. That may lead to the conclusion that the disparities are not, after all, so great as was suggested above.

There are, however, important variations around the Community average. In two large European areas, Southern Italy and Ireland, which

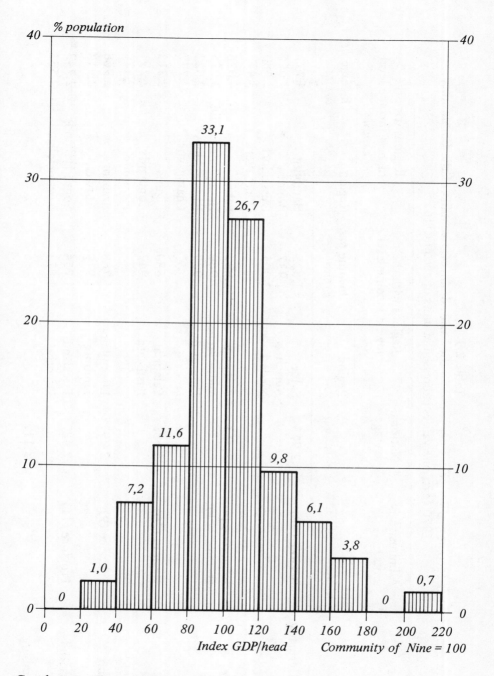

Graph 2.2: The population distribution in the EEC according to the GDP at market prices per head and per region in 1970.

69

Table 2.3

The gross value added at market prices *per capita* in the basic administrative units of the Community, 1970 (extreme values expressed in units of account) [6]

Country	Administrative units	National average	Regions with the lowest income level *per capita*		Regions with the highest income level *per capita*	
			Region	Income *per capita*	Region	Income *per capita*
West-Germany	Bezirke (38)	2.973	Stade	1.825	Hamburg	4.777
			Aurich	1.937	Bremen	3.665
			Niederbayern	2.005	Düsseldorf	3.480
					Oberbayern	3.477
France	Région de pro-gramme (21)	2.713	Bretagne	1.927	Paris	4.026
			Midi-Pyrénées	1.969	Haute-Normandie	3.025
			Limousin	1.973	Rhône-Alpes	2.822
					Champagne	2.777
Italy	Regioni (20)	1.683	Calabria	880	Liguria	2.312
			Basilicata	947	Lombardy	2.291
					Piemonte	2,170
Belgium	Province (9)	2.297	Luxemburg	1.788	Brabant	2.968
			Limburg	1.919	Antwerp	2.917
Netherlands	Province (11)	2.487	Friesland	1.754	South-Holland	2.743
			Drenthe	1.871	North-Holland	2.533
Luxemburg	—	3.117	—		—	—

United Kingdom	Standard regions (11)	2.170	North	1.745	South-East	2.494
			Northern Ireland	1.764	East-Midlands	2.201
Ireland	Planning regions (9)	1.318	West	995	East	1.590
			Donegal	1.002	South-West	1.320
Denmark	Zones (3)	3.160	Jylland	2.595	Sjaelland	3.775
Community		2.399				

Source: Eurostat, Regional accounts, economic aggregates, 1970;
Report on the regional problems in the Enlarged Community.

Table 2.4
Gross value added at factor costs per head of population and per
head of employment per region, 1950, 1960 and 1970 (in $ per head)

Region	GDP *per capita*			GDP per head of employment		
	1950	1960	1970	1950	1960	1970
EEC	489	1022	2180	1201	2465	5530
Germany (FR)	400	1124	2720	960	2369	6312
Schleswig-Holstein	290	925	2167	927	2372	6027
Hamburg	709	1783	3977	1628	3210	7332
Niedersachsen	323	967	2306	850	2190	5662
Bremen	583	1519	3156	1325	2860	6186
Nordrhein-Westfalen	468	1230	2831	1142	2697	6960
Hessen	390	1157	2967	955	2361	6596
Rheinland-Pfalz	325	867	2494	711	1941	6290
Baden-Württemberg	402	1170	2816	834	2200	5975
Bayern	343	989	2608	776	2005	5834
Saarland	490	1064	2264	1172	2470	5890
Berlin (West)	407	1142	2800	1195	2501	6235
United Kingdom	632	1203	1844	1471	2742	4337
England	660	1246	1896	1516	2793	4386
North	537	1091	1553	1331	2712	3856
Yorkshire-Humberside	643	1239	1704	1446	2741	4009
East-Midlands	567	1213	1783	1284	2705	4131
East-Anglia	551	1042	1725	1437	2534	4261
South-East	776	1348	2139	1785	2974	4790
South-West	460	1066	1715	1215	2686	4380
West-Midlands	660	1305	1922	1427	2763	4264
North-West	622	1186	1757	1344	2588	4077
Wales	454	1057	1578	1173	2673	4066
Scotland	560	1041	1684	1350	2488	4170
Northern Ireland	393	756	1332	998	2033	3725
Italy	307	626	1560	823	1663	4552
Piemonte	442	877	1987	988	1971	5071
Valle d'Aoste	473	920	2018	1071	2214	5285
Liguria	509	916	2053	1304	2286	5884
Lombardia	466	937	2102	1132	2218	5432
Trentino-Alto Adige	337	611	1596	888	1525	4506
Veneto	274	602	1539	745	1581	4444
Friuli-Venezia Giulia	311	642	1686	859	1645	4851

Table 2.4 continued:

	1950	1960	1970	1950	1960	1970
Emilia-Romagna	328	716	1821	779	1667	4547
Marche	261	467	1349	576	1006	3323
Toscane	324	623	1614	837	1567	4502
Umbria	266	471	1387	661	1128	3929
Lazio	341	732	1646	930	2157	5544
Campania	208	435	1063	639	1341	3537
Abruzzi·	201	421	1178	553	1145	3563
Molise	170	359	976	369	697	2642
Puglia	200	400	1107	607	1249	3643
Basilicata	173	302	1008	453	816	2948
Calabria	171	311	895	505	954	2982
Sicilia	201	387	1134	690	1307	3875
Sardegna	235	448	1215	777	1486	4415
France	587	1141	2498	1366	2926	6399
Région Parisienne	952	1733	3704	2160	3909	7760
Champagne	545	1082	2489	1331	2886	6547
Picardie	546	1034	2277	1403	2882	6328
Haute Normandie	590	1299	2864	1419	3362	7325
Centre	435	972	2264	1011	2558	5960
Basse Normandie	453	873	1983	998	2187	5027
Bourgogne	466	915	2160	1108	2447	5793
Nord	616	1133	2275	1569	3129	6552
Lorraine	659	1160	2359	1684	3241	6618
Alsace	629	1089	2453	1459	2778	6360
Franche-Comté	543	1027	2235	1258	2654	5749
Pays de la Loire	462	925	2126	1025	2353	5498
Bretagne	423	791	1782	947	2013	4833
Poitou-Charentes	403	833	1958	937	2352	5486
Aquitaine	448	1020	2199	974	2621	6055
Midi-Pyrénées	394	817	1791	858	2125	5013
Limousin	494	854	1894	1000	2032	4885
Rhône-Alpes	586	1117	2581	1287	2708	6300
Auvergne	489	905	1917	1069	2314	4959
Languedoc-Roussillon	434	882	1828	1114	2660	5782
Provence-Côte d'Azur	566	1141	2324	1481	3321	6673
Corse	478	892	1768	1380	3488	7346
Netherlands	430	888	2226	1237	2606	6382
North	363	782	2011	1059	2374	6125
East	355	791	1998	984	2350	5874
West	479	970	2449	1381	2781	6830
South	414	831	2031	1207	2513	5893

Table 2.4 continued:

	1950	1960	1970	1950	1960	1970
Belgium	717	1109	2373	1944	3238	6935
Vlaanderen	642	1010	2336	1887	3133	7011
Wallonie	730	1052	2130	1990	3243	6868
Brabant	859	1406	2779	1981	3407	6872
Denmark	663	1141	2689	1565	2670	6081
Sjaelland-Lolland-Falster	711	1254	2896	1619	2765	6224
Fyn	646	1086	2545	1523	2577	5861
Jylland	616	1034	2499	1513	2576	5958
Ireland	351	639	1315	907	1793	3823
Luxemburg	868	1479	2820	2015	3727	7210

Source: W.T.M. Molle, B. van Holst and H. Smit, 'Regional Disparity and Economic Development in the European Community', op.cit., Appendix 3.

contain about 8 per cent of the population, there is undoubtedly a serious lag: the gross regional product per head does not attain 60 per cent of the average for the Community. In Ireland, only the East region has a higher index (67), (see Map 2.3). Alongside these two areas and towards the centre of the Community, there are two other areas where the situation is better but which are nonetheless well below the Community average, with gross regional products *per capita* of between 60 and 80 per cent of the Community average. These are Central Italy and the North-East of Italy and the North and West of the United Kingdom.

On the other hand the EEC has a number of regions which have an income level considerably above the Community average. A high or very high level of income (GDP per head exceeding 20 per cent of the Community average) is found in the regions of the capital cities of France, West Germany, Belgium (including the Province of Antwerp), and Denmark, and in the Land-cities and a few other regions of Germany. These regions account for 20.6 per cent of the EEC population.

Although it is not our intention to explain the regional income disparities — for a general explanation refer to chapter 1 — a number of relationships are worth emphasising.

(a) It cannot be denied that peripheral situation, unequal activity rates, and/or predominance of agriculture in the economic structure are largely responsible for the inequalities. The comparison of Map 2.3 and the orientation of employment to agriculture mentioned in Table 2.2, is indicative in this matter. GDP per head

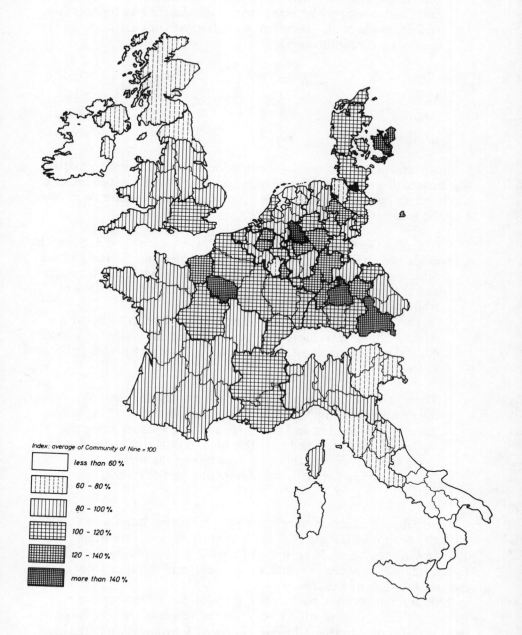

Index: average of Community of Nine = 100

less than 60 %

60 – 80 %

80 – 100 %

100 – 120 %

120 – 140 %

more than 140 %

Map 2.3: The gross domestic product at market prices per head and by region, 1970

75

correlates negatively with the share of agriculture in total employment and positively with the shares of industry and services (see W.T.M. Molle et al.: correlation coefficients of GDP and employment-structure indicators).

	Agriculture	Industry	Services
1950	−0.70	+0.61	+0.62
1960	−0.79	+0.62	+0.70
1970	−0.62	+0.32	+0.55

However, agriculture employment alone is not sufficient to explain the income disparities in Europe. Certain agricultural regions are in a much better position. For a more detailed analysis we refer to chapter 4 of the study of W.T.M. Molle et al.

(b) The German authors D. Biehl, E. Hussmann, and S. Schnyder made the interesting remark that income per head in the EEC of Six appears to fall steadily with the distance between the region and the European Community's industrial centre in the lower Rhine valley (see Graph 2.3):[7]
   This general statement would still apply if we considered the EEC of Nine. It is, moreover, borne out by the following consideration of A. Cairncross, H. Giersch, A. Lamfalussy, G. Petrilli, and P. Uri:

There is also evidence of a kind of curved development axis running down from a high point near the mouth of the Rhine in one direction to London and Coventry and in the other along the Valley of the Rhine and over the Alps to Milan. The area lying along this axis covers about one-quarter of the surface of the Community and contributes almost one-half to its total product. [8]

We shall have occasion to return to the subject in hand when we deal with the economic potential of the European regions (see chapter 4). [9] It will then be made clear that Graph 2.3 incorporates in fact a causal relation between regional income level and distance from the industrial centre of Europe.
   The German authors, basing their calculations on the regions of Europe of the Six, have tried to express the relation between income level and distance to the industrial centre of Europe (Köln-Düsseldorf) in the following equations.

$$\ln Y_i = 7{,}97387 - 0{,}00086\,X_i \quad N = 61 \quad R^2 = 0.71 \qquad (2.1)$$
$$(\pm\ 0{,}00007)$$

$$\ln Y_i = 7{,}86149 - 0{,}00079\,X_i + 0{,}00019\,Z_i \quad N = 61 \quad R^2 = 0.81 \quad (2.2)$$
$$(\pm\ 0{,}00006) \quad (\pm\ (0{,}00003))$$

where:

Y_i = income per head in region i;

X_i = distance of region i from the area Köln-Düsseldorf;

Z_i = population density of region i;

N = number of observations.

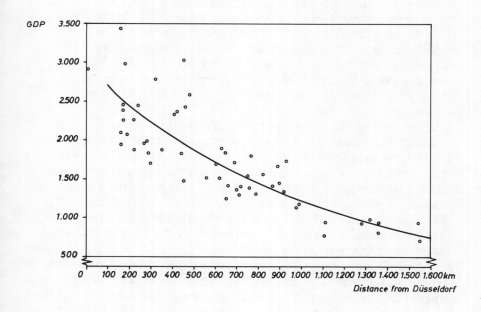

Graph 2.3: Relation between regional product per head and the distance of regions from the economic centre (the area Köln-Düsseldorf in Nordrhein-Westfalen) of the European Community of Six, 1968.

Such an analysis, which does not take any causal factors into account is, of course, an extremely simple one.

Further on we shall see that the population density or the degree of urbanisation stands for a number of very important location factors.

(c) The differences in activity rate or employment rate by region form a third general factor explaining the income disparities. The highest employment rate is registered in Land Hamburg (54 per cent), the lowest in the region Sardegna (27 per cent).

Some very important remarks should be made to complete this section.

1. The regional product per head is only a rough indicator of the real welfare disparities between the different regions, even if we disregard such non-economic factors as the environment in the broad sense. Many factors support that thesis. [10] In the first place there is the difference between gross regional product and regional income. The product of a region is the total sum of the value added created there without taking into consideration the contribution to the regional income of production factors located or working elsewhere. Unfortunately the income created by commuters is unknown.

In the second place transfer incomes should be taken into account. The transfer can take different forms such as incomes from labour, profits, capital income. This transfer can be positive or negative for any region, a distinction which is very important if we take small regions into consideration. A region with a high product may have a rather low welfare level due to this transfer. [11] For the regions taken into consideration in this chapter, the distinction has not too much importance. A third factor that may disturb the picture is depreciation.

2. More important is the distinction between product or money income on the one hand and real income on the other. We can expect that the difference in purchasing power between the regions is less than the disparity based on regional product. To measure the former, we need to work with purchasing power parities (PPP). Indeed in the poor regions, the price level for a number of products and services is lower and their home consumption higher than in the industrial regions. It is unlikely, however, that correction would change the general picture of inequalities between the regions. Probably the psychological income due to environmental factors is more important.

3.   The disparities between the regions are further lessened by unequal tax burdens. Income taxes are progressive. Sometimes it is stated that we must also consider public transfers in the form of social security and infrastructure aid. In general this consideration is correct.

4.   In comparing the income levels of regions in different countries attention should be paid to the exchange rate chosen; that is well illustrated in the above mentioned contribution of D. Biehl, E. Hussmann, and S. Schnyder.[12]

In this chapter we are concerned with the lessening of regional income disparities on the national level. It is quite possible, however, that — after the movements in the exchange rates during the 1970s — the EEC regions as a whole present a different picture as far as income disparity is concerned.

5.   In this section and the preceding sections we analysed briefly a number of indicators of regional disparity. Other indicators can be added to the analysis such as income per head of the working population.

To conclude our disparity analyses it would be interesting to make a ranking of the regions; however, the unequal breakdown of the different statistical resources makes this rather difficult. So we shall just refer to a study made by G. Tagliacarne,[14] who ranked the 119 regions of the European Community (such as they are defined by the Commission) according to four separate indicators: (a) the GDP per head; (b) the ratio of agricultural to total employment; (c) the ratio of total employment to population, and (d) the ratio of net migration to total population.

Such a ranking of the regions is to a certain extent a synthesis of the factors discussed in the preceding sections of this chapter and the migration factor mentioned in the theoretical considerations of the first chapter. Among the top twenty regions, there are 11 German regions (of which 8 Bezirke), 4 French regions (Région Parisienne in first place), one region each for Belgium, the United Kingdom, Denmark, and Italy, and, finally, Luxemburg. All but 2 of the 20 lower-ranked regions are in Italy (10 regions), and Ireland (8 regions), the exceptions being Northern Ireland and Friesland.

The example of the United States

In the section 'The geographical distribution of employment' we came to the conclusion that within the EEC income disparities are rather high and, indeed, within most individual Member States. In the context of this study it seems interesting to compare the regional income disparities in the EEC with those in the United States.

But in making such a comparison it is important to avoid a common

Table 2.5
The evolution of the *per capita* personal income in the United States by region, 1929—76 (average of US = 100)*

Region	1929	1948	1965	1976
New England	125	104	108	103
Mid-East	138	115	114	108
Great Lakes	114	112	108	105
Plains	81	101	96	95
South-East	52	69	77	86
South-West	67	83	86	94
Rocky Mountain	85	99	91	94
Far West	129	120	114	110
United States	100	100	100	100
Typical states				
Connecticut	146	120	126	115
New York	165	126	122	110
South Carolina	38	62	69	80
Mississippi	41	55	60	71
Alabama	46	61	70	80

* See also Appendix 2.1

mistake. The regional breakdown has a very great influence on the final disparities perceived. The smaller is the number of regions the less are the inequalities. This general remark should be taken into account in the interpretation of the results.

The first conclusion that can be drawn from Table 2.5 and more precisely from Appendix 2.1 (*per capita* personal income by State) concerns the overall disparity. The index of income per head varies between 163 and 77, high indexes being scored by Alaska (163), (with a very high price level), District of Columbia (126), Connecticut, Illinois, and New Jersey (115), and low scores being reached for Mississippi (79), Arkansas (77), and Alabama, South Carolina and four states of the South-East region (80). That comes to a national disparity of about 1 to 2.3 or 1 to 1.8 if we drop the region of Alaska. Even if we take the size of the American States into consideration, this disparity is much smaller than the income disparities observed in the EEC. The disparity between economic regions in the United States is even smaller, with indexes ranging from 110 for the Far West to 86 for the South-

East in 1976. Comparison of this disparity with that of the European national income levels of 1970 sustains our general conclusion. The extreme indexes for the EEC were 126 for France, 118 for Denmark on the one hand, and 68 for Italy and 53 for Ireland[15] on the other.

One fundamental remark should be made here. The European figures relate to gross value added and the American ones to personal income, which greatly influences the results. Disparities expressed in terms of *per capita* product are generally far greater than those expressed in terms of *per capita* disposable income. Without changing the trend of our general conclusion that the disparity in income tends to be greater in Europe than in the US, our remark points out that inter-regional income transfers are sizeable, and help to correct the imbalance in the regional distribution of product.

A second general conclusion concerns the evolution of the disparities. Table 2.5 shows a net decrease in the income inequalities in the United States during the period 1929–76.

While the extreme values on the states level were 1 to 4 in 1929, they became 1 to 2.5 in 1950 and 1 to 2.3 (1.8) in 1976. The evolution in the last decade is very striking, and is to be attributed largely to migration out of the cities.

The trend towards lower regional disparities in the United States started long before 1929. Some figures of R.A. Easterlin and G.C. Bjork may illustrate that. R.A. Easterlin has calculated the arithmetic mean deviation of regional *per capita* income from national level (per cent) for the period 1880–1950 (based on nine regions).[16]

1880:	45.6
1900:	36.6
1920:	25.7
1930:	31.1
1940:	25.0
1950:	16.9

The decline of inter-regional income differentials in the United States can, according to B. Balassa, be attributed to migration, to shifts in the composition of output, to shifts of location affecting some industries, and lately to increased government spending in the South.[17]

Two determining factors seem to be mainly responsible for the inter-regional differences in income level in Europe and the United States, viz:

(a)   low productivity per head in all sectors of a region, and

(b) a high percentage of low productivity sectors in a region.

The importance of the first factor is stressed by J. Viner: 'The real problem . . . is not agriculture as such, or the absence of manufacturing as such, but poverty and backwardness, or poor agriculture and poor manufacturing'.[18] The second factor has been emphasised in the discussion of regional disparities in the United States, where it has been shown that about 80 per cent of the variation in *per capita* incomes can be explained by differences in occupational distribution.[19]

G.C. Bjork gives a good idea of the convergence (or lack of it) in the regional incomes in the United States. His research work, also related to the period 1880–1950,[20] can give us some indication of what may happen in the EEC regions.

Table 2.6
Weighted mean percentage deviation of individual states in the
United States from the national averages of income and
demographic variables

	1880	1900	1920	1950
1 Personal income *per capita*	35.2	33.3	27.5	19.2
2 Labour income *per capita*	33.3	30.3	34.3	18.1
3 Labour force as % of population	8.2	6.3	6.1	4.7
4 Labour income per worker	30.6	27.6	18.9	13.6
5 Agricultural labour income per worker	33.8	35.7	33.1	32.3
6 Non-agricultural labour income per worker	12.4	11.8	10.0	11.8
7 Non-agricultural workers as % of labour force	38.5	31.3	21.2	8.6
8 Property income *per capita*	51.1	51.1	42.3	29.3

Source: G.C. Bjork, op.cit., p.84

From this Table 2.6 two conclusions can be drawn. First, the convergence in *per capita* income between states was largely due to the growing similarity in the proportion of the labour force engaged in agriculture. The convergence of labour income per worker coupled with the narrowing of differences in labour force participation and the interstate equalisation of property income also contributed to *per capita* income equalisation.

Secondly, the most interesting point presented by the table is that there is no strong movement toward convergence in labour income per worker in non-agricultural employment.

According to G.C. Bjork one might have expected a more marked convergence in labour income per worker in non-agricultural employment for three reasons, namely, (a) lower barriers to interstate migration due to improved transportation and better information about economic opportunities, (b) the growth of national labour unions (see chapter 1), and (c) the greater mobility of capital (economic theory postulates that factor prices will tend to become equal when either factors of production or goods are free to move among regions).

The author attributes the lack of convergence or insufficient convergence to three factors. The first factor is the fact that regional price differences may conceal a convergence in 'real' as opposed to money wages. The second factor is that there are structural differences in employment even though labour in the same type of employment receives equal wages. Does the existence of high wages permit the establishment and expansion of only those industries in which labour productivity is high enough for the industry to compete successfully in the labour market? An example of that phenomenon might be spotted in Massachusetts, where the textile industry emigrated to a lower wage area but was replaced with electronics and light manufacturing, which have in turn raised the wages further and started to drive out the shoe industry. The third factor is the demand for labour relative to supply. Bjork tries to explain changes in relative wages by predicted changes in relative labour scarcity in places where labour scarcity is not balanced by migration. The relatively static demand for food and the increasing demand for consumer durables and services have an effect on the location of employment opportunities. At the same time significant differences in the rates of natural population growth occurred in a pattern opposite to that of the changes in labour demand.

Measurement of regional disparities and the evolution of income disparities in the countries of the Community

Measurement of the dispersion of extreme values [21]

So far this chapter has been descriptive. Given the aim of this study, it seems necessary to draw attention to a number of techniques for measuring employment or income disparities; that will provide the opportunity to study the evolution of these disparities in the countries of the Community.

A large number of techniques can be used to analyse disparities. A first group of measuring techniques can be called 'measurement of the dispersion of extreme values'. We distinguish three measures:

1 The range of variation

$$v = x_1 - x_2 \text{ (}x_1 \text{ being the highest value and } x_2 \text{ the lowest).}$$

2 Relation between extreme values

$$R = x_1/x_2$$

Instead of this simple ratio, the ratio between extreme 'quantiles' can be taken, that is, for instance, the ratio between the means of the upper and lower 10 per cent, or that between upper and lower 'quartiles', that is 25 per cent.

3 Deviation of extreme value

This measure gives a better method of dealing with disparities, in which the extreme values are compared, not with each other, but to the arithmetical mean of the series ($\bar{x}$).
The characteristic of dispersion is then: $E = e_1 - e_2$, where e_1 and e_2 can be calculated alternatively:

by difference: $e_1 = x_1 - \bar{x}$ and $e_2 = x_2 - \bar{x}$
by ratio: $e_1 = x_1/\bar{x}$ and $e_2 = x_2/\bar{x}$

This first group of measuring techniques has only a limited value because they consider only the extreme values; it was this type of measurement that was used in the preceding sections.

Measurement of total dispersion

The measuring techniques examined in the previous section have in common that they take into consideration only the extreme values and do not measure the dispersion of the observations as a whole. We distinguish three measures of total dispersion:

(a) the mean deviation;
(b) the standard deviation;
(c) the variance (the variance can be decomposed into a 'within-group' and a 'between-groups' variance);
(d) the coefficient of variation (this coefficient can be decomposed in the same way as the variance into a within-set and a

84

between set variation).

To compare countries and periods, the coefficient of variation is the only adequate indication of dispersion. The coefficient of variation is defined as: $CV = 100 \, s/\bar{x}$ in which s is the standard deviation and $\bar{x}$ the mean. According to W.T.M. Molle et al. the coefficient of variation took the following values for the period 1950–70.[22]

	1950	1960	1970
EEC programming regions	36.2	32.8	29.3
EEC countries	32.3	25.0	22.8
West Germany	28.5	22.5	17.6
United Kingdom	18.2	13.9	11.4
Italy	35.6	35.6	26.0
France	22.6	19.8	19.0

The disparity between the countries of the EEC decreased during the whole period 1950–70, albeit more in a pronounced way in the 1950s than in the 1960s. The disparity decreased also between the regions of each of the four large countries considered. The decrease in the disparities in Italy was entirely achieved during the 1960s, the coefficient of variation decreased from 35.6 to 26.0.[23] The CV coefficients illustrate that the highest income disparities are to be found in Italy.

Measurement of concentration

Two measures of concentration can be derived from the concentration curve established by Lorenz (see graph 2.4). The Lorenz curve shows the relationship between regional distribution of the product, as an ordinate, and of the population, on the abscissa.[24] The concentration curve L is nearer to the diagonal of equidistribution OA as income disparities are lower. From the application of the Lorenz curve we can derive two coefficients:

(a) *the coefficient of concentration.*
The coefficient of concentration R is defined as:

$$R = \frac{\sum\limits_{i=1}^{n} \left| P_i - Y_i \right|}{2\Sigma\, P_i}$$

in which

P_i = share in population of region i;

Y_i = share in product of region i.

The R-value varies between 0 (the L curve coinciding with the diagonal of equidistribution) and 1 (the product being produced virtually in one region only).

This coefficient has a strong similarity with the coefficient of geographic association (coefficient of Florence):

$$F = 1 - \frac{1}{2} \sum\limits_{i=1}^{n} \left| P_i - Y_i \right|$$

where 1 means complete equality and 0 complete inequality.

(b) *Gini's coefficient of concentration.*
Gini's coefficient of concentration corresponds to twice the area enclosed between the diagonal of equidistribution and the concentration curve. It varies, therefore, between 0 and 1, the former value indicating absolute equality, the latter absolute inequality. It is defined as:

$$G = \frac{1}{2} \sum\limits_{i=1}^{n} \sum\limits_{j=1}^{n} P_i P_j \left| \frac{Y_i}{P_i} - \frac{Y_j}{P_j} \right|$$

where P and Y are, respectively, the shares of total population and of product in each region. If ten regions are considered, there are 10 times 9 differences $\left| \dfrac{Y_i}{P_i} - \dfrac{Y_j}{P_j} \right|$, each weighted by the corresponding $P_i P_j$.

Because it gives a variable weighting to different observations, Gini's coefficient constitutes a better methodological approach than previously mentioned ways to measure dispersion. However, the coefficient of variation can also be weighted. We draw attention to the fact that

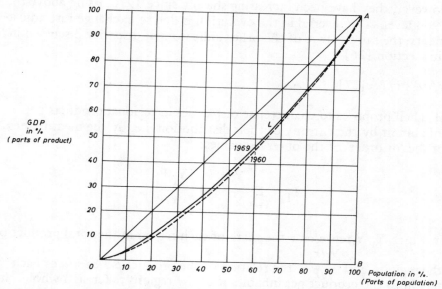

Graph 2.4: The cumulative contribution of the EEC regions to the GDP, 1960 and 1969.

Gini's coefficient like any measure of dispersion, is influenced by the number of regions considered. The Gini coefficient for Belgium based on nine provinces equals G = 0.104; when only three regions were considered, G would become 0.070.

The following figures show the evolution of the G-values between 1950 and 1970 for estimated regional GDP at factor cost.[25]

	1950	1960	1970
EEC-programming regions	0.207	0.162	0.155
EEC-countries	0.156	0.106	0.118
West Germany	0.096	0.071	0.049
United Kingdom	0.101	0.062	0.067
Italy	0.190	0.191	0.144
France	0.159	0.138	0.132

In all countries considered the regional income equality had become somewhat smaller in the course of the study period. The figures show once more that disparity was greater in Italy than in the other EEC countries. Income equalities between the regions of the EEC as a whole also narrowed, most perceptively so in the first decade; probably, however, they have been increasing sharply since 1970, rising above the 1960 level. The reversal in the evolution is due to exchange-rate adjustments; the same is true of the other indicators of disparity discussed in this section.[26]

Theil's index[27]

H. Theil proposes to characterise disparities in regional products per inhabitant by the entropy of their distribution, i.e. by the measurement of the 'disorder' of the observed values.

$$I_T = \sum_{i=1}^{n} \frac{Y_i}{Y} \; \log \; \frac{Y_i/P_i}{Y/P}$$

in which Y_i/Y represents the share of each region in the total product of the regions, and $\dfrac{Y_i/P_i}{Y/P}$ the relation of the product *per capita* of each region to the product per inhabitant of the regions taken as a whole. It can vary between 0 and $\log P/P_i$. The value 0 corresponds to the case of perfect equality in regional products per head. The value $\log P/P_i$ corresponds to the case of maximum inequality in regional products per inhabitant, in which the whole of the product is concentrated in the region where the population is smallest.

Gini's coefficient of concentration and Theil's index are both weighted. But while the former is weighted by population, the latter is weighted by product to conform more to the economic significance of the desired measurement.

Theil's index has, in addition, possibilities of aggregation into sub-assemblies (e.g. groups of regions) which make it particularly interesting from the point of view of analysis of regional disparities: total variation = variation of national average incomes *per capita* between the EEC countries + variations of regional average income *per capita* in the EEC countries.

$$I_T = \sum_{i=1}^{n} Y_i \log \frac{Y_i}{P_i} = \sum_{g=1}^{G} Y_g \log \frac{Y_g}{P_g} + \sum_{g=1}^{G} Y_g \left[\sum_{i \in S_g} \frac{Y_i}{Y_g} \log \frac{Y_i/Y_g}{P_i/P_g} \right]$$

where:

Y_i = part of region i in the EEC product;

P_i = part of region i in the EEC population;

Y_g = part of country g in the EEC product;

P_g = part of country g in the EEC population;

G = number of countries;

S_g = number of regions in country g ($i \epsilon S_g$: i is one element of the group S_g);

N = number of regions in the EEC.

W.T.M. Molle et al. calculated for the period 1950—70 the following I_T values: [28]

	1950	1960	1970
EEC-programming regions	0.068	0.047	0.039
EEC countries	0.040	0.026	0.023
West Germany	0.017	0.010	0.005
United Kingdom	0.017	0.007	0.007
Italy	0.057	0.057	0.033
France	0.043	0.033	0.030

Once again for all EEC countries considered, regional disparities are decreasing, if much more pronounced in the first decade than the second. It must be emphasised that the results obtained with the Theil-coefficients do not correspond entirely with those based on the Gini-coefficients.

How total disparity is built up out of disparities between whole countries and between the regions of the individual countries can be seen by decomposing the I_T coefficient into a between-sets (countries of the EEC) and a within-set inequality (regions within a country).

W.T.M. Molle et al. observed that the larger part of total regional disparity in levels of GDP per head in the European Community is due to disparities between the levels of GDP per head of countries. As a matter of fact, in all three reference years the 'between-sets inequality' accounted for 55 to 60 per cent of total inequality between EEC programming regions as far as GDP/population was concerned (57 to 60 per cent with regard to GDP per head of employment). They derive one important conclusion from these findings: 'That is why policies setting out first and foremost to reduce imbalances between member states are likely to do more towards diminishing overall disparity than "regional" policies in the narrow sense of the word'.[29]

The decrease in disparity between levels of GDP *per capita* may have been brought about by two different developments: (a) redistribution of people and (b) redistribution of income. If the population grows in core regions while declining in laggard regions, the disparity will go down. But regional policy aims at decreasing disparity by the distribution of GDP, by stimulating GDP to grow faster in the regions with low income per head. The conclusion of W.T.M. Molle's analysis with respect to that point can be summarised as follows: '. . . on the regional level, the observed tendency towards less disparity in GDP per head across the European Community is largely due to a shift in the distribution of people and employment from regions with low to regions with high GDP per head, and only for a small part to GDP redistribution, while on the national level it is entirely due to the redistribution of GDP'.[30]

Regional disparities, economic structure and shift-share analysis

In chapter 1, but also in this chapter, we have referred to the impact of the economic structure on employment and income. The relation between orientation to agriculture and the evolution of total employment was already demonstrated on page 67. Agriculture is only one facet of the economic structure. In this part of the study we define the economic structure of a region as the employment composition by economic sectors. The number of sectors can be large or limited. The greater the breakdown the better the information we get.

To analyse regional employment changes — and, for that matter, the regional income changes — shift-share analysis can be applied. This section will first deal very briefly with the method.[31] In a second step we apply the method to two Belgian regions, Flanders and Wallonie, using basic material from the FLEUR study. Finally a few remarks will be made about the interpretation of the results.

The shift-share method

Shift-share analysis is a method of standardising data on regional employment change (or regional income change) which takes account of the particular economic structure of regions and of the different national growth rates of sectors.

Two main variations of the technique have been developed. The first one, called structural base standardisation, adjusts the region's sectoral structure to the national pattern. The second one, called national growth rate standardisation, adjusts regional sectoral growth rates to national sectoral changes. In the application which follows in the next section national growth rate standardisation is used.

In the traditional shift-share analysis (also called components of change analysis) three components of employment (value added) change are identified: the national component (N), the structural component (S), and the differential or regional component (D). We shall explain the method in five steps.

90

1   The national growth component (N) shows the employment change expected from the overall national employment growth rate. It measures the change in employment that would take place in a given region if the economy had grown at the same rate as total employment in all regions considered.

$$N_{ij} = b_{ij} \, g_n \tag{2.3}$$

in which:

b_{ij} =   level of employment in sector i in region j;

g_n =   the national (or EEC) rate of growth of total employment.

2   The structural component (S) shows for each sector the employment change expected from the national growth rate of that sector after allowing for the overall growth rate. In other words it measures the portion of regional growth that is due to an abundance of either quickly or slowly growing sectors.

$$S_{ij} = b_{ij} \, (g_{in} - g_n) \tag{2.4}$$

where g_{in} is the national (or EEC) growth rate of industry i.

3   The differential component (D) is the difference between the actual employment change in the region and the sum of the other two components. It is the element of regional change that takes place within the sectoral groups used. If positive, it represents a beneficial interaction between sector and region, possibly due to a comparative cost advantage although the fundamental factors explaining this phenomenon cannot be derived from the analysis. A negative differential component is evidence of a lack of regional competitiveness; the differential component regroups all influences on total regional employment that are not accounted for by the sectoral structure. It is given by:

$$D_{ij} = b_{ij} \, (g_{ij} - g_{in}) \tag{2.5}$$

where g_{ij} is the rate of growth of sector i in region j.

4   The total change in employment within a given sector is the sum of the three components:

$$C_{ij} = N_{ij} + S_{ij} + D_{ij} \tag{2.6}$$

5   For convenience, the difference between actual employment change and the national or EEC growth component is expressed as

the net relative change (NRC), which can then be attributed to the two remaining components:

$$NRC = S_{ij} + D_{ij}$$

An application of shift-share analysis

In this section the technique of shift-share analysis is applied to two regions of Belgium, namely Flanders and Wallonie, for the period 1950—70.[32] We make use of the basic figures in the FLEUR study of the Netherlands Economic Institute. The sectors taken into consideration are the two-digit sectors of the standard activity classification used in FLEUR; there are thirty-three of these in all. The reference base is the EEC growth rate rather than the national growth rate. The basic figures are given in Appendix 2.2 and the implementation of the method is to be found in Table 2.7.

The figures for Italy and the Netherlands not being available, the EEC growth rates refer to seven countries instead of nine.

Table 2.7 shows that over the twenty year period considered, employment increased by 116,300 in Flanders and declined in Wallonie by 135,700 at a time when, had the EEC overall employment growth rate (+ 13.8 per cent) applied, an increase of, respectively, 186,200 and 143,800 would have taken place.

The Flanders net relative change of − 19,900 can be attributed entirely to the structural component. In fact, it was even higher (− 22,800) than the total net relative change, from which it must be concluded that the differential component was positive (+ 3,100). In relative terms the net relative change is very small (− 1.5 per cent); the structural and differential components are, respectively, − 1.7 and + 0.2 per cent. In other words, the Flanders economy behaved very much like the economy of the EEC as a whole.

The situation of Wallonie is quite different. With a much lower total employment, the net relative change amounts to − 279,508, of which by far the greater part (98 per cent) can be attributed to the differential component, and only the remaining 2 per cent to the structural component. In relative terms the negative differential component is very high (− 26.3 per cent). In other words, the poor economic performance of Wallonie in the period 1950—70 seems due not so much to the often-stressed poor economic structure as to the regional or differential component. An examination of the differential components in Table 2.7 shows that within Wallonie's economy only 6 out of the 32 sectors have a positive differential change, while Flanders has 13 sectors with a positive differential change.

The sectors with the largest differential losses in Wallonie are coal-

Table 2.7
Shift-share analysis of employment change in Flanders and Wallonie, 1950–70

Flanders (a)

No.	Sector	Actual change Nos. (1)	% (2)	EEC growth (b) Nos. (3)	Net relative change Nos. (4)	% (5)	Structural Nos. (6)	% (7)	Differential Nos. (8)	% (9)
11	Agriculture	-116.8	-58.6	27.5	-144.3	-72.4	-142.1	-71.3	-2.2	-1.1
12	Forestry	-0.8	-72.7	0.2	-1.0	-96.5	-0.8	-72.7	-0.2	-18.2
13	Fishing	-1.2	-44.4	0.4	-1.6	-58.2	-1.2	-44.4	-0.3	-11.1
21	Coal mining	-19.4	-47.4	5.6	-25.0	-61.2	-29.8	-72.9	+4.8	+11.7
22	Crude petroleum & nat. gas	—	—	—	—	-13.8	—	—	—	—
23	Metal ore mining	0	—	—	—	-13.8	—	—	—	—
24	Other mining and quarrying	-0.6	-42.9	0.2	-0.8	-56.7	-0.5	-35.7	-0.3	-21.4
31	Food and beverages	-4.4	-6.2	9.8	-14.2	-20.0	-3.8	-5.3	-10.4	-14.6
32	Textile, leather	-48.8	-24.6	27.3	-76.1	-38.4	-87.7	-44.3	+11.7	+5.9
33	Wood & wood products	+6.0	+14.5	5.7	-0.3	+0.7	-9.8	-23.6	+10.0	+24.1
34	Paper & paper products	+8.2	+44.3	2.6	+5.6	+30.5	+6.1	+33.0	-0.5	-2.7
35	Chemicals	+17.6	+64.2	3.8	+13.8	+50.4	+12.7	+46.4	+1.2	+4.4
36	Non-metallic mineral products	+4.0	+16.4	3.4	+0.6	+2.6	+1.5	+6.1	-0.9	-3.7
37	Metal industries	+60.5	+71.7	11.6	+48.9	+57.9	+33.8	+40.0	+15.1	+17.9
38	Transport equipment	+33.0	+84.4	5.4	+27.5	+70.6	+11.9	+30.4	+15.7	+40.2
39	Other manufacturing	+5.8	+25.7	3.1	+2.7	+11.9	+12.2	+54.0	-9.6	-42.5
41	Electricity, gas & steam	+0.8	+8.0	1.4	-0.6	-5.8	—	—	-0.6	-6.0
42	Water works	+0.9	+81.8	0.2	+0.7	+68.0	+0.2	+18.2	+0.5	+45.5
50	Construction	+52.6	+60.6	12.0	+40.6	+46.8	+23.8	+27.4	+16.8	+19.4
61/2	Wholesale & retail trade	+18.6	+10.4	24.6	-6.0	-3.4	+40.7	+22.8	-46.8	-26.2
63	Restaurants and hotels	+5.9	+18.6	4.4	+1.5	+4.8	-1.8	-5.7	+3.4	+10.7
71	Transport	-6.7	-7.6	12.1	-18.8	-21.4	-16.6	-19.0	-2.1	-2.4
72	Communication	+5.9	+39.9	2.0	+3.9	+26.1	+3.3	+22.3	+0.5	+3.4
81	Financial institutions	+10.2	+127.5	1.1	+9.1	+113.7	+10.0	+125.0	-0.9	-11.3
82	Insurance	+5.0	+71.4	1.0	+4.0	+57.6	+5.1	+72.9	-1.0	-14.3
83	Real estate & business serv.	+10.3	+93.6	1.5	+8.8	+79.8	+15.5	+140.9	-6.7	-60.9
84	Laundry & cleaning services	+14.5	+116.0	1.7	+12.8	+102.2	+3.6	+28.8	+9.2	+73.6
91	Public administration	+17.3	+32.6	7.3	+10.0	+18.8	+20.2	+38.1	-10.2	-19.2
92	Education services	+55.0	+136.5	5.6	+49.4	+122.7	+50.7	+125.8	-1.2	-3.0
93	Medical services	+21.2	+131.0	2.2	+18.9	+117.2	+10.6	+65.8	+8.3	+51.6
94	Other social services	+10.8	+82.4	1.8	+9.0	+68.6	+8.1	+61.8	+0.8	+6.1
95	Recreational & cultural serv.	+1.0	+18.9	0.8	+0.2	+5.1	+1.4	+25.5	+1.1	-20.0
	Total employment	+166.3	+12.3	186.2	-19.9	-1.5	-22.8	-1.7	+3.1	+0.2

Wallonie (a)

No.	Sector	Actual change Nos. (1)	% (2)	EEC growth (b) Nos. (3)	Net relative change Nos. (4)	% (5)	Structural Nos. (6)	% (7)	Differential Nos. (8)	% (9)
11	Agriculture	-62.8	-55.2	15.7	-78.5	-69.0	-81.1	-71.3	+2.6	+2.3
12	Forestry	-3.1	-56.4	0.8	-3.9	-70.2	-4.0	-72.7	+0.2	+3.6
13	Fishing	—	—	—	—	-13.8	—	—	—	—
21	Coal mining	-93.3	-83.5	15.4	-108.7	-97.3	-81.4	-72.9	-27.3	-24.4
22	Crude petroleum & nat. gas	—	—	—	—	-13.8	—	—	—	—
23	Metal ore mining	-0.5	-83.3	0.1	-0.6	-97.1	-0.4	-66.7	-0.2	-33.3
24	Other mining and quarrying	-9.5	-56.5	2.3	-11.8	-70.3	-6.1	-36.3	-5.7	-33.9
31	Food and beverages	-11.8	-30.0	5.4	-17.2	-43.8	-2.1	-5.3	-15.1	-38.4
32	Textile, leather	-47.6	-54.9	12.0	-59.6	-68.7	-38.4	-44.3	-21.2	-24.5
33	Wood & wood products	-5.6	-30.4	2.5	-8.1	-44.2	-4.3	-23.4	-3.8	-20.7
34	Paper & paper products	+1.8	+14.8	1.7	+0.1	+1.0	+4.0	+32.8	-3.9	-32.0
35	Chemicals	-1.6	-9.8	2.2	-3.8	-23.6	+7.5	+46.0	-11.4	-69.9
36	Non-metallic mineral products	-1.8	-5.2	4.8	-6.6	-19.0	+2.1	+6.1	-8.7	-25.1
37	Metal industries	-0.5	-0.3	22.1	-22.6	-14.1	+64.0	+40.0	-86.5	-54.1
38	Transport equipment	+3.2	+17.3	2.6	+0.6	+3.5	+5.6	+30.3	-5.0	-27.0
39	Other manufacturing	+1.4	+37.8	0.5	+0.9	+24.0	+2.0	+54.1	-1.1	-29.7
41	Electricity, gas & steam	+1.0	+13.9	1.0	—	+1.0	0.0	0.0	0.0	0.0
42	Water works	+0.8	+72.7	0.2	+0.6	+58.9	+0.2	+18.2	+0.4	+36.4
50	Construction	+9.9	+15.1	9.0	+0.9	+1.3	+17.9	+27.4	-17.1	-26.1
61/2	Wholesale & retail trade	+9.0	+7.8	16.0	-7.0	-6.0	+26.4	+22.8	-33.4	-28.8
63	Restaurants and hotels	+2.9	+15.3	2.6	+0.3	+1.5	-1.1	-5.8	+1.4	+7.4
71	Transport	-15.3	-26.9	7.9	-23.2	-40.7	-10.8	-19.0	-12.3	-21.6
72	Communication	+2.5	+16.7	2.1	+0.4	+2.9	+3.4	+22.7	-2.9	-19.2
81	Financial institutions	+3.3	+56.9	0.8	+2.5	+43.1	+7.2	+124.1	-4.7	-81.0
82	Insurance	+2.1	+55.3	0.5	+1.6	+41.5	+2.7	+71.1	-1.2	-31.6
83	Real estate & business serv.	+6.7	+109.8	0.8	+5.9	+96.0	+8.6	+141.0	-2.7	-44.3
84	Laundry & cleaning services	+6.9	+74.2	1.3	+5.6	+60.4	+2.7	+29.0	+2.9	+31.2
91	Public administration	+11.2	+27.4	5.6	+5.6	+13.6	+15.6	+38.1	-10.0	-24.4
92	Education services	+39.7	+127.7	4.3	+35.4	+113.9	+39.1	+125.7	-3.7	-11.9
93	Medical services	+13.1	+91.6	2.0	+11.1	+77.8	+9.4	+65.7	+1.7	+11.9
94	Other social services	+2.0	+24.1	1.1	+0.9	+10.3	+5.2	+62.7	-4.3	-51.8
95	Recreational & cultural serv.	+0.2	+4.8	0.6	-0.4	-9.0	+1.1	+26.2	-1.4	-33.3
	Total employment	-135.7	-13.0	143.8 13.8	-279.5	-26.8	-5.0	-0.5	-274.4	-26.3

(a) Except the part in the province Brabant

(b) The EEC growth rate is 13.8 per cent for all sectors

(4)=[(1) –(3)] = [(6) +(8)] or (5)=[(2) –(13.8%)] = [(7) +(9)]

mining (− 24 per cent), metal-ore mining (− 33 per cent), other mining and quarrying (− 34 per cent), food and beverages (− 38 per cent), textile (− 24 per cent), wood (− 21 per cent), paper (− 32 per cent), chemicals (− 70 per cent), non-metallic mineral products (− 25 per cent), metal industries (− 54 per cent), transport equipment (− 27 per cent), other manufacturing (− 30 per cent), construction (− 26 per cent), wholesale and retail trade (− 29 per cent), transport (− 22 per cent), communication (− 19 per cent), financial institutions (− 81 per cent), insurance (− 32 per cent), real estate and business services (− 44 per cent), public administration (− 24 per cent), education services (− 12 per cent), other social services (− 52 per cent), and recreational and cultural services (− 33 per cent). It is striking that all manufacturing sectors show a differential loss. In Flanders that is only the case for six out of the twelve manufacturing sectors.

The greatest differences in differential components between Flanders and Wallonie can be listed as follows:

> relatively better performances in Wallonie than in Flanders in the following sectors: forestry, fishing, other manufacturing, and real estate and business services;

> relatively weaker performances in Wallonie than in Flanders in the following sectors: coal mining, metal-ore mining, other mining and quarrying, food and beverages, textile, wood, paper, chemicals, non-metallic mineral products, metal industries, transport equipment, construction, transport, communication, financial institutions, insurance, education services, medical services, other social services, recreational and cultural services.

The many differential losses of Flanders and Wallonie in the tertiary sector indicate how strongly the growth of employment in the tertiary sector is concentrated within the Brussels region. Flanders shows a differential loss in 9 out of the 16 tertiary sectors; in Wallonie the number is 11. The losses are, moreover, more pronounced in Wallonie than in Flanders.

It is not excluded that some structural differences are concealed within the individual sectors in Wallonie, especially as far as manufacturing is concerned. Nevertheless, it looks as if the poor performance of Wallonie is due to its weak competitive position. However, shift-share analysis fails to show up how that weakness has come about; to that end, further research is needed.

Some technical remarks should be made first.[33] To begin with, the
results obtained can be sensitive to the level of data disaggregation used,
whether by sectoral breakdown, spatial boundaries or time period. The
sectoral breakdown is especially important. Even with a relatively
detailed level of classification, some structural differences are hidden.
T.W. Buck gives a good illustration of the phenomenon in his example
concerning Merseyside.[34]

Fluctuations in the results may also occur between different periods,
especially when very short periods are chosen. It is necessary to choose
a time period sufficiently long for basic trends to become apparent.

A more fundamental limitation is that the technique fails to take
account of relationships between the sectors distinguished. Because of
regional linkages and a corresponding regional multiplier effect, it may
be that the performance of one or two leading sectors of the economy
is of paramount importance to the pattern of regional change, yet the
technique will treat each industrial grouping as being equally important.
The growth or decline of one sector such as ship building, affects other
groups related to it, such as steel and engineering, Above all, the
growth of service industries responds in large measure to the growth of
incomes and the expansion in other sectors. A poor regional rate of
growth in services is, therefore, much more likely to be a consequence
of regional dispersion than of locational disadvantage.

The 'shift-share' technique also fails to take labour productivity into
account. A negative differential employment component may reflect
above average labour productivity growth rather than slow growth of
output.

As far as the real interpretation of results is concerned, it should be
emphasised that shift-share analysis is not a theory of regional growth,
but integrates fairly well with some theories of regional growth.[35]
The structural component gives only an indication of the extent to
which the basic economic structure was favourable or unfavourable to
the growth of employment (or income).

There is a tendency to infer that the differential component stands
for regional competitiveness. Competitive position is a very vague
notion because many factors can be responsible for it, such as locational
advantages or disadvantages,[36] availability or lack of availability of
entrepreneurial ability, local services or financial agencies, and special
labour or capital investment aspects. However, a positive differential
component can also reflect the efficiency of a regional policy affecting
the region during the period considered. In that case there is no direct
link with regional competitiveness.

Even using the minimum list heading some structural differences are concealed in the differential component, and to test this thoroughly it is necessary to build up information on individual establishments. Some firms are making products with an income elasticity of demand very different from that for the products of their industry as a whole.

The above remarks lead to the conclusion that we have to be careful using shift share analysis as a guide to regional policy. We must ask whether differential growth, as opposed to the structural component, is evidence of the aggregate efficiency of industry in a region. If a region's growth deficiency can be attributed to the structural component, the situation can conceivably be rectified by policies affecting the regional distribution of economic activities. If differential growth and not structure is held responsible for any shortfall, the implications for policy are different. In the latter case, a general improvement in infrastructure and other instruments needed.

A regional comparative model

In the preceding sections we dealt with a few aspects of regional disparities and of structural elements responsible for them. A few years ago we elaborated a basically very simple comparative model in which most of these aspects are incorporated.[37] It may be worth while to mention the essential elements of this model as a synthesis of this chapter. The model tries to explain the regional population growth and income disparities. For its use as a labour market model see chapter 9, page 371.

The structural equations
The supply equations:

$$P_t = P_{t-1} + \Delta P + M \tag{2.7}$$

$$M = a\,(w - \overline{w}) \tag{2.8}$$

$$L_s = P \tag{2.9}$$

in which:

P_t = total population (active population is proportional to total population);

ΔP = national increase of population;

M = net migration (commuting included);

W = wage level in the region;

96

$\overline{w}$ = average wage level outside the region;

a = parameter which stands for mobility of labour.

The demand equations:

$$L_{nd} = \Upsilon P \qquad (2.10)$$

$$L_{db} = -\beta(w - \overline{w}) + Z \qquad (2.11)$$

$$L_d = L_{nd} + L_{db} \qquad (2.12)$$

$$L_d = L_s \text{ (hypothesis of full employment)} \qquad (2.13)$$

in which:

L_{nd} = demand for labour force in non-basic activities; L_{nd} is proportional to P (based on the method of minimum requirements);

L_{db} = demand for labour in basic activities;

L_d = total demand for labour;

Z = autonomous demand for labour, independent to wage level. The factor Z is related to the industrial structure; it follows the fluctuations in the different industrial sectors weighted by the relative importance of the sectors in the region;

Υ = constant factor;

β = represents the mobility of the demand for labour (linked to the mobility of capital).

The reduced form equations:

From the above mentioned structural equations we can derive two important reduced form equations. The first (2.14) concerns population growth, the second (2.15) income changes.

$$P = \frac{\beta}{\beta + a(1 - \Upsilon)}(p_{t-1} + \Delta P) + \frac{a}{\beta + a(1 - \Upsilon)} Z \qquad (2.14)$$

$$w - \overline{w} = \frac{1 - \Upsilon}{\beta + a(1 - \Upsilon)}(p_{t-1} + \Delta P) + \frac{1}{\beta + a(1 - \Upsilon)} Z \qquad (2.15)$$

Equation 2.14 shows that the total population in period t is determined by the total population in the preceding period, the natural increase of population realised meanwhile, and the potential growth of industry. Equation 2.15 indicates the influence of the same variables on the difference between the wage level of the region and the average wage level outside the region.

These two equations lead to two conclusions. First, total population varies in the same direction as the increase of natural population and the potential growth of industry. Second, income *per capita* varies in the same sense as the potential increase of industrial employment and inversely to the natural increase of population.

The coefficients a, β and Υ determine the sensitivity of P and $(w - \overline{w})$ to either of the two variables: natural increase of population and potential increase of industrial employment.

The coefficient a can take two extreme values: $a = 0$ and $a = \infty$. If $a = 0$, then:

$$P = P_{t-1} + \Delta P$$

$$w - \overline{w} = \frac{1 - \Upsilon}{\beta} (P_{t-1} + {}^{\Delta}P) + \frac{1}{\beta} Z$$

If $a = \infty$, then:

$$P = \frac{1}{1 - \Upsilon} Z$$

$$w - \overline{w} = 0 \qquad (2.16)$$

The coefficient β stands for the mobility of demand for labour. In the case of extreme values for β we get:
If $\beta = 0$, then:

$$P = \frac{1}{1 - \Upsilon} Z$$

$$w - \overline{w} = -\frac{1}{a} (P_{t-1} + \Delta P) + \frac{1}{a (1 - \Upsilon)} Z \qquad (2.17)$$

If $\beta = \infty$, then:

$$P = P_{t-1} + \Delta P$$

$$w - \overline{w} = 0.$$

In chapter 9, page 358, an implicit application of this model will be presented. It seems useful, however, to mention here two more applications of a version of the model, namely to the regions of the Netherlands[38] and to Belgium.[39] Although both studies were carried out a few years ago, they indicate that the model works reasonably well. The somewhat more sophisticated application indicated above (in chapter 9) is of a later year (1972) and affirms the applicability of the model also to smaller regions.

The form of the reduced-form equation tested for fifty-four regions in the Netherlands on income data for the years between 1952 and 1955 (see later) is the following.

$$y_t = \delta_0 - \delta_1 r_t - \delta_2 z_t + \delta_3 a_t - \delta_4 u_t \qquad (2.18)$$

in which:

y_t = income *per capita* (for the available year 1955);

r_t = net natural increase of population (in 1952);

a_t = agglomeration factor (per 1,000) defined as the fraction of the total population living in communities with more than 40,000 inhabitants (in 1952);

u_t = (structural) unemployment (as full employment in the normal sense prevailed all over the Netherlands, total and structural unemployment are supposed to be identical);

z_t = an indicator of the region's economic structure (this factor is actually very difficult to define statistically, as it differs in character from region to region; as a general indicator of the economic structure of a region could be used, however, the percentage of active population working in the most dynamic branches; equivalently, in the most static branches: employment in agriculture was chosen, and since the relevant percentage equals 100 minus the percentage of the working population employed in industry and services, the influence of this factor should be negative. A somewhat more refined approach was used in the Belgian study (see later in this section).

The formula tested for fifty-four regions gave the following result:

$$y_t = 2098.8 - 28.4\, r_t - 3.5\, z_t + 38.1\, a_t - 107.3\, u_t + \epsilon \qquad (2.19)$$
$$\qquad\quad (5.7) \qquad (2.0) \quad (10.5) \qquad (32.6)$$
$$R = 0.84$$

The standard errors of the parameters are shown in brackets. The interpretation of this result was the following.

1   Income differences are (in 1955) largely determined by

99

differences in the natural growth rate of the population in the regions;

2   the influence of the proportion of working population in agriculture is less important than population growth and not significant on the 3σ level;

3   the influence of the agglomeration factor is relatively large and is, of course, of special importance in West Central Holland; and

4   the effect of the structural-unemployment factors is exactly equal to the expected loss in total income (10,730 guilders per year).

It could be questioned if the introduction of both the agglomeration factor and the factor indicating the economic structure is useful. The agglomeration factor could also work via the economic structure if the latter was defined more precisely; this was done in the Belgian study.[39]

The formula tested in that study was originally identical to (2.15). The test was carried out for the nine provinces of Belgium.

In order to compare relative increases only, both P_{-1} and Z_{-1} were put equal to unity, with $P = P_{-1} + \Delta P$ and $Z = Z_{-1} + \Delta Z$, equation (2.15) becomes:

$$w - \overline{w} = - \frac{1 - \Upsilon}{\beta + a(1 - \Upsilon)} \Delta^n P + \frac{1}{\beta + a(1 - \Upsilon)} \Delta Z + \frac{\Upsilon}{\beta + a(1 - \Upsilon)} \quad (2.20)$$

In this equation $\Delta^n P$ and ΔZ are fractions and may be expressed as percentage increases. ΔZ is the relative increase in the performance of basic industries. ΔZ is directly related to the economic structure index. The index is the average of the national growth potentials of all industries when weighted for each region with the regional structure (compare chapter 1, page 5). If we call $\Delta Z'$ the corresponding rate of increase in total employment, and if we accept a value of 0.5 as a fair estimate for Υ, we may say that ΔZ will be about equal to half $\Delta Z'$; the coefficient of ΔZ will then be of the same order of magnitude as the coefficient of the natural increase of population.

It is somewhat more difficult to estimate $\Delta^n P$, which relates to the working rather than to the total population. In the absence of reliable data on the natural increase of the working population, it is the natural rate of increase of total population that must be used as an approximation.

With a correlation coefficient of 0.85, we obtain the following fit:

$$\omega - 100 = - 2.75 \Delta^n P + 2.27 \Delta Z - 4.3 \quad (2.21)$$

the standard error for the coefficient of $\Delta^n P$ being 1.02, while that for the coefficient of ΔZ is 0.85.

The interpretation of this result, presented by the author after comparing actual results and expected values for each of the nine provinces is the following:

1   The fact that Antwerp's income is above average is due to a very favourable economic structure which dominates the negative influence of population increase;

2   Brabant's high income is due to a very low population growth combined with a very favourable industrial structure;

3   the income of Hainaut is about average. The very unfavourable structure is to a large extent compensated by a very low natural population growth;

4   in Limburg the unfavourable economic structure and the very high natural increase in population both contribute to a very low income level;

5   in the province of Luxemburg the negative influence of the unfavourable structure is the cause of the low income.

If it had been possible to introduce the capital intensity of industry into the model, a considerably better fit would very likely have been obtained. Unfortunately, the data concerning this factor in the different provinces were inadequate. Consideration of this factor would no doubt help to explain the higher than predicted income levels of Liège and Hainaut, and the correspondingly lower levels prevailing in West and East Flanders.

The foregoing models are, of course, (multi) regional and not inter-regional models. In subsequent chapters (4 and 11) it will be indicated how inter-regional models could in principle be set up. In this chapter regional models were used to show how relatively simple types of models can contribute to our insight into the causes of regional disparity.

Types of problem regions in the EEC

At the end of this chapter about the regional disparities in the EEC we shall distinguish a number of types of problem areas in Europe of the Nine. The classification is not based on former sections; it is a synthesis of classifications proposed by many authors. It is not our intention to summarise their different ideas but only to make a distinction between types of problem regions. This classification is related to the definition of problem regions given in the first chapter. For each type of problem region a corresponding regional policy must be implemented (see chapter 7). Six types of problem regions are distinguished:

1   In the first group we have the peripheral regions of the EEC characterised by a predominance of agricultural activity. These regions have a double handicap: they are peripheral on the one hand, and oriented to a stagnating sector as far as employment is concerned on the other. Underdevelopment in the broad sense is a common characteristic. Typical examples are Southern Italy, Ireland, and the West and South-West of France.

2   A second group consists of the other agricultural regions. These regions have, in comparison to the first group, the advantage that they are not peripheral. Of course 'peripheral' is a relative notion. In general this type of region is not so far removed from a big urban centre as the regions in the first group. Furthermore, their population density is much higher than that of the regions of the first group. Schleswig-Holstein in West Germany and the North of the Netherlands are typical members of this group.

3   A different kind of problem is the stranded region (depressed area, declining region). They may be coal mining areas, textile regions, regions dominated by ship building activity. South-Wales, the North of England, and Wallonie in Belgium are a few of many examples. A regional development programme for these areas will be quite different from one elaborated for the peripheral and non-peripheral agricultural areas.

4   A special type of problem area is formed by the frontier regions, affected by the stopping of traditional trade flows due to political events. Of these we have only one in the EEC, viz. the set of the administrative units of West Germany along the iron curtain.

5   In many documents of the European Commission, a few years ago, the frontier regions on either side of a border were looked upon as very important problem regions. In fact, they are not in a very bad situation, for they are the first to benefit from economic integration. In former days the parts on either side of the border belonged to the same economic region. However, they have one common characteristic, namely the lack of, or in any case, the insufficient coordination of infrastructure (roads, railways, canals, etc.).

6   The sixth group of problem regions are the conurbation regions. It may be surprising that the conurbation regions are classified as a special group since the income levels in these regions belong to the highest in Europe. With reference to the first chapter, it may be evident that no real Community regional policy

can be conceived without paying attention to the economic, social, and environmental problems of the big conurbation regions. British and French regional policy sustain that thesis.

Notes

[1] EEC 'Report on the regional problems in the enlarged Community', Brussels, 1973. See also Molle, W., 'Regional disparities in the European Community', Association de Science Régionale de Langue Française, Fribourg, 1978. See also Thoss, R., 'Regional concentrations in the countries of the European Community', *Regional Policy Studies,* no.4, Brussels.

[2] NEI, 'Population by region and employment by region and industry in the European Community, 1950, 1960, 1970', Rotterdam, 1975. See also, Molle, W., Van Holst, B. and Smit, H., *Regional Economic Development in the European Community,* London, 1979.

[3] Figures based on the NEI report.

[4] Evolution of total employment is a function of orientation to agriculture.

[5] CEE, *L'évolution régionale dans la Communauté — Bilan analytique,* Brussels, 1971. EEC, 'Report on the regional problems of the enlarged Community', Brussels, 1973.

[6] The values expressed in national currencies have been calculated in units of account of the European Communities, at 1970 rates. It should be stressed that these monetary parities do not represent the ratio's between the domestic purchasing powers of the various countries.

[7] Biehl, D., Hussmann, E. and Schnyder, S., 'Zur regionalen Einkommensverteilung in der Europäischen Wirtschaftsgemeinschaft', *Die Weltwirtschaft,* Heft 1, 1972, pp.66—78.

[8] Cairncross, A., Giersch, H., Lamfalussy, A., Petrilli, G., and Uri, P., *Economic Policy for the European Community,* Kiel, 1974, chapter 3.

[9] Clark, C., Wilson, F., and Bradley, J., 'Industrial location and economic potential in Western Europe', *Regional Studies,* vol.3, no.2, 1969, pp.197—212.

[10] Biehl, D., Hussmann, E. and Schnyder, S., op.cit., pp.64—6.

[11] The gross value added at market prices *per capita* is 60,7 per cent and 23,3 per cent above the average in the regions Hamburg and Bremen; if we take gross disposable income the above mentioned figures become much lower, namely 28,0 and 11,6 per cent.
A better example can be found in France.

	Gross value added per capita (France = 100)	Gross disposable income per capita (France = 100)
Région Parisienne	148,4	134,1
Haute Normandie	111,5	98,8
Bretagne	71,0	85,1
Limousin	72,7	88,1

Unfortunately only three countries can provide figures for the gross disposable income by region.

[12] Biehl, D., Hussmann, E. and Schnyder, S., op.cit., pp.67—8.
[13] Conversion factors based on the ratio of the US consumers price index to the consumers price index of each country.
[14] Tagliacarne, G., 'Le regioni forti e le regioni deboli della Communita allargata: indicatiori socio-economica per la politica regionale della Communita', *Note Economiche*, no.4, 1973.
[15] EEC, 'Report on the regional problems in the enlarged Community', op.cit., p.52.
[16] Easterlin, R.A., 'Long term regional income changes: some suggested factors', *Regional Science Association, Papers and Proceedings*, vol.IV, 1958, p.315.
[17] Balassa, B., *The Theory of Economic Integration*, London, 1962, p.199.
[18] Viner, J., *International Trade and Economic Development*, Oxford, 1953, p.52.
[19] Hanna, F.A., 'Analysis of Interstate Income Differentials: Theory and Practice', *Regional Income, Studies in Income and Wealth*, no.21, 1957, pp.113—61.
[20] Bjork, G.C., 'Regional adjustment to economic growth: the United States, 1880—1950', *Oxford Economic Papers*, no.1, 1968.
[21] OSCE, Regional statistics, 1972.
[22] Molle, W.T.M. et al., op.cit., Annex 3.
[23] In an OECD working party on policies for regional development Prof. Vicinelli emphasised that the evolution of regional income *per capita* in Italy was influenced by the important migration flows from the South to the North. He also pointed out to the working group that the growth of consumption in the South over the period 1951—67 had been faster than the growth of income and that in consequence Southern Italy was still far from attaining the objective of self sustaining growth.
[24] Biehl, D., Hussmann, E., and Schnyder, S., op.cit., p.69.
[25] Molle, W.T.M. et al., op.cit., Annex 3.
[26] van Ginderachter, J., 'Economic Integration and Regional Imbalance', *Tijdschrift voor Economie en Management*, no.1, 1974, p.51.

[27] Theil, H., *Economics and Information Theory,* Amsterdam, 1967, pp.121–3.

[28] Molle, W.T.M. et al., op.cit., Annex 3.

[29] Molle, W.T.M. et al., op.cit., chapter 3.

[30] Molle, W.T.M.,et al., op.cit., pp 10-16.

[31] Dunn, E.S., 'A statistical and analytical technique for regional analysis', *Regional Science Association, Paper,* vol.6, 1960. Thirlwall, A.P., 'A measure of the proper distribution of industry', *Oxford Economic Papers,* March, 1967. Stilwell, F.J.B., 'Regional growth and structural adaptation', *Urban Studies,* vol.6, 1969. Stilwell, F.J.B., 'Further thoughts on the shift and share approach', *Regional Studies,* vol.4, 1970. Buck, T.W. 'Shift and share analysis — a guide to regional policy', *Regional Studies,* no.4, 1970. Bishop, K.C. and Simpson, C.E., 'Components of change analysis: problems of alternative approaches to industrial structure', *Regional Studies,* vol.6, 1972. 'West Central Scotland Plan', Glasgow, 1974.

[32] It would be too demanding to apply the method to all the regions of the EEC. This application has the advantage of comparing a growing and a stagnating region which belong to the same country.

[33] West Central Scotland Plan, op.cit., p.17.

[34] Buck, T.W., op.cit., p.447.

[35] Stilwell, F.J.B., op.cit., p.452 and 453.

[36] There is a group of industries for which locational disadvantages may be serious. This group consists of:
> firms which derive important benefit from being near the centre of the national market;
> branches of existing firms where the organisational difficulties of being separated by a long distance from the parent plant imposes additional costs;
> firms relying on external economies derived from close proximity to related industries and suppliers.

[37] Klaassen, L.H., *Aménagement économique et social du territoire, Directives pour les programmes,* OCDE, Paris, 1965.

[38] Klaassen, L.H., Kroft, W.C. and Voskuil, R., 'Regional income differences in Holland', *Papers of the Regional Science Association,* vol. X, 1963, p.77 ff.

[39] Klaassen, L.H., *Aménagement économique et social du territoire, Directives pour les programmes,* OCDE, Paris, 1965.

The evolution of *per capita* personal income by states and regions in the United States in comparison to the national average, selected years 1929–76

Region/State	1929	1948	1957	1965	1972	1976 in $	1976 Index
USA							
– income per head in $	705	1,430	2,045	2,770	4,492	6,399	100
– Index. Per cent of national average	100	100	100	100	100		100
New England	125	104	110	108	106	6,573	103
Maine	85	86	82	82	80	5,366	84
New Hampshire	98	90	94	93	94	6,010	94
Vermont	89	79	80	86	82	5,411	84
Massachusetts	130	105	110	108	108	6,588	103
Rhode Island	124	104	98	102	100	6,331	99
Connecticut	146	120	133	126	119	7,356	115
Mid-East	138	115	116	114	112	6,924	108
New York	165	126	122	122	117	7,019	110
New Jersey	132	118	124	118	117	7,381	115
Pennsylvania	110	100	104	99	99	6,439	101
Delaware	145	120	129	120	116	7,030	110
Maryland	111	103	107	107	109	6,880	108
District of Columbia	181	137	132	134	140	8,067	126
Great Lakes	114	112	110	108	105	6,687	105
Michigan	113	109	109	110	109	6,754	106
Ohio	111	109	109	104	101	6,412	100

Region/State	1929	1948	1957	1965	1972	1976 in $	Index
Indiana	87	101	99	103	97	6,222	97
Illinois	136	127	122	119	114	7,347	115
Wisconsin	97	99	97	97	97	6,117	96
Plains	81	101	91	96	95	6,105	95
Minnesota	85	100	92	96	96	6,183	97
Iowa	82	111	91	100	96	6,245	98
Missouri	89	97	94	97	96	5,963	93
North Dakota	53	98	72	84	83	5,846	91
South Dakota	59	105	78	80	82	5,120	80
Nebraska	84	106	92	95	97	6,086	95
Kansas	76	93	92	99	99	6,469	101
South-East	52	69	72	77	85	5,526	86
Virginia	62	79	81	88	96	6,341	99
West Virginia	66	78	79	75	80	5,460	85
Kentucky	56	69	72	75	80	5,379	84
Tennessee	54	66	69	75	82	5,364	84
North Carolina	48	68	67	75	85	5,453	85
South Carolina	38	62	60	69	77	5,147	80
Georgia	50	68	72	80	87	5,548	87
Florida	74	83	86	86	98	6,020	94
Alabama	46	61	67	70	76	5,106	80
Mississippi	41	55	51	60	70	4,529	71
Louisiana	59	72	79	76	79	5,405	84
Arkansas	43	61	59	68	75	4,934	77

Region/State	1929	1948	1957	1965	1972	1976 in $	1976 Index
South-West	67	83	87	86	88	6,024	94
Oklahoma	65	80	80	84	84	5,707	89
Texas	68	84	89	87	89	6,201	97
New Mexico	58	76	83	81	79	5,322	83
Arizona	84	89	88	86	95	5,799	91
Rocky Mountain	85	99	94	91	93	6,010	94
Montana	85	113	95	88	89	5,689	89
Idaho	72	92	84	88	84	5,640	88
Wyoming	96	112	100	93	97	6,642	104
Colorado	91	100	99	96	102	6,440	101
Utah	80	87	88	86	83	5,350	84
Far West	129	120	117	114	108	7,033	110
Washington	107	112	106	106	100	6,802	106
Oregon	97	113	98	100	95	6,261	98
Nevada	125	127	127	117	113	7,162	112
California	142	123	122	117	111	7,151	112
Alaska	—	—	114	114	114	10,415	163
Hawaii	—	98	95	104	112	7,080	111

Source: Survey of Current Business.

APPENDIX 2.2: The evolution of employment by sector in Flanders, Wallonie and the EEC, 1950–70 (x 1,000)

No.	Sector	Flanders *			Wallonie *			EEC (without Italy and Netherlands)		
		1950	1970	Actual change	1950	1970	Actual change	1950	1970	Relative change
11	Agriculture	199.3	82.5	- 116.8	113.8	51.0	- 62.8	13,437.9	5,714.9	- 57.5
12	Forestry	1.1	0.3	- 0.8	5.5	2.4	- 3.1	249.4	100.3	- 59.8
13	Fishing	2.7	1.5	- 1.2	0.0	0.1	—	128.4	87.5	- 31.9
21	Coal mining	40.9	21.5	- 19.4	111.7	18.4	- 93.3	1,759.8	720.2	- 59.1
22	Crude petroleum & nat.gas	0.0	0.1	—	0.0	0.0	0	14.6	17.9	+ 22.6
23	Metal ore mining	0.1	0.1	0	0.6	0.1	- 0.5	73.4	32.0	- 56.4
24	Other mining & quarrying	1.4	0.8	- 0.6	16.8	7.3	- 9.5	267.9	207.5	- 22.5
31	Food and beverages	71.1	66.7	- 4.4	39.3	27.5	- 11.8	2,437.6	2,642.9	+ 8.4
32	Textile, leather	198.0	149.2	- 48.8	86.7	39.1	- 47.6	5,231.3	3,635.6	- 30.5
33	Wood & wood products	41.5	47.5	+ 6.0	18.4	12.8	- 5.6	1,344.2	1,214.1	- 9.7
34	Paper & paper products	18.5	26.7	+ 8.2	12.2	14.0	+ 1.8	1,196.0	1,756.0	+ 46.8
35	Chemicals	27.4	45.0	+ 17.6	16.3	14.7	- 1.6	1,317.8	2,109.0	+ 60.0
36	Non-metallic mineral prod.	24.4	28.4	+ 4.0	34.6	32.8	- 1.8	952.2	1,143.1	+ 20.0
37	Metal industries	84.4	144.9	+ 60.5	159.9	159.4	- 0.5	6,331.2	9,734.7	+ 53.8
38	Transport equipment	39.1	72.1	+ 33.0	18.5	21.7	+ 3.2	2,427.0	3,501.9	+ 44.3
39	Other manufacturing	22.6	28.4	+ 5.8	3.7	5.1	+ 1.4	789.7	1,327.0	+ 68.0
41	Electricity, gas & steam	10.0	10.8	+ 0.8	7.2	8.2	+ 1.0	635.4	723.2	+ 13.8
42	Water works	1.1	2.0	+ 0.9	1.1	1.9	+ 0.8	64.1	87.1	+ 35.9
50	Construction	86.8	139.4	+ 52.6	65.4	75.3	+ 9.9	4,727.7	6,675.3	+ 41.2
61/2	Wholesale & retail trade	178.5	197.1	+ 18.6	115.9	124.9	+ 9.0	7,626.2	10,416.7	+ 36.6
63	Restaurants and hotels	31.7	37.6	+ 5.9	19.0	21.9	+ 2.9	1,952.1	2,109.1	+ 8.0

No.	Sector	1950	1970	Actual change	1950	1970	Actual change	1950	1970	Relative change
71	Transport	87.4	80.7	- 6.7	56.9	41.6	- 15.3	3,527.9	3,343.6	- 5.2
72	Communication	14.8	20.7	+ 5.9	15.0	17.5	+ 2.5	998.8	1,361.6	+ 36.3
81	Financial institutions	8.0	18.2	+ 10.2	5.8	9.1	+ 3.3	521.4	1,244.5	+138.7
82	Insurance	7.0	12.0	+ 5.0	3.8	5.9	+ 2.1	413.7	769.8	+ 86.1
83	Real estate & business serv.	11.0	21.3	+ 10.3	6.1	12.8	+ 6.7	820.3	2,086.3	+154.3
84	Laundry & cleaning serv.	12.5	27.0	+ 14.5	9.3	16.2	+ 6.9	887.4	1,265.4	+ 42.6
91	Public administration	53.0	70.3	+ 17.3	40.9	52.1	+ 11.2	2,857.5	4,339.9	+ 51.9
92	Education services	40.3	95.3	+ 55.0	31.1	70.8	+ 39.7	1,478.0	3,541.6	+139.6
93	Medical services	16.1	37.2	+ 21.1	14.3	27.4	+ 13.1	1,518.1	2,724.4	+ 79.5
94	Other social services	13.1	23.8	+ 10.8	8.3	10.3	+ 2.0	642.1	1,130.0	+ 76.0
95	Recreational & cult. serv.	5.5	6.5	+ 1.0	4.2	4.4	+ 0.2	492.5	685.9	+ 39.3
	Total	1349.3	1515.6	+166.3	1042.3	906.7	- 135.6	67,121.6	76,449.0	+ 13.8

* Except the part in the province Brabant

3 'Region', a relative notion

Definition of an economic region

Careful consideration of what constitutes a region and how the national economy may be subdivided into a system of regions would seem an essential prerequisite for the analysis of regional phenomena. However, the definition of an economic region is rather ambiguous. Certain authors (see, e.g., W. Leontief) even have the idea that the definition of an economic region has to be looked upon as a political option.

A major ambiguity arises from the fact that the size of a region may vary from a small population centre and its environment to a vast massive subregion within a continent, or even to a whole continent, depending on the range and type of questions under study.

In his book, *Regional Economic Growth: Theory and Policy*, H. Siebert describes a region as an intermediate category:

> The concept of a region is an intermediate category between an aggregate economy with no spatial dimension and a highly disaggregated economic system defined as a set of spatial points . . .
> . . . The new concept is an in-between category similar to the sector, which makes possible some aggregation of the multitude of individual firms without requiring a complete aggregation into a national economic system.[1]

How the national economy should be subdivided into regions in a meaningful way is, however, not evident from the above definition. There are constraints and different criteria.

A first question is how many regions are to be considered; even to that question there is no uniform answer. The only thing to say is that the number depends on the size of the country and on the form and the nature of the analysis. In many cases regional analysis is understood as an adjunct of national planning, and that usually means that only a small number of regions are considered. On the other hand physical planners prefer to work with a much more numerous set of regions, because the kind of work they perform can only be carried out successfully on a basis of small units. In all cases, however, the requirement of contiguity is put forward; it means that each area of country forms part of one region and that all regions together should add up to the country as a whole. The contiguity constraint is an essential element of the definition given by H.S. Perloff, E.S. Dunn, E.E. Lampard and R.F. Muth, in

111

which they say: 'The term "region" is generally used to describe a group of geographically contiguous areas which have certain common or complementary characteristics or which are tied by extensive inter-areal activity flows'.[2]

In general it may be said that there is no absolute criterion for the division of a country into regions. There are, indeed, many criteria, and very often they lead to completely different results. That will become clear when we analyse the classification of regions in the next section.

Regional prototypes

Classification according to
J.R. Boudeville [3]

1 *Uniform or homogeneous regions* (espace homogène)

The view of a region as a homogeneous area is based on the idea that separate spatial units can be linked together because of certain common characteristics. Some are homogeneous with respect to such physical characteristics as geography and natural resource endowment, while others are defined as similar in their economic and social characteristics, e.g.:

> production structure;
> consumption pattern;
> occupational distribution of the labour force;
> ubiquity of a dominant natural resource;
> topography;
> climate;
> social attitude;
> *per capita* income level;[4]
> business-cycle concept.

A major problem in attempting to delimit homogeneous regions is that regions tend to be similar to another region in some respects but in other respects show a closer link with a third region. Moreover, most regions will contain both rural and urban areas.

2 *Nodal or polarised regions* (région polarisée)

'A polarized space is a set of units or economic poles maintaining more trade or connections with a pole of the next superior order than with any other pole of the same order'.[5]

According to this definition, Mulhouse belongs to the region of Basel if it has more trade relations with Basel than with the region of

Strasbourg.

A nodal region has two characteristics, viz. intra-regional functional interconnections and a hierarchical structure.

(a) *Functional interconnections* (notion de connectivité)
A nodal region is composed of heterogeneous units, but these are closely interrelated with each other functionally. The functional interconnections are most clearly visible as flow phenomena. The flow can be represented as (a) a regional account system, (b) an input-output system, or (c) a graph. The matrix and graph presentations are given below.

Matrix

	A	B	C
A	–	t_{ab}	t_{ac}
B	t_{ba}	=	t_{bc}
C	t_{ca}	t_{bc}	–

Graph

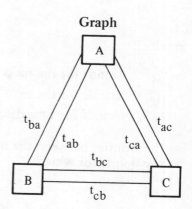

The t-flows above could, of course, refer to different flow phenomena. One could think of:

    population flows (migration and commuting);
    trade in goods and services;
    communication (telephone calls);
    traffic flows;
    retail and wholesale good flows;
    service connections;
    newspaper circulation;
    financial flows.

(b) *Hierarchy*
These flows do not occur at random and at even rates across a region. Rather, the heaviest flows tend to polarise towards and from one or two dominant centres, usually large cities. In that sense, the nodal region focusses attention on the controlling centre of the region rather than on its boundaries, which, to a certain extent at least, are less important.

The nodal approach demonstrates the functional interdependence not only between a region's internal components but also between its nodes and the nodes of other regions.

We find here in fact an application of the law of W.J. Reilly[6] according to which the traffic between two poles is directly related to their mass and inversely related to the square of the distance between them.

$$t_{12} = c \frac{M_1 . M_2}{d_{12}^2} \qquad (3.1)$$

in which:

M_1 stands for the mass of town 1;

M_2 stands for the mass of town 2;

d_{12} stands for time distance.

The frontier between the market areas of two centres is determined by the points for which:

$$\frac{M_1}{M_2} = \frac{(d_{b_1})^2}{(d_{b_2})^2} \qquad (3.2)$$

d_{b_1} and d_{b_2} being the distance from, respectively, pole 1 and pole 2 to a point on the frontier line (the breaking point).

3 *Planning or programming regions* (région plan)
According to J. Boudeville[7] a planning region 'is a continuous space permitting to attain a certain objective in the most economic way: a maximum of trade or of urban income, moving the polarisation border in order to achieve better collective exploitation in a larger framework'.

There should be a close relationship between planning regions and nodal regions. If planning regions are defined indiscriminately without regard to functional linkages between separate spatial results, so that areas are included in the planning region which have a higher degree of interdependence with nodes outside the region, planning decisions may become ineffective.

It is obvious that a programming region cannot always be based on a nodal region. That is particularly evident when there is no nodal region

114

or when the nodal region is deformed by national frontiers (custom barriers).

Classification according to the rate of growth

We can make a distinction between growing, stagnating, and regressive regions (by income and/or population criteria), a classification that leads to the notion of underdeveloped regions. How an underdeveloped region is defined depends on two elements viz. the average to which the region is compared and the criteria applied (unemployment, activity level, income level). It is a bit dangerous to define underdeveloped regions only in a static way; a dynamic viewpoint seems more fruitful. Barkin[8] says about this:

> The destiny of such regions could well be the same as that of others that are now at the summit of their economic progress. Economic and technical changes continuing they will in future transform the situation in many regions. Not a single group is protected from the ravages of our so turbulent and dynamic economy. Those who today are the most prosperous will perhaps be the vanquished of tomorrow.

The dynamic viewpoint leads us to the incorporation of two basic elements:

(a) the income level in comparison to the national level;
(b) the expected growth rate in comparison to the national rate.

Thus we arrive at the classification proposed by L.H. Klaassen:

Growth rate in respect to national growth rate	Income level in comparison to national average	
	high (≥ 1)	low (< 1)
high (≥ 1)	prosperous region	underdeveloped region in expansion
low (< 1)	potentially underdeveloped region	underdeveloped region

Since each class of regions has certain definite characteristics, differently structured policies will have to be applied in each case.

*Classification according to
the reciprocal influence*

According to this classification we speak of complementary regions whenever the development of region A has a positive impact on region B and vice versa, and of substitutive regions if the development of region A puts a brake on the development of region C, and vice versa.

Regional prototypes of N. Hansen [9]

Hansen uses three kinds of capital (and investments), viz.

 (a) direct production activities (DPA);
 (b) economic overhead capital (EOC)
      oriented to support DPA or
      towards the movement of economic resources
 (c) social overhead capital (SOC) (education, cultural projects, health programmes, etc.).

Considering these three types of activities, Hansen arrives at a division of regions in three groups:

(a) *Congested regions*
In these regions marginal social costs (private costs plus external effects) of further expansion are equal to or higher than the concomitant marginal social benefit (MSC $\geqslant$ MSB). Congested regions are considered by Hansen as products of unbalanced growth.

(b) *Intermediate regions*
These regions offer significant advantages to private firms for which in general MSB $>$ MSC. It means that the marginal net social product resulting from direct private investments in these regions is greater than would accrue from the same investments in congested regions.

(c) *Lagging regions*
These regions present few attributes that could attract new economic activities. Their economic structure is characterised by small scale agriculture and/or declining or stagnant industries.

Some further considerations

Wherever the foregoing considerations might have led, three things seem certain, viz.

116

1   Because the delimination of regions leads to the determination of regional income, regional employment, etc., for the set of regions as a whole as well as to their regional distribution, it should be such that all the variables are relevant and meaningful. A set of regions defined in such a way that the resulting regional characteristics are meaningless does not make sense;

2   Delimination of regions without any reference to political boundaries does not seem very efficient either. Since political boundaries are subject to change over time, the link between the two need not be strict, but a certain coordination seems to be in order;

3   A regional division that serves *all* purposes (analytical as well as political) does not exist. For the analysis of different activities, different regions are relevant; the same is true for policies concerning these activities. No region can be expected to serve equally well the analysis of the spatial distribution of oil refineries and that of the location of, say, drugstores. Oil refineries and drugstores have completely different relevant regions, and their spread should, therefore, be studied within regions of different size.

The conclusion from these three points is easy: the regions for which data are collected should be as small as possible, or rather, as large as is required for the analysis and the policy of the activity with the smallest relevant region.

If statistical data were available for such regions, every analysis could in principle be performed on the basis of the data for the small regions, which could then be grouped into data for larger regions as required for the activity to be studied. It seems that, if the data on the smallest scales were studied thoroughly, and particularly if they informed us about inter-regional relations as well as development through time, regions of higher order would suggest themselves logically. We should, however, always be aware that divisions derived in the way indicated are also subject to change through time, and should, therefore, be adjusted to changed circumstances. The advantage of the suggested system is that the division into the smallest units could be maintained even when macrodivisions have to be adjusted.

In this context, the following considerations seem relevant. [10] They refer to the difficulties that are often experienced in the construction of general models (comprising economic, social, and environmental variables) and inter-regional models. If we accept that it will be extremely difficult, if at all possible, to construct such general disaggregated models, two questions suggest themselves:

1   If general models in which all the relevant variables play their

117

proper roles are so complex that our present knowledge is inadequate to construct them successfully, how would we then construct meaningful sub-models (i.e. sub-models that are to some extent operational)?

2   If we were able to construct meaningful sub-models, would they be relevant for government policy? In other words, is the best way to break down the general model also the best way to structure government policy?

The first question touches in fact on the problem how to break down a general model into sub-models without violating too much its main object, viz. registration of all interaction between all variables. When we cut out a piece from the large model, we implicitly cut interaction flows (one way as well as two way flows) between variables in the sub-model and in the remaining part of the general model. The first and general principle should be, then, to cut the sub-models out of the general model in such a way that a minimum number of interaction flows are interrupted.

The second principle is based on the assumption that the intensity of interaction decreases with physical distance. This is supposed to hold not only for consumer activities such as recreation, shopping, or more general, the use of social infrastructural elements, but also, and just as much, for deliveries by industrial firms and for interindustrial relations. Therefore, the larger the regions chosen as a basis for the analysis, the smaller the size of the interaction flows will be in relation to the total size of inter-regional activities.

The final principle derives from the fact that the distance-decay function is different for each activity. For that reason it is essentially possible to rank each activity according to the influence distance exerts on the demand for its products and/or the supply of its inputs. Obviously this influence is smaller with most services, particularly those for which the consumer has to move in person to the place of production, than with industrial products, which can be transported over larger distances at relatively low cost. In a ranking, we shall find most industrial activities in the bracket of low distance elasticities and most service activities in the high distance elasticity bracket. High distance elasticities may be called low order activities, and activities characterised by low distance elasticities may be denoted as high order activities.

If we start with relatively large regions we shall find that the flows of goods and services passing the borders consist mainly of flows resulting from high order activities, and that they are characterised by a high degree of autarchy as far as lower order activities are concerned. Low order activities are, in fact, irrelevant when we study the development of and the inter-relations between large regions.

It seems natural to use the results of these larger regions (such as industrial location studies) as inputs in studies of medium sized regions, making them serve as quasi exogenous variables.

The same process can be repeated in a study of smaller regions, the results obtained for the medium sized regions serving in turn as quasi exogenous variables.

In this way a hierarchy of models is created in which each activity, according to the size of its distance elasticity, is studied in a relevant regional context.

The foregoing implies that for a proper division into large, medium sized, and small regions the distance elasticities of the different activities need to be studied. In practice, because of the structure of the available data, one is often forced to use existent administrative divisions. That is a disadvantage inasmuch such a division might not correspond with a set of different sized relevant regions, but an advantage inasmuch as such a division usually corresponds with administrative boundaries regular adjustments, particularly to municipal ones, prevent the differences between administrative units and analytical regions from becoming prohibitive for a proper analysis.

If we assume further that a government on a given level (*de facto* the government of a region of a given size) is responsible for all activities for the corresponding level or lower levels, which means in practice all activities for which the relevant region is equal to or smaller than the region for which this government is held responsible, we have implicitly answered the second question put forward in the beginning of this section. In this construction the regional government is not responsible for activities with large external effects, since these, by definition, fall under the jurisdiction of a higher level government.

Final remark

One final remark seems to be in order. In chapter 4 we shall have the opportunity to present in more detail the notion of a potential. A potential for a given facility is defined as:

$$\pi_i = \sum_j x_j e^{-a d_{ij}} \qquad (3.3)$$

where

π_i = potential for a given facility;

119

x_j = size of facility in region j;

d_{ij} = distance between i and j or generalised transportation costs.

It appears that if the regions are not too large, this concept, which is of strategical importance in regional analysis, is in principle *independent of the regional divisions* used, if the distance between the regions is properly defined. This is a characteristic of the potential which makes it even more valuable. The other important characteristic of the potential is, that, if used in a regional model, it turns this model into an *interregional* model, as it indicates the influence of all j variables on the variable in region i. It is, however, the former characteristic that is the most important in the context of this chapter. It contributes in a modest way to the solution of the problem how to define a region by lessening the necessity of defining a region.

Notes

[1] Siebert, H., *Regional Economic Growth: Theory and Policy*, Sranton, 1969.
[2] Perloff, H.S., Dunn, E.S., Lampard, E.E. and Muth, R.F., *Regions, Resources and Economic Growth*, Baltimore, 1960, p.4.
[3] Boudeville, J.R., *L'espace et les pôles de croissance*, Paris, 1968, chapter I.
[4] Richardson, H.W., *Regional Economics: Location Theory, Urban Structure and Regional Change*, London, 1969, p.225.
[5] Boudeville, J.R., op.cit., p.27.
[6] Reilly, W.J., *The Law of Retail Gravitation*, New York, 1931.
[7] Boudeville, J.R., *L'espace et les pôles de croissance*, op.cit., p.35.
[8] See Barkin, S., 'Principles for area redevelopment legislation', *Labor Law Journal*, August 1959.
[9] Hansen, N., *French Regional Planning*, Edinburgh, 1968.
[10] Klaassen, L.H., Paelinck, J.H.P., and Wagenaar, Sj., *Spatial Systems*, Farnborough, 1978, chapter VIII.

4 Micro and macro aspects of the location of firms

Introduction

Theories about the location of firms and theories about the regional distribution of industries are in fact closely related to one another. Although the location of a firm is of course a precisely defined concept, an exact point in space, for many reasons the region within which a location takes place is a much more convenient geographical concept to handle, particularly since from many a point of view the knowledge about the exact location is irrelevant for a proper regional analysis. An important restriction should, of course, be made here. Regional analysis may serve different purposes. An analysis of the location of shops requires much smaller regions than one of the location of international airports. The relevant size of a region depends on the activity that is being considered. This should always be kept in mind whenever a study of a particular activity is undertaken. In the next chapter we shall have the opportunity to explain the consequences in some more detail.

A. Weber, the father of location theory[1] [2]

A location factor is, according to A. Weber, 'ein seiner Art nach scharf begrenzter Kostenvorteil, der einen bestimmten Industrieprozess hierhin oder dorthin zieht'. In his analysis he makes a distinction between factors that determine the distribution of industries among regions (general location factors) and those which determine the location within a region (specific factors). He considers as costs the costs of the inputs (raw materials), labour, and transport. As price differences of raw materials can be reduced to differences in the costs of transporting these raw materials, only two differences in costs are actually relevant: those of labour and transport. When there are no differences in labour costs, the location chosen will coincide with the point of minimum transportation costs (determined by weight and distance).

The point of optimum location is in general determined by three factors:

(a)   the index of materials (defined as the ratio between the

121

weight of raw materials and the weight of final products);
(b)   the labour-coefficient;
(c)   economies of agglomeration and deglomeration.

It is the merit of A. Weber to have developed a theory that embraces a number of important factors in one system. Despite the criticisms that followed, his theory had and still has a considerable influence on thinking about the location of firms.

As will be clear from the short presentation of his analysis, his theory was in principle entirely cost oriented. He searched for the point in space where, ceteris paribus, the sum of production and transportation costs was lowest. A. Lösch has pointed out that for a more complete analysis not only the costs side but also the demand side should be taken into consideration. Only if demand were completely inelastic would the location of the firm not influence the size of demand for the firm's product and therefore the volume of its production. In practice the effect of location on production varies considerably from one sector to another (services versus steel production).

The consequence of Lösch's remark is that the optimum location of a firm is determined neither by the minimum costs nor by maximum gross revenues but by the maximum difference (net revenues) between the two. [3] The location theory of A. Lösch leads to a specific spatial distribution of economic activities. We will come to this later.

A macro-economic approach. The gravitation and potentiality models

In the foregoing analyses of both Weber and Lösch it is assumed that each firm has a good knowledge of the size of the potential market for its products. As this is usually not the case, simple devices have been developed for a quick (and dirty) evaluation of the size of the potential market. These devices find their origin in the gravitation model: [4]

$$M_{ij} = k. \frac{P_i P_j}{D_{ij}^a} \tag{4.1}$$

in which

M_{ij} =   movement or flows (migration, commuting, shopping, trade, etc.) between locality i and locality j (in which the 'locality' can be a region or a country);

P_i =   population of locality i;

122

$$P_j \quad = \quad \text{population of locality } j;$$
$$D_{ij} \quad = \quad \text{distance between } i \text{ and } j;$$
$$k \text{ and } a = \quad \text{constant factors.}$$

Applied to inter-regional or international trade, formula (4.1) may be rewritten as

$$X_{ij} = c \, \frac{Y_i Y_j}{D_{ij}} \tag{4.2}$$

in which

$$X_{ij} \quad = \quad \text{the export of region (country) } i \text{ to region (country) } j;$$
$$Y_i \text{ and } Y_j = \quad \text{regional (national) product of region (country) } i \text{ and } j.$$

The transition from the gravitation model to the potentiality model is easy.

Assume that firm A of region (country) i has a new product. If we accept that the export of the new product to each region (country) j can be forecast by formula (4.2), total export possibilities $\sum_j X_{ij}$ equal

$$\sum_j X_{ij} = cY_i \sum_j \frac{Y_j}{D_{ij}} \tag{4.3}$$

Since cY_i is a constant factor, we need only calculate the sum of the ratios of the regional (national) products to the respective distances to have an idea of the potential market. By comparing the potential market of the firm in location (country or region) A with that in B, C, etc., we can easily find the most promising location.[5]

No need to say that the foregoing analyses are both crude and superficial. The relevant demand variables are either population or national (regional) income without indication of the importance of these factors for the markets under study. Trade in the potentiality model is assumed to be proportional to the simple reciprocal of physical distance. What is essentially lacking in these analyses is the behaviour of the producers including their reaction to different circumstances in the regions under consideration. It appears that even for simple demand oriented industries the analysis could be improved considerably by a somewhat different approach.

In order to keep the argument simple we will start with a sector that is completely demand oriented, which means that its location is completely geared to the location of effective demand.

We assume that potential demand is a weighted sum of actual demands in all regions j corrected for distance as well as for the accessibility index for each region:

$$d_i^p = \sum_j d_j \, \frac{\exp\left\{-\rho^c{}_{ij}\right\}}{\varphi j} \tag{4.4}$$

in which

d_i^p = demand potential of region i;

d_j = effective demand in j;

φ_j = accessibility of region j (to be defined later).

(4.4) represents the weighted sum of demand in all regions j, deflated by communication costs. φ_j represents the accessibility of region j from all regions. The easier j is accessible from all directions, the more difficult it will be for a producer in i to penetrate into the market of this region.

The value of φ_j can be found as follows:

$$\sum_i d_i^p = \sum_j d_j = d \tag{4.5}$$

The sum of all potential demands has been defined here as the sum of all effective demands. This is, of course, not necessarily true. It is not difficult to give an example (e.g. relating to the labour market) where there is in some regions open demand (potential demand larger than effective demand) as well as open supply (potential supply larger than effective supply). In this example we will assume that the sum of all effective demands equals the sum of all potential demands, so that there are no changes in stocks.

Consequently, we may write

$$d = \sum_i \sum_j \frac{d_j}{\varphi_j} \exp\left\{-\rho c_{ij}\right\} = \sum_j \frac{d_j}{\varphi_j} \sum_i \exp\left\{-\rho c_{ij}\right\} \tag{4.6}$$

One obvious solution for φ_j is

$$\varphi_j = \sum_i \exp\left\{-\rho c_{ij}\right\} \tag{4.7}$$

The maximum value of φ_j is reached for all $c_{ij} = 0$; then $\varphi_j = n$ (= number of regions). Its minimum value is reached for all $c_{ij} = \infty$. Then $\varphi_j = 0$.

The accessibility coefficient $(0 \leqslant a \leqslant 1)$ may now be written as

$$a_j = \frac{\varphi_j}{n} = \frac{\sum\limits_i \exp\left\{-\rho c_{ij}\right\}}{n} \tag{4.8}$$

and (4.4) may be rewritten as

$$d_1^p = \sum_j d_j \frac{\exp\left\{-\rho c_{ij}\right\}}{\sum\limits_i \exp\left\{-\rho c_{ij}\right\}} \tag{4.9}$$

in which potential demand is defined as a realistic estimate of sales in all regions j of the industry(ies) located in i. Since φ is sector-specific, this equation holds only for a well-defined sector. [6]

Transportation costs and distance costs (frais de communication)

The c_{ij} in the foregoing section was supposed to represent not only the physical transportation costs but also all the costs in time, money, and risk that are in one way or another related to the need for communication, an extremely important subject in location theory. Communication costs have become essential in this theory particularly since the rapid growth of the service sector, which neither uses nor produces physical products, but depends for its production completely on all sorts of communication with other industries. Nevertheless some more detailed information about the importance of the transportation costs 'tout court' seems useful. It appears that a number of quite interesting studies have been made on this subject. [7]

(1) *Relative importance of transportation costs*
In a variety of studies it has been attempted to assess the importance of transportation costs. A number of interesting conclusions can be drawn from the findings of these studies.

(a) It appears that the location of firms is often either concentrated in the market or at one of the sources of raw materials. In principle, that can only be in accordance with Weberian theory if the different cost categories are linear functions of distance.
(b) For a wide range of economic activities transportation costs

125

are not an important element of total costs. The Toothill Committee studied the effect of transportation costs on firms which had chosen a location in Scotland and found them to amount to less than 2 per cent of production costs. That does not mean, of course, that 2 per cent transportation costs account for 2 per cent of an article's total costs. The two relate to the specific level of production considered. If we were to consider the accumulated quota of transportation costs including all former stages of production, the share of transportation costs in total costs would be considerably higher.

Remarkably, it is often forgotten to accumulate transportation costs. A similar phenomenon can be observed for energy costs; one often points to the extremely low energy costs at a given production stage, without referring to the accumulated energy costs, which might be very high, and in some cases even extremely high, in comparison to the non-accumulated energy costs.

(c) Transportation costs are not proportional to distance as the simple Weber model assumes, for the obvious reason that the costs of loading and unloading are fixed costs, independent of distance.

(d) Lutrell found that the majority of manufacturing in Britain was footloose in the sense that it could operate satisfactorily in any of the major industrial centres in Britain. This fact seems extremely important within the context of location theory, and therefore deserves some further attention.

(2) *Distance costs* (frais de communication)[8]
Despite the findings of Lutrell and Toothill it would be a mistake to assume that location is a matter of indifference and that distance has no meaning economically.

Businessmen are influenced to a significant extent by the factor of distance in choosing a new location. The advantage of being in daily contact with raw material and component suppliers, with customers and distributors, is great; that is one of L.H. Klaassen's theses.

In many cases, the notion of the distance to be bridged in the physical sense does not coincide with the notion of distance on which, implicitly or explicitly, the entrepreneur relies. The same material distance may indeed, from an economic and social point of view, vary widely in importance according to the interindustrial relation that is at stake. The outlays made to bridge a material distance will be called transportation costs, while those that make it possible to reduce an economic gap will be called communication costs.

This concept of communication costs, which obviously is very much wider than that of transportation costs, appears to be much more relevant particularly now that service industries have become more important than manufacturing industries, at least in the Western world. On the assumption that communication costs are a function of distance and could — and are in fact — also be called distance costs, the concept comes very close to that of 'economies of agglomeration'. These costs, too, are a function of the geographical association. Distance costs express the costs disadvantage of not communicating easily with suppliers, buyers, and auxiliary services.

The assumption that communication costs are a very important factor in determining international trade was confirmed by the results of a study on international trade as early as 1960.[9] In this study the influence of distance on the origin of the imports in the Netherlands was examined. It was assumed that there exists a relation of the general form

$$\ln S = a_1 A + a_2 P + a_o \qquad (4.10)$$

in which

S = imports in tons;
A = distance from the exporting country;
P = export price per unit of product;
a_1, a_2, a_o = parameters.

It appeared that the average import elasticity with respect to distance was about -2, while the average price elasticity was -0.2. These conclusions show how important distance is and how much more important than transportation costs. If the transport quota in the total price were, say, 10 per cent, the expected value for the distance elasticity would be 10 per cent of the price elasticity or roughly 0.02. In reality the influence of distance is about a hundred times higher. From the analysis for different products it emerged furthermore that distance elasticities are much higher for complex products than for simpler products, which is what might be expected, the former products being considerably more 'communication intensive' than the latter.

Industrial location and economic potential in Western Europe

The aim of the study of Clark et al. on industrial location and economic potential[10] was to examine which regions in Western Europe are most attractive to industry and what effect an enlarged Customs Union was likely to have on the distribution of the most favoured regions. This study set out to discover whether, if Britain were a member of the Common Market, any part of Britain would be included in the region of greatest potential for economic growth in Europe, or if Britain would be relegated to a position on the periphery.

The starting point of the study is the idea that the majority of industries can now be described as footloose. Technical developments in processing and transport tend to increase their number. Other than conditional factors are now considered for the location decision. Even though theoretically there is a wide range of reasonable locations for a footloose industry, it is found that entrepreneurs tend to respond to certain definite factors. A general description of what is happening in the modern industrial world is that while the macro-location of industry (and population) is tending towards increasing concentration in a limited number of areas, their micro-location tends towards increasing diffusion.

The concept of economic potential

The method chosen to measure the attraction for industry of the regions in Western Europe was that of calculating the economic potential for each region. The economic potential of any region is defined by summating the regional incomes in and around it, each regional income having first been divided by the distance costs of reaching it. These two factors are explicitly or implicitly taken into consideration: (1) the main sources of inputs and the main markets for the product; (2) the cost of bridging the distance from any given point of area. Concerning the first point we must be aware of the fact that areas of dense population are sources of some of the most vital inputs (diversified labour force, specialised services, repair services, low communication costs) as well as the main markets. The capacity of a region to act as a market for outputs as well as a supplier of inputs can be measured by the regional income.

The area of greatest attraction to industry will be the region where the distance costs to all possible markets are lowest.

The estimation of economic potentials

The economic potential for any one region is expressed by the following formula:

128

$$P_i = \frac{I_i}{M} + \sum_{\substack{j=1 \\ j \neq i}}^{m} \frac{I_j}{M + T_{ij} + F} \qquad (4.11)$$

in which

P_i = potential of region i;

I_i = income of region i;

M = minimum cost ($ 28 per 10 ton load)

T_{ij} = transport cost from i to j;

F = tariff (the surcharge incurred when 10 ton load of goods crosses the frontier);[11]

1 to n = 103 regions of Western Europe; and n + 1 to m = all non-West European regions.

For convenience, all costs and values are expressed in US dollars. In the measurement of the distance costs, all calculations have been made on the basis of the average cost of moving a 10 ton load of a heavy commodity.

There is no need to say that this formula has some arbitrary features. The first is that the potential of a market is assumed to be proportional to income. This is rather a rough assumption, particularly because it does not discriminate between different products, some of which will be income inelastic while others are income elastic. The approach followed assumes for all products, or at least, for all industrial products together, an income elasticity equal to unity.

The second decision is that an *a priori* coefficient of value one is attached to transportation costs in the denominator. In the preceding section we already indicated a possible alternative approach in which such a coefficient would be dependent upon the nature of the product studied.

If we simplify the formula a little by writing $c_{ij} = M + T_{ij} + F$ and $c_{ii} = M$, we can write

$$P_i = \sum_j \frac{Y_j}{c_{ij}} \qquad (4.12)$$

which means that the potential is defined as the quantity of products that could be transported from i to j if the total income in j were spent on transportation costs!

In spite of what is said in the foregoing paragraph it is, of course, rational to assume that the potential of a market for a given region is a positive function of the income in that region and a negative function of the distance from the region to the market. It is only the somewhat primitive way in which the two factors are accounted for that warrants the above criticism.

Application

Five different values have been estimated for each region describing its economic potential, and thus implicitly the changes of the potential for manufacturing industry under five sets of conditions:

    1 the situation existing prior to the Treaty of Rome;
    2 the situation in 1969;
    3 the assumed situation of an enlarged Common Market;
    4 the assumed situation of lower shipping costs in Europe;
    5 the assumed situation with a Channel Tunnel.

In order to show the distribution of potentials, five maps were drawn, using the potential values and regional boundaries to locate the position of iso-potentials. The higher a region's potential figure, the greater its attraction to manufacturing industry (see C. Clark, F. Wilson and J. Bradley, pp.203 to 207).

The economic potentials calculated suggest that in future manufacturing industries will tend to locate and become concentrated within the Rhine valley of West Germany, Eastern Belgium, and the South-East Netherlands (see chapter 6).

From the increase or decrease of employment in the pre Treaty of Rome period of 1950—60 and the period 1960—65, it can be seen that regions with the greatest rise in potential values also experienced the greatest increase in employment. Very substantial increases in employment were found in the Eastern and Southern parts of the Netherlands and in Eastern Belgium. In the more remote regions, such as South-West France, Southern Italy, and Northern Germany, employment tended to decline or to grow more slowly in the years between 1960—65 than in the earlier period. The conclusion is that there is some indication of employment responding to the changed locational value of certain regions following upon the Treaty of Rome.

We have to make one remark. Availability of labour was probably an important factor in favour of Southern Netherlands and Eastern Belgium. This factor, and some others, have not been taken into consideration.

Importance of location factors

In the last decade several inquiries were held among industries to get an idea of the relative importance of different location factors; in this section the results of two research projects are presented.

Motives behind the location of
international investments in North-West Europe [12]

This study presents the results of a research project executed by the French 'Centre de Recherches Economiques et de Gestion' on the request of the 'Organisation d'Etude et d'Aménagement de l'Aire Métropolitaine du Nord' (OREAM Nord).

The OREAM was interested in the behaviour of international firms as to the location of their new direct investment. In the analysis a distinction was made between national and regional factors. 'Why does firm X prefer country A to B' and 'If country A is chosen, why region P and not G' were the questions asked. The answers given to both questions could possibly be valuable indications for policy on the national and regional level.

The inquiry was organised among forty international firms (50 per cent of which were intermediate agencies such as international bankers and location experts; their role in the location (decisions) is very important. The interviewed firms could answer the two main questions with the appreciation 'very important' (3 points), 'important' (2 points), and 'less important' (1 point). The fact that we have forty cases means that the maximum a location factor could obtain was 120 points (coefficient of importance).

From the level of the coefficients in Table 4.1, printed hereafter, we can draw two conclusions:

(a)   National factors are very important especially the image of the country.
(b)   On the regional level factors that intervene directly in the cost price are considered more important than factors falling under the category 'environment'.

An evaluation of location factors of
900 industrial firms in Flanders (1971) [13]

In this inquiry more than 4,000 industrial firms with a minimum of twenty workers were requested to collaborate; in total 900 firms effectively assisted in the research project. A list of location factors was prepared. Each firm was requested to answer the following question:

Table 4.1
Coefficient of importance of the location factors
(maximum = 100%; minimum = 33.3%)

Object of the question	Firms	Inter-mediaries	Total
The choice of a nation			
Tax system	80.3	82.4	81.2
Administrative efficiency	69.5	74.5	71.7
Conditions of credit and aid			
(a) credit	76.4	76.5	76.4
(b) public aid	72.2	78.4	74.8
The choice of a region			
1. Direct components of the company's economic accounting			
Proximity of sales markets	68.1	64.1	66.7
Natural resources:			
a. raw materials	51.4	—	—
b. energy	55.6	—	—
c. water	66.7	—	—
Labour:			
a. quantity	63.8	62.2	63.2
b. qualification	75.0	88.9	81.0
c. technical schools	65.3	77.8	70.1
d. wages	45.8	50.0	47.5
Economic infrastructure:			
a. passenger transport	58.3	79.6	67.5
b. goods transport	79.2	—	—
c. links with European decision centres	58.0	64.8	61.0
d. telecommunications	80.6	91.1	84.6
Industrial sites and zones:			
a. price of sites	72.2	55.6	65.8
b. availability of sites	71.9	72.5	72.2
c. industrial zones	63.0	80.0	69.0
2. Environment			
Economic environment:			
a. industries	59.4	64.3	61.3
b. services	44.9	51.1	47.4
c. university and research	53.6	58.8	55.8
Social climate:			
a. power of the trade unions	51.4	66.7	57.0
b. number of strikes	50.0	63.0	55.6

Table 4.1 continued:

	Firms	Inter-mediaries	Total
Socio-cultural environment:			
a. 'structures d'accueil'	44.4	59.3	50.8
b. international schools	42.4	60.4	50.0
c. leisure organisations	40.6	44.4	42.1
d. reception of wives	40.6	53.3	45.6
Regional pression groups	50.7	41.7	47.0

'In case you would have to take a decision regarding the location of your firm in 1971, how would you appreciate the various factors: dominant influence, very important, important, less important, no importance at all'. To measure the relative importance of the different factors a production scale per factor was elaborated (from 4 to 0 points).

From Table 4.2 it seems that the availability of labour is the most important among the location factors. Of course, we must not generalise. For certain industrial sectors the traditional factors are still the most important; the steel industry and oil refineries are good examples. Burchard and Capanna have written some noteworthy essays on the subject.[14]

Table 4.2
A general estimation of the location factors
(maximum 400 points − minimum 0 points)

Category	Location factors	Points
Labour (193)	Availability of unskilled and trained male workers	220
	Availability of unskilled and trained female workers	140
	Availability of skilled male workers	210
	Availability of skilled female workers	99
	Availability of staff	176
	Wage level	199
	The faithfulness of labour to the firm	253
	The social climate in the region	250
Infrastructure (112)	Availability of good water connections	83
	Availability of good railway connections	85
	Availability of good road connections	255
	Situated at a highway	163
	Nearness of a seaport	75

133

Table 4.2 continued:

Category	Location factors	Points
[Infra- structure (112)]	Nearness of an airport	34
	Possibilities of pipeline connections	30
	Availability of equipped industrial sites	148
	Availability of equipped industrial sites at a canal	53
	Price per m2 of industrial sites	195
Input (108)	Availability of raw materials in the region	123
	Low transport cost on raw materials and components	198
	Availability of cooling water	87
	Availability of processing water	121
	Possibility to avoid waste water	109
	Nearness of similar firms	56
	Nearness of other industries	69
	Presence of annex firms (backward linkage)	97
Output (138)	Presence of annex firms (forward linkage)	116
	Local market (in the region)	162
	Access to the Belgian market	227
	Nearness of the German market	115
	Nearness of the Dutch market	144
	Nearness of the French market	130
	Nearness of the British market	72
	Central position in Europe	137
Environment (133)	Availability of social and cultural amenities in the region	127
	Nearness of a big town	122
	Suitable housing accommodation for workers	156
	Presence of auxiliary firms	139
	Nearness of financial firms	145
	Easy contact— personal or by telephone — with suppliers and the demand	225
	Nearness of an attractive recreation area	64
	Nearness of the headquarters of the firm	96
	Living habits in the region	126
Regional Financial Aids (215)	Financial stimulus in the framework of regional expansion laws in favour of firms set up in an underdeveloped region	215

Theories on the spatial distribution of economic activities

Models of spatial organisation

We cannot say that theory about the spatial distribution of economic activities is well developed. The reasons are not very clear, but one of them might be that the interest in control and direction of spatial organisation has in fact only come up recently. Two principal pioneering works are those of W. Christaller and A. Lösch. A good analysis of these theories was made by T. Hermansen and H.C. Bos. Their theories have a number of important points in common: [15]

(a) both develop a system of hexagonal markets;
(b) both offer an explanation for the simultaneous existence of urban settlements of different size;
(c) both rely very heavily on differences in transportation costs;
(d) both theories are extremely simple and tend to lead to unrealistic conclusions.

The assumptions on which both theories (as well as Tinbergen's theory) were based are:

there exist homogeneous plains with an even distribution and quality of agricultural conditions and natural resources;
in all subareas of this plain, the population density is the same (and so are consumer preferences and production techniques for each product);
transportation costs and economies of scale differ from product to product;
for each product there is a specific demand function;
it is assumed that all producers behave rationally.

Given these basic assumptions, the question is what is the spatial distribution of plants producing products with different (a) costs of transportation, (b) demand functions and (c) economies of scale.

Similar approaches have been developed during the 1960s by J. Tinbergen and J. Friedman. Recently, development has gone more in the direction of the growth pole theory of Perroux and the attraction model of L.H. Klaassen and A.C. van Wickeren. In the following we will pay attention to each of the theories mentioned above.

Christaller's theory of central places[16]

The basic elements of Christaller's theory of central places are:

central places are centres supplying their environment;

central places can be of different order or rank;

the order of the central place is by definition determined by the radius of the goods or services the centre supplies;

the radius is the maximum distance over which a dispersed population will buy the product;

a system of central places is derived from the consideration that neighbouring central places must be located at equal distances from one another. That is only the case if the centres are located at the corners of equilateral triangles. The market areas are consequently of a regular hexagonal shape;

the structure of the system of central places is further based on the principle that in the gravity centres of triangles formed by three equidistant centres, new centres of lower order will be located until the smallest market area and the central places of lowest order are reached. The result is a geometrically (with a ratio of 3) increasing number of centres of different order.

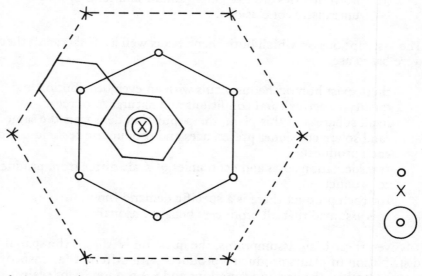

Graph 4.1: Optimum spatial pattern of centres according to W. Christaller

Christaller found support for this theory in data about the number, size, and location of centres in South Germany.

It is obvious that Christaller's system does not allow for specialisation among central places or division of labour other than is consistent with higher order centres providing goods to lower order ones. We shall come back to this point later on.

Lösch's theory of location [17]
This theory starts by assuming that there is a plain on which agricultural population and natural resources are evenly dispersed. On this plain, the settlement of industrial activity depends on:

> transportation costs;
> possibilities of exploiting economies of scale;
> demand structure.

It follows that an activity is centralised if the economies of scale are infinite or if the costs of transport are insignificant, and would be dispersed if economies of scale were completely lacking and if the costs of transport were high. A well known example used by Lösch is that of the brewing industry. In this industry economies of scale exist: not every family brews its own beer; but transportation costs are not insignificant. Both points make for circular market areas. As Lösch assumes that the transport costs are borne by the consumer, market areas are clearly defined by the limits of demand.

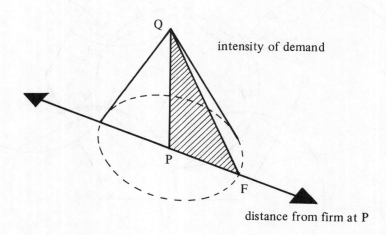

Graph 4.2: Lösch demand 'cone'.

At the centre of the cone transportation cost will be minimum and the cost of the product to the consumer at its lowest. Demand for the product will here be at its greatest and output PQ will be sold. For places located at a distance the demand will gradually become less until the circle through F is reached. Beyond this point no sales take place. The circular market area is described by the radius PF. If there is more than one supplier, the limit of the market area will for each firm be set by the competition from other firms. The market areas will lose their circular shape and assume that of hexagons if two conditions are fulfilled:

(a)   the firm is situated in the centre of the market area;
(b)   transportation costs are identical in every direction.

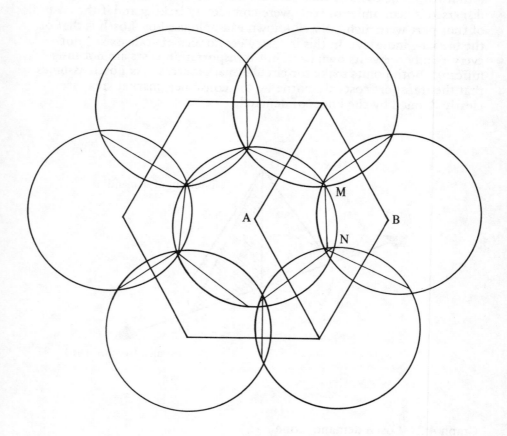

Graph 4.3: Lösch's market areas

138

The resulting hexagonal market areas prove to be the ideal shape in a competitive situation. As conditions of transport and economies of scale differ from industry to industry, the size of the hexagonal market areas will be different from one industry to another.

Lösch shows that there are three possible types of hexagonal market forms. They are of different size and can be repeated at different scales. The market size for the various commodities will have to deviate from their original specific optimum size to fit the closest of the standard networks.

In order to get a completely determined system, Lösch seeks the pattern in which total costs of transportation are minimised, that is, where as many production sites as possible have agglomerated, by rotating the networks around the central place. In this system the costs of transportation are minimised. He obtains six regions (sectors) with many, and six with few agglomerations.

The characteristics of the resulting system of spatial clusterings can be summarised as follows:

(a) there is a superior centre where all kinds of goods are produced;

(b) there is real specialisation, division of labour and trade between centres. Smaller centres supply larger centres with their specialised products;

(c) there is a concentration of centres in city rich areas (6 in total) separated by sectors with a lower density of centres;

(d) nothing can be said about the relative sizes of centres, except that the superior one is larger than all others. Centres with the same number of functions do not necessarily provide the same kinds of services.

The basic differences between the theories of Christaller and Lösch are:

(a) Lösch begins at the bottom with the goods of the smallest spatial range;

(b) in both cases there is one centre where all commodities are produced, but in Christaller's system a hierarchic ranking of centres is possible, in Lösch's system not. Here, we find a greater variation in types of centres; several are specialised in the production of one or a few commodities, in varying combinations.

(c) Lösch's and Christaller's models can be regarded as supplementing each other; the former explaining the spatial organisation of secondary activities and the latter that of service activities.

139

(d) Christaller's model can be looked upon both from a micro and from a macro point of view; Lösch's model does not have any aggregate feature.

It is clear that both systems depend on the initial assumption of agricultural population and natural resources being evenly distributed across economic space, which is a rather doubtful starting point. A second point of criticism concerns the importance attached to transportation costs, these costs being assumed to be proportional with distance in every direction. The fact that for a considerable range of economic activities transport is not an important cost element, is neglected. Finally it can be observed that the models are entirely static and therefore unable to explain changes in regional economic structure other than by changes in autonomous variables.

Tinbergen's hypothesis on spatial dispersion [18]
The problem posed by Tinbergen is how to combine the production units of the various industries in centres in such a way that production and transportation costs are minimised. The solution has to specify the numbers of centres, their industrial composition (first part), and their location (second part).
As starting points Tinbergen chooses:

a closed economy with agricultural production evenly spread over the area;
the non-agricultural part of the economy is divided into an arbitrary number of sectors, each of which has a characteristic minimum size of enterprise at which unit production costs reach a minimum and above which they remain constant;
all products are final consumer goods and the production is organised in plants producing only one good;
all transportation costs are paid by the producers;
all consumers spend their income in the same way;
the population is constant.

On the basis of total demand for each product and knowing the minimum plant size, one can derive the number of plants needed to serve the country in each sector. Then each industry is ranked in accordance with the number of plants.
The next step is to find the combination of plants belonging to each sector in each centre that minimises the total costs of transportation and production. To that end Tinbergen introduces three hypotheses (bringing a solution for the first part of the problem):

1   Each centre containing an industry of rank h, contains also all industries belonging to lower ranked industries. Thus, the centres can be ranked according to their highest ranking industry.
2   From each centre only goods from the highest ranking industry are exported. The export pays for the import of agricultural products and for goods produced by higher ranking industries not represented in the centre.
3   Each highest ranking industry in a centre is represented by only one plant.

From these hypotheses follows a hierarchy of groups of centres. There are as many groups of centres as there are kinds of industries. Each group can be distinguished according to the highest ranking industry and is given a corresponding rank. Centres of the lowest rank consist of one production unit of the lowest ranking industry only. They export part of their production to the agricultural area and have to import all other products. The centres of the next higher rank 2 consist each of one company of industry 2 exporting part of its production to centres of rank 1 and to the agricultural area, and of production units of industry 1, which supply only the population of centres 2, etc. The number of centres in each group diminishes with an increase in the rank of the centre. There is only one centre of the highest rank that locates production units of all industries. The company of the highest ranking industry exports to all lower centres and to the agricultural areas. The only imports in this centre are agricultural products. With given value for total production, given composition of demand, and given minimum plant sizes in all industries, the three hypotheses permit the determination of the number of centres in each group and their industrial composition. The question now is whether the solution arrived at is optimal or not. Tinbergen posed this problem as one of minimising total costs of transportation.

Empirical tests conducted with data for the Netherlands showed a very good fit to the model, while a similar test on a French material showed significant deviations between the real size distribution and industrial composition of centres and those suggested by the model.

The shortcomings of the model are obviously

(a)   it is basically a model applicable only to the demand oriented service sector;
(b)   the assumptions are very unrealistic;
(c)   no attempt is made to integrate location of natural resources, external economies arising from intermediary goods and interplant linkages;
(d)   the model is static and unhistoric.

H.C. Bos has elaborated and amended the approach of Tinbergen in his book *Spatial Dispersion of Economic Activity*. [19]

Growth pole theory

Functional and geographical concepts of the development pole

The development pole concept has provoked a number of interpretations and controversies. The primary cause of the controversies was that F. Perroux's original definition was unclear. That gave rise to confusion of the development-pole concept with related notions. Furthermore, F. Perroux did not reason in terms of geographical space but in terms of economic space. [20] Moreover, the notion was used for different purposes in the framework of regional economic policy, and this did not contribute very much to the clarity of the concepts used.

As we said, the notion was introduced by F. Perroux: 'However basic it may seem, the fact of the matter is that growth does not appear everywhere and all at once; it appears in points or growth poles with variable intensities; it spreads along diverse channels and with varying terminal effects for the whole of the economy'. [21]

It was this definition, and Perroux's description of economic space — 'As a field of forces, economic space consists of centres (or poles or foci) from which centrifugal forces emanate and to which centripetal forces are attracted . . . The firm considered as a centre releases centrifugal and centripetal forces' [22] — that accounted for much of the confusion and gave rise to different interpretations. Other definitions formulated later on, such as 'A development pole is an ensemble of propulsive units which exercises "stimulation effects" with respect to another ensemble economically or territorially defined' [23] and 'a growth pole is a propulsive unit in a determined environment; the propulsive unit is simple or complex; (a) a firm, (b) group of firms not institutionalised (industry), (c) institutionalised group of firms (private combines), semi-public combines etc . . . ', [24] made matters even worse.

The functional interpretation, which has been developed by Belgian economists belonging to the French school of Perroux and Boudeville, is based on the above definition of economic space and is well represented by the following quotation:

> A growth pole is formed when an industry, through the flow of goods and incomes which it is able to provoke, stimulates the development and growth of the industries that are technically related to it (technical polarisation), determines the prosperity of the tertiary sector by means of the incomes which it promotes (income polarisation), or stimulates an increase of the regional

income by causing a progressive concentration of new activities, attracted to a given place by the prospect of finding there certain factors or production facilities (psychological and geographical polarisation).[25]

We return to the different forms of polarisation later on. From these definitions we have to retain one essential point: the links between economic elements.

According to O. Vanneste, the geographical interpretation of the development pole concept finds its origin in the use by F. Perroux of the word 'points' in his definition. The idea is that of a limited geographical place of location. We can find a practical application of this idea in the regional policy of certain countries (e.g. the Netherlands).[26]

> The impression left by the growth pole concept, particularly in Dutch literature, is that of the association arising from the Dutch notion of a 'centre' or 'nucleus'. Industry has by nature a tendency to agglomerate. As the even distribution of industry is an economic impossibility, the Netherlands have upheld in their regional economic policy the principle of the distribution of industry by regional concentration. This finds its confirmation in practice in a series of measures in favour of the so-called industrialisation centres. In this way, the Dutch hoped to channel the industrial growth of their backward areas into a few chosen industrial centres. Most of the centres had little success as points of attraction for new industry. Thus new centres, the so-called development centres, were indicated in the second phase of Dutch regional economic policy. The new term contains far more of the growth element. In their choice of new centres the Dutch were guided especially by the principle that a centre has to be a point of support for a wider structure; that is, it must possess a centre function.[27]

'The presence of a centre function implies exercising a power of attraction on the environment and the presence of, to-quote L.H. Klaassen, some "secondary factors of location".' [28]

Although A.O. Hirschman emphasises technical polarisation in his book *The Strategy of Economic Development,* there are parts which refer to a geographic interpretation. A.O. Hirschman was convinced that in order to get a higher income level in a region 'it must and will first develop within itself one or several regional centres of economic strength. The need for the emergence of "growing points" or "growth poles" in the course of the development process means that international and inter-regional inequality of growth is an inevitable concomitant

143

and condition of growth itself'.[29]

While assuming that the growth pole has, in particular, a functional character, one would be wrong to neglect the spatial aspect and the geographical implications of the idea. Since each location and each economic activity take place within a defined space, they must have spatial consequences. An author who has made the link between the functional and geographical concepts is J. Albertini. The following reflection on the growth pole concept is to be found in his study 'Options pour une méthode d'aménagement. Les pôles de développement':

> Their study began from the empirical observation of the growth phenomenon. Economic progress does not appear everywhere at the same time. It propagates itself from within certain strong areas. In this sense, economic space is essentially a polarised space. However, it would be misleading to call all poles of development, generators of activity.[30]

Indeed the two interpretations — functional and geographical — are not independent from each other. Each activity takes place in a defined space and provokes spatial consequences. In Davin, Degeer and Paelinck we detect already the geographical interpretation. Later on several authors made the link between the schools. In this context we must mention J. Boudeville who emphasised the polarised space and the polarised region created around a core point or a centre.[31]

For such a relationship T. Hermansen uses a very remarkable and meaningful expression 'localised functional growth pole'.[32] This presupposes a polarisation in the functional as well as in the geographical sense.

O. Vanneste tried to make a synthesis of the foregoing approaches: 'A growth pole can be defined as a set of economic elements concentrated in a geographical space, among which certain links exist which sustain growth'.[33]

Three characteristics are to be observed in this definition, viz:

> inter-relations between the economic elements,
> the multiplier effect,
> geographical concentration.

This author also distinguishes between effective and potential growth poles. A potential growth pole forms the basis for attracting other economic elements, which, however, are still lacking. Their introduction could give impetus to a possible growth process. Basing himself on the different kinds of propulsive units, L. Davin differentiates between

144

'functional polarisation' and 'investment polarisation' (infrastructure works, a university, a port, etc.).

To the characteristic multiplier effect we would like to add, in the light of recent developments, the idea of 'sustained growth'. We find this idea very clearly expressed in V. Nichols's definition quoted by N. Hansen: 'A growth pole is an urban centre of economic activity which can achieve self-sustaining growth to the point that growth is diffused outward into the pole region and eventually beyond into the less developed regions of the nation'.[34]

Evolution in ideas about the growth pole concept
In its short history, growth pole theory has evolved significantly.[35] Furthermore, it has been integrated into regional economic policy and regional economic thinking.

In essence the growth pole concept of F. Perroux was an instrument of regional development in an abstract space. T. Hermansen was the first to emphasise this:

> This theory is essentially a theory of development, a theory which purports to explain the entire process of structural change in the economic as well as in the social and even institutional systems, as opposed to a theory of economic growth which concentrates upon the conditions for expansion of aggregate production and total income. Although, as will be seen, Perroux was at the outset not particularly concerned with the spatial aspects of development in its purely geographical sense.[36]

> Perroux's concept of a growth pole is a highly abstract one. It was introduced as a tool to explore the process by which economic activities, i.e. firms and industries are born, grow, and as a rule, stagnate and sometimes disappear.[37]

Nevertheless, F. Perroux was thinking in terms of concentration of economic elements, albeit in an abstract rather than a geographical sense. His approach to the industrial complex is indicative of this. Two cornerstones of F. Perroux's theory are industrial interdependence, and the Schumpeterian ideas about innovation and the role of the big firms. To the first cornerstone belong the notions 'dominant industries', 'backward and forward linkage', and 'industrial complexes'. There is a close link between the cornerstones, leading to the concepts of dynamic companies and leading industries. The notion 'propulsive unit' or 'unité motrice' is derived from these ideas. We will return to it later on.

Two of the above mentioned features of a growth pole, namely interrelations between economic activities (backward and forward linkage),

145

and multiplier and growth effects, are clearly contained in F. Perroux's ideas. Moreover we should note the concept of 'dominance via the propulsive unit'.[38] However, there is no question of geographical concentration.

We should also note the distinction in F. Perroux's publication between growth and development. He emphasises development (structural mutation) much more than growth (increase in the magnitude of economic variables such as income, employment, etc.); that leads M. Penouil to distinguish between 'growth poles' and 'development poles'.

> This basic distinction leads us to oppose growth poles and development poles. In the former case we are concerned with the combination in a particular centre of certain propulsive activities of which the combined action permits a regular increase of the local product. Thanks to its repercussions on incomes and consumption this growth could attract to the centre new activities and new services that will exert an attraction effect on the population and producers of the neighbouring areas. If one admits, however, that the development of the area considered is obstructed by a number of restraining factors (ill-adapted agricultural structures, inadequate staff, conservative mentality, demographic ageing, absence of local consuming markets, insufficient infrastructure, insufficient local saving), it will not get under way by the action of the growth pole alone. The growth pole does not alter, or contribute towards the disturbance of, the existing socio-economic balance; it simply improves the situation of the inhabitants by increasing their income.
>
> In contrast, the development pole questions the former structural balance and contributes towards the elimination of the obstacles that maintain the economy in relative stagnation. It moulds a new society with dynamic people and it opens up new avenues to manifold innovations. From that time onwards a cumulative process is established leading to a continuous amelioration of the situation.[39]

With respect to the notion 'growth pole', M. Penouil makes a further distinction between three types of centres or attraction zones: growth points, growth poles and growth axes.[40]

K. Allen and T. Hermansen also distinguish between 'growth pole' and 'growth centre'.[41] According to these authors the former is more or less synonymous with 'growth area' and 'core region'; it refers to national polarisation, reflecting the location and expansion of national growth poles. The term 'growth centre' or 'growth point' refers to the process of concentration and polarisation within regions. They define a growth centre as 'being a main centre at the regional level which, in addition to its function as a regional service centre, also provides a prosperous and reasonably diversified industrial structure. The centre should either be growing or show potential for growth of economic activity, employment, population and income' . . . 'Growth centres play their important role in transmitting growth to the regions and in restoring the balance between regions which would otherwise arise during the 'process of economic growth'.

The functional role of a growth centre is reflected in its linkages within the region and with other regions. Allen and Hermansen distinguish the following functions.[42] Within the region: (a) it is the centre of the regional labour market — the travel to work centre and centre for intra-regional migration; (b) it is the region's major retail, wholesale and service centre; (c) it is the regional communication, administrative and information centre.

In an extra-regional context, a growth centre has the following functional roles: (a) it is the main centre for external communications; (b) it is the main centre for the movement of export products from the surrounding region as well as the centre itself; (c) it is the main centre for the exchange of information and of financial flows between the region and the rest of the country.

A second evolution in growth pole concept has taken place on the policy level. The growth pole has become significant as a tool of regional development strategy (see chapter 7).

Closely related to this second evolution is a third. For a long time the growth pole theory was isolated. On the basis of the abstract content provided by F. Perroux, the theory was closer to development theory than to any other. Later on, it became an instrument of regional economic policy. We cannot describe the recent trends in location theory without mentioning the growth pole concept.

The shifting of the accent from the growth pole in a functional space to the growth pole in a geographical and/or geo-functional space signifies also an integration of the growth pole concept in the theory of urban economics. When we are confronted with the choice of the growth centres, we cannot deny several aspects of urban economics. We find the same ideas in the contribution of T. Hermansen, N. Hansen and J. Boudeville.

The propulsive unit (unité motrice) in the growth pole
The growth pole notion acquires more precise content with the defining of the propulsive unit of a growth pole. Originally, 'propulsive unit' meant a propulsive industry, but later on a broader context was created (see F. Perroux, L. Davin, J. Baillargeon and J. Milhau). A propulsive unit might be an industrial sector, a firm, or even an element of

infrastructure; highway, port, airport, university, etc. Some related definitions of propulsive units are to be found in J. Baillargeon's contribution: 'In a set of complexes, a propulsive unit causes an increase in the size of the other firms through capital investment and the introduction of technical innovation. It modifies the economic structure and the organisation of the enterprises and it stimulates economic growth of the whole region',[43] and J. Milhau: 'The growth pole is an "ensemble fonctionnel" capable of acting upon the environment with a cumulative effect, leading to a structural transformation of the region ... Its propulsive units could be a big hydro-agricultural infrastructure project, the location of a key industry, or the simple creation of an industrial site'. [44] In spite of the widening of the propulsive unit concept, industry still occupies a dominant position. Many development plans reflect that view.[45] That is, in any case, the opinion of N. Hansen.[46] N. Hansen attaches three main characteristics to a propulsive unit:

> it must be relatively large in order to assure that it will generate sufficient direct and potential direct effects to have a significant impact on the economy;
> it must be a relatively fast growing sector;
> the quantity and intensity of its inter-relations with other sectors should be important so that a large number of induced effects will indeed be transmitted.

A firm with these characteristics (size, growth, and intersector relations) probably guarantees the creation of a development pole as intended by F. Perroux, but not necessarily a localised functional growth pole. The propulsive unit influences other elements, but this may happen entirely or partially outside the region (see Lorraine and Lacq in France).

Ph. Aydalot further widened the propulsive unit concept. According to this author external economies had been neglected for too long in the whole approach to a definition of propulsive units:

> It is necessary to situate properly the notion of propulsive industry. If a propulsive industry plays a stimulating role, it is also a derived role and only represents a stage in the process(es) of polarised growth. It is the notion of propulsive *activity* which becomes the key notion. It can take different forms; it is the real producer of external economies.[47]

Many firms are indeed reluctant to locate a production unit in a region without sufficient infrastructure and secondary factors of location. Infrastructures and services are contained in 'propulsive activity'. Propulsive activities can also be found in medium sized and large cities. A passage from N. Hansen's critical analysis is important here:

> . . . the industries which are most attracted by the external economies generated by large urban areas are not characterised by a highly oligopolistic structure, but are rather industries with numerous small and medium sized firms which are highly dependent upon auxiliary business services and which need frequent direct personal contacts with buyers and sellers.[48]

This brings us back to the notion of distance costs.

The above mentioned idea of Ph. Aydalot is put in the right perspective by asking: if it is the propulsive unit that creates external economies in a region, why then did the propulsive unit itself settle there in the first place? Indeed a propulsive unit — e.g. a firm — is not the backbone of the growth pole. Ph. Aydalot emphasises the role of agglomeration effects through tertiary activities.[49]

Instead of using the term 'propulsive unit' or, for that matter, 'propulsive industry' it does indeed make more sense to use the notion 'propulsive activity' introduced by Aydalot, or 'propulsive space' (espace moteur), put forward by M. Penouil. 'The power of attraction over people and activities is exerted less by productive units than by an ensemble of activities, collective equipment, commercial and administrative centres'.[50] Such considerations lead to an extended vision of the propulsive unit.

Related notions

A number of notions used in regional economic literature are in one way or another related to that of a propulsive unit.

1 *Development block* (E. Dahmen) '. . . a concept emphasising the interdependence of industrial development'.[51] It concerns a network of industrial branches which are economically and technically related to one another. To E. Dahmen, however, the spatial aspect of the phenomenon is completely absent.

2 *Industrial complex* (W. Isard and E.W. Schooler) 'One or more activities occurring at a given location and belonging to a group of activities which are subject to important production, marketing, and other inter-relations'.[52]

3 *Axis of development* (L. Davin, L. Degeer and J. Paelinck) '. . . all auxiliary infrastructure which favour a flexible functioning of

the studied industrial complex and particularly the flow of goods'.
[53] A zone of development is defined by the same authors as:
' . . . a geographical unit of activities of which the technico-
economic adaptation is strategic to the validity of a great economic
space'.[53]

4 *Primary and service activities* (Basic and non-basic activities)
Many look upon W. Sombart as the forerunner of those who make
the distinction between primary and residential activities.[54]
However, the founder in the Netherlands is Th. van Lohuizen.[55]
For him an industry is primary if it is not immediately dependent
upon the size of the population of the area where it is situated. By
disposing of its products either partly or wholly beyond it's own
territorial limits, the circulation of money extends to other areas.
Service industries, on the contrary, provide for the needs of the
local population and the local primary industries and find their
market chiefly within the region. In economic literature, primary
industries are often called agglomeration-forming while residential
industries are called agglomeration following.[56]

5 *External economies and agglomeration effects.*

6 *Secondary location factors* (L.H. Klaassen) e.g. skilled labour,
industrial climate, amenities of life, satellite industries, transport
facilities, etc.

The forms of polarisation in a growth pole
What matters fundamentally is the nature of the links between the
active element, or propulsive unit, and the other economic components
of a growth pole. In the economic literature four kinds of polarisation
phenomena can be distinguished: (a) technical polarisation, (b) income
polarisation, (c) psychological polarisation, and (d) geographical polarisation.

1 *Technical polarisation.* Technical polarisation that arises through
technical links between the active element and the economic activity
attracted. Two kinds of technical linkage must be distinguished: backward linkage and forward linkage. In French literature, the same notions
are known as 'polarisation en amont' and 'polarisation en aval'.

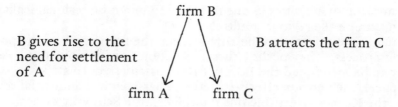

firm B

B gives rise to the need for settlement of A

B attracts the firm C

firm A   firm C

Between the companies A and B, and between A and C there exist flows of goods such that it becomes more profitable for the firms A and C to be located in the neighbourhood of company B. The economic advantages of concentrated development fall into two broad categories: (a) technical economies (proximity of suppliers and customers), and (b) external economies (they occur when the production costs of one firm are lowered by the actions of other firms).

Such polarisation is in line with what L.E. Davin calls 'functional polarisation'. This author clearly separates this idea from that of 'investment polarisation'. The latter is also a technical polarisation form which might consist of an industrial site, a port, a highway, a university, an extended residential centre, etc. The distinction made by L.E. Davin is well justified. In the following statements the term 'technical links' means simply 'polarisation de fonctionnement'.

What activities cause the greatest technical polarisation? This is an important question to which a general and permanent answer cannot be given. In view of the dynamic character of the economy, every answer is linked to time, and to a certain degree, to space. In general terms, four major factors determine the intensity of the polarising activity:

1 the growth rate of an industry;
2. the number of phases in the production process;
3 the intersectoral degree of linkage of an industrial branch;
4 the diversity of the regional economic structure.

Some remarks could be made regarding the relations that exist between technical polarisation and input-output analysis. The first is that there may be important technical relationships between sectors, in the sense of the input-output table, i.e. one sector may be an important purchaser of, or seller to, another sector even if they are located in two completely different regions. The second is that in input-output analysis technical relations are exclusively demand relations. The supply effects are often of paramount importance (petro-chemical or carbochemical industries based on the presence of oil refineries or coal mines are an example in point). In technical polarisation such possible interrelations are explicitly included. A third point is that technical polarisation is directed towards 'bouclage régional', that is towards such a concentration of activities in one region as to minimise regional leakages or to maximise the regional multiplier.[57]

A number of effects may be noted within the framework of the polarisation process. They occur either in isolation or in combination. As such may be mentioned the Leontief-Rasmussen effect (matrix-multiplier), the Perroux effect (structural change in interindustrial relations), the Keynes effect (income multiplier), the Scitovsky effect (effects on higher productivity via the effects of external or internal economies on prices), the Aftalion effect (acceleration), the Matilla or association effect (effect on social amenities), and the Capet effect (internal and external 'bouclage').

In practice technical polarisation is very often less important than theory suggests. O. Vanneste's research is relevant in this respect.[58]

2 *Technical polarisation in a larger context.* During the nineteenth and the twentieth centuries several industrial complexes were created in Europe. In view of the inter-relations between the industries in one region, they were in fact growth poles. Heavy industries formed the basis and at that time they were the growing industries. Transportation costs were a factor that stimulated concentration. Although later on transportation systems were improved and technological progress was made, the concentration of industry did not decrease. On the contrary, the action radius of the original poles became wider. How can we explain that tendency? The explanation is to be found in (a) the new interrelation between firms due to the efforts made to raise efficiency (lower production costs), (b) the efforts made to reduce distance costs, and (c) the influence of secondary location factors. This can be illustrated in the following way:

(a) technological development and large scale production bring about a specialisation of the production processes. Greater specialisation increases interindustrial linkages. 'While in the twentieth century production in manufacturing industry was still characterised by vertical integration, in the most dynamic production sectors, manufacturing becomes more and more quasi-horizontally integrated. The production in a production unit is concentrated on the major activities; the others are committed to subcontractors and other firms which supply products or intermediate products to large numbers of customers. This allows large production units to produce on a large scale, to apply the most productive techniques, to assure a better utilisation of resources and labour, and consequently to produce at lower costs'.[59]

(b) Around the major firms auxiliary firms (e.g. repair shops, maintenance firms) and subcontractors (subcontracting firms,

152

service industries) will develop. In a modern economy a manufacturing firm performs itself the principal activities and makes more and more use of auxiliary firms and subcontractors. The latter are viable only if a sufficient number of firms are located nearby.

(c) The manufacturing firms are mutually linked through the common use of socio-cultural infrastructure, economic infrastructure, and facilities.

A corollary of increasing specialisation is the greater dependence of each firm on 'industrial environment', to use the expression of A. Tosco. The efforts made in Southern Italy (Bari-Tarente-Brindisi) and in Canada (New Brunswick) to create a 'localised functional growth pole' must be seen in this context. This implies a geographical concentration and the choice of a number of 'similar manufacturing activities', with a high growth rate. In the Italian projects branches of the metal industry were chosen, which all have similar inputs and which appeal to similar auxiliary firms and subcontractors.

3 *Income polarisation.* In addition to the flow of goods, one must take into consideration the parallel current of the economic circuit — the flow of expenditure and its effects. The prices paid for the production factors, e.g. land, labour, capital, and also the profits of the entrepreneur are passed on by consumers to producers via expenditure. All sorts of activities owe their existence to these circular flows.

The degree of polarisation within the economic regions is influenced by the following factors:

(a) the regional consumption quota;
(b) the rate at which money flows out to other regions by attracting outside workers;
(c) the extent to which the profit of the entrepreneurs remains within the economic group;
(d) the extension and diversity of economic activities.

In fact, the phenomenon of income polarisation is very close to that of the regional multiplier.

4 *Psychological polarisation.* Psychological polarisation can be exerted in three ways:

(a) through the imitation effect: polarisation as a consequence of the location of a dominant firm is of a psychological nature. Large shopping units are often seen to attract a number of smaller shops to their area;

153

(b) through information about location possibilities;
(c) through a work of infrastructure.

5 *Geographical polarisation.* Geographical polarisation is directly related to growth centre policy. Two things are of interest:

(a) the number of centres or nuclei, and
(b) the choice of the centres or nuclei. We return to this point in chapter 7 dealing with methods of regional development.

The growth pole concept and regional economic policy
The relation between the growth pole idea and regional economic policy must be seen from the point of view of two interpretations of the growth pole concept: the functional and the geographical interpretation (see also chapter 7). The usefulness of the growth pole concept appears immediately when we start from the geographical interpretation, especially if we consider the nucleus or centre as the propulsive unit (Zentrale Orte, Métropoles d'équilibres, etc.).[60]
There is less unanimity concerning the application of the growth pole concept in its functional form. O. Vanneste raises the question: 'Growth pole theory: concentration or spreading?'
Indeed, on the basis of growth pole theory one could deduce not only that the polarising action of the active elements promotes a concentration, but also that the concentration must be stimulated in order to effect an optimum flow of goods and incomes.
When such polarisation is carried through further, free from other very important economic considerations, the statement of L.E. Davin '. . . then, one may wonder whether the best method to fight against structural regional unemployment does not consist in multiplying the activities of the industrial branches in fundamental expansion, and in encouraging them to the maximum in the big zones of development, which are themselves also in expansion' becomes logical.[61]
Such a theory supposes, however: (a) a blind belief in polarisation as such, (b) the neglecting of many other location factors, (c) complete mobility of labour, (d) a disregard for many social costs *per capita* in agglomerations with growing populations (see chapter 5).[62]
The theory of polarisation — as it is put forward by many authors — takes into account the mutual relationship between many factors. The decision to maximise economic effects by concentration originates from the fact that L.E. Davin starts from technical polarisation as the cornerstone of the whole polarisation process. However, that starting point overestimates the importance of technical polarisation in the development of an area on the one hand, and, on the other hand, underestimates the effects of income and psychological polarisations as well as

of the authority's or welfare body's possibilities of contributing to the development of an area through 'voluntary geography'.

Rather than an inducement to concentration, growth pole theory must be considered as the opening of a gate to the dispersal of economic prosperity across a limited number of regions by means of the location of active elements.

To extend the scope of growth pole theory, it is necessary, in the first place, to shift the accent to the active element, and, secondly, to accept the relative character of technical linkages. With the accent on the active element, growth pole theory becomes a positive contribution to the promotion of regional development in structurally weak as well as in structurally strong areas. It may also be assumed that the stimulating of a large number of active elements of divergent character in a region will *ipso facto* lead to the highest possible number of links.

Growth pole theory offers a positive contribution to the explanation of economic phenomena and of shifts in space. It is also a cornerstone for an efficient regional policy, provided it is not based exclusively on technical links. In chapter 7 we return to the relationship between this theory and regional economic policy.

The attraction model[63]

Basic and non-basic activities
By definition, a non-basic activity is an activity that for economic reasons necessarily has to be performed within the area considered. It follows that a basic activity, although performed within the boundaries of the area, need not necessarily be located there. A subdivision of all activities into basic and non-basic activities enables us to derive the average demand multiplier (see chapter 1).

Reconsideration of the notion of a non-basic activity leads us to the conclusion that there are two sources of non-basic activities: (a) the spending of consumers' income earned in basic activities; and (b) the spending by the basic industries themselves (induced or secondary production); it must be produced within the area.

It follows logically that we should distinguish regional demand multipliers for all sectors.

The difference between the basic — non-basic (BNB) approach and the input-output (IO) approach
There are some fundamental differences between the basic — non-basic approach and the input-output approach. They can be listed as follows:

BNB	IO
An autonomous increase of activity in NB activities is unrealistic	An increase of the final demand may be assumed; we can calculate the total effect in each sector
A basic activity has no effects on other basic activities	Relationship between the basic activities
An increase in the demand for basic activities creates income and the NB activities are a function of income	Analyses the technical relationship between the production in the different sectors and the inputs

It appears that in spite of these differences both approaches concentrate exclusively on the demand side.

The supply factors
So far, we have considered only the effects on demand resulting from the location of the basic activity (final demand and industrial demand). However, considerable influence may be exerted by the supply effects. Supply considerations are relevant for the location of a given industry in a given area and will induce other industries to locate in the neighbourhood of the first one (example of forward linkage). Taking both effects into consideration we arrive at three kinds of secondary effects: (a) demand effects, (b) supply effects, and (c) demand effects resulting from the supply effects.

Since one industry might create considerably more supply effects than another we again have to reconsider the regional multiplier. The greater both supply and demand effects of a given industry are, the higher will be its total regional multiplier. The industries with the highest total regional multiplier are called the propulsive or strategic industries.

Usefulness of the input-output table
The input-output approach suggests that the larger the money flow from one industry to another, the more intense their connection and thus the stronger the tendency for the two to be located in close proximity. Some remarks should be made in this context:

the attraction between two industries may be very strong even if the money flow between them is small;
the attraction between two industries may be quite strong, even

though the money flow between them would not be greatly affected by a larger distance (and may appear small in the input-output table).

To approach the problem of the spatial proximity of activities, the concept of communication costs (distance costs), as the widest concept for describing the costs of interaction between economic activities, could be useful. The costs of communication cannot be defined directly; the attraction that industries exert upon one another has to be measured indirectly. The principle is: 'If two or more types of industries are mutually attractive, they will frequently be located in one another's neighbourhood. The higher this frequency, the more attraction they are supposed to exert'.

The elements of attraction theory
According to attraction theory, the size of an industry in a region is determined by:

> final demand
> interindustry demand $\Big\{$ total demand
> supply

Consequently we may distinguish three categories of industries:

> demand-oriented industries,
> supply-oriented industries,
> 'industries équilibrées' (balanced industries, oriented to demand as well as to supply).

It is not the transportation costs that are regarded as the principle factor of an industry's location choice, but the hypothetical sum of the transportation costs and other costs incurred in connection with markets and suppliers; attempts are being made to find out how far these costs — the 'communication costs' which include transportation — determine location in the sense that industries will have a stronger tendency to locate in one another's neighbourhood as the communication costs are higher.

The mathematical model
(a)
$$x_{kj} = g_{kj} - d_{kj} \tag{4.13}$$
in which

x_{kj} =   exports of products k from region j;

157

$$g_{kj} = \text{production of products k in region j};$$

g_{kj} = production of products k in region j;

d_{kj} = demand for products k in region j.

(b)
$$m_{klj} = \beta_{kl}g_{kj} - a_{lk}g_{lj} \qquad (4.14)$$

in which

m_{klj} = imports of products of industry l by industry k in region j;

β_{kl} = the fraction of gross production of industry k required from industry l in region j;

a_{lk} = the fraction of gross production of industry l sold to industry k in region j.

(c) Communication costs (transportation costs included)

equal zero for one unit of sales of product k within the region;
equal t_d for one unit sold outside the region;
equal zero for one unit of requirements l bought within the region;
equal t_l if the requirement is imported.

The total communication costs for industry k in region j are by definition:

$$t_{kj} = t_d x_{kj} + \Sigma\, t_l m_{klj} \qquad (4.15)$$

We replace x_{kj} and m_{klj}, it then follows

$$g_{kj} = \underbrace{\frac{t_d}{t_d + t_l\beta_{kl}}}_{\lambda_d} d_{kj} + \Sigma\, \underbrace{\frac{t_l\beta_{kl}}{t_d + \Sigma\, t_l\beta_{kl}}}_{\lambda_l} \cdot \frac{a_{lk}}{\beta_{kl}} g_{lj} \qquad (4.16)$$

then (4.16) becomes

$$g_{kj} = \lambda_d d_{kj} + \Sigma\, \lambda_l \frac{a_{lk}}{\beta_{kl}} g_{lj} \qquad (4.17)$$

in which

$$\lambda_d + \Sigma\, \lambda_l = 1.$$

Table 4.3
Some attraction equations

No.	Sector	Equation	R
4	Foodstuffs (assim.products)	$g_{4j} = 0,408d_{4j} + 0,592g_{15j}$	0,594
5	Foodstuffs (oth.products)	$g_{5j} = 0,195d_{5j} + 0,2472g_{5j} + 0,557g_{20j}$	0,986
6	Production of drinks & tobaccos	$g_{6j} = 1000g_{5j}$	0,981
7	Textiles	$g_{7j} = 0,419d_{7j} + 0,581g_{7j}$	0,938
8	Footwear & clothing	$g_{8j} = 0,539d_{8j} + 0,461g_{12j}$	0,777
9	Wood & furniture	$g_{9j} = 0,904d_{9j} + 0,096g_{9j}$	0,799
10	Papermills	$g_{10j} = 0,541d_{10j} + 0,459g_{10j}$	0,986
11	Printers & publishers	$g_{11j} = 1000g_{11j}$	0,991
12	Leather & rubber industry	$g_{12j} = 0,591d_{12j} + 0,409g_{12j}$	0,879
13	Chemicals incl. oil refineries	$g_{13j} = 0,886d_{13j} + 0,114g_{13j}$	0,996
14	Production of pottery, glass, stones	$g_{14j} = 0,557d_{14j} + 0,206g_{14j} + 0,236g_{14j}$	0,977
15	Metal/production & machine building	$g_{15j} = 0,757d_{15j} + 0,243g_{15j}$	0,922
16	Transport articles	$g_{16j} = 0,863d_{16j} + 0,137g_{16j}$	0,982
17	Other metal/industry & diamond cuttery	$g_{17j} = 0,483d_{17j} + 0,516g_{17j}$	0,842
19	Public utilities	$g_{19j} = 1000d_{19j}$	0,996
20	Services	$g_{20j} = 0,877d_{20j} + 0,123g_{20j}$	0,995

(d) The λ's are called attraction coefficients:

λ_d represents demand attraction;

λ_l represents supply attraction;

If λ_d = 1: the industry is completely demand-oriented,

If λ_l = 1: the industry is completely l-supply-oriented.

The industry is footloose if all t's are zero.

(e) The λ's are empirically estimated, i.e. by regression analysis. The λ's and the coefficient of correlation must be significant.

The results of the multiple regression analysis have been calculated for the Netherlands (on the basis of provincial input-output tables).

(f) This enables us to rank the industries by demand orientation or supply orientation and to determine how the growth of one industry in a particular region influences the growth of other industries in a direct way.

Remark: The attraction coefficients are not comparable to the technical coefficients in a normal input-output table. They represent the influence of the growth of a given industry in a given region upon the growth industries in *the same* region through stimulation of both *demand and supply.*

An inter-regional attraction model

A basic assumption of the conventional attraction analysis presented in the foregoing is that communication costs within the 'relevant region' are zero. If we put their value outside the relevant region at c, this assumption may be presented as in Graph 4.4

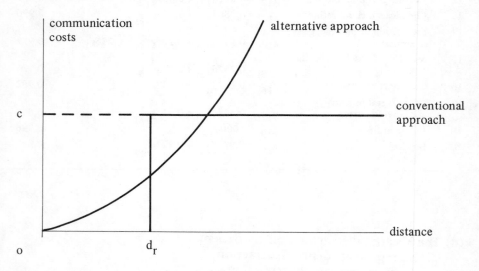

Graph 4.4: Communication costs and distance

The radius of the relevant region is represented by d_r. For distances smaller than d_r communication costs are zero.

In an alternative approach, communication costs are low for small distances and steadily increase with distance. This at the same time more general and more realistic assumption implies that, e.g. the demand in all regions is of importance for a producing firm in a given region, but that the degree of importance decreases as the distance from that region increases.

It follows logically from this assumption that to make it operational in attraction analysis it is sufficient to replace the concept of demand in a given region with the concept of the weighted demand of all regions involved for products given from that region.

The foregoing means that potential demands as well as potential outputs should be defined as a function of their regional accessibility. This is identical to saying that the notion of a demand or supply potential should be used instead of demand or supply itself.

Now write [64]

$$D^p_i = \sum_{j=1}^{n} \Phi_j \, D_j \, e^{-\varphi d_{ij}} \qquad (4.18)$$

in which

D^p_i = the potential total demand for a given product produced in region i

D_j = actual demand for the product in region j

$e^{-\varphi d_{ij}}$ = the 'resistance' function, indicating the influence of the distance between regions i and j (d_{ij}) on the importance of D_j for D^p_i.

Φ_j = a coefficient representing the 'openness' of region j to competition from all regions i, to be defined more precisely later.

n = number of regions.

The coefficient Φ_j is important. In general, a region will be more open to competition from outside if the average distance to other regions is small. Evidently, regions at the periphery of a country will be considerably less 'open' than those situated in the centre.

If it is now, realistically, assumed that the sum of all potential demands is equal to actual demand, then the following equation should hold:

$$\sum_i D^p_i = \sum_j D_j = D \qquad (4.19)$$

We may write, then,

$$D = \sum_i \sum_j \Phi_j \, D_j \, e^{-\varphi d_{ij}} \qquad (4.20)$$

$$D = \sum_j \Phi_j \, D_j \sum_i e^{-\varphi d_{ij}} \qquad (4.21)$$

The obvious solution for Φ_j is

$$\Phi_j = \left[\sum_i e^{-\varphi d_{ij}} \right]^{-1} \qquad (4.22)$$

so that we may write

$$D_i^P = \sum_j D_j \frac{e^{-\varphi d_{ij}}}{\sum_i e^{-\varphi d_{ij}}} = \sum_j a_{ij} \, D_j \qquad (4.23)$$

in which a_{ij} is the *relative accessibility* of region j from i compared to the accessibility of j from all regions i.

(4.23) presents the potential demand for products produced in region i as the sum of all regional demands D_j, corrected for the distance from region i to j as well as for the 'openness' of region j to competition from all regions i.

If distance plays no role, in other words, if the costs of communication with consumers are zero, then $\varphi = 0$. In this case $a_{ij} = \frac{1}{n}$ for each region j. This implies that potential demand

$$D_i^P = \sum_j \frac{D_j}{n} = \frac{1}{n} D \qquad (4.24)$$

In this case all regions are equally open to competition from other regions.

When communication costs are very important, φ approaches infinity. Consequently a_{ij} approaches unity (assuming that $d_{jj} = 0$) and $D_i^P = D_i$. In this case the potential is limited to the region i itself.

The coefficient φ represents the influence of distance and reflects the influence of the absolute size of the costs of communication with the market.

Obviously φ is closely related to the size of the relevant region. The larger the value of φ, the smaller the so-called relevant region (as far as demand is concerned). The smaller φ, the larger the relevant region. The approach suggested here, in which the size of the relevant region is implicit in the analysis, seems more elegant than the conventional approach which was essentially a trial and error method, albeit a more systematic one than most.

The above considerations are still incomplete. As in the conventional approach, the availability of inputs has to be taken into consideration as well. When there are s inputs, we shall get in principle s input-availability potentials analogous to the market potentials. The attractiveness of location in a given region for a given industry is then determined by the weighted sum of all demand and supply potentials or symbolically, by

$$G = \lambda_D D^P + \sum_1 \lambda_1 \frac{a_{1k}}{\beta_{kl}} G_1^P \tag{4.25}$$

which is formally identical to (4.17) with the exception of the production and demand variables, which in (4.24) represent potentials.

When (4.25) is summed over all regions we get

$$\Sigma G = \lambda_D \Sigma D^P + \sum \sum_1 \frac{a_{1k}}{\beta_{kl}} G_1^P$$

$$\Sigma G = \lambda_D \Sigma G + \Sigma \lambda_1 \Sigma G \tag{4.26}$$

so that evidently again

$$\lambda_D + \Sigma \lambda_1 = 1 \tag{4.27}$$

The model is elaborated further in the Mathematical Appendix.

In fact (4.25) represents an inter-regional attraction model, which can be applied as an instrument for regional industrialisation policy as well as for regional infrastructure policy. The latter influences the distance matrix. In many cases this will be a time distance rather than a physical distance matrix, which does not make much difference in practical research. If a time distance matrix is used, improvements in the transportation system that result in time savings will exert a similar influence as improvements that shorten distances.

It may be remarked that the model enables us to determine the influence of any increase in production in any region. The total effect of the location of an industry on all industries in a given region is called the regional multiplier. Obviously the model can be used just as well by regional authorities for the industrialisation policy of a given region as by the national authorities for the purpose of obtaining a balanced regional development in a country as a whole. In the former case the objective will be to adjust the structure of the region's economy in such a way as to maximise the regional multiplier; the introduction into the region of such activities as fill the 'gaps' in the economic structure may help bring about the desired effect. In the latter case the national multiplier will be maximised within the boundary condition that the degrees of development are distributed over the country in an acceptable way.

As in the conventional attraction approach, the inter-regional attraction model has to be completed by the introduction of the secondary factors of location. From the foregoing it can be derived that the expected level of production of a given sector in a given region depends upon the weighted demands and supplies in all other regions. The weights decrease with distance, but the decrease is slight when the φ's are small. In that case the expected production in all regions will approach the same value, since the 'openness' of all regions in this case also approaches the same value. The smaller the φ's the more even the industry is expected to be distributed over all regions.

In actual fact, a given size of regions is always used in the analysis. Provinces, départements, Kreise, are all examples of administrative levels on which statistical data are collected and on which, consequently, any analysis has to be based. To the radius of these regions an average value of $\overline{d}_{ij}$ can be related, and consequently a value of φ which makes $\overline{d}_{ij}$ a reasonable substitute for the radius of the 'relevant region'.

Formally, write

$$a = e^{-\varphi \overline{d}_{ij}} \qquad (4.28)$$

in which $0 \leqslant a \leqslant 1$.

An acceptable value for a would be 0.9 or 0.95, meaning that 90 or 95 per cent of the value of the resistance function is reached. The value of $\overline{d}_{ij}$ for which this equation holds equals

$$\overline{d}_{ij} = -\frac{1}{\varphi} \ln a$$

$$\text{If } a = 0.95, \ \overline{d}_{ij} = \frac{0.05}{\varphi}$$

The industries for which $\overline{d}_{ij} > d_{ij}$, being the industries for which the relevant region is larger than the regions used in the analysis, should receive special attention as far as the secondary factors of location are concerned. For such activities the secondary factors should be taken

164

implicitly into account, albeit under the condition that the average influence of these factors equals zero.

Applied to a region of a given size, the foregoing means that the secondary factors of location are the most important ones when the size of the relevant region largely exceeds that of the region itself. The activity is then, as far as interindustry and market relations are concerned, 'footloose' within its relevant region (which includes the region under consideration): an industry looking for a site might locate within the area under consideration, but might as readily choose any other part of the relevant region. Since for the location within the relevent region the secondary factors are decisive, they are also decisive for the decision to locate or not to locate in the area under consideration. For the regional authorities, this is the essential point.

Is the relevant region smaller than the area studied, then the location of the firm will in any case take place within the boundaries of the area. Its exact location may be important for e.g. a balanced spatial structure of the area but not for the level of activities in the area as a whole.

In fact, the factors called secondary are not very well defined. They represent all 'other factors' that are of importance on a level lower than that of the relevant region. But since the definition of the relevant region, or rather, the possibility of defining the relevant region, depends upon the quality and level of disaggregation of the available statistical material, it can easily happen that factors belonging essentially to the category of interindustry relations appear as secondary factors of location. An example might be a brewery for which the quality of water is important. If the availability of water in general, regardless of its quality, is analysed as to its importance for the location of breweries, probably no influence of any significance will be found. The quality of the water will then be considered a secondary factor of location. If, however, the availability of water had been subdivided according to the quality of the water, then it might have been found a primary factor of location.

This example shows that the boundary between secondary factors and primary factors of location is not a very precise one and that the denomination of a factor may within certain limits depend upon the quality of the information available to the researcher and upon his personal judgement.

Environmental factors

A special group of secondary factors are formed by the environmental factors. The quality of the environment is the joint product of a number of influences, amongst which those of the structure of the industrial activities in a given region. The willingness to start a new activity in such a region will depend not only upon purely economic factors such as interindustry and market relations, labour market factors and other secondary factors of production, but just as much on the quality of the environment. In fact the relation between production and environmental qualities is twofold. The first part of this relation is the influence exerted directly on production. Food industries or other 'clean' industries are apt to be not very enthusiastic about locating in an area polluted by refineries or steel industries, as is indeed confirmed in practice. The same relation exists between polluting industries and tourism.

The second part is an indirect relationship. Pollution makes a region less attractive for living and if pollution is heavy, out-migration, particularly of higher skilled labour, might be the result. For industries that depend heavily on this kind of labour, its scarcity will negatively influence a region's attractiveness.

With either influence, the value of the secondary factor of production (environment) is determined by the production levels, which in turn react to the quality of the environment. Of course, each activity will react in its own way and with its own intensity. It would not be right, therefore, to assume a direct relationship between the production levels of certain pairs of sectors and to introduce, e.g., negative attraction coefficients (repulsion coefficients) between these sectors. The repulsion of the one sector is caused by the pollution resulting from the production of the other industry and not by that production itself. Measures taken to reduce pollution will also decrease the negative influence of the environment on other sectors.

If we write E for the quality of the environment and $\underline{k}$ for the vector of the coefficients of the different sectors' reaction to pollution, we may rewrite the basic equation as follows:

$$\underline{g} = \hat{\Lambda}_D \, B\underline{g} + \Lambda_{\underline{AB}} \, \underline{g} + \hat{\Lambda}_D \, \underline{f} + \underline{k}E \qquad (4.29)$$

Evidently, the scalar E is a function of the different production levels in the region. If c is the vector of the pollution coefficeints per unit production we may write

$$E = c'\underline{g} \qquad (4.30)$$

so that (4.29) can be written

$$\underline{g} = \hat{\Lambda}_D \, B\underline{g} + \Lambda_{\underline{AB}} \, \underline{g} + \hat{\Lambda}_D \, \underline{f} + \underline{k}c'\underline{g} \qquad (4.31)$$

for which the solution reads

$$\underline{g} = \left[I - \hat{\Lambda}_D B - \Lambda_{\underline{AB}} - \underline{k}c' \right]^{-1} \hat{\Lambda}_D \underline{f} \qquad (4.32)$$

It appears that the influence of the environment does not change the values of the attraction coefficients but does alter the value of the multipliers.

Analytical elements of a regional industrialisation policy

In the foregoing we concentrated on the factors that determine the decision of an entrepreneur to locate his firm in a given region. Attraction analysis was treated as one method of finding an explanation for the actual behaviour of entrepreneurs.

As already said before, it has been a long time, however, since the location of an industry in a given area was considered a matter to be decided by the entrepreneur only. For a multitude of reasons that idea has been abandoned. It is now generally recognised that every industry causes a number of external effects in the economic, social, and environmental fields, which may be so serious that the decision of the entrepreneur, although rational enough from a purely commercial point of view, might not be at all favourable from the point of view of society as a whole. In that case society should have power to prevent the location of that particular industry altogether, to grant permission to start production under certain constraints only, or to permit location in certain well defined regions only.

The more insight is gained into the linkages between activities and into the consequences of the location of a particular firm on social, environmental and traffic conditions in the region involved, the more and the narrower will be the boundary conditions within which the entrepreneur is allowed to take his final decision to start or not to start production.

It seems that this development is not typical of specific economic regimes. In both capitalist and socialist countries recognition of the favourable and unfavourable consequences of industrial growth has gradually grown, leading in both groups of countries to more rational decision making in the field of industrial location. The only basic difference between the two groups of countries is that in capitalist countries the entrepreneur takes the final decision to accept or not to accept the conditions set, while in socialist countries the decision is taken, at least formally, by the government. This implies that in capitalist countries the decision is conditioned by two groups, in socialist

167

countries by one. Consequently, there is a possibility of actual industrial development in the one group of countries deviating from that in the other group. Symbolically we can present this as follows

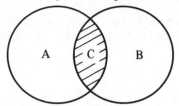

Let A be the set of alternatives for the location of an industry acceptable to the government in a capitalist country and B the set of alternatives acceptable to the entrepreneur, then the alternative finally chosen will be located in C, which only exists in so far as A and B overlap. In a socialist country any alternative within A might be chosen. That means that the decisions in the two cases may be identical (if the socialist government chooses an alternative in C) but are not necessarily so. The probability that they are depends on the nature of the alternative acceptable to the entrepreneurs and the degree to which these appear acceptable to the government.

Now A and B are not fixed. Projects may seem so attractive to the government that it decides to subsidise them so as to make them attractive to the entrepreneur as well. Others may be so unattractive to the government that it decides to levy a special tax on them, thus greatly reducing the number of alternatives acceptable to the entrepreneur. In the case of a subsidy A and B might even come to coincide; in the case of tax C will decrease in size or even disappear completely.

Evidently, the A set in a capitalist country does not necessarily coincide with the A set in a socialist country. In a socialist country A represents the set of *preferred* or desired alternatives, in a capitalist country it is the set of *permissible* alternatives, the latter being essentially wider than the former.

Imperfect knowledge about the ultimate importance of the projects might in a socialist country lead to the exclusion of desirable alternatives and the inclusion of undesirable alternatives, in a capitalist country to the permission of inacceptable projects and the exclusion of acceptable projects.

In fact, imperfect knowledge is the main cause of wrong decisions in both groups of countries. The more insight is gained into all the effects of given projects, the smaller the probability that an undesirable project is permitted or a desirable project excluded.

In a report on this subject now being organised and coordinated by the Centre de Coordination des Sciences Sociales in Vienna [65] an attempt is made to gain more insight into the factors determining the location of industries in a number of capitalist and socialist countries. It is felt that either group of countries could profit from the experiences gained in the other group in their efforts to promote the well being of their societies. The study undertaken by the Centre concentrates on the factors determining the location of growth industries.

The foregoing argument gives rise to the question what criteria a government should apply in its efforts to promote industrial growth, in other words, what industries serve the purpose of the region best. Attraction analysis might provide us with a first criterion, viz. that industries creating larger secondary effects than others are to be preferred, in other words, that industries are to be ranked according to the level of their (regional) multiplier. To the same class of criteria belongs the detection of leakages or gaps in the existing structure. A gap in the structure might be the cause of low multipliers in a number of sectors and the filling of such a gap could contribute considerably to the growth rate and the stability of the system.

The problem of the stability of the structure is particularly urgent in so called monostructured regions, i.e. in regions where one specific industry is of dominant importance. From the past we know that such regions may be hit very hard by the decline of their dominant industry. Textile and coal mining regions are clear cut examples of regions where the whole economy got in distress because of the heavy decrease in employment in the dominant activities. Regional governments should try in its industrialisation policy to avoid such onesidedness, even if the dominant industry is a marked growth industry, and to strike a balance between growth and stability of the economy in their regions by a programme of diversification. Growth is promoted by the introduction of growth industries, stability by diversification. In order to reach a balanced situation a sacrifice in growth may be called for.

This point is of particular importance in discussing the concept of growth industry. Usually industries are defined as growth industries if in comparison with other industries they have shown considerable growth in some relevant variable, such as employment or gross production. But obviously such growth always relates to the circumstances as they were in the past. And as experience shows, an industry that has been a growth industry in the past will not necessarily remain a growth industry in the future. Conventional products may be replaced with new ones or, as may now be expected, new products may again be replaced with other ones. Technological innovation may cause a sharp decrease in employment, even with production still rising. A possibility to be especially kept in mind by those responsible for regional industrialisation, is that rising wages may cause the shift of a whole industry (even a precious growth industry) from one country to another or from one region to another. Electric components industries are certainly growth industries in the sense that their production is expected to grow in the near future, but it is not at all sure that their location will prove to be stable. Rising wages in developed countries might in the near future make a location in a low wage country preferable by far to the present one. Although in this case the industry is a growth industry for the world as a whole, it is certainly not a growth industry for the region from which the industry moves. The same reasoning holds for chemical industry, which in the past developed on the basis of coal mining, shifted to oil as its main input and may now shift back again to coal. Here, too, the shift brings decline to the region from which the industry moves, although it simultaneously brings prosperity to the area of new location.

These considerations lead us to the conclusion that those in charge of industrialisation policy should not concentrate their preparatory research solely on the preferences of a new industry for a given location, but also give attention to the preferences of existing industries so as to be informed about the stability of employment in these branches.

Unfortunately there is not much information available on the migration of industries, but from German and Dutch data it has become clear that in many regions the relatively small net growth of a given activity may be the result of relatively large mutually compensating mutations. Immigration, out-migration, closing down and newly locating have much greater dimensions than net figures show. In other words: the study of the location of growth industries, if based on net figures, might show us only the top of the iceberg and nothing of the 90 per cent that is below the surface.

The arguments evolved in this chapter lead us to the following procedure for the preparation of a sound regional industrialisation policy.

1 Draw up a list of growth industries, defined e.g. as industries that are expected to grow in the coming decade.
2 Estimate by means of attraction analysis the size of the multiplier of each growth industry.
3 Determine which new growth industries could contribute most to the increase of the multipliers in some or all sectors ('gap' analysis).[66]
4 Prepare on the basis of 1, 2 and 3 a provisional list of desirable activities.
5 Carry out a diversification analysis in order to determine which of the industries mentioned in that first list contribute most to the stability of the economy in the region. Correct, with the help of this information, the priority list.
6 Analyse the social and environmental effects of a potential

introduction of each of these activities.

7 Draw up a final priority list of desirable activities.

8 Define, on the basis of the analyses carried out, the requirements that have to be met in order to attract these activities (sectoral profile).

9 Design a policy to meet these requirements if the existing regional profile is inadequate.

10 Contact the relevant entrepreneurs and discuss the proposals.

It should be remarked here that the proposed procedure is similar to the one suggested by Jean H.P. Paelinck [67] when he introduced the notions of sectoral and regional profiles and derived from the confrontation of the two profiles the growth potentials of regions.

Final observations

The observations presented in the foregoing are considerably more general than those usually made in industrial location analysis. It should be realised, however, that the real world is still much more complex than any location model could suggest. After all, an industrial location model is only one part of the general model in which several submodels are contained. Industrial developments influence developments in transportation and on the labour market. Transportation again influences locational decisions of both firms and individuals, who in turn exert their influence on the labour market and thus on the location of industries. Environmental factors also play a significant role in location while — as indicated earlier — being themselves determined by distribution of industries, and so on, and so forth.

It was, however, not the object of this chapter to go into all that; the object was to show how different sorts of analyses can be used within a limited framework for designing a proper industrialisation policy.

It is, no doubt, possible to refine the models presented. A promising approach might be found in using comparative statics, and possibly also in dynamisation of the model. A dynamic model could enable us to determine optimum development paths for regions.

APPENDIX 4.1

Mathematical appendix on the interregional attraction model

1 Write $\underline{g}$ for the vector of production levels in a given region;

$\hat{\Lambda}_D$ for the diagonal matrix of λ_D-coefficients;

$B\underline{g}_p^D$ for the vector of intermediary demand potentials. The element β_{lk} in the B-matrix represents the fraction of gross production of sector l demanded by sector k;

$\underline{f}_p$ for the vector of final demand potentials;

Λ_{SA} for the matrix of coefficients of the supply potentials. A typical element of this matrix is $\lambda_S^{lk} \times a_{lk}/\beta_{kl}$ in which λ_S^{lk} is the attraction on industry k exerted by the supply of industry l and a_{lk} the fraction of gross production of industry k sold to industry l.

2 The attraction equation can now be written as

$$\hat{\underline{g}} = \Lambda_D \, B\underline{g}_p^D + \Lambda_{SA}\, \underline{g}_p^S + \hat{\Lambda}_D \underline{f}_p \tag{1}$$

3 Now write

$$\underline{g}_r = \begin{bmatrix} \underline{g}^1 \\ \underline{g}^2 \\ \vdots \\ \underline{g}^r \end{bmatrix}$$

in which $\underline{g}^i$ is the vector of gross productions in region i

$$\underline{f}_r = \begin{bmatrix} \underline{f}^1 \\ \underline{f}^2 \\ \vdots \\ \underline{f}^r \end{bmatrix}$$

in which $\underline{f}^i$ is the vector of final demand in region i

$$\hat{\Lambda}_D = \begin{bmatrix} \hat{\Lambda}_D & & 0 \\ & & \\ 0 & & \hat{\Lambda}_D \end{bmatrix}$$

$$\hat{\Lambda}_{SA} = \begin{bmatrix} \Lambda_{SA} & & 0 \\ & & \\ 0 & & \Lambda_{SA} \end{bmatrix}$$

$$\hat{B} = \begin{bmatrix} B & & 0 \\ & & \\ 0 & & B \end{bmatrix}$$

The distance factors are introduced for demand as a Δ-matrix and for supply as a Γ-matrix. The structure is basically the same and is for the Δ-matrix (3 sectors and 2 regions):

$$\Delta = \begin{bmatrix}
\delta_{11} & 0 & 0 & \delta_{12} & 0 & 0 \\
0 & \delta_{11} & 0 & 0 & \delta_{12} & 0 \\
0 & 0 & \delta_{11} & 0 & 0 & \delta_{12} \\
\delta_{21} & 0 & 0 & \delta_{22} & 0 & 0 \\
0 & \delta_{21} & 0 & 0 & \delta_{22} & 0 \\
0 & 0 & \delta_{21} & 0 & 0 & \delta_{22}
\end{bmatrix}$$

4   The final equation can now be written as

$$\underline{g}_r = \hat{\hat{\Lambda}}_D B \Delta \underline{g}_r + \hat{\Lambda}_{SA} \Gamma \underline{g}_r + \hat{\hat{\Lambda}} \Delta \underline{f}_r \tag{2}$$

for which the solution reads

$$\underline{g}_r = \left[I - \hat{\hat{\Lambda}}_D \, B\Delta - \hat{\Lambda}_{SA} \, \Gamma \right]^{-1} \hat{\hat{\Lambda}}_D \, \Delta \underline{f}_r \qquad (3)$$

The model thus simultaneously determines the influence of a final demand increase in a given region in a given sector on all levels of production in all regions.

If for each activity a region called relevant region is determined within which communication costs are negligible and outside which they are infinitely large, the model can be adjusted by assuming $\Delta = \Gamma = I$. In that case (3) reads

$$\underline{g}_r = \left[I - \hat{\hat{\Lambda}}_D B - \hat{\Lambda}_{SA} \right]^{-1} \hat{\hat{\Lambda}}_D \, \underline{f}_r \qquad (4)$$

which is formally identical to

$$\underline{g} = \left[I - \hat{\Lambda}_D B - \Lambda_{SA} \right]^{-1} \hat{\Lambda}_D \underline{f} \qquad (5)$$

representing the final equation of the conventional attraction model.

In case $\hat{\Lambda}_D = I$ the model reduces to

$$\underline{g} = \left[I - B \right]^{-1} \underline{f}$$

which is the ordinary input-output approach.

Notes

[1]   Weber, A., *Über den Standort der Industrien*, Tübingen, 1909 (translated: *Theory of the Location of Industries*, Chicago, 1929). See also Christaller, W., *Die zentralen Orte in Süddeutschland*, Jena, 1933 (translated: *Central Places in Southern Germany*, Prentice Hall, 1966); Lösch, A., *Die raumliche Ordnung der Wirtschaft*, Jena, 1940 (translated: *Economics of Location*, Yale University Press, 1954); Hoover, E.M., *The Location of Economic Activity*, New York, 1948. See also Von Thünen, J.H., *Der isolierte Staat in Beziehung auf Landwirtschaft und National-ökonomie*, Hamburg, 1926 (translated: *Von Thünen's Isolated State*, Pergamon Press, 1966).

[2]   For a more selected bibliography see Townroe, P.M., *Industrial Location and Regional Economic Policy*, Birmingham, 1968.

[3]   Proper account being taken of the differences between the short and the long run.

[4]   See Zipf, G.K., 'The P_1P_2/D hypothesis on the intercity movement of persons', *American Sociological Review*, vol.11, 1946.

[5]   See also Clark, C., 'Industrial location and economic potential', *Lloyds Bank Review*, October 1966.

[6]   Klaassen, L.H., Paelinck, J.H.P., Wagenaar, Sj., *Spatial Systems,* op. cit., pp.55—6.

[7]   Lutrell, W.F., *Factory, Location and Industrial Movement*, NIESR, 2 vols., 1962. Toothill Report, 'Report of the Committee Inquiry into the Scottish Economy', Scottish Council of Development of Industry, 1969. See also Hoover, E.M., op.cit.

[8]   Klaassen, L.H., *Méthodes de sélection d'industries pour les régions en stagnation*, OECD, p.51. See also Cameron, G.C., and Clark, B.D., 'Industrial movement and the regional problem', *University of Glasgow, Social and Economic Studies,* 1966; and Cameron, G.C. and Reid, G.L., 'Scottish economic planning and the attraction of industry', *University of Glasgow, Social and Economic Studies,* 1966.

[9]   Mulder, E.H. and Klaassen, L.H., *De gevolgen van de realisatie van de Euromarkt voor de intra-Europese handel*, Rotterdam, NEI, 1960.

[10] Clark, C., Wilson, F. and Bradley, J., 'Industrial location and economic potential in Western Europe', *Regional Studies*, vol.2, 1969.

[11] Within Western Europe, the tariff was arbitrary estimated as $ 210 per 10 ton load and represented not only the tariff levied, but also imputed costs of uncertainty arising out of trade with a foreign country.

[12] Falise, M. and Lepas, A., 'Les motivations de localisation des investissements internationaux dans l'Europe du Nord-Ouest', *Revue Economique*, no.1, 1970.

[13] Vanhove, N., *De ontwikkeling van de Vlaamse economie in internationaal perspectief — Synthese en beleidsopties*, Brussels, 1973

(translated into the languages of the Community).

[14] Burchard, H.J., 'The principles determining the localisation of refineries and petro-chemical industry', in Regul, R. (ed.), *The Future of European Ports*, Bruges, 1971. Capanna, A. 'Aspects et problèmes de la sidérurgie côtière dans le monde et dans la CEE', Regul, R. (ed.), *The Future of European Ports*, op.cit.

[15] Hermansen, T., 'Development poles and development centres in national and regional development.— elements of a theoretical framework', Kuklinski, A. (ed.), *Growth Poles and Growth Centres in Regional Planning*, Paris, 1972.

[16] Christaller, W., *Die zentralen Orte in Süddeutschland,* op.cit., see also Bos, H.C., *Spatial Dispersion of Economic Activity,* Rotterdam, 1964.

[17] Lösch, A., *Raumliche Ordnung der Wirtschaft,* op.cit.

[18] Tinbergen, J., 'The spatial dispersion of production: a hypothesis', *Schweizerische Zeitschrift für Volkswirtschaft und Statistik,* vol.97, no. 4, 1961. Tinbergen, J., 'Sur un modèle de la dispersion géographique de l'activité économique', *Revue d'économie politique,* numéro spécial, Janvier-Février, 1964, pp.30—44.

[19] Bos, H.C., op.cit.

[20] Aydalot, Ph., 'Note sur les économies externes et quelques notions connexes', *Revue économique,* no.6, 1965.

[21] Perroux, F., 'Note sur la notion de pôle de croissance', *Economie Appliquée,* no.1—2, 1955, p.309.

[22] Perroux, F., 'Economic space: theory and applications', *The Quarterly Journal of Economics,* no.1, 1950, p.105.

[23] Perroux, F., 'La méthode de l'économie généralisée et l'économie de l'homme', *Science Economique et Développement,* Paris, 1958, p. 115.

[24] Perroux, F., 'La firme motrice dans la région et la région motrice', *Théorie et Politique de l'Expansion Régionale,* Brussels, 1961, p.302.

[25] Davin, L.E., Degeer, L., and Paelinck, J.H.P., *Dynamique économique de la région Liégeoise,* Liège, 1959, p.96.

[26] Vanneste, O., *The Growth Pole Concept and the Regional Economic Policy,* Bruges, 1971, p.21.

[27] Vanhove, N., *De doelmatigheid van het regionaal economisch beleid in Nederland,* Gent, 1962, p.118.

[28] Klaassen, L.H., *Regionale welvaartsverschillen en regionale politiek,* Haarlem, 1959, p.6.

[29] Hirschman, A.O., *The Strategy of Economic Development,* New Haven, 1958, p.183.

[30] Albertini, J., 'Options pour une méthode d'aménagement. Les pôles de développement', *Economie et Humanisme,* no.127, 1960, p.41.

[31] Boudeville, J., 'Les notions d'espace et d'intégration', Boudeville, J.

(ed.), *Les pôles de croissance,* Paris, 1968, pp.23—41. Boudeville, J., 'Polarisation and urbanisation — the Canadian and French Examples', *Economie Appliquée,* no.1, 1975.

[32] Hermansen, T., op.cit., p.29.

[33] Vanneste, O., op.cit., p.25.

[34] Hansen, N., 'Criteria for a growth centre policy', Kuklinski, A. (ed.), *Growth Poles and Growth Centres in Regional Planning,* op.cit., p.105.

[35] Vanneste, O., 'Het groeipoolconcept als strategisch element in het regionaal beleid', Liber Amicorum Prof. Dr. G. Eyskens, Leuven, 1975.

[36] Hermansen, T., op.cit., p.3.

[37] Ibid, p.21.

[38] Penouil, M., 'Politique régionale et pôles de croissance', Petrella, R., (ed.), *Le développement régional en Europe,* Paris, 1971, p.105. 'On the other hand, even if the settled industrial activity has a stimulating characteristic, it does not automatically constitute a pole. A pole implies another feature: it must exercise a dominant effect on all of the activities within the zone in which it is located'.

[39] Ibid, pp.108—9.

[40] Ibid, p.107. 'Those different criteria lead us to distinguish three types of centres or attraction zones. First the *growth points* character-ised by the presence of propulsory industries that ensure the regular, sometimes rapid, growth of a micro-region, but without causing impor-tant effects outside the zone, and more in particular in the macro-region. Thus complementarities are established within the centre, but without external effects. By contrast, with *growth poles* the repercuss-ions are felt outside the direct location of the pole. The many activities present in the propulsory micro-zone, which are sometimes totally independent of one another, contribute to that extension of the comm-ercial and industrial attraction effects. Finally, one might encounter *growth axes;* these are constituted by a series of growth points (or, more rarely, poles), between which fairly close relations are established mostly thanks to the presence of well developed means of transporta-tion: rivers, canals, railroads, roads. The effects on the overall set of industries and businesses can then be considerable'. (translation). See also Kuklinski, A., *Growth Poles and Growth Centres in Regional Policies and Planning: an institutional perspective; remarks for discuss-ion,* Geneva, 1969. See also Gohman, V.M. and Karpov, L.N., *Growth Poles and Growth Centres,* Kuklinski, A. (ed.), op.cit., p.126.

[41] Allen, K. and Hermansen, T., 'Economic growth — regional prob-lems and growth centres', *Regional Policy in EFTA — an examination of the growth centre idea,* Edinburgh, 1968, chapter 2, pp.64—5.

[42] Ibid, p.65.

[43] Baillargeon, J., 'Le rôle des pôles dans le développement', *Développement et Civilizations,* no.5, 1961, p.31.

[44] Milhau, J., 'Problèmes de l'élaboration et de l'exécution des plans régionaux', *Conseil Economique et Social*, 26.4.1960, p.355

[45] CEE, 'Etude pour la création d'un pôle industriel de développement en Italie Méridionale', *Série Economie et Finances,* no5, Brussels, 1966 (Study directed by A. Tosco .)

[46] Hansen, N., 'Development pole theory in a regional context', *Kyklos,* no.3, 1967, p.717. See also Klemmer, P., 'Die Theorie der Entwicklungspole — strategische Konzept für die regionale Wirtschaftspolitik?', *Raumforschung und Raumordnung,* June, 1972. See also Aydalot, Ph., op.cit., p.963.

[47] Aydalot, Ph., op.cit., p.967.

[48] Hansen, N., op.cit., p.722.

[49] Aydalot, Ph., op.cit., p.965. 'The propulsory industry clearly does not represent the origin of polarisation, it is only its effect. The real hierarchy as it can be derived from the previously made observations, would be the following:

> The major, first fact is the occurrence in a certain place of agglomeration effects. These agglomeration effects are 'produced' by the existence of various activities at the present moment mainly by 'services rendered to industries' and 'services rendered to private persons', that is, by tertiary activities.
> Then follows the appearance of industries: among them there are propulsory industries producing effects of real dependence.
> These propulsory, but not autonomous, industries induce in turn new activities, called induced activities'. (Translation)

[50] Penouil, M., op.cit., p.906.

[51] Dahmen, E., 'Technology, innovation and international industrial transformation', *Le Progrès Economique,* Leuven, 1955, p.297.

[52] Isard, W. and Schooler, E.W., 'Industrial complex analysis, agglomeration economies, and regional development', *Journal of Regional Science,* 1959, p.21.

[53] Davin, L.E., Degeer, L., and Paelinck, J., op.cit., p.83.

[54] Sombart, W., 'Der moderne Kapitalismus', München, 1928, pp.131 —2.

[55] Commissie Van Lohuizen, 'Stuwende en verzorgende bedrijven', *Rijksdienst van het Nationale Plan,* no.51, 1952.

[56] Vining, R., 'Location of industry and regional patterns of business cycle behaviour', *Econometrica,* no.1, 1946, p.42.

[57] See Klaassen, L.H. and Paelinck, J.H.P., op.cit.

[58] Vanneste, O., op.cit.. See also Vanhove, N., 'The development of the Flemish economy in an international perspective', Synthesis and policy options, *EEC Regional Policy Series,* no.1, 1973. See also Klemmer, P.., op.cit.

[59] CEE, *Etude pour la création d'un pôle industriel de développement en Italie Méridionale,* op.cit., pp.40—1.

[60] Vanneste, O., op.cit., chapter IV.

[61] Davin, L.E., *Conditions de croissance des économies régionales en état de suremploi,* op.cit., p.6.

[62] See also West Central Scotland Plan, op.cit., pp.365—6.

[63] Klaassen, L.H. and Van Wickeren, A.C., 'Interindustry relations; an attraction model', Bos, H.C., (ed.), *Towards Balanced International Growth,* Amsterdam, 1969. Klaassen, L.H., 'Location of industries in depressed areas', OECD, Paris, 1968. For a full mathematical treatment see, Klaassen, L.H., Paelinck, J.H.P., and Wagenaar, Sj., *Spatial Systems,* op.cit.

[64] Compare page 122.

[65] R. Petrella is the director of this study.

[66] Klaassen, L.H. and Paelinck, J.H.P., *Uncovering Regional Growth Potentials from an input-output Table,* FEER, NEI, 1975/4.

[67] Paelinck, J.H.P. (with collaboration of Jaumotte, C.), 'Avantages et inconvénients des régions industrielles en stagnation et des zones rurales pour l'implantation d'industries automatisées. In *Automation, Progrès Technique et Main-d'Oeuvre,* OECD, Paris, 1966, pp.331—6.

5 Urban developments and costs related to urban growth

Introduction

The gradually increasing importance of the secondary and tertiary sectors in Western Europe was one of the most important factors behind urban development. Growing interdependence of different sectors in the economy required concentration of production in larger economic units as well as spatial clustering of interdependent units in the same place or at least the same region. At a time when transportation possibilities were limited, such concentration of employment compelled workers to choose as their residence a place close to their working place.

It seems worthwhile to consider in this context the different stages by which the process of urban development has been characterised, the stages of urbanisation, suburbanisation, and desurbanisation.[1]

A general presentation of the stages of urban development

The first stage

During the first of the three stages distinguished, when a country or region can grow no further as an agricultural economy and gradually changes to an industrial country, the chain of events is fairly obvious. Owing to population growth and limited possibilities of extending the available agricultural land, rural districts will have increasing redundant labour, entailing a corresponding decrease in income level. When new industrial employment is created, a migration flow will be initiated from the country to the towns where it is concentrated. Because in the early days of the process the level of income and the number of hours to be worked daily do not permit living too far from one's work, that flow will lead to strong urban concentrations and to relative decrease of the rural population. The newcomers are obliged to live in the town itself, in new residential quarters built around the existing centre and near the factories. This first phase is characterised, therefore, by fast expansion of towns with massive, concentrated town quarters. Similarly, new towns can spring up at places that appear favourable to industrialisation.

180

Such a process or urbanisation has developed in all the countries in Europe since the beginning of the Industrial Revolution in England, for most of them already in the nineteenth century, but for some only since the Second World War.

The phenomenon of accelerating urbanisation can manifest itself in different ways. If the country to town movement in a country is oriented largely towards one particular town which embodies all modern development, that town has a chance of growing into the national metropolis. However, the movement may just as well orient itself to a number of smaller towns scattered across the country. Whether one or the other development occurs depends not so much on the urbanisation process itself as on the historical situation in the country involved, the degree of political centralisation or decentralisation, and the propensities of a region, or town within a region, for industrialisation. Those propensities in turn depend on the town's location in the national and international contexts, the physical circumstances, the facilities for the supply of raw materials and the dispatch of final products, and on more political factors such as the policy pursued by the government in point of industrialisation and facilities for the establishing of industries and the expansion of the town. Together such factors constitute the conditions and limitations for the locational behaviour of industries as described earlier. Most of the urban development of this stage is linked up with existing urban centres, which up till then have functioned as an administrative, cultural, religious, commercial, or military centre.

That supports the hypothesis that an existing urban nucleus, with its attendant agglomeration advantages, is highly conducive to successful industrialisation, and that its diversification is important for further growth prospects (see chapters 4 and 7). Yet, at places where the presence of raw materials, a favourable labour market, or good transportation prospects compensate for the lack of an existing urban milieu, entirely new industrial towns may come into being.

As far as the spatial structure of a town is concerned, the most important feature at this stage of the urban process is the concentration of the development. Towns go through a phase of concentrated growth amid a stagnant surrounding territory. If there are several urban centres near enough to one another, there is a chance of their growing together to form one agglomeration.

The spatial form of a town is determined to a great extent by the transportation facilities and traffic provisions available. The stage of economic development and the level of income force the townsman who works in the town to go on living in that town; his choice of residence is limited by the available traffic provisions. As traffic technologies develop, the spatial shape of the town also evolves. In the early days of the Industrial Revolution labourers had to walk to their work, so that houses must necessarily be built near to the factories. With the advent of railways and tramways larger distances could be bridged, and towns are observed to expand along the tracks and around the stations. Public transport in town being the main mode of conveyance, the townsman's mobility is restricted to the town where he lives, which consequently is characterised by a dense population. Within the town all sorts of public amenities have to be provided for the fast growing population, in the fields of medical care, hygiene, education, and recreation. As a rule, the creation of amenities follows the growth of employment and of the attracted population with a considerable lag. Without denying the resulting social abuses we conclude on the ground of our assumptions and with the help of the set of concepts used that many people increased their well being in this period by moving from country to town. It is not difficult to imagine that having a job and hence being sure of one's livelihood, however poor, has the highest priority, and that the house and its surroundings do not count so heavily, no more than the availability of public amenities. It is in the next stage that increase of welfare will be looked for exactly in the elements that are still lacking.

The second stage

The second stage is referred to as one of further development of the industrial era. Speaking in broad, schematic terms one might say that urban development, after a period of factories springing up everywhere and of a fast and accelerating evolution of the economic structure in which towns grow at the cost of rural areas, has now entered a stage of consolidation, with its own characteristic changes in urban structure. Although the towns continue to grow and to attract people from outside, the accent in this stage is on qualitative improvement. In terms of the objective functions of the actors postulated in previous sections, it could be stated that – with the work available and increasing – priority shifts to better houses and public amenities, come within reach thanks to the increased income, which individually and collectively is being spent according to the new preferences.

The traffic evolution is decisive for the spatial changes of the town. Extended public transport facilities, and the introduction of buses and private cars which open up areas not connected with the network of trains and tramways, widen the scope of residential location. New spacious residential quarters in more pleasant surroundings, 'garden towns' sometimes, can now be added to the city. Town parks and green belts are designed; museums, theatres, schools, and hospitals are built in other empty places. In the very city centre space is reserved for new employment in the tertiary sector, or existing monumental buildings are given a new function as office buildings.

Factories are moved as much as possible to the town's periphery where they are less of a nuisance and yet, thanks to the new modes of transport, accessible. In the town banks, offices, and the whole complex of administrative and personal services inherent to the complicated, industrial society, are accommodated. It is in this period, too, that people begin to live out of town while working in the city. The movement is started by small well to do groups who in point of leisure, income, and transport facilities can afford to move out, and it develops into an inverse migration flow fast growing in volume. To the people involved, living in a quiet rural environment is important enough to outbalance the sacrifices in money and time required for bridging the distance to their work and the provisions of the town. Given their objective function, they have again increased their welfare, provided that the infrastructure between their new residence and the town is adequate. In very nearly all cases it is the government that is responsible for that infrastructure, and that gives the government a powerful instrument to influence the spatial pattern or urbanisation. Through the construction of infrastructure and the provision of certain forms of transport the government can reinforce or check certain spatial tendencies. The better the transport system, the more a town can expand. In the next stage that will become increasingly evident.

The third stage

We shall not try to define the exact point in economic development where the second stage can be considered finished and the third begun. We have defined that third stage as the transition to a post-industrial era, typified by a high proportion of workers in the tertiary sector and a relatively high income for large groups of population. A feature to be underlined in particular is the tremendous expansion of the private car, which in the course of the process is coming within almost everybody's reach. The consequences, both positive and negative, for urban spatial structure can hardly be overestimated. The possession of a private car makes it easier to bridge distances independently from the location of the public transport network. Home to work travel is affected in particular: it becomes less necessary to choose a place to live near one's work or near public transport facilities. For large categories of society an entirely new situation is created: they now have a much wider area in which to find a location from which, given their preferences, they still have adequate access to all elements that contribute to their welfare. Working in town can easily be combined with living at considerable distance from one's job, and a number of central provisions in the city still remain within reach. The tendency that first manifested itself in the building of garden towns, is now continued on a vast scale.

Typically, in all European countries where cars are common, many people aspire to a house of their own in green surroundings outside the town. Governments and house building corporations rarely resist that tendency by their policy; on the contrary, they stimulate the outward movement by large scale building outside the towns. Thus is initiated the massive suburbanisation that marks the present spatial changes in many European towns. It is now in the suburbs of central towns that the population grows, while in the cities themselves the number of inhabitants is decreasing.

Now that the towns are spreading over an ever-increasing territory, 'urban area' or 'urban district' has become a more accurate term than 'town'. Central city and suburban surroundings are functionally united, and within the larger area living and working are being spatially distributed, as are other activities such as recreation, which also puts in a claim for the empty places of that area.

Towards an optimum?

The development may be called positive in that it meets prevailing wants as regards housing, that it makes for more living comfort and has done away with overcrowded town quarters. But there are also obvious negative consequences, and they are getting worse as the scale of suburbanisation becomes larger, the worst problems being those relating to traffic.

Quite soon the day will come when existing road infrastructure can no longer cope with the thousands of commuters who on weekdays try to get into the town and find a parking space. The resulting congestion makes all kinds of work places and central provisions in the city centre less and less attainable. Attempts are being made to better the centre's accessibility by improving the infrastructure and stimulating the use of public transport.

To improve infrastructure, it will be necessary to clear areas for new access roads, modify the lay out of streets, and provide extensive parking facilities. The space needed is found mostly where the old residential quarters are, dating from the time when urbanisation first started; they are sacrificed to the modernisation and reconstruction of the centre. People living there find themselves compelled to seek refuge in the outskirts or join those who have moved to suburban municipalities.

When the traffic measures taken prove indeed effective, increasing the centre's accessibility for cars, there is a good chance of new service activities deciding to settle in the city centre. Of course, increased traffic intensity will once more lead to congestion, and to additional nuisance to townspeople, giving them an additional stimulus to suburbanise. Indeed, improvement of the situation will grow more and more difficult and require even higher investments.

Measures that aim at transferring an increasing proportion of traffic in the city centre from private cars to public transport, have the same indirect result. Improvement of the public transport facilities and their extension to the suburban municipalities around the town does indeed make for easier access to the town by the suburbanites, but at the same time makes it even more attractive for people to leave the town for the suburbs. The tendency of progressive suburbanisation and the attending continuous need for adapting and extending infrastructure and public transport at even higher cost, will be maintained for as long as tertiary industries are preferably located in the town centre. Owing to enlarging scales and expansion, the tertiary sector needs more and more space, to be claimed from the older living quarters in the town. Wherever the process described here occurs, the number of inhabitants of the central town is observed to decrease continually.

Ultimately, this development may to a growing extent threaten the prosperous existence of a town as such. When the inhabitants leave town, provisions such as shops, schools and medical care will follow presently. If the city centre remains congested, there comes a point where for offices, too, it becomes more attractive to choose a location in the suburbs, or even outside the urban district in other parts of the country, which so far have escaped full urbanisation and remained more accessible because there is no congestion. If that happens, not only towns but whole urban districts will decline in population, while elsewhere areas now still rural will be transformed into urban areas, often at the cost of the natural environment and valuable scenery.

It seems that towns are facing either the sad prospect of a centre being progressively reconstructed and 'enriched' with traffic provisions, road crossings, and a surfeit of shopping centres and office buildings, realised at the cost of the residential function, or the even more disheartening threat of total decline, with all activities that so far have determined the central function moving away, leaving in their wake an eroded area without any hope of ever being once more the living heart of an urban district.

Against both alternatives the government as well as the population are beginning to demur. Awareness of the processes going on has opened the eyes to the many negative external effects that attend the spatial changes described above. In terms of the concepts developed earlier it can be said that government and industries as well as individuals have sought to attain their objective of increased well being without heed to the social cost involved in their individual actions. It has been explained above how governmental policy, which ought to be corrective, in reality tends to reinforce the tendencies leading to, e.g., worse congestion.

Traffic problems dominate the present urban problems, and to resist urban decline it will be necessary first of all to solve these problems. Experience has taught that the desired effect can be expected only from measures that manage to reduce traffic demand. Such measures must bridle suburbanisation, and accomplish the reurbanisation of central towns by giving new support to their residential function. To that end, industries will have to be redistributed across the whole urban district in such a way that home to work distances are reduced and the use of the existing infrastructure is less one way than it is now. Concrete measures to reach these goals have already been introduced in several European countries; they will be discussed further on.

It is not very likely that these measures will meet with considerable success at short notice. Particularly in the countries in Western Europe the larger cities are showing signs of decline, not just in the central cities of the agglomerations but actually for the agglomeration as a whole. The increase in the population in suburban regions around the central city is no longer able to compensate the decrease in the population of the central city and the result is an absolute decline both in population and employment of the agglomeration as a whole. This is the stage of desurbanisation, becoming evident now in many large urban areas in Western Europe.

In Graph 5.1, the different stages of urban development are presented. [2] During the first stage the central city is growing fast, and the suburban (in this case rather: rural) ring around the central city remains constant in population. This is the stage of urbanisation. In the second stage the growth of the central city starts to slacken while gradually the suburban ring increases in population. The proportion of the population living in the ring increases considerably, particularly after the point has been reached where the population of the central city starts declining. In the third stage, that of suburbanisation/desurbanisation, this decline accelerates, finally resulting in an absolute decline of the population of the whole urban agglomeration.

In the graph an alternative possibility is indicated, viz. that of reurbanisation. In many large cities in Western Europe both local and central governments have become active in a policy aimed at turning the tide for these cities, and through measures of rehabilitation of the existing housing stock, urban renewal programmes, measures for improvement of the traffic situation, pedestrian zones, creation of a more adequate social infrastructure etc. try to improve the image of large cities. It is hoped that these measures will make more people decide to stay in the city as well as influence favourably the decision of people from outside the city to locate there. It is questionable whether these measures will be successful. The trend towards desurbanisation for the largest cities seems so general and so strong that only a very rigorous

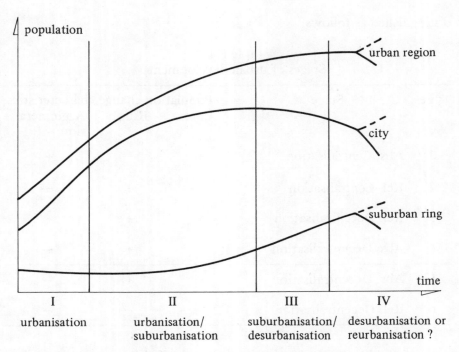

Graph 5.1: Size of population and stages of urban development

---

policy could be expected to show significant results. That kind of policy, however, has not been invented yet.

Simultaneous development

The foregoing might have given the impression that economic progress in a country will lead more or less automatically to desurbanisation for all cities in a country. In fact, the situation is much more complicated than that. The study of urban developments in a country leads to the conclusion that each of the cities of that country follows a certain pattern. The largest cities find themselves in the most 'advanced' stages of development, the smaller cities in one of the earlier stages. For both groups of cities holds that in the countries with the highest level of industrial development they find themselves in a later stage than in the less developed, less industrialised countries.

That phenomenon can be observed clearly in a table produced by the 'CURB project' directed by Roy Drewett of the London School of Economics.[3] In this table six stages of urban development are distinguished as follows:

Table 5.1
Stages of urban development

| Type | Stage | Population change characteristics | | |
		Core	Ring	Agglomeration
1	Abs. Centralisation	+	−	+
2	Rel. Centralisation	++	+	++
3	Rel. Decentralisation	+	++	+
4	Abs. Decentralisation	−	+	+
5	Abs. Decentralisation	−	+	−
6	Rel. Decentralisation	− −	−	−

In this table the first four stages are stages of cities growing in population. The last two stages are the stages of absolute decline (agglomeration −).

In Table 5.2 the 115 agglomerations with a population of over 200,000 in 1970 are classified according to their stage of development. The countries are ranked according to the distribution of the agglomerations in each country.

It appears that four groups of countries may be distinguished. The first group is formed by the Eastern European countries Hungary, Bulgaria and Yugoslavia. Their cities are all in the first two stages of urban development. The next group − Italy, Denmark, Austria and France − concentrate in the stages 2, 3, and 4. The third group is formed by the Netherlands, F.R. of Germany and Switzerland. In this group the first cities appear in the first absolute decline stage.[5] In the last group (UK and Belgium) 9 cities out of the 27, that is one third of the largest cities, are declining (stages 5 and 6).

The phenomenon of declining population in large agglomerations is in fact a recent phenomenon and the consequences have not yet been studied thoroughly. Neither can it be said that urban policy, either carried out by the local city councils or by regional and national authorities, explicitly focuses on this development other than by making financial means available for improvement of the housing stock or urban

Table 5.2
Stages of urban development in 12 European countries*

Country	Classification groups 1 – 6						
	1	2	3	4	5	6	Total
Hungary	4	2	–	–	–	–	6
Bulgaria	2	3	–	–	–	–	5
Yugoslavia	2	3	–	–	–	–	5
Italy	–	6	4	–	–	–	10
Denmark	–	2	1	1	–	–	4
Austria	–	2	2	1	–	–	5
France	–	7	1	6	–	–	14
Netherlands	–	1	3	2	1	–	7
FR of Germany	–	3	14	9	1	–	27
Switzerland	–	–	2	3	–	–	5
United Kingdom	–	–	4	12	5	1	22
Belgium	–	–	–	2	2	1	5
Total	8	29	31	36	9	2	115
		Growth			Decline		

*Figures relate to urban agglomeration with a population of over 200,000 in 1970.

renewal in large cities. The problem is very seldom seen as a structural phenomenon regarding the whole hierarchical system of cities in each country.

The rationale of the decreasing immigration towards and the increased emigration from large cities is all too often sought in the living conditions prevailing in large cities; very likely, however, the more favourable conditions elsewhere combined with an increased appreciation for good environmental and traffic conditions as well as decreasing quality of life in spite of measures locally taken form the basic reasons for the developments.

Whether such developments could be corrected by urban policy at all, is an extremely important question, closely related to another, namely whether or not there is an optimum size of cities. If people's behaviour is not related in any way to the actual size of a city, the concept of optimum city size remains an empty box, interesting perhaps from an analytical point of view, but without any practical value. Nevertheless, in later sections we shall review efforts that have been made to determine the optimum size of a city. First, however, we will concentrate somewhat more on actual urban development in the EEC countries.

Urban development in the EEC

Urban concentration in the European Community manifested itself very strongly since the First World War; particularly the number of agglomerations of 1 million inhabitants and over have increased considerably. In the countries that now make up the EEC there were in 1920 10 agglomerations in that group, and their number had increased to 23 in 1970. The total population of these two groups of cities was 28 million in 1920 and 60 million in 1970. In Table 5.3 the evolution per decade and per country is given.[4]

Very important urban concentration areas in the EEC are indicated in Table 5.4.

As indicated earlier, in recent years the larger cities have evidently entered a period of absolute decline of the population caused by a decrease in the natural growth of the population as well as by a decrease in immigration and an increase in outmigration. Particularly the emigration effects are considerable, even if the change in the socio-economic structure of the population that goes hand in hand with the changed pattern of migration is left out of account.

In Table 5.5 figures are presented for a number of declining agglomerations in the EEC.

Originally this decline of population in the large cities was caused by outmigration; this was, however, mainly directed towards the immediate neighbourhood of the agglomeration of origin. This means in practice that outmigrants only changed their residence but maintained their working place in the agglomeration. In more recent years deconcentration tendencies have no longer been limited to residence, but extended

190

Table 5.3

Population levy in the agglomerations of more than one million inhabitants
(in thousands of inhabitants)

		B	DK	D	F	IRL	I	L	NL	UK	EEC
1920	Total pop.	7,521	3,243	44,531	39,000	3,100	37,766	261	6,820	43,552	185,594
	Agglom. pop.	—	—	7,875	4,965	—	—	—	—	15,512	28,352
	%	—	—	17.8	12.7	—	—	—	—	35.6	15.3
1930	Total pop.	8,076	3,542	47,381	41,610	2,946	40,888	297	7,884	46,069	198,693
	Agglom. pop.	—	—	8,495	5,884	—	—	—	—	17,108	31,488
	%	—	—	17.9	14.1	—	—	—	—	37.1	15.8
1940	Total pop.	8,389	3,832	50,955	41,200	2,958	44,673	296	8,897	48,226	209,426
	Agglom. pop.	—	1,001	9,735	6,050	—	2,426	—	—	17,530	36,742
	%	—	26.1	19.1	14.7	—	5.4	—	—	36.3	17.5
1950	Total pop.	8,639	4,270	50,600	41,736	2,969	46,603	297	10,114	50,325	215,553
	Agglom. pop.	—	1,163	7,999	6,300	—	2,856	—	—	17,864	36,182
	%	—	27.2	15.8	15.1	—	6.1	—	—	35.5	16.8
1960	Total pop.	9,153	4,581	55,423	45,684	2,834	49,642	314	11,480	52,352	231,463
	Agglom. pop.	1,014	1,260	14,229	7,140	—	4,671	—	—	17,820	46,134
	%	11.1	27.5	25.7	15.6	—	9.4	—	—	34.0	19.9
1970	Total pop.	9,676	4,921	61,688	50,775	2,944	53,670	339	13,019	55,711	252,743
1968–1970	Agglom. pop.	1,730	1,381	22,046	9,272	—	6,842	—	2,103	17,500	60,217
	%	11.1	28.1	35.7	18.3	—	12.7	—	16.2	31.4	23.8

191

Table 5.4
Important urban concentrations in EEC

	% Surface (a)	% Popula- tion(a)	% Income (a)	% Index of income *per capita*(a)
Paris region (1968)	2.2	19.0	26.2	137.9
Greater London (1971)	0.65	13.3	17.4	130.8
Rimcity (Neth.) (1970)	20.7	46.3	51.4	110.0
Rhein-Ruhr (1970)	2.6	18.0	21.0	116.7
Milano-Torino-Genova (1971)	3.8	13.5	19.7	145.9

(a) relative to the national figures

Table 5.5
Recent evolution of the population of a few big agglomerations

Country	Agglomerations	Year	No. of inhabitants	Year	No. of inhabitants
Belgium	Brussels (19 c.)	1965	1,079,181	1972	1,069,005
	Antwerp (14 c.)	1965	675,268	1972	671,872
	Liege (27 c.)	1965	452,713	1972	438,825
	Ghent (6 c.)	1965	232,915	1972	223,145
	Charleroi (13 c.)	1965	220,032	1972	212,559
	TOTAL		2,660,109		2,615,406
Denmark	Copenhagen	1970	1,380,204	1974	1,335,069
Germany	Ruhrkohlenbez*	1961	5,619,300	1973	5,546,500
Netherlands	Amsterdam	1967	1,049,113	1972	1,018,641
	Rotterdam	1971	1,064,095	1972	1,055,157
	The Hague	1963	746,556	1972	693,890
United Kingdom	Greater London	1951	8,197,000	1971	7,452,000
	Merseyside	1951	1,386,000	1971	1,267,000
	West Midlands	1961	2,378,000	1971	2,372,000
	S.E. Lancashire	1961	2,428,000	1971	2,393,000
	Tyneside	1961	856,000	1971	805,000
	Central Clydeside	1961	1,802,000	1971	1,728,000

* Siedlungsverband Ruhrkohlenbezirk

Sources: Belgium: Bulletin de Statistique démographique, n.4/73, p.21.
Denmark: Københavens Statistiske Årbog, 1974.
Germany: Statistische Rundschau für das Ruhrgebiet, 1973.
Netherlands: Statistical Yearbook of the Netherlands, 1973.
United Kingdom: Central Statistical Office — Annual Abstract of Statistics, 1973, p.12.

to working places. Middle sized towns farther removed from the larger cities are growing relatively fast both in number of inhabitants and in workplaces, while both are decreasing rapidly in the larger agglomerations.

The final result of such a movement of population and its impact on the urban structure are shown for the Netherlands in Table 5.6.[5] It is very clear from the table that 'the most rapid growth occurred in places with a population of between 20 and 30 thousands at the end of the period, closely followed by those in the groups with 30 − 40 thousands (28.1 per cent) and 10 − 20 thousands (25.5 per cent). Together these places accounted for more than 73 per cent of total urban change. On a lower level, but still above the average rate of growth, scored the groups 40 − 50 thousands (15.6 per cent) and 50 − 100 thousands of inhabitants (17.3 per cent). The next groups of towns with 100−200 and 200−500 thousands of inhabitants remained below the national average growth, while the three largest towns of over 500,000 inhabitants experience a considerable decline of population (7.4 per cent).[6]

Table 5.6
Urban population change 1960−70 by size group*

Size group (x 1,000)	Number of places	Total urban population			Urban change 1960-70		
		1960 (x 1,000)	1970 (x 1,000)	Abs (x 1,000)	%	Migra-tion %	Nat. in-crease %
10 −< 20	163	1,849	2,320	472	25.5	6.1	19.4
20 −< 30	50	935	1,238	303	32.4	13.1	19.3
30 −< 40	22	593	759	166	28.1	9.3	18.8
40 −< 50	10	375	434	59	15.6	− 1.2	16.8
50 −< 100	25	1,496	1,756	259	17.3	3.0	14.3
100−< 200	12	1,508	1,673	165	10.9	− 2.5	13.4
200−< 500	1	255	278	23	9.2	− 1.8	11.0
500−<1,000	3	2,199	2,037	−162	− 7.4	−14.0	6.6
Nation total	286	9,210	10,495	1,286	14.0	− 0.2	14.2

*Figures relate to municipalities

This table adequately illustrates for the Netherlands the tendencies described earlier in this section.

It has often been stated that the distribution of growth between cities or groups of cities is important from the point of view of efficient overall growth. A suggestion to that effect is given by G.M. Neutze when he states:

> The distribution of growth between cities is one dimension of the pattern of economic development. It can make a large difference to the economic efficiency of a country.[7]

It is a very difficult task actually to prove the truth of such a statement. One would be inclined to argue that the economic performance of a country like France with heavy urban concentration is not very much different from that of a country with a much more dispersed urban pattern like the Federal Republic of Germany. On the other hand it seems plausible that social and environmental conditions, which are definitely worse in larger agglomerations than in small towns, should in the long run influence the attractiveness of these large agglomerations and thus indirectly their economic performance. In this context a number of studies could be mentioned that occupy themselves with the question how economic and other variables are related to the size of a city and if so whether there could not be something like an optimum size for cities. In the past decade this question has been raised in a number of countries (France, Great Britain, the Netherlands, Italy, etc.). The fact that it is of vital importance because of its implications in the social field in general and the regional and urban policy in particular, justifies giving it some more attention. The following sections do not pretend to answer the question clearly; they only try and give an idea of the many aspects involved.

Considerations on city size

The minimum size approach

As early as 1945, Colin Clark started to analyse, for the United States, Canada, and Queensland, the relations between economic and other variables and the size of a city's population. He formulated his approach as follows: 'Our problems remain to determine what size of city is necessary for the efficient performance of the functions that a modern community requires',[8] [9] and somewhat farther on: 'We must answer this question primarily in the light of the ability of cities of different sizes to provide services rather than their ability to manufacture'.[10]

The procedure followed by Colin Clark is the following. He started from regional employment figures for different service sectors. The next step was to divide these figures by regional income measured in millions of dollars. The result was the variable PS/Y, which was then related to the size of the population in the largest city in the region. The outcomes were ranked according to size in order to determine from which city size onwards the ratio PS/Y remained constant. In this way it could be determined what size city could provide adequate services for the population. For retailing his analysis is somewhat more sophisticated due to the introduction of national figures as normative figures.

On the basis of his statistical material Clark reached the conclusions: [11]

> 1 that the principal function of the city is now to provide service rather than manufactures, and will be so to an increasing degree;
> 2 that a region can give its inhabitants an adequate range of commercial services when the population of its principal city is somewhere between 100,000 to 200,000;
> 3 that, in the case of the other service industries, a smaller population will generally suffice;
> 4 that manufactures tend to be concentrated in the older settled communities; in the more lately settled communities, where the manufacturing population is smaller, a city somewhere between 200,000 and 500,000 is necessary for full development of manufacture.

Although much of what Clark did is quite interesting, some doubt may arise as far as his measure for the quality of services is concerned. Let us write

$$S_i = a_o Y_i \qquad (5.1)$$

a simple assumption, indicating that sales in a given service sector in region i are proportional with income in that region (which is true to a considerable extent).

Write furthermore

$$\frac{S_i}{P_{si}} = \beta_o \frac{Y_i}{P_i} \qquad (5.2)$$

stating that the sales in the service sector under consideration in region i per employee is proportional to the average income in the region (overall productivity, also quite a plausible hypothesis).

195

It follows from (5.1) and (5.2) that

$$\frac{P_{si}}{Y_i} = \frac{a_o}{\beta_o} y_i^{-1}$$

(5.3)

which means that the measure 'number of employees per million dollar regional income' is a decreasing function of average regional income itself and not of population size.

A simple regression analysis carried out on Colin Clark's statistical material indicates that there is a negative influence of income on P_{si}/Y_i and that the influence of population is very weak. The states with the lowest income per head do indeed show the highest values for P_{si}/Y_i. It must therefore be regarded as questionable that the results of Colin Clark's analyses could form the basis for any statement about minimum city sizes,[12] however plausible his results otherwise may sound. More research in the direction indicated by Colin Clark, in other words, more studies concerning different possible measures for the quality of services in a city and the relation between them and city size, seems extremely useful, not only for the problem of minimum city size itself but also in the wider context of the relation between indicators of the quality of life and city size.

The minimum cost approach

A European study
The minimum cost approach starts from the assumption that the optimum size of a city is reached when *per capita* costs of 'running' the city are at a minimum. Although the definition of costs in this context is not a simple matter, all authors finally arrive at a U-shaped cost curve as presented in Graph 5.2.

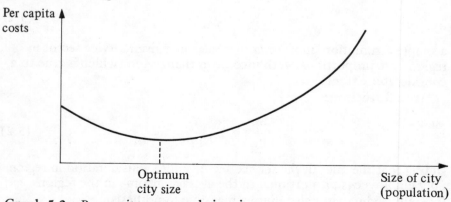

Graph 5.2: *Per capita* costs and city size

That is also the case in the EEC analysis mentioned earlier;[13] Table 5.7 is taken from it. It is based on budgetary costs of local authorities.

One of the conclusions of the EEC report is very important in this context: 'The detailed effect one observes is indeed so marked as to make it very unlikely that it can be explained exclusively from the additional services'.[14]

It appears that the increase in expenditure for the larger cities is very often due to the increase in the costs of: staff; sanitation and social affairs; cultural affairs; public security; infrastructure and transport.

The degree to which increases manifest themselves is greatly influenced by the hierarchy in the municipal structure, the specialisation and responsibility of the towns, especially in the field of education and infrastructure (what is paid for by which level of government), and the grants that local authorities receive from authorities on the provincial or national level.

Some important remarks should be made regarding the conclusion of the EEC report.

1 The higher expenditure in larger cities might be due to the higher quality of the services there. That would mean that, although the *per capita* expenditure in large cities might be higher, real costs are not necessarily so; they might even be lower.

2 Many cities provide services not only for their own population but also for the population of other municipalities in their neighbourhood.

3 Frequently certain investments (capital expenditure) are financed not by the local government but directly by the national government.

4 Expenditure in cities may be higher because salaries are higher there; that leads to higher expenditure *per capita* but also to higher income *per capita*.

5 Expenditure in the larger cities may be higher because they provide a more varied assortment of services.

6 It could be that for some services production costs decrease with the size of the population while distribution costs increase; the total sum of the two might be U-shaped.

Similar studies

Many other authors have undertaken similar studies. Practically all of them arrive at a U-shaped cost curve but the optimum size derived from their analyses is very different from author to author. Table 5.8 indicates a number of them.

It seems likely that the differences in the results of the studies are due to the following factors:

Table 5.7
Index of expenditures according to the size of the villages and towns

Country	Small villages	Index	Small towns	Index	Medium sized towns	Index	Large towns	Index
B	less than 20,000 inhab.	83 to 52	20 to 30,000 inhab.	100	30 to 100,000 inhab.	108 to 125	Brussels, Antwerp, Liège, Ghent	353
DK	less than 20,000 inhab.	96 to 99	20 to 50,000 inhab.	100	50 to 30,000 inhab.	106 to 108	Copenhagen-city	149
D	less than 20,000 inhab.		20 to 50,000 inhab.	100	50 to 200,000 inhab.	118 to 131	+ 200,000 inhab.	153
F	less than 20,000 inhab.	52 to 84	20 to 50,000 inhab.	100	50 to 500,000 inhab.	108 to 111	Paris	180
IRL	less than 14,000 inhab.	61 to 78	14 to 52,000 inhab.	100	55 to 125,000 inhab.	108 to 120	Dublin	138
I	less than 15,000 inhab.	87 to 94	15 to 30,000 inhab.	100	30 to 500,000 inhab.	128 to 213	+ 500,000 inhab.	484
NL	less than 20,000 inhab.	92	10 to 50,000 inhab.	100	50 to 500,000 inhab.	105	+ 500,000 inhab.	164
UK	Wales	116	Counties and non-metropolitan districts	100	Counties and metropolitan districts	115	Greater London	157

Source: CEE, Le coût des concentrations urbaines et de la dépopulation rurale dans la CEE, 1975, published working document, p.13.

Table 5.8
Studies on city size[15]

Authors	Year	The most efficient size (x 1,000 inhabitants)
W.Z. Hirsch	1959	50 — 100
K.S. Lomax	1943	100 — 150
O.D. Duncan	1956	500 — 1,000
C. Clark	1945	100 — 200
Svimez[16]	1967	30 — 325
Royal Commission on Local Government in Greater London	1960	100 — 250
Redcliffe-Maud Commission	1969	250 — 1,000
P. Pinchemel, A. Vakili and J. Gozzi	1959	300
Z. Driembowski	1976	100 — 200

(a) different definition of costs;
(b) different methods;
(c) different fields of application of the methods (in some countries the numbers of large towns is limited);
(d) different periods.

In this context a study made by C. van den Berg[17] in 1956 is worth mentioning. He tried to identify the variables that could explain the differences in municipal expenditures *per capita* in the Netherlands. The author did not intend to determine the optimum size of a city but was only interested in the relation between expenditure and population size. For the towns with more than 20,000 inhabitants (from which in the first part of his study Amsterdam, Rotterdam, and The Hague were excluded) he derived the following regression equation:

$$U_{54} = 0.200 \, B + 1.327 \, C + 0.534 \, I + 0.940 \, F + 62.28 \quad (R = 0.837)$$
$$\quad\;\; (0.028) \quad (0.196) \quad (0.157) \quad (0.226)$$

$$(5.4)$$

in which

U_{54} = expenditure *per capita* in guilders in 1954;

B   =   population size in thousands;

C   =   index for the degree to which the town carries out central functions for a larger region;

I   =   degree of industrialisation;

F   =   quality of the soil (building costs).

It appears that the population size has a definite positive effect on average expenditure *per capita*. By multiplying (5.4) by B and differentiating the results it can easily be shown that the marginal costs with respect to population are 0.40 *per capita* for any increase in population of 1,000 inhabitants.

General considerations on the cost approach

A study of the relations between a city's population size and its expenditure is quite useful as long as the study's outcomes are not used indiscriminately. There are, in fact, several remarks to be made.

First and foremost, studies of urban expenditure (or urban cost) consider only one side of the medal — the cost side — while completely ignoring the other side, that of the benefits. Now it is easy to see that such a one sided approach would almost certainly lead us astray if urban benefits, too, turn out to be a function of a city's population size. We shall go into that point in the next section.

Second, the optimum size of a city should refer not only to the budget of the local government, but also to the purse of the private individual living in that city. So, if only public costs are measured, a very important element, the private costs, is neglected.

The third remark refers to a point already mentioned, viz. that larger cities provide more and better services. We quote W. Alonso: 'If the demand for public goods and services is at all income elastic, cities with higher incomes would be spending more to get more, so that rising expenditures are not strong evidence of rising expensiveness'.[18]

This implies that, in order to detect the differences in 'expensiveness' between different cities, it would be absolutely necessary to compare exactly the same sort and quality of services, which in fact is never done.

A final point to be made concerns the translation of expenditure into costs. It could be, for example, that teachers in a large town receive a higher salary than their small town colleagues because in the large town the teachers are unionised. In fact, the difference in salary represents a transfer payment within the city rather than a true resource cost.

Naturally, it would not be a simple job to incorporate all these elements in a proper investigation of the differences between cost levels in different cities. To get at least a fairly standardised approach a number of standardisations would have to be carried through.

First of all it seems useful to make a distinction in the analysis between the costs of production of a good or a service and the costs of its distribution. In the case of electricity, e.g., this means that we shall do well to distinguish between the costs of production of electricity at the plant and the costs of its distribution (net work costs and running costs) across the urban area. Similar approaches seem useful for gas and water. Measuring the costs of a sewage system we can in a comparable way divide the costs into costs of collecting the 'goods' and costs of processing them at the sewage plant.

With most services the costs of distribution are borne by the consumers. They have to betake themselves to the place where the service is being produced (school, recreation area, medical centre, etc.). The distribution costs then consist in the transportation efforts to be made by the consumers.

The distinction between production costs and distribution costs seems relevant to the problem studied because it may be expected that production costs are a non-increasing function, and distribution costs a non-decreasing function of the size of the city. It can be safely assumed that production costs per unit of water, gas, and electricity are subject to considerable economies of scale and are, therefore, probably appreciably lower in large cities than in small cities, while distribution costs are more likely to increase with the size of the city.

The sort of analysis resulting from the foregoing considerations may be demonstrated by the following example relating to school of a given type.

1 Production costs

Production costs consist of three elements

(a) *capital costs* $= rK_0 + \dfrac{K_0}{\lambda}$

    in which K_0 =   value in current prices of a new school

                r =   interest rate;

                λ =   lifetime of the school.

(b) *employee* (teacher) *costs* $= \bar{s}T$

    in which $\bar{s}$ =   average salary;

               T =   number of teachers.

(c) *pupil costs* $= cP$

    in which c =   costs per pupil;

201

$$P \quad = \quad \text{number of pupils.}$$

2 *Consumption costs* equal $a\bar{t}P$

in which $\bar{t}$ = average time needed per pupil per period to visit the school regularly;

a = valuation of pupil's time (including efforts to be made for bridging the distance between school and house). Other transportation costs (such as bus-fares) could be added, but are left out for the sake of simplicity.

The total costs thus equal

$$C = (r + \frac{1}{\lambda}) K_O + \bar{s} T + cP + a\bar{t} P \qquad (5.5)$$

Now assume

$$K_O = k_O P \qquad (5.6)$$

which means that the amount of capital investment of the school is proportional to the number of pupils, and

$$T = t_O P \qquad (5.7)$$

in which $1/t_O$ is the pupil/teacher ratio. After substituting (5.6) and (5.7) into (5.5) we obtain:

$$\frac{C}{P} = (r + \frac{1}{\lambda}) k_O + \bar{s} t_O + c_O + a\bar{t} \qquad (5.8)$$

which says that the costs per pupil of a school equal the interest and depreciation of the capital needed as investment per pupil, increased by the salary costs per pupil plus the other costs per pupil (e.g. books) and the valuated average time spent per pupil in transportation to and from the school.

(5.8) can be written differently if we add a suffix i to each variable or coefficient in the equation that is supposed to be city specific, or rather, of which the value can be expected to differ from city to city.

We may then write

$$(\frac{C}{P})_i = (r + \frac{1}{\lambda}) k_{oi} + \bar{s}_i t_O + c_O + a\bar{t}_i \qquad (5.9)$$

in which three elements have been given a suffix, viz. the capital investment per pupil k_{oi}, the average salary of the teacher $\bar{s}_i$ and the average time spent in transportation $\bar{\tau}_i$.

When comparing two urban areas i and j we thus find

$$(\frac{C}{p})_i - (\frac{C}{p})_j = (r+\frac{1}{\lambda})(k_{oi} - k_{oj}) + (\bar{s}_i - \bar{s}_j)t_o + a\,(\bar{\tau}_i - \bar{\tau}_j) \qquad (5.10)$$

or in words: the difference between costs per pupil in i and j equals the interest on and depreciation of the difference in the investment costs per pupil, the difference in salary per pupil and the valuation of the difference in time needed in transportation. It is likely that this difference is positive if the population of i is larger than that of j — as wages and land costs will be higher in the larger city (which means $k_{oi} > k_{oj}$ and $\bar{s}_i > \bar{s}_j$) while distances to be covered will certainly not be smaller in the larger city than in the smaller one.

The foregoing shows that a cost comparison between i and j can only be made if all elements of (5.9) (or, at least, (5.10)) are known. Obviously, however, τ_i can never be found from official financial records nor from budget data. The value of $\bar{t}$ will have to be derived from a survey on private costs. For a the values applied in traffic studies may be used. For the other data the most fruitful approach seems to be to estimate, with the assistance of the relevant local authorities, the values of k_{oi}, $\bar{s}_i$ and $\bar{\tau}_i$, and to take for c_o and t_o average values for the country. By aggregating the weighted cost functions for different elements the total cost function of the most important elements can then be calculated.

The relation between cost functions and physical planning approaches (threshold analysis)

In recent years considerable attention has been paid — in Poland and Scotland — to the so-called threshold analysis, originally introduced by B. Malisz in the early 1960s[19] and applied by the Planning Research Unit in its Regional Plan for the Grangemouth/Falkirk Growth Area in Scotland (HMSO, 1968). In the manual it is stated:

> Threshold theory is based on observations that towns encounter limitations to their expansion due to physiographic features, existing land uses, and infrastructure services. An important inference from these observations is that the physical growth of towns is not smoothly continuous but proceeds in stages marked by successive limitations which have been called development thresholds. Some development thresholds can be identified on the ground (e.g. physiographic limitations) but others can only be expressed numerically as a capacity limitation (e.g. water supply limitations). Development thresholds are not insurmountable but they can be

overcome by incurring additional (often very high) investment costs, known as threshold costs. The investment necessary to overcome thresholds must be committed either before the land can be opened up for development, or during the course of development.

The total cost, (C_t) of providing an accommodation for a new inhabitant in a town can be seen as including:

(i)   'normal' costs (C_n). These costs are dependent on the the type of density of dwellings, site servicing and development, and the costs of materials, labour, etc. They are not dependent upon the location of development.

(ii)   'Additional'costs (C_a), i.e. threshold costs. These costs result from land characteristics, new services, the form and scale of development. They may vary substantially from one location to another.

$$Therefore\ C_t = C_n + C_a.$$

If conditions are 'normal', i.e. the land is relatively flat, is served by public utility networks and has direct access to the existing road system, the cost of development at a given density is 'normal'.

The division of costs into 'normal' and 'additional' is fundamental to threshold theory, and threshold analysis concentrates on studying and analysing 'additional' or threshold costs. When carrying out threshold analysis, 'normal' costs must be held constant. This is done through the adoption of basic residential units for which a standard residential density and mix of dwellings has been set. In 'normal' conditions the cost of all basic residential units will be the same.[20]

Thresholds have been classified into two types — grade thresholds and stepped thresholds. The distinction is based on the way in which investment is made to overcome the thresholds. A stepped threshold is overcome by the investment of a 'lump sum' before new inhabitants can be accommodated in new basic residential units. In contrast, a grade threshold is overcome by additional investment during the development. Stepped thresholds are usually cuased by limitation in the infrastructure services whereas grade thresholds are generally caused by site conditions.[21]

In the manual some graphs are presented, indicating the influence of both types of thresholds on total costs of the expansion of the town. They are, with a slight modification for graph (c)[22] presented below.

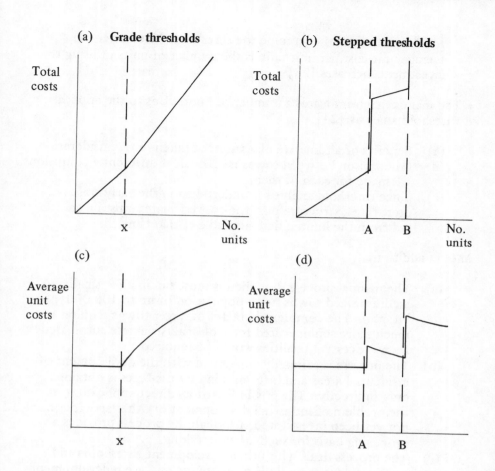

These illustrations relate to the following cases:

In (a), the total cost increases in proportion to the number of new basic residential units up to point x when this cost is increased at a higher rate as a result of overcoming the threshold.

In (b), the total cost increases in proportion to the number of new basic residential units up to point A when a 'lump sum' is required for the development of additional units. This investment enables further units to be developed up to point B when a similar 'lump sum' will be required to cross the threshold.

In (c), the average unit cost remains the same up to point x when the threshold is reached, thereafter it increases as a result of overcoming the threshold.

In (d), the average unit cost remains constant up to point A when there is a dramatic rise as a result of a 'lump sum' investment which

which is required to overcome the threshold. Thereafter the average unit cost per unit falls as the number of units utilising the investment increases.[23]

The manual itself indicates a number of limitations to the application of threshold analysis: [24]

(a) Benefits of alternative plans are not taken into consideration.
(b) Comparison between towns is difficult if different assumptions are made for each of them.
(c) Since threshold analysis is undertaken in the early stages of preparing a structure plan the cost estimates must be calculated from the limited data available at that time.

And, in addition:

(a) The manual process described is most suitable for small and medium sized towns (with population of up to 100,000 inhabitants). The complex character of larger towns requires a much more sophisticated form of analysis where automated Data Processing facilities would be required.
(b) The process is primarily concerned with the development of residential areas and information on other uses is obtained only indirectly. The possibility of its direct application to the problem of industrial development or other activities has not yet been investigated, although the process provides a promising basis for such an undertaking.
(c) The process deals with urban development thresholds and only provides general ideas on how to analyse redevelopment thresholds.
(d) The process concentrates on comparing the threshold cost of various sites. The relationship between threshold costs and total development costs can be established if required and this would put threshold costs in their proper perspective.
(e) The process concentrates on calculating 'direct' threshold costs (capital costs) and gives only general guidance on the calculation of 'indirect' threshold costs (exploitation costs). Running costs are particularly difficult to deal with as there is no uniform basis for calculating them for all functions.[25]

The foregoing considerations are interesting in the context of this chapter on urban development and costs related to urban growth. In threshold analysis the costs are used as an indicator of the direction in which cost minimising solutions for urban expansion can be found, but at the same time cost functions are produced as a result of the general analysis.

The important element introduced is that one cannot expect smooth continuous cost functions, but that at certain points in time bottlenecks have to be overcome which results in considerable jumps in the cost curve. In this context it is understandable that the manual suggests using threshold analysis only for smaller towns. It uses as an argument that for larger towns computer techniques will have to be developed, but a more realistic argument would probably be that in larger cities so many thresholds have to be overcome in one year's time as development proceeds, that the total cost curve would become a smooth continuously increasing function of population size. In other words, thresholds may result in a poor fit as far as the relation between population size and costs for smaller towns is concerned, but the goodness of fit is likely to increase with the size of the cities studied. Therefore, the main importance of threshold analysis does not seem to lie in its contribution to the general analysis of functional relationships between costs and population, but in its use for the selection of alternative plans. Its potential importance is that it can help city planners to decide in what direction to develop a city, especially as far as its residential facilities and social infrastructure elements are concerned. In view of the long term character of city planning it is obvious, however, that it is not the short term thresholds that determine in what direction the optimum solution is to be sought, but rather the discounted flow of the costs of sequences of thresholds that could be considered as possible solutions for future development problems. In other words, threshold analysis should concentrate on finding the optimum sequence of thresholds to be crossed during the long term development process of a city.

Anyhow, threshold analysis can be most helpful, especially when applied to expenditure time series for individual cities. It would be very interesting to use it not only to determine optimum development paths for the future, but also to analyse solutions of the past, and the influence certain decisions have had on the outlays of certain cities.

The maximising of net income

W. Alonso has persuasively argued that minimising the *per capita* public costs associated with urban size is a poor objective of public policy.[26] L.H. Klaassen, as we indicated in chapter 1, shares Alonso's ideas on this point.

W. Alonso (and also L.H. Klaassen) take the view that efficiency would be much better served in maximising the difference between income and costs. This view is illustrated in Graph 5.3. This figure is analogous to the usual setting of costs and revenues for a firm except

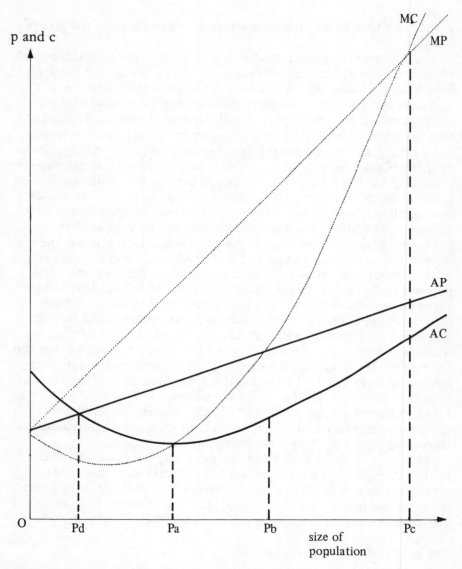

Graph 5.3: Relations between urban cost, urban product, and city size

that the horizontal axis relates to population size rather than to quantity of output. The curves of this graph are

AC — the average cost curve indicating the total costs of the city per head of the population. In the preceding sections when we were considering minimum cost approaches, we were indeed referring to this function and the point Pa, indicating the minimum average cost level.

AP — the average product *per capita*. This function increases monotonically.

MC — Marginal costs, a function that naturally intersects the average cost function in its minimum.

MP — Marginal product.

From the graph we now easily derive that the point of maximum local contribution to national income is P_c (where MC = MP). Obviously, a policy that is aiming at maximising national income will try to realise P_c only if there is a national surplus of labour. With a limited supply of labour, the national product would be maximised at a lower level, where the difference between MP and MC exceeds an amount equal to the opportunity cost of siting the population in alternative cities (see chapter 1). The optimum point for the inhabitants of the city is found where disposable income is at a maximum. It is P_b, where the difference between AP and AC is maximum.

With respect to W. Alonso's approach we may point out that the author considers the optimum size of one city without taking into account the size of other cities. He states: 'In brief, the optimal population will differ according to whether a national or a local viewpoint is assumed . . . '.[27] In reality we are concerned with the size of a city within the framework of an existing settlement pattern. In other words, in what city or cities should population increase be promoted? L.H. Klaassen does take the pattern of dispersion into account.

It should be recognised that the path of the curves is unsure and changes with different time horizon perspectives, which in turn depend on the adaptability of the urban system.[28]

An important remark has been made by L. Wingo.[29] He argues that if income *per capita* rises with city size, that could be interpreted to mean not only that larger cities are more productive but also that firms can benefit from external economies only because they entice workers to leave smaller places by paying higher wages. Thus, the extra wage required to compensate workers for living in big cities is included in the costs of production in those big cities. When the goods produced in big cities are sold in the local market, the diseconomies are reflected in a higher cost of living. When they are exported, the purchasers bear the cost of these diseconomies. A plausible reasoning, but one to be handled with caution; figures quoted by W. Alonso from a paper by R. Douglas[30] seem to suggest that the external economies may well outrank the disadvantages pointed out by L. Wingo (see Table 5.9).

Table 5.9
Index of salaries, value added, value added minus salaries per worker of
67 Standard Metropolitan Statistical Areas, 1963*

City size (x 1,000)	Index salaries	Value added index	Index value-added minus salaries	Index net investment per worker
250— 500	0.994	0,970	0.943	0.967
500—1,000	1.029	1.047	1.099	1.028
1,000—5,000	1.061	1.046	1.029	0.925
5,000 and more	1.058	1.053	1.129	0.784

*Standardised to industrial composition.

The advantages of urban concentration

It is' often suggested that large agglomerations imply benefits from agglomeration economies or higher efficiency. However, one should be more precise and ask 'for whom?'. To find out, we shall consider different groups: firms, households, and the community.

A. *Agglomeration advantages for the firms*

G.M. Neutze basing his arguments on the Australian situation,[31] distinguishes three groups of factors: [32]

1 Direct economies resulting from location in a large centre
  (a) Labour of all types is available; in turn the large town has a particular attraction for workers with special skills.
  (b) Large cities provide a much wider range of educational opportunities than small ones.
  (c) There is less pressure on firms in a recession period (in a small town alternative jobs are scarce).
  (d) Cost of local authority services is lower (is not always true).
  (e) In the case of a forced sale, the sales value of buildings is high.
  (f) A large centre has direct transport and communication links with all parts of the hinterland.
  (g) Modern industrial firms are highly interdependent;

frequently one firm specialises in just small parts of a complete manufacturing process (see chapter 4 — The polarisation theory).

2 Savings on the costs of communication and transport between the plant and the large centre
   (a) Savings on the costs of communication (see chapter 4):
      with other firms;
      with the demand (one also saves on distribution costs);
      with government agencies.
   (b) Neither the supplier nor the receiver needs to keep large stocks.
   (c) Lower freight costs are involved in getting materials and sending the product to the market.
   (d) Packaging costs are lower.

3 Other advantages
   (a) Firms belonging to the same sector may be interested in location in one another's neighbourhood.
   (b) The presence of supplying and repair firms.
   (c) Provision of a good economic infrastructure.
   (d) Availability of capital.
   (e) Existence of all kinds of service firms (bookkeeping firms, fiscal counsellors, publicity firms, etc.).

It may be remarked in this context that a considerable number of the above mentioned advantages is also available in cities of 500,000 and even 200,000 inhabitants.

B   *Agglomeration advantages for households*

Agglomerations offer certain advantages to households as well; the most important ones are listed below.
   1 Better job opportunities, particularly for skilled persons.
   2 Better educational facilities.
   3 Higher level of income.
     The relation between income level and the size of the villages and towns in Belgium (1967) can be expressed by the following equation: [33]

$$\text{Log } Y = 0.089 \log X + 1.20761 \quad (R=0.97)$$

This relation implies that the average income level of a town becomes 0.09 per cent higher when its population gets 1 per cent larger.

Here we have to make an important remark:

On the one hand the size of city is, of course, not the only variable to be taken into account and, on the other hand, the variable 'population size' can have an effect on other variables (economic structure). The income level *per capita* in agglomerations is also influenced by property income; earners of high property income often live in large agglomerations.

4 A wider range, and better quality, of goods and services (shops, education, sanitation, cultural manifestations, etc.).

With respect to Belgium we found:

$$Y = 52.3 - 1,354.8 \ 1/X + 20.0 \log X$$

in which

Y = number of service functions in a city;
X = population size.

The diversity of functions is positively related to population size but it grows less rapidly as population increases.

We agree with H.W. Richardson that the various functions do have an unequal importance for the different income groups. [34]

C   *Agglomeration advantages for the community*

Among the advantages for the community the following are worth mentioning:

1 Higher efficiency of public services (cfr. minimum size approach).
2 The impact on the national economy.
   (a) A big city has international prestige (e.g. the role of Paris);
   (b) A large agglomeration promotes research and innovation, at least according to some authors.[35] H.W. Richardson is of a different opinion. [36]

The disadvantages of urban concentration

Earlier we cited some writers who feel that the degree or the nature of urban concentration influences national welfare. In the first chapter we already indicated how the concentration of people might influence the rate of inflation in a country. It would be quite interesting to study the spatial diffusion of inflation in a country by identifying its original sources.

The influence of population size is much clearer. In the beginning of this chapter we introduced, in the context of the considerations around the optimum city size, the U-shaped expenditure functions. Table 5.10 shows how this function works out for Belgian municipalities.

Table 5.10
Expenditure *per capita* in Belgian municipalities,
per size class, 1966—68

Size class (population)	Current expenditure ** (x 1,000 BF)	Capital expenditure *** (x 1,000 BF)	Total (x 1,000 BF)
— 1,000	3.7	2.8	6.5
1,000— 2,500	2.6	2.2	4.8
2,500— 5,000	2.5	2.2	4.7
5,000— 10,000	2.8	2.2	5.0
10,000— 20,000	3.3	3.0	6.3
20,000— 30,000	3.9	3.0	6.9
30,000— 40,000	6.3	3.7	10.0
40,000— 50,000	4.4	4.4	8.8
50,000— 60,000	7.1	3.0	10.1
60,000—100,000	7.1	4.1	11.1
100,000 and more *	11.8	5.5	17.3

* The agglomerations Antwerp, Bruges, Brussels, Charleroi, Ghent and Liège.
** The average for the years 1967—68.
*** The average for the years 1966—68.

Although the total expenditure pattern is somewhat irregular, the larger municipalities appear to have significantly higher expenditure *per capita* than medium sized and small municipalities. The function for current expenditure is clearly U-shaped with a very low minimum (2,500—5,000 inhabitants).

In his article 'Les coûts de la croissance urbaine', P.H. Derycke[37] quotes the results of a study of CERAU[38] concerning the average annual infrastructure costs *per capita* in a number of French cities (see Table 5.11).

Table 5.11
Average annual infrastructure costs *per capita* according
to the size of the city, 1960–67 (FF)

Equipment	32 agglomerations of more than 100,000 inhabitants	20 cities with 20,000 to 100,000 inhabitants	27 cities with less than 20,000 inhabitants
Roads, etc.	63	43	23
Water distribution	21	17	18
Hygiene	25	17	12
Services (lighting, public transport, green spaces etc.)	20.7	15.2	11.8
Other expenditure	4.3	5.8	1.2
Total	134	98	66

Source: CERAU

The picture is essentially the same as for the Belgian municipalities; a steady increase in infrastructure costs with a rise in population size can be observed.

The EEC document[39] quoted earlier presents the results of a study by Lajugie in which the author gives the expenditure for public equipment per marginal inhabitant (see Table 5.12).

Table 5.12
Expenditure for public equipment per marginal inhabitant
in France (1970)

Size of municipality	Marginal costs (FF 1970)
200,000 and more	37,000
100–200,000	36,700
50– 10,000	33,400
20– 50,000	24,400
10– 20,000	24,100
–10,000	17,300

Again, the picture is similar, the expenditure in the group of largest municipalities exceeding by more than 100 per cent that in the group of smallest municipalities.

The results suggest that a settlement structure consisting of small and medium sized towns is more economical than concentration in one very large agglomeration.[40]

J.R. Boudeville opposes polarised and mononuclear regions to the urban region which he describes as: 'large homogeneous space, with a high demographic, industrial and tertiary density, showing a diversified, discontinuous urbanisation'.[41] The urban region is to be preferred for various reasons, as has also been pointed out by L.H. Klaassen.[42] The advantages of a 'structure multipolaire', that is a multipolar structure, are:

reduction of the distance between home and workplace,
reduction of peak traffic,
better utilisation of transport infrastructure and means of transport,
more human living conditions.

Urban concentration and individual preferences

Location patterns in space are determined not only by economic factors; locational preferences also play a part. The latter explain why profit maximising models for the industrial locations and income maximising models for the households determine the factual location.

We can follow H.W. Richardson when he states:

However, it is probable that locational preferences for households are more significant in the sense of having a large impact on the spatial distribution of population and, hence, of economic activity. The reason for this is that in the absence of locational preferences we would expect households to crowd into the centres of agglomeration at least until the effects of immigration equalised incomes between areas. Yet because of locational preferences substantial numbers of people choose to live away from the centres of agglomeration even when this involves sacrifices in income.[43]

Locational preferences contain to a considerable extent non-economic elements that does not make them irrational. The psychical income one derives from living in a particular town is not always translated into monetary income. It should be pointed out, moreover,

215

that the impact of locational preferences on the spatial patterns of the production factors labour and capital is contradictory.

> . . . locational preferences for households tend to foster dispersion by maintaining population in lagging regions at higher levels than justified by income differentials. Locational preferences for firms, on the other hand, tend to perpetuate concentration and agglomeration. Since many firms refuse to relocate away from centres of agglomeration even in cases when more profitable sites are available elsewhere. [44]

Recent trends seem to indicate that firms which are particularly dependent on labour tend to follow labour in its tendency to migrate to medium sized towns.

Urban concentration and living costs

It is often said that living costs are much higher in a large city than in a small place. The research results available do not confirm that hypothesis. Let us quote a few such results:

(a) W. Alonso and M. Fajans: 'It appears that one can live as cheaply in big cities as in small ones, but that the more varied opportunities of large cities raise expectations'. [45]

(b) Bureau of Labor Statistics City Workers' Family Budget Index: [46] The relation between living costs and city size is weak.

(c) WES-research (situation in Belgium, 1973): An analysis of the price level of consumption goods retained in the consumption price index for 35 villages and towns gives the following disparities:

	Lowest Index	Highest Index
Foodstuffs	96,8	102,0 (Hoei)
Non-foods	95,9	102,7 (Antwerp)
Services	90	109,6 (Liège)
Total	96,6	103,1 (Antwerp)

In these figures the rents of houses are not included, for one thing because it is difficult to find houses of equal quality to compare, and for another, because tastes in and preferences for houses are strongly related with income and class. For a good comparison it would be necessary to make a division into houses for the lower and medium income groups on the one hand, and houses for the

216

higher income groups on the other.

Probably in the large agglomerations the rents are tempered by the low quality of the housing stock (the houses available for the lower income classes). [47]

In this context it is interesting to compare the price levels of building land as a function of the size of the city. There are figures available for Belgium and France. In these countries, the average price per are of building land was, in 1967, in cities of

less than 1,000 inhabitants	12,446 BF
5,000 — 10,000	22,917 BF
10,000 — 20,000	30,095 BF
20,000 and more	35,060 BF
agglomerations	76,144 BF.

According to P.H. Derycke the costs of building land represent on an average 48 per cent of the total cost of a building operation. This author also gives an indication of the relation between the price of building land and the size of towns (situation 1962): [48]

	Price per m^2 in the centre of the town (FF)
100,000 inhabitants	100
300,000 — 500,000 inhabitants	400 to 600
800,000 — 900,000 inhabitants	1,000
Paris	$\pm$ 6,000 (right bank)

The higher price paid by the inhabitants of large agglomerations represents in fact a land surplus paid to reduce the transportation costs.

Urban concentration and the quality of urban life

There are many factors which seem to indicate that the quality of life in large agglomerations is lower than that in smaller cities as far as: air pollution; noise; hygiene; psychological stress; criminality; traffic congestion; are concerned.

In Paris, Professor Truhaut succeeded in provoking cancers in laboratory animals simply by making them inhale substances contained in the air which people in Paris breathe every day.

In his study 'Les villes prolétaires' Ph. Saint-Marc mentions a number of figures relative to mortality due to pulmonary cancer in Great Britain:

	Male	Female
Very large cities	125	121
+ 100,000 inhabitants	112	101
50,000—100,000 inhabitants	93	88
—50,000 inhabitants	84	86
Rural areas	64	77

The air pollution based on SO_2 (sulphur dioxyde) has been measured for Belgian towns and villages [49] [50] in winter periods:

	Highest monthly average of SO_2, during the winter 1970—71, 1971—72 and 1972—73 (in microgram per m^3 air)
—5,000 inhabitants	93
5,000—10,000 inhabitants	128
10,000—20,000 inhabitants	135
20,000—30,000 inhabitants	163
30,000—40,000 inhabitants	175
40,000—100,000 inhabitants	215
Agglomeration of Bruges	184
Agglomeration of Charleroi	182 (centre)
Agglomeration of Ghent	237 (centre)
Agglomeration of Liege	219 (centre)
Agglomeration of Antwerp	303 (centre)
Agglomeration of Brussels	364 (centre)

The relationship between air pollution (SO_2 pollution) and population size is given by the following equation (based on the Belgian situation)

$$\log Y = 0,190 \log X + 1,347 \quad (R = 0,95)$$

After all, air, water, nature, silence, have become economic goods. They are, indeed, scarce in big cities, and scarcity is a characteristic of economic goods. There can only be an increase in the welfare level if we succeed in alleviating the scarcity of economic goods.

There is obviously a close link between air pollution and traffic volume and congestion. Structural developments in practically all large cities have not only aggravated traffic congestion but also lead to unbalanced traffic flows and an excessive demand for parking places.

The structure of the problem is well known and can be summarised in a few lines:

(a)   Most cities are mononuclear in structure with the central business district (a nasty word) representing the main attraction centre as both a working and a shopping place.

(b)   Motorisation enables people formerly living in the urban core to move out to more pleasant places which combine the nearness of urban amenities with the advantages of a house 'in the green'.

(c)   The increased traffic flows resulting from these moves endanger the chances of survival of the CBD and induce activities to decentralisation to places on the outskirts of the city.

(d)   Space in the CBD becoming available by this process is rapidly occupied by offices and banks, worsening again traffic problems.

(e)   As a result of this process, the quality of life in the urban core deteriorates rapidly, stimulating further downward trends.

(f)   The principal solution prepared by local government is improvement of public transport and restriction of private car traffic in certain areas of the CBD.

Although these developments are certainly not the only ones influencing the quality of urban life, their importance is vital.[51]

Urban policy measures are now gradually being introduced; in essence they aim at a more equal distribution of population and activities among the different parts of the city, just as regional policy does with respect to regions.

Obviously a large number of problems is posed in the implementation of this policy. The first problem is how to make the centre of our cities an attractive place to live in. Recent trends in Europe have shown that young people in particular appreciate living in town centres and do so the readier, the more intimate the atmosphere in the centre is. Old towns like Cologne, Munich, and Amsterdam offer splendid opportunities for living in historical places in the middle of everything that a city of some size and character has to offer. By living there they themselves contribute to the atmosphere of the city. By demanding amenities available in the urban core, they stimulate the typical centre activities, they make the city more attractive by their mere presence after working hours and, above all, they prevent the city from being 'bought' by bankers and insurance companies who would build enormous so-called representative offices in the city centre and turn the area into a dead and unpleasant place during most of the day. Frank-furt is a unique example of the quick death of a beautiful centre as a result of this very process and Paris is going rapidly in the same direction.[52]

Although it is not very likely that a government by its policy will be able to check the dynamic developments that are leading European cities towards desurbanisation, there are at least clear signs that govern-ments have begun to recognise the problem and are willing to take appropriate measures.[53] Should such policy measures prove unsucc-essful, then especially the larger agglomerations will in the not too distant future face great and grave problems. The following somewhat pessimistic considerations might help[54] to visualise the kind of problems we mean.

By definition, the total demand for land in an agglomeration equals the demand for land per household multiplied by the number of house-holds. This number equals total population divided by the average size of a household.

So, we may write:

$$S = s \frac{B}{f} \tag{5.11}$$

in which
S = total effective demand for land for urban purposes;
s = same per household;
B = total population of the agglomeration;
f = average size of a household.

To simplify the argument we write (5.11) in relative changes, indicated by a dot over the relevant symbol; then

$$\dot{S} = \dot{s} + \dot{B} - \dot{f} \tag{5.12}$$

holds.

It is known that $\dot{s}$, one of the three variables in the right hand part of the equation, representing the relative increase in the demand for land per household, is positive. It is not a simple matter to forecast this variable for the future: in view of the expected lower growth rates for income, it will be assumed that the increase expected for the future will gradually decrease.

There is enough evidence now to assume that population growth,

220

which used to be positive in all agglomerations, is now in many cases decreasing through time (see the beginning of this chapter). The function for $\dot{B}$ then decreases through time intersecting the horizontal axis and becoming negative beyond the intersection.

The average size of a household is decreasing and the function of $\dot{f}$ is, therefore, negative; it may be assumed to approach the horizontal axis asymptotically.

In Graph 5.4 the developments for $\dot{s}$, $\dot{f}$ and $\dot{B}$ are indicated. The function for $\dot{S}$ is derived from these three by addition. In this figure there are a number of important points to be indicated. The first is, t_A, representing the moment which the population of the agglomeration starts declining; it marks the beginning of desurbanisation, in many Western European countries now a common phenomenon. The second point is t_B, marking the time when the decrease in population size is no longer compensated by the decrease in family size, and consequently the absolute number of households starts declining.

On the assumption that each household in the city occupies one dwelling, from this point onwards the demand for dwellings is declining in an absolute sense.

The last interesting point is t_C, beyond which the increase in the demand for land per household and the decrease of the average household size are no longer able to compensate for the decrease in population, and an absolute decrease in the demand for land will become manifest. Beyond this point the city just will have to shrink. It is in particular the description of the last development phase that congenes up a glooming picture of the future of our great cities.[55]

In that last phase, the phenomena are the same as in the two previous ones, but the results are worse. For there will be no people and no activities to replace these that move out, no useful employ for empty houses and vacant lots. There will be less demand for dwellings, schools, shops and transportation; as the congestion of private vehicles is letting up, public transport will be losing much of its 'raison d'être'. There will be nothing for it but to raise certain parts of the agglomeration, pulling down houses and other buildings.

But where to start the raising operation? It seems logical, perhaps, to start by tearing down the 'worst' parts of a city transforming them into parks. Doing that, we shall end up with a city core sitting in the hub of a green area, with an urban outer ring, a ring that will be in decline itself, for that matter. That may seem a logical solution, but it is open to query all the same: the very costly rehabilitation programmes of recent years have been focussed on that very ring of old town quarters, and city planners will have no mind to have the capital invested there depreciated in just a few years.

Razing the outer urban ring is not an attractive proposition either:

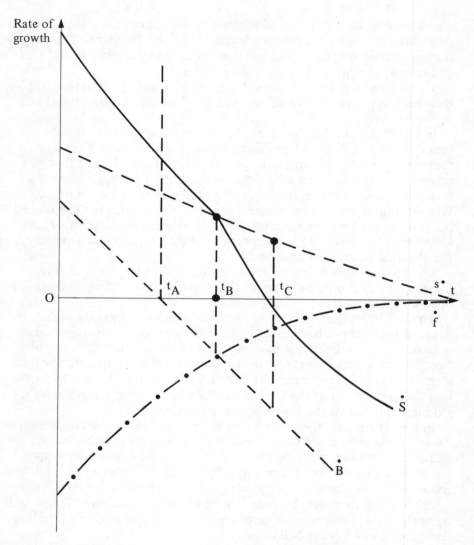

Graph 5.4: Developments in relative changes of important urban
          variables

that, too, would involve large scale destruction of capital, the houses
there being among the newest and most expensive to be found in the
agglomeration. True, the land thus falling vacant could be, as it were,
restored to its original agricultural use, but at what cost . . .

Whatever the outcome, there is bound to be a surplus of land,
dwellings and facilities. Empty city quarters or land lying fallow do not

make for an attractive town; they are symbols of decline, of a living city turning into a ghost town.

Perhaps living in large agglomerations was a way of life that belonged to a past period of great dynamism and empestuous growth. Perhaps large agglomerations do not fit the picture we have of the future quality of life. On the other hand, effective policies might perhaps turn the tide and make the city once more attractive to people and activities. The first signs of desurbanisation might induce local governments to a policy of active reurbanisation; except in a few places, there are no signs of such a policy, and the outlook is far from bright.

Notes

[1] The considerations on page 180 are derived from 'Elements of theory or urban development', Vijverberg, C., van den Berg, L. and Klaassen, L.H., Foundations of Empirical Economic Research, NEI, Rotterdam, 1977/1.

[2] Adjusted Graph 5.1, taken from Vijverberg, C., van den Berg, L. and Klaassen, L.H., op.cit.

[3] Project of the Vienna Center for documentation and coordination of social research: 'The costs of urban growth'. First results published in 1978.

[4] This table is presented in an unpublished working document of the Commission of the European Communities 'Le coût des concentrations urbaines et de la dépopulation rurale dans la CEE', Bruxelles, 1975.

[5] van den Berg, L., Boeckhout, Sj. and Vijverberg, C., 'Urban development and policy response in the Netherlands', NEI-Erasmus University, Rotterdam, 1977, p.11. Figures relate to municipalities.

[6] Ibid., p.11.

[7] Neutze, G.M., Economic Policy and the Size of Cities, Camberra, 1965, p.7.

[8] Clark, C., 'The economic functions of a city in relation to its size', Econometrica, no.2, 1945, p.97 ff.

[9] Ibid., p.100.

[10] Ibid., p.100.

[11] Ibid., p.112.

[12] See Klaassen, L.H. and Verster, A.C.P., De optimale structuur van stedelijke gebieden, Rotterdam, 1970.

[13] CEE, 'Le coût des concentrations urbaines et de la dépopulation rurale dans la CEE', op.cit.

[14] Ibid., p.13.

[15] Hirsch, W.Z., 'Expenditure implications of metropolitan growth and consolidation', Review of Economics and Statistics, vol.41, 1959.

Lomax, K.S., 'Expenditure per head and size of population', *Journal of the Royal Statistical Society*, vol.106, 1943. Duncan, O.D., 'The optimum size of cities', Spengler, J.J. and Duncan, O.D. (eds), *Demographic Analysis*, 1956. Clark, C., 'The economic functions of a city in relation to its size', *Econometrica*, vol.13, 1954. Royal Commission on Local Government in Greater London, 1960, Cmnd.1164. Redcliffe-Maud Royal Commission on Local Government in England, 1969, Cmnd.4040, HMSO. Pinchemel, P., Vakili, A. and Gozzi, J., *Nouveaux optima des villes*, Lille, 1959. See also: Goze, M. and Leymarie, O., 'Naissance des agglomérations et villes centres', *Revue du Sud-Ouest*, no.2, 1978. Driembowski, Z., *Synthetic Indices of Social Costs of Local Economic Infrastructure in Cities of Different Size*, Warszawa, 1976 (unpublished).

[16] See Cameron, G.C., 'Growth areas, growth centres and regional conversion', *Scottish Journal of Political Economy*, vol.21, 1970.

[17] van den Berg, C., *De structuur van de gemeentelijke uitgaven*, Leiden, 1956.

[18] Alonso, W., 'The economics of urban size', *Papers Regional Science Association*, vol.26, 1971, p.68.

[19] For a systematic treatment of threshold analysis and its possible applications see: Scottish Development Department, *Threshold Analysis Manual*, HMSO, Edinburgh, 1973.

[20] Ibid., p.3.

[21] Ibid., p.4.

[22] Average unit costs are past x a non-linear function of the number of units and not a linear as suggested in the manual.

[23] Ibid., p.4.

[24] Ibid., pp.8–9.

[25] Ibid., pp.8–9.

[26] Alonso, W., 'The economics of urban size, *Papers RSA*, vol.26, 1971. See also Alonso, W., 'The question of city size and national policy', Center for Planning and Development Research, *Institute of Urban and Regional Development*, University of California, Berkeley, Discussion Paper no.125, 1970.

[27] Alonso, W., op.cit., p.72.

[28] Hansen, N., *Public Policy and Regional Economic Development — the experiences of nine Western countries*, Cambridge, 1974, p.15.

[29] Wingo, L., 'Issues in a national urban development strategy for the United States', *Urban Studies*, no.9, 1972.

[30] Douglas, R., 'Selected indices of industrial characteristics for US standard metropolitan statistical areas', 1963, Discussion Paper no.20, Regional Science Research Institute, Philadelphia, 1967.

[31] Comparison of Sydney and Melbourne with cities of less than 100,000 inhabitants.

[32] Neutze, G.M., op.cit., chapter 6.

[33] WES, *Optimale grootte van een stad — Proeve van synthese,* Brugge, 1974.

[34] Richardson, H.W., *Regional Growth Theory,* p.186.

[35] Hägerstrand, T., 'Aspects of the spatial structure of social communication and the diffusion of information', *PPRSA,* no.16, 1966.

[36] Richardson, H.W., op.cit., p.195.

[37] Derycke, P.H., 'Les coûts de la croissance urbaine', *Revue d'Economie Politique,* no.1, 1973.

[37] CERAU, *Les coûts des infrastructures urbaines en France — 1960—1967,* Paris, 1970.

[39] CEE, 'Le coût des concentrations urbaines . . .', op.cit., p.22.

[40] Alonso, W., *The question of city size and national policy,* op.cit. *Medium sized cities clustered in urban regions seem to offer the best solution.*

[41] Boudeville, J., 'Les régions de villes et l'Europe', Meeting of the Association de Science régionale de langue française, Rotterdam, 1974.

[42] Klaassen, L.H., *De optimale structuur van stedelijke gebieden,* Rotterdam, 1971, p.127.

[43] Richardson, H.W., 'Regional growth theory', op.cit., p.196. See also chapter 1, p. 28.

[44] Ibid., p.196.

[45] Alonso, W. and Fajans, M., 'Cost of living and income by urban size', *Working Paper no.128, Center for Planning and Development Research,* University of California, Berkeley, 1970.

[46] Brackett, J.C. and Lamale, H., 'Area differences in living costs', *American Statistical Association, Proceedings of Social Statistics,* Section, 1967.

[47] See also CEE, *Le coût des concentrations urbaines . . . ,* op.cit., pp. 25—6.

[48] Derycke, P.H., op.cit., p.128.

[49] We refer also to the EEC report: 'Air sulphur dioxyde concentration in the European Community', *Yearly Report,* April 1971, March 1972, Luxemburg.

[50] For air pollution based on CO (carbon monoxide) we refer to the EEC publication, 'Atmospheric carbon monoxide pollution in urban thoroughfares and road tunnels in the EEC countries', Luxemburg, 1973.

[51] Klaassen, L.H., 'Urban planning and its impact on the quality of life', Kuklinski, A. (ed.), *Social Issues in Regional Policy and Regional Planning,* The Hague/Paris, 1977, pp.283—4.

[52] Ibid., p.285.

[53] A notable example is the city of Rotterdam. See, 'Structuurplan Rotterdam binnen de ruit', Municipality of Rotterdam, 1977.

[54] Klaassen, L.H., 'Het desurbanisatieproces in de grote steden', *ESB*, 1978, no.3136, p.8 ff.
[55] Harrison, A.J., and Whitehead, M.E., 'Is there an inner city problem', *The Three Banks Review,* September 1978.

6 The regional impact of the integration process

The fear of repercussions

In the late 1950s and the beginning of the 1960s some personalities of the scientific and political world expressed their anxiety about the impact of the economic integration process on the problem regions within each country and in the EEC in general.

In his introduction to the book *Espace Economique et Intégration Européenne,* by H. Bourginat, J.B. Merigot wrote in 1962:

> Among the serious problems raised by the creation of the European Economic Community is that of its compatibility with the policy developed in our countries during the last few years towards fewer inter-regional disequilibria through the elaboration of a regional policy, economic decentralisation, and development of the backward regions. Do not the creation and the development of the Common Market threaten to increase the existing inequalities between the different French regions? [1]

J.B. Merigot and H. Bourginat were not the first to draw attention to the negative impact of economic integration on regional disparities. H. Giersch and M. Byé examined the relationship between agglomeration economies and regional development in an integrated area. H. Giersch emphasised that, with the abolition of restrictions on trade and factor movement, the exploitation of agglomeration economies would enhance the attractiveness of highly industrialised centres to both labour and capital.[2] M. Byé maintained that 'Because of agglomeration economies, a customs union can increase the attractiveness of the industrialised centres to factors of production'.[3]

A warning was also given by the ideas of F. Perroux, published in the late 1950s. F. Perroux asserted that integration and the development of backward regions are incompatible, and maintained that a policy aimed at integration favours the regions possessing poles of development at the expense of the now underdeveloped regions. With regard to the European Common Market, F. Perroux expressed the view that 'the policy of so-called integration does not assert itself to the benefit of an abstract Europe, but very concretely, to the benefit of the Ruhr and of those industries which are most directly animated by it'.[4]   Integration

227

would intensify the agglomerative tendencies in the Common Market.

> The development and growth resulting from the realisation of the Common Market will strengthen the principal development poles to the extent that it is unprofitable to trade on markets whose position is spatially far from perfect and which are subject to monopolistic competition.[5]

Although he subscribed to the ideas of F. Perroux, B. Balassa was of the opinion that the economic attraction of the Ruhr might have been somewhat overrated.

> Two considerations seem to be neglected by those who lay great emphasis on the intensification of regional imbalances in an integrated area: first, the impact of the abolition of trade and other barriers on frontier regions; second, the possibility of beneficial effects of increased inter-regional intercourse for poor regions . . . spread effects, emanating from highly developed regions, would also benefit the backward regions in the framework of a European union.[6]

Anxiety is also expressed in official documents. In this respect we refer to three publications. First, the *Economic Survey of Europe Since the War,* a publication of the United Nations Economic Commission for Europe. Referring to the Italian example, the Commission found that 'In the absence of positive intervention . . . disparities in income levels, once established, have a vicious tendency to become more pronounced' [7] and, furthermore, 'this is tantamount to saying that the gap between levels of development in the high income and the low income areas of Europe would continue to widen, which could hardly be regarded as an achievement in economic integration'.[8]   Secondly, we should mention the Birkelbach report.[9] W. Birkelbach emphasised four factors or phenomena that could or would deteriorate the position of backward areas in Europe: (a) the risk of increasing economic difficulties in peripheral regions due to increasing competition and the threat to small firms; (b) the changed geo-economic position of the frontier regions within the EEC; (c) the impact of an intensified competition between the industries in the Community on one-sided regions; (d) the impact of the Common Agricultural Policy on certain agricultural regions of the EEC. Thirdly, the Bersani report stressed the ideas prevailing at the time of the signing of the Treaty of Rome. 'One was afraid that the abolition of economic barriers would only accentuate disparities in the development of the different regions of the Community, provoking serious difficulties in the economic and political field and one was assured that this would happen'.[10]

Although the Treaty of Rome does not contain a special chapter dealing with regional policy, one cannot deny that implicitly and sometimes explicitly, the fear of undesired regional repercussions of the integration process is present; we return to that point in chapter 10. Such fear is in contradiction to the neoclassical theory of international trade, which leaves little doubt that the establishment of a Common Market would narrow differences in *per capita* income between member countries.

The ideas of several prominent scientists and politicians lead us to one general conclusion: there was in the EEC a general feeling that the integration process would alter the European region economic map. There were five underlying factors:

(a)   increased competition would be harmful to firms with relatively low competitive power, especially in the peripheral regions;

(b)   integration would necessitate the reconversion of a number of one-sided regions relying too much on stagnating activities;

(c)   the influence of external economies on the location of new firms would increase the attractiveness of the existing industrial centre. In other words, an intensification of agglomerative tendencies could be expected;

(d)   a modification of the geo-economic position of certain regions on both sides of a border would alter, a phenomenon that, as we shall see, need not by definition be detrimental to the regions concerned;

(e)   the evolution of agricultural structures.

The events in the United States, reported in chapter 2, did not seem to justify the anxieties expressed above. Yet, European experiences in the 1960s and 1970s made it clear that in the case of the EEC they are well founded. The question can now be raised, 'What can we learn from economic theory?'. The subject is very complex: not only are we confronted with many types of regions,[11] but economic integration itself is, after all, a process with different phases, ranging from customs union to economic union. That alone explains the diversity of opinions within economic theory.

In the following sections of this chapter we shall pay attention to a number of theories and models concerning the regional impact of an integration process.

The spatial impact of a customs union:
the Giersch model

It is very difficult to predict the consequences of an integration process for the location determinants of existing firms and new projects. H. Bourginat has tried to form an opinion about the impact of the EEC as a customs union on the regions in France.[12] Largely inspired by the Giersch model,[13] Bourginat approaches the real world by way of successive approximations.

The Giersch model

The starting point is a vast homogeneous economic space ('un espace économique indifférencié') surrounded by an insurmountable barrier, within which the population is evenly spread, and where there are no cost differences between the regions. Under such conditions the location of firms will be determined by the transportation costs. As these costs are a function of distance, economic activities will tend to locate in the centre of the economic space, and the result will be overemployment in the centre and underemployment in the peripheral zones.

Now, let us suppose that the homogeneous economic space is divided into two countries, and that a customs barrier is raised between them; see Graph 6.1.

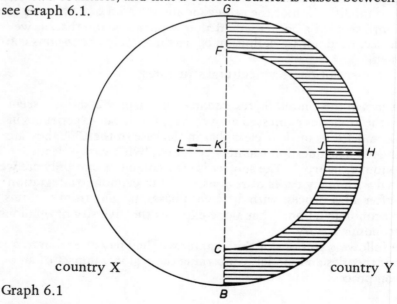

Graph 6.1

in which
     L = location of firm A before the introduction of the barrier GB;

LH = the market radius of firm A;
X and Y = two countries after the division of the homogeneous
economic space.

The introduction of the customs barrier decreases the market radius of firm A in country Y. The hatched zone BCJFG is lost to the products of firm A. If K is the only border passage along which a product of firm A can be delivered to country Y, the market radius of firm A in country Y is limited to a circle with K as the centre and KJ as the radius. The proper strategy for firm A is to move away from the frontier to a more central situation with respect to suppliers and the separate national markets.

It is easy to imagine what will happen when the countries X and Y form a customs union: the tendency of firm A will be to approach the frontier zone between the two countries. The frontier region must surely benefit from the new circumstances.

The Giersch model and reality

Reality is not a homogeneous economic space but a structured economic space in which cost levels are not uniform and population is not evenly spaced. By dropping the model's hypotheses or simplifications one by one, it is possible to assess the impact of creating a customs union in the real world.

Taking into consideration the concentration of people and economic activities along the Rhine-Meuse axis, H. Bourginat came to the following conclusions: 'If theoretical firms demonstrate a tendency to approach the centre of the market in the case of the abolition of economic barriers in a theoretical homogeneous space, real firms will have an even greater tendency to do so in a real economic space in view of the fact that the regions to which firms move, are already in a favoured position'.[14] In other words, when we start with different costs per region and with an uneven spread of population, the conclusions drawn from the Giersch model are strengthened.

Increase of competition in an economic space constitutes a very strong factor in favour of agglomeration. Each country has a number of growth poles; accentuation of polarisation effects can be expected. Formerly the field of action of the national poles was limited. With the formation of a customs union, their radius will extend and new firms will look for new optimum locations. Of course, each pole must be considered in the light of its particular characteristics. This brings H. Bourginat to a second conclusion: 'The region with the strongest propulsive units will have the best chance of cumulative development. The realisation of a customs union should, in normal circumstances, benefit the existing national agglomerations and accelerate the deterioration of the backward regions'.[15]

The possible evolution of regional disparities in the case of a customs union

In the preceding section, we discussed the Giersch model. Its approach is, by definition, very simplified and theoretical. Therefore it is necessary to tackle the question: 'What can be the impact of a customs union on the difference between the incomes and employment created by existing activities and the incomes and employment created by new locations?'.

The possible evolution of existing activities

In chapter 1 we saw that the theory of comparative advantage cannot be applied to regions within a common market. The theory does apply to a certain extent to a country as a whole but not to all the regions of a country. It is possible that, while the overall situation of a country improves, the disparities within that country become worse. Moreover, even if the situation improves in all individual regions in an absolute sense, the relative disparities between regions may be left intact. It should also be remembered that the theory presupposes the reorientation of factors of production; in reality conversion of labour and capital tends to meet with strong resistance.

The neoclassical theory of international trade leaves little doubt that the creation of a common market would narrow differences in *per capita* incomes between member countries, because (a) free markets in principle lead to the equalisation of factor prices, and (b) free movement of goods is a substitute for free movement of factors. In chapter 1, we stressed that many basic assumptions are not fulfilled (it is not realistic, e.g., to assume perfect international mobility of factors, transportation costs are not zero, etc.). These imperfections are accepted by international trade theorists. Nevertheless they are of the opinion that although a common market cannot lead to a full equalisation of factor prices, the market mechanism will induce a narrowing of income differences.

We have already expressed our doubt about the situation in the real world. The deepening of the analysis will justify our reservations.

In the preceding section we mentioned increased competition as a direct consequence of the creation of a common market. Firms will seek better organisation; they may be interested in cooperation in certain fields and possibly in merging. The strongest firms will increase their power; the marginal ones are condemned to disappear.

The link between such competition effects and regional disparities depends on the location of the marginal firms. If they are relatively concentrated in the less developed regions, a customs union is apt to increase the imbalance. There is no evidence about the location of marginal firms, but it is known that backward regions have more small and medium sized firms than developed regions. In general we can assume that there exists a certain relation between the size of firms and productivity; the relationship varies from sector to sector. Furthermore, we may safely state that the economic climate in the backward areas does not stimulate dynamic industrial management. Firms in the peripheral regions are distant from the most important consumption markets in Europe (cf. the distribution of the population in the EEC countries and in the EEC as a whole). In fact there is a widening of the distance between the consumption centres and the peripheral regions. This brings about higher distribution and transport costs. All these factors lead to the assumption that the decrease of employment and income due to the behaviour of marginal firms will be relatively higher in the problem regions and, consequently, lead to greater regional disparities.

The peripheral regions are in an unfavourable position not only as far as costs are concerned, but also from the viewpoint of demand. Most of these regions are agricultural. The income elasticity for most agricultural products is rather low (see chapter 1). The elasticity consideration applies also to certain regions based on fuel industries.

One important remark should be made here. A theoretical approach always leads to generalisation. However, not all activities feel the impact of economic integration. Industries in which the constituent firms have an almost exclusively regional outlet will not be affected much. Firms based on the transformation of local natural resources are also better off. They profit from a spatial monopoly.[16] Such residential industries can stabilise regional employment and income but they are unable to stimulate export led growth.

As a general conclusion it can be stated that the overall employment opportunities and income levels in regions depend to a large extent on the growth or stagnation of existing activities. They are determined by the demand for regional products as well as by the competitive position. Although it may be impossible to indicate the impact of a common market on each region, the already underdeveloped regions are, after all, in a rather bad position as far as demand is concerned. From the viewpoint of costs, many peripheral regions are in a less favourable position than the central areas of the EEC. The problem regions are at a disadvantage in terms of competition, costs, and demand.

233

Although it may be difficult to express in a few lines how the creation of a common market affects the location of new firms, the general tendency can be distinguished. Among the many determinants of location, three important groups should be retained: (a) production costs, (b) demand factors, and (c) availability of external economies.

It is hard to say to what extent production costs favour the less developed regions. Disregarding external economies for a while, one must take into account the relative wage level, productivity, the social climate, distribution and transportation costs (see page 232), the availability of natural resources, the existence of port facilities, and aids in the framework of regional policy. There is one danger. The Common Market (we take the EEC as an example) may aggravate regional problems through a gradual tendency to equalise factor earnings. Freedom of factor movements and collective wage bargaining at Common Market level may cause regional factor earnings to approach equality.

One can be more conclusive in relation to the other two groups of location factors. Demand factors and the availability of external economies favour the industrialised and/or central regions of the EEC. The densely populated areas of the EEC are practically all situated in the centre and together represent about 50 per cent of the European market. G. McCrone has the same idea when he writes:

> The gradual replacement of national markets by a European market may lead firms increasingly to prefer a location at the centre of Europe . . . Suffice it to note that, in the past, within the national economies there has been a marked tendency for economic activity to be attracted to the market centres or areas of highest economic potential as defined by Clark.[17]

Demand factors and external economies will reinforce the existing industrial centres of the EEC because they will have a dominant influence on the location of new activities. One exception must be made. Problem areas in the centre of the EEC close to large industrial centres can become attractive location areas. They very often offer lower production costs than the existing centres and are close enough to the highly developed regions to benefit from the proximity of the market and from external economies. The location pattern of new firms in the 1960s sustains our thesis.

C. Clark, F. Wilson and J. Bradley come to the same conclusion in their study.[18] The aim of their research work was to examine which regions in Western Europe are most attractive to industry, and the effect which an enlarged customs union and developments in transport was

234

likely to have on the distribution of the most favoured regions.[19] Their original approach starting from the Clark idea of economic potential, merits special attention. (For an elaboration see chapter 4.)

To an increasing extent the regions of dense population provide some of the most vital inputs (diversified labour force, specialised services, repair services, easy contact with suppliers, government agencies, etc.) as well as the main markets. The capacity of a region to act as a market and as a supplier of inputs can be measured by its regional income. The area of greatest attraction to industry will be the region where the distance costs to all possible markets are the lowest. Central location is likely to become of increasing importance as the productive capacity of firms expands owing to economies of scale, and each firm becomes able to supply a larger market. Therefore, the further away a market is from a firm, the less attractive it will be.

An underlying hypothesis of the authors is the idea that the majority of industries can be described as footloose. The final conclusion of the authors sustains indeed the general conclusion formulated above.

> The economic potentials suggest that in future manufacturing industries will tend to locate and become concentrated within the Rhine valley of West Germany, eastern Belgium and the south-east Netherlands. Before the Treaty of Rome, one of the three areas of high potential was in Britain, but since that date and despite the assumptions made which directly improved Britain's position relative to the rest of Europe, the country has been shown to lie outside the central area of greatest potential in Europe. Since the Customs Union agreement entails not only the unhindered movement of goods across frontiers but also freedom of labour and capital, the possibility arises that the labour and capital of Common Market countries which are remote from the centre, will migrate to the centre, to the detriment of the countries on the periphery.[20]

The frontier regions

In chapter 1 we mentioned the fact that in many documents of the European Commission, the internal frontier regions are considered real problem regions.[21] The figures of chapter 2 do not sustain this thesis. We do not deny that there are problems specifically related to frontier regions. After all, they are peripheral regions with respect to the national core regions, although from a European point of view the income levels and the employment possibilities are not always that bad. We agree that a number of frontier regions are at the same time stranded areas, but that is another problem.

What are the specific problems of the internal frontier regions and how may they be affected by the creation of a Common Market?

Frontier problems

G. van der Auwera has summarised the problems of frontier regions.[22] They can be classified in two main groups: (a) socio-economic problems and (b) problems on the administrative and social levels.

The socio-economic problems may result from several different sources:

> monetary disparities;
> lack of harmonisation of legislation;
> structural differences and unequal development;
> insufficient employment stability;
> insufficient coordination of economic infrastructure.

Exchange rate changes due to devaluations, revaluations, or floating have an impact on the movement of the frontier workers and on international trade between the regions on both sides of the common border. Changes in competitive position caused by exchange rate changes have an important influence on the trade flows of the firms in the frontier regions. These firms are generally export oriented. The neighbour regions are very often a natural market.

Lack of harmonisation of legislation has an effect in such fields as social security (unequal contribution for employees and employers, unequal relief), environment regulations and tax systems. In the choice of working place, frontier workers are guided more by net direct income than by indirect social reliefs and advantages.

The frontier regions on both sides of the internal borders can have identical structures, complementary structures, or completely different structures. In the case of equal structures with identical structural problems, national concern for these regions may be unequal. There is no harmonisation of national regional economic policies; this implies the danger of unfair competition.

Frontier commuting is influenced not only by the above mentioned monetary disparities and the lack of harmonisation of social security, but also by the simple fact that frontier workers do not have the same employment stability as the national labour force. Frontier workers are the first to be dismissed in the event of an economic downturn.

As far as infrastructure is concerned (railways, highways, roads, canals, etc.) the lack of trans-border links is a well known phenomenon. Although a certain improvement can be observed as far as the basic economic infrastructure is concerned, there is little or no coordination in relation to medical infrastructure, power stations, airports, recreation facilities, etc.

The problems at the administrative and cultural levels can be summarised under three headings. First, there are the different institutional structures combined with unequal competence of the local authorities on either side of the frontier. Secondly, a number of purely administrative problems are very annoying, for example frontier controls, the absence of a good public trans-border transport system, the tarification of telephone connections. Thirdly, the non-equivalence of diplomas is another factor which limits the free movement of labour. We have to admit that very often the language differences constitute a real barrier to trans-border coordination.

A number of efforts have been made to cope with these problems. Here we should mention trans-border cooperation on the intergovernmental level, particularly intergovernmental agreements, and the trans-border agreements on the level of local and regional authorities.[23] The integration process stimulates such trans-border cooperation to a large extent. The results are not always what one would expect, however.

The economic impact of economic
integration on the frontier regions

It is evident that the creation of a customs union causes certain modifications in the structures of the frontier regions. The economic structures of the regions on either side are very often largely influenced by an economic barrier. That can be seen with respect to economic activities as well as infrastructure. The modifications entailed by a customs union depend on the degree of parallelism in the economic structures of the frontier regions.

In the case of identical structures, increased competition must follow. Closing of firms, mergers and concentrations are the consequence of a rationalisation process, which in the long run will benefit the frontier regions.

But also in the case of complementary structures, the frontier regions will profit by an integration process. The advantages may take two forms: (a) trade advantages, and (b) inter-change of factors of production.

There are two other fields in which the integration process will influence the frontier regions. First, it is very likely that the integration will increase the economic potential of the frontier regions for new locations. Secondly, and there is evidence of it within the EEC, better coordination of the economic infrastructure — railways, highways, canals — can be expected.

Rigidities within countries that do not exist between them

In his contribution to which we referred in chapter 1, 'Regional problems and common currencies', E.V. Morgan deals with the impact of a common currency on regional problems.[24] In many respects this contribution is original and provides an insight to the potential repercussions of a monetary union on the problem regions of the EEC (see page 240). Morgan's central thesis is 'There are rigidities within countries that do not exist between them'.

A region is a community trading with the rest of the world (other regions of the country included). There are three ways in which a region might run into balance of payments problems: (a) a fall in demand for its exports, (b) an increase in its imports (centralisation of services), and (c) the exportation of too much capital (centralisation of capital markets). As we have seen in chapter 1 these three factors explain, according to E.V. Morgan, how regions become depressed. If a region is unable to reduce its costs and prices relative to those of other regions, or if it cannot allow the value of its currency (in principle there is no regional currency) to fall on the foreign exchange market, the balance of payment deficit tends to depress demand and create stagnation and unemployment. The region stays depressed because 'there are important rigidities that impede the normal ways in which a market economy adjusts to changes in supply and demand'.[25] E.V. Morgan takes the example of South Wales confronted with a fall in sales of coal. The rigidities are numerous. First, a fall in the price of coal is unlikely because of the rigidity of costs and, possibly, monopolistic arrangements among producers. Second, the wages of mining labour are also very rigid. Their relative position on the pay scale (in comparison with other sectors) is an important factor in union bargaining, probably more important within a national community than in relation to other nations. Third, as spending power is reduced, South Wales is bound to have less demand for imported goods and a fall in demand for domestic products. On the other hand, the rigidity in factor markets leaves little hope of a fall in the prices of final products; indeed there are some constraints on price flexibility between regions that do not operate between nations:

(a)   Many of the firms operating in the depressed regions are branches of multi-plant organisations. Sometimes they produce similar products or components.
(b)   There seem to exist rigidities in relative wages between one

region and another. National bargaining imposes rigidities between regions that do not exist between nations.

(c) In a deficit region one would expect a rise in interest rates. The fact that the regions all have access to a centralised capital market prevents this.

(d) A common currency rules out any possibility of exchange rate fluctuations.

The question can be raised whether South Wales has been better off with the combination of relatively high income for those in employment, relatively heavy unemployment, and external aid, than it would have been if it could have devaluated its 'currency', dispensing with aid, reducing the real earnings of those in work, but also reducing unemployment and probably accelerating growth. A similar question was raised by G. McCrone[26] 'does it follow that some of the problem regions might do better as sovereign states?'. There is no universal answer to this question. In any case we have to be very wary of too simple an approach.

According to E.V. Morgan, aid can be available for one region but it is highly unlikely that Britain would get much in the way of aid from other members of a European Monetary Union. A decline in the demand for exports has to be met by a great number of individual price adjustments in individual markets for goods and factors, or by a general adjustment operating through the exchange rate. Devaluation may reduce or avoid many of the frictions that impede price changes. Account being taken of the influence of incentives in the framework of regional policy and the need to develop new industries in the depressed regions, and in the absence of wage flexibility, devaluation is the only way to create a generalised incentive to exploit new opportunities. In Europe we are confronted with the inverse question; what may be the regional impact of a monetary union with one currency or with fixed exchange rates?

By the above reasoning, many problem regions may get in a difficult position within a monetary union. That may particularly be true of the British and Italian backward areas.

The development of the Common Market must make its member states more like regions and less like 'old fashioned' countries. The abolition of trade restrictions and the 'harmonisation' of fiscal policies, social security, hours and conditions of work and legal systems will all reduce the number of instruments available to national governments for the regulation of their own economies. Already, international companies are extending their activities over Europe in the same way as national companies were extending over the regions two generations ago; already trade unions are paying increasing attention to wages and conditions in Europe; and already financial institutions are making the first move in a process that is likely to culminate in a European capital market. [27]

After all, the final suggestion of E.V. Morgan is not surprising. 'In these circumstances, the retention of national currencies with some flexibility in exchange rates could help to prevent temporary setbacks, at the national level, from turning into chronic depression'.[27]

The impact of a monetary union

The last section has brought us to one of the most important points of the regional impact of an integration process. If on the one hand a European regional policy is essential to the realisation of a monetary union (see chapter 10), on the other hand the latter may have a very great influence on the problem regions within the EEC. This explains the attitude of the United Kingdom and Italy during the discussions about an economic and monetary union in the early 1970s, and recently when the Summit discussed the European monetary system.

According to E. Nevin, there are three forces at work which explain regional imbalances as we know them in most countries.[28] (a) The declining use of labour in agriculture and the corresponding urbanisation of society; (b) the decreasing reliance of manufacturing industry on natural materials and the consequent emphasis on proximity to the final market, and (c) the increasing importance of the consumption of services leading to the backwardness of the peripheral regions and the concentration of economic activity in the centre in most European countries.

E. Nevin's line of thought is that differences in absolute costs of production in different countries can be largely eliminated by one or both of two very powerful national instruments: a tariff (or other trade restrictions) and the exchange rate of the national currency.

Hence the probability that any centripetal tendency inherent in the growth process will be stronger within countries than between them . . . Hence cost differences within a country are minimised, in the long run, by movements of labour and capital from areas in which returns are low to those in which they are high . . . It is precisely because that factor mobility is relatively high (to repeat, in the long run) that the problem of declining regions arises. Depopulation and decline do no more than confirm the proposition that

240

regional prosperity within any single country tends to depend on absolute, not relative, costs . . . [29]

The implication of an economic and monetary union for problem regions emerges very clearly. There are no more trade barriers and the power to vary exchange rates disappears. Therefore increased specialisation and the exploitation of economies of scale will accentuate, rather than reduce, the adverse pressures operating on areas in decline.[30] One can also expect that the centripetal tendencies clearly in evidence within individual countries must *a fortiori* exert themselves on the EEC level. The centripetal tendencies are also treated in the publications of H. Giersch and H.M. Stahl. H. Giersch wrote already in 1949:

The abolition of barriers to inter-European trade and to inter-European movement of factors will weaken the deglomeration effect of national agglomerations and will thus enforce international or more precisely, inter-European, agglomeration. It will strengthen the attractiveness of the highly industrialised centre both for labour and capital.[31]   (See also the Giersch model page 231.)

H.M. Stahl states:

It is indisputable that the creation of a monetary union may lead to savings of costs in view of the falling transaction costs and the elimination of deficiencies of the capital market. From a regional-political point of view this implies that the economic distance of the peripheral areas in the EEC, still accentuated by the situation of the consuming markets, is relatively diminished for the areas lying closer to the EEC centre. This shift of locational potential applies to both the EEC countries among themselves and to the regions of the member states . . . The centripetal powers coming into action in this way are characteristic for any integration process and should not be considered as specific to monetary integration. [32]

As far as the location of firms is concerned, one incentive to set up a branch firm in a peripheral country of the EEC disappears and the locational advantages of the regions close to common barriers increase. But H.M. Stahl does not overestimate this phenomenon.

However, the costs inherent to the existence of various currencies are only of little importance; when they are eliminated by the creation of a monetary union, the consequent shift of locational potential between the partner countries in favour of the centre and at the expense of the periphery and the resulting relocation of production in the EEC area is probably comparatively negligible. [33]

We agree that the thesis of H. Giersch and H.M. Stahl is not typical of a monetary union but, primarily, of a customs union.

Their pessimism is not shared by everybody. E. Nevin is the first to make two important remarks. In the first place it is extremely dangerous to generalise at industry level. Secondly, the integration process may stimulate economic growth. Regional policy intervention aimed at the improvement of the economic position of peripheral regions is easier in a climate of growth than in a stagnant economy. An economic and monetary union is one factor of economic growth.

Some ideas of E. Nevin can also be found in 'The All Saints' day manifesto for European monetary union'.[34] In this document nine prominent European economists recognise that the tendency for labour and capital to move to the central developed regions from the peripheral regions may be accentuated by a monetary union. They attribute it to the fact that wages in the peripheral low productivity areas may be increased to the level of those of the high productivity areas while differences in productivity remain unchanged.

> Consequently, unit labour costs in the peripheral areas may become so high that firms which previously were viable may no longer be able to pay their way and the prospect of a satisfactory return on new investment may disappear. Should that happen, capital would tend to move to the high productivity areas and thereby attract labour to move from the peripheral to the central areas. In Europe regional diversity is highly, and in our view rightly, valued. We consider, therefore, that monetary union should not be permitted to encourage the movement of labour and capital to the central developed areas at the expense of the peripheral and less developed regions. For this reason we look upon a vigorous regional policy as an integral part of monetary unification in the European community. We regard it as essential that such a policy should concentrate on eliminating the causes of regional imbalance by raising productivity levels in the poorer areas and that income transfers to alleviate the consequences of low productivity should be used as an interim measure only.[34]

The thesis expressed in the manifesto is known in the United Kingdom as the 'Pearce theory'. J. Williamson recently criticised this theory and stated that the Pearce theory must be rejected in its extreme form, as wage rates can and do differ between regions within a monetary union. However, J. Williamson agrees that there is some suggestion that wage differentials tend to be smaller within a monetary unit.[35] Basing himself on a purely formal model, J. Williamson states:

> The second effect will be that of adding higher paid populations to the reference group taken into account in the formulation and pursuit of wage claims. This will tend to lead to an increase in the level of wages in the region, but at the cost of a permanent rise in the level of unemployment. The region's disadvantage will be manifested to a greater degree in above-average unemployment and to a lesser degree than before in below-average wages. This will be disadvantageous to the Community as a whole, since output in the peripheral region will fall and there will not be symmetrical rise in output in the high productivity regions at the centre if demand management policy is dominated by a concern to avoid overheating in the central regions.[36]

Before the All Saint's Manifesto a similar reasoning was developed by H.M. Stahl.[37] His thesis with corresponding findings are most interesting.

Shifts in the spatial economic structure are the result of two influences. In the first place there is the abolition of trade barriers; the centripetal impact has been demonstrated above; it has only a relative importance. The second cause of regional distortion is the creation of a real monetary union. The very existence of the monetary union makes it impossible to neutralise certain competitive disequilibria between the regions within the union. If the member states of the monetary union harmonise their wage policies, either institutionally or de facto, wage costs per production unit may, from non-monetary causes, develop differently in the individual regions. Indeed, the impact of harmonisation measures is a function of differences in economic development between the member countries of the monetary union. Two situations must be distinguished: for countries with a similar development, which form a homogeneous group, monetary integration is not necessarily detrimental to the poorer regions or member states; if, however, the member states of a monetary union are in very unequal stages of economic development, locational advantages will accrue to the richer regions or countries. From the regional point of view, a monetary union between countries or regions with pronounced differences in development should be discouraged.

In the former situation the relatively greater increase of wages in the poorer regions or countries will not be pronounced or permanent. It is highly probable that the relative wage increase will be compensated by a relatively greater increase in productivity, by the abolition of other hindrances to integration (e.g. tax systems, equalisation of sectoral and regional aid systems), or by equalisation of profits. In the long run harmonisation of wage policy in these countries must lead to equalisation of wage increases. Insofar as regional policy measures or other instruments lead to relatively high increases in productivity in the poorer regions, a monetary union may guarantee the shifts in competitive power which are necessary for reallocations to the benefit of the less developed areas.

The latter situation is completely different. A monetary union of pronouncedly unequal regions should be avoided because of the real danger of a worsening of regional imbalance. The increase of wages in the poor regions may be so great that it cannot be compensated by growth in productivity. That leads to a disparity of remunerativeness between regions in favour of the richer ones. This confirms a well known thesis of H. Giersch 'The creation of a monetary union transforms balance of payments problems into regional problems'.[38]

The conclusion can be that a monetary union of regions or countries with small differences in development may help to make regional imbalances smaller. On the other hand a monetary union between regions or countries with important differences in development must provoke a worsening of regional imbalance.

The two cases are illustrated by regional developments in two independent states of the Community, West Germany and Italy, during the period 1961—69. The former stands for the above described first situation; the latter is a monetary union of regions with very high disparities.

H.M. Stahl takes as a measurement of the changed profitability of a region the change of wage costs per production unit, or, conversely, the change in the ratio of product per employee to wage per employee. The tests are based on the 11 Länder of West Germany and the 20 regioni of Italy.

The results for Italy can be summarised in a number of equations.[39]

$$\ln y = 10.207 - 0.351 \ln x \quad R^2 = 0.816[40] \qquad (6.1)$$
$$(8.426)$$

in which
  y = wage increase by region, 1961—69;
  x = wage level by region, 1961.

$$\ln y = 8.222 - 0.204 \ln x \quad R^2 = 0.731 \qquad (6.2)$$
$$(6.591)$$

in which
  y = increase of net domestic product per employee by region, 1961

−69;
x = net domestic product per employee by region, 1961.

$$\ln y = 2.157 + 0.176 \ln x \quad R^2 = 0.224 [41] \qquad (6.3)$$
$$(2.146)$$

in which
    y = profitability change by region, 1961−69;
    x = net domestic product per employee by region, 1961.

$$y = -175.422 + 20.146 \ln x \quad R^2 = 0.481 \qquad (6.4)$$
$$(3.848)$$

in which
    y = see eq. (6.3);
    x = wage per employee by region, 1961.

$$\ln y = 5.232 - 0.0028 \times R^2 = 0.775 \qquad (6.5)$$

in which
    y = see eq. (6.3);
    x = increase of wage per employee by region, 1961−69.

$$\ln y = 3.473 + 0.252 \ln x \quad R^2 = 0.397 \qquad (6.6)$$
$$(3.243)$$

in which
    y = index of employment growth by region, 1961−69;
    x = profitability change by region, 1961−69.

The main conclusions to be drawn from these results are:

(a)   wage increase, but also productivity growth was highest in the poor regions;
(b)   the regional levelling of wages in Italy overcompensated the regional levelling of productivity. In other words the most developed regions were able to improve their profitability in comparison to the poorer ones (see equations (6.3), (6.4), and (6.5));
(c)   given the improved profitability situation in the developed regions, we can expect a more rapid growth of employment in the North than the South. Equation (6.6) confirms that for the Italian case. The relative increase of employment was greatest in the regions with the highest profitability index.

These results completely conform to the theory. The author states further that the existence of two currencies in Italy (one for the North and one for the South) could have avoided such a strong wage levelling. In that case the Southern regions would have improved their profitability position in comparison to the North.

An analogous study was made for West Germany. The main results are to be found in the following equations. To facilitate comparison with the results for Italy and in order to avoid repetition, we use the same equation numbers as for Italy.

$$\ln y = 7.566 - 0.267 \ln x \quad R^2 = 0.247 \, [42] \qquad (6.1)$$
$$(1.716)$$

$$y = 6.84.612 - 53.344 \ln x \; R^2 = 0.534 \, [43] \qquad (6.2)$$
$$(3.213)$$

$$\ln y = 7.777 - 0.334 \ln x \quad R^2 = 0.736 \qquad (6.3)$$
$$(5.004)$$

$$y = 25.809 + 0.419 x \qquad R^2 = 0.597 \qquad (6.7)$$
$$(0.12)$$

in which
  y = profitability change by region, 1961–69;
  x = productivity index by region, 1961–69.

$$y = - 192.791 + 63.21 \ln x \quad R^2 = 0.453 \qquad (6.6)$$
$$(2.409)$$

The main conclusions with respect to the German case are:

(a) the wage increase is not significantly higher in the poor than in the rich regions; this is different from the Italian case;
(b) productivity increased most in the poor regions;
(c) the higher (lower) the productivity level of the regions was in the base years, the more strongly did the profitability position deteriorate (improve) (see the difference with Italy);
(d) the fact that the employment has increased most in the regions where profitability improved in relation to that in other regions, has led to a shift of economic activity towards the poorer regions.

In the context of the results obtained for Italy and West Germany another important conclusion should be underlined: migration was not influenced by inter-regional wage disparities. Migration was related to the unemployment rate, out migration being in favour of the regions that could improve their profitability situation and had a greater supply of jobs. That brings us to the conclusion that migration flows, in a case like the Italian, have a destabilising impact. They do not lessen the shifts between the regions' relative positions; on the contrary, they stimulate them.

The impacts of a monetary union on regions so far considered, namely (a) the tendency towards equalisation of money wage rates without a corresponding evolution of productivity levels and (b) the centripetal tendency, are also to be found in the well known study by G. Magnifico *European Monetary Unification.*

> . . . monetary unification is bound to strengthen the tendency towards equalisation of money wage rates, and to do so at a pace which might, on balance, be faster than that of the rapprochement of levels of productivity. The low activity regions will be more vulnerable to cost-push inflation caused by demand-pull in high activity regions. Other things being equal, their competitiveness will suffer. Of course, other things will not be equal. The depressed peripheral regions of member countries, countries which themselves happen to be in peripheral position within the larger Community area, will see the stimuli emanating from the national growth poles grow weaker, while finding themselves farther removed from over-expanding European centres.[44]

The impact of a monetary union on problem regions must be considered from another point of view as well. We have seen in chapter 1 that regional imbalances contribute to inflation; countries with severe regional imbalances are likely to have a greater propensity to inflation than countries where regional imbalances are less acute, and will therefore sooner resort to downward parity changes. But in a monetary union parity changes become more difficult. As a result, countries which face balance of payment problems are forced to rely on traditional, deflationary policies. It will be the weaker regions that suffer most.[45] [46]

This impact is very close to the Fleming/Cordon theory (see Graph 6.2). This theory is based on the assumption that each region has its own Phillips curve. Exchange rate flexibility permits each region to select its preferred position on its own Phillips curve, whereas monetary union compels all regions to accept a common rate of inflation. In equilibrium the region with the stronger inflationary tendencies does not have more inflation, but more unemployment.

J. Williamson makes one important remark in relation to this theory. 'The difficulty with this theory is that it provides no reason for expecting the peripheral regions to be the ones with the highest unemploy-

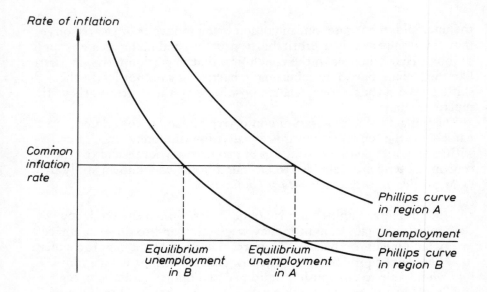

Graph 6.2

---

ment, since the theory does not offer a rational for supposing that the peripheral regions will be prone to suffer more serious wage push pressures than the others'.[47]

It should be emphasised that we disregard for the moment any regional economic policy on the Community level aiming at avoiding detrimental effects upon the less developed regions. In that respect the propositions of G. Magnifico are very interesting[48] (e.g. credit policy and twin economic policies for the high and the low activity regional groups, respectively).

In this context we must mention that fiscal transfers generally accompany monetary unions. Such transfers enable a low productivity region to cash in on some of the benefits of devaluation as far as unit labour costs are concerned, without the accompanying terms of trade losses.

A last aspect should not be ignored: the more open an economy, the greater the balance of payment effects of regional aid systems financed locally. The multiplier effects on income and employment tend to leak into other regions of the union.

H.M. Stahl proposed the introduction of two or more currency areas within the EEC to avoid the negative impact of a monetary union on a number of problem regions in Italy, United Kingdom, and Ireland, or on each of the three countries. Belgium, Luxembourg, the Federal

Republic of Germany, Denmark, France, and the Netherlands qualify for membership of a monetary union; Italy, United Kingdom, and Ireland, however, should remain independent currency areas. He even considers splitting up national currency areas into two parts.[49]

Not every author is of the opinion that a region would be better off with an independent currency. S. Holland states: 'For less developed regions in single currency areas there is little practical prospect of a unilateral declaration of monetary independence'.[50] The question can be raised what kind of region we are considering, for instance as far as size is concerned. The statement of S. Holland is based on three arguments.

First, the advantage of having an independent currency lies in being able to change the rate of exchange. The effect of a change depends on the region's structure of production, the structure of its foreign trade, and the size of its foreign trade sector. The larger the foreign trade sector, the lower will be the price elasticity of demand for imported products. For the price elasticity to be significant, there must be considerable possibilities of substituting imported articles by home produced ones. Those possibilities depend again on the structure of production. In view of the small scale, low income elasticity, and technological deficiency of the export sector in some of the backward regions, devaluation might well work adversely.

Secondly, devaluation alone cannot assure to a region the benefits of cumulative export led growth under any conditions, and cannot be a substitute for structural adaptation.

Thirdly, less developed regions, by resorting to devaluation of their currencies, stand to lose certain transfers and put in jeopardy the willingness of core regions to finance and help with their economic adjustment.

So far we have reviewed only the more traditional types of monetary union. In theory at least a strategy of parallel currencies also comes into consideration. According to R. Vaubel a European parallel currency could be a helpful instrument of EEC regional policy;[51] similar ideas are to be found in the work of G. Magnifico.[52] Because they differ in their propensity to inflation, EEC countries do not constitute an optimum currency area; therefore, G. Magnifico considers it undesirable and hardly feasible to form instantly a full monetary union, with one overall currency or currencies linked through rates that are irrevocably fixed, a common central banking system and a unified monetary policy.

If, however, there is the political will to unite, the question arises of how those countries could be made to meet the requirements of an optimum currency area. In my analytical framework, the compact answer would be that European countries would have to close the gaps in their NPI's (national propensity to inflation). This means that the process of effective integration of member countries needs to be pursued much further than is the case today. To second that process, a much wider and deeper opening of national markets is needed; also a series of convergent steps must be taken through the whole range of industrial relations, market monopoly and social exclusionist practices, education and social security, taxation, and general economic and monetary policies.

As far as these latter are concerned, I have put forward proposals with whose implementation a start could be made in the near future. The operations of a Multi-role European Bank could help to relieve an important cause of gaps in member countries NPI's. The creation of an additional European currency would represent a big step forward towards monetary unification, but in a way that would not do violence to the fact that NPI's differ, that member countries do not yet comprise an optimum currency area. It would make possible a gradual approach to integration, which would start now and be accomplished over a number of years (a quarter of a century?), thus bridging the gap, which is also psychological, between those who would like to see an instant monetary union and those who would prefer as remote a date as possible for departing from the traditional forms of national monetary power.

Final remarks

The analysis of the different theoretical approaches leads to the general conclusion that the fear of repercussion, expressed in the introduction to this chapter is fully justified: the creation of a customs union and also the formation of a monetary union may well lead to increased regional disparities. The founders of the EEC had too optimistic a view, in the late 1950s, of the positive impact on inter-regional trade. Perhaps that explains why such scant attention was paid to regional economic policy in the Treaty of Rome.

It would be incorrect, however, to deny any positive effect of the integration process on less developed regions. For one thing it makes for more economic growth (economies of scale effects),[53] *a conditio sine qua non* for a successful regional policy (see chapter 1); in a period of full employment the availability of labour becomes one of the most important location factors. For another it improves the geo-economic position. Moreover, certain specialisation effects through reallocation of output can be expected. Specialisation effects stem from differences in natural factor endowments; land and climate may be important in this respect. Actually the facts do not seem to confirm the theory.[54]

The theoretical approach was to a large extent based on a black and white situation: we have distinguished only rich and poor regions. That does not correspond to reality. In chapter 2 we made a distinction between several types of problem regions. It is one of the merits of L. Frey to define four types of regions as far as the integration impact is concerned,[55] namely: (a) highly industrialised regions, (b) stranded regions, (c) less industrialised regions situated near to a strong region, and (d) less industrialised regions situated a long distance from industrialised ones. For each of these types of regions he indicates the possible theoretical effects of market enlargement through economic integration (see Table 6.1). The two basic conclusions of L. Frey are in line with the ideas developed in the preceding sections:

(a) The productive structure of the different regions affects very strongly the distribution of gains from an enlargement of markets related to a process of international economic integration. The more a region presents a developed productive structure, open to technical progress, the higher will be the advantage of market enlargements. In the regions with a weaker productive structure, one can register the disadvantages due to the presence of less dynamic industries less capable of realising economies of scale.
(b) The effect of an economic integration process on the productive development of the different regions is profoundly conditioned by the rate and characteristics of the movements of population (and consequently labour force) and of capital in the medium and the long term. [56]

To relieve the rather gloomy prospects for the less developed regions, only a very pronounced regional policy on the Community level can help. Apart from that, some autonomous factors may work in favour of certain problem regions; they can be classified under four headings:

1 greater locational flexibility of basic activities due to fewer links with the soil, a changing economic structure, and the increasing significance of mobile external economies;
2 the diminishing share of transportation costs in the value added and the evolution of transport technology (size of ships, pipelines, slurry systems, gazoducs, containerisation, etc.);
3 modification in the supply of energy; think of new energy resources (natural gas, nuclear energy and the location of power stations);
4 the increasing importance of ports due to their industrial function and the switch from European to non-European raw

251

Table 6.1

The distribution of the integration effects in the different regions

Theoretical effects	Industrialised regions Type A	Stranded regions Type B	Underdeveloped regions near to an industrialised region Type C	Underdeveloped peripheral regions Type D
1 Economies of scale or mass production	higher than in B, C and D	higher than in C and D	higher than in D	less important than in other regions
2 Better utilisation of disposable resources (due to reduction of costs and geographical and sectorial mobility)	—Afflux of productive resources of high value —Increase of the LQ/L (LQ= qualified labour) —Technical adaptations to the higher capital intensity	—Efflux of LQ and capital —Afflux of non-qualified workers —Decrease of the LQ/L ratio —Difficulties in attracting capital on favourable terms	See type 3	—Efflux of labour and capital —Difficulties in attracting capital on favourable terms
3 Increase of resources (due to adoption of new techniques)	—A higher quantity of capital and LQ detrimental to other regions (in particular to the nearby regions)	—Difficulty in adapting to new techniques		

	A	B	C	D
4 Acceleration of specialisation on the international level	—Acquisition of the greatest part of the positive effects	—Possible negative consequences on the local balance of trade	See type B	less important than in other regions
5 Greater choice for the consumer	—More important than in region C and D		more important than in region D	
6 Greater mobility of factors of production (in particular labour)	—Afflux as mentioned in point 2	—Afflux and afflux (see point 2)		Efflux as in point 2
7 Increase of the competitive power on extra Community markets	—Positive effects very important	—Positive effects less important	possible negative effects on economic development	
8 Attraction of foreign capital	—Very important	—Rather limited (too great a specialisation in stagnating activities)	Less important than in the other regions due to the proximity to regions of type A	unimportant
9 Amelioration of the terms of trade	Highly in favour of the specific trade balance	Uncertain	Uncertain: possible deterioration	possible deterioration to the detriment of the specific trade balance

Source: L. Frey, op.cit., pp.136—7.

materials.[57]

Notes

[1] Bourginat, H., *Espace Economique et Intégration Européenne,* Paris, 1962. See also Bourginat, H., 'Inégalités régionales de développement et Marché Commun', *Bulletin Sedeis,* July 1962.
[2] Giersch, H., 'Economic union between nations and the location of industries', *Review of Economics Studies,* vol.17, 1949—50, p.91.
[3] Byé, M., 'Localisation de l'investissement et communauté économique européenne', *Revue Economique,* March 1958, pp.188—212.
[4] Perroux, F., 'La coexistence pacifique', vol. II, *Pôles de développement ou nations,* Paris, 1958, p.261.
[5] Perroux, F., 'Les formes de concurrence dans le marché commun', *Revue d'économie politique,* no.1, 1959, pp.357—9.
[6] Balassa, B., *The Theory of Economic Integration,* pp.203—4.
[7] UN Economic Commission for Europe, *Economic Survey of Europe Since the War,* p.218.
[8] Ibid., p.220.
[9] Birkelbach, W., *Rapport fait au nom de la Commission économique et financière, sur la politique régionale dans la CEE,* European Parliament, Document 99, 1963—64.
[10] Bersani, G., *Rapport fait au nom de la Commission économique et financière, sur la Première communication de la Commission de la CEE sur la politique régionale dans la CEE,* European Parliament, Document 58, 1966—67.
[11] See Frey, L., 'Intégration économique européenne et développement régional', Petrella, R. (ed.), *Le développement régional en Europe,* The Hague, 1971.
[12] Bourginat, H., op.cit.
[13] Giersch, H., op.cit.
[14] Bourginat, H., op.cit., p.8.
[15] Ibid., p.10.
[16] Bourginat, H., op.cit., p.15.
[17] McCrone, G., op.cit., pp.251—2.
[18] Clark, C., Wilson, F. and Bradley, J., op.cit.
[19] Ibid., p.197. Their study attempts to discover whether, if Britain were a member of the Common Market, any part of Britain would be included within the region of greatest potential for economic growth in Europe, or whether Britain would be relegated to a position on the periphery, and likely to decline in importance relative to the other countries of Europe.
[20] Clark, C.. Wilson, F. and Bradley, J., op.cit., p.208.

[21] CEE, *Première communication de la Commission sur la politique régionale dans la communauté économique européenne*, 1965. 'Proposition d'une décision du Conseil relative à l'organisation de moyens d'action de la communauté en matière de développement régional', *Journal officiel des communautés européennes*, no.C 152, 28.11.1969.

[22] Van Der Auwera, G., 'Les régions frontalières et l'intégration européenne', *Revue du Marché Commun*, no.182, 1975. See also Vanhove, N., *The Development of Flemish Economy in the International Perspective — synthesis and options of policy*, Commission of the European Communities, *Regional Policy Series*, no.1, 1973.

[23] Van Der Auwera, op.cit., p.72.

[24] Morgan, E.V., op.cit.

[25] Ibid., p.22.

[26] McCrone, G., op.cit., p.82.

[27] Morgan, E.V., op.cit., p.30.

[28] Nevin, E., 'Europe and the regions', *The Three Banks Review*, no.2, 1972, pp.56—7.

[29] Nevin, E., op.cit., p.58.

[30] See Also Marquand, *Report on Repercussions of Economic and Monetary Union on Regional Development*, Consultative Assembly of the Council of Europe, Document 3282, 1973, p.11. 'The abolition of tariff barriers between north and south after reunification led to the collapse of southern industries in the face of competition from the north. Industrial development was still further concentrated in the north, where there was more capital available for investment and where geographical factors were more favourable'.

[31] Giersch, H., 'Economic union between nations and the location of industries', op.cit., p.91.

[32] Stahl, H.M., *Regionalpolitische Implikationen einer EWG — Währungsunion*, Tübingen, 1974, pp 47-9.

[33] Ibid., p.220.

[34] 'The All Saints' Day manifesto for European monetary union', *The Economist*, 1—7 November 1975.

[35] Williamson, J., 'The implication of European Monetary Integration for the peripheral areas', in Vaizey, J., (ed.), *Economic Sovereignty and Regional Policy*, London, 1976, pp.105—6.

[36] Ibid., p.117.

[37] Stahl, H.M., op.cit.

[38] Giersch, H., *Marktintegration, Wechselkurs und Standortstruktur*, Fundamentale Fragen künftiger Währungspolitik. Frankfurter Gespräch der List Gesellschaft, 1965 (quoted by H.M. Stahl, op.cit., p.51).

[39] Stahl, H.M., op.cit., chapter D.

[40] (8.426) is a t-value.

[41] From the statistical point of view significant.

[42] From the statistical point of view there is no significant result.

[43] Gross domestic product instead of net domestic product.

[44] Magnifico, G., op.cit., p.90.

[45] Marquand, op.cit., p.26.

[46] See also T. Buck, 'Regional policy and European integration', *Journal of Common Market Studies,* June 1975, p.373. See also Magnifico, G., op.cit., p.10.

[47] Williamson, J., op.cit., p.110. He refers to Fleming, J.M., 'On exchange rate unification', *Economic Journal,* September 1971. Cordon, W.M., 'Monetary integration', *Essays in international finance,* no.93, Princeton, April 1972.

[48] Magnifico, G., op.cit., p.19 and also pp.279—320. 'The two policies would not need to be harmonised in actual detail. They might even diverge, for achievement of a common strategic aim might require action in opposite directions. In conditions usually described as "overheating of the economy" it might be appropriate to switch to restriction in the high activity group while pursuing more or less moderate stimulation in the group in need of economic invigoration'.

[49] Stahl, H.M., op.cit., pp.224—5.

[50] Holland, S., *Capital Versus the Regions,* 1976, p.95.

[51] Vaubel, R., 'Die Pläne für eine europaïsche Parallelwährung', *Die Weltwirtschaft,* no.2, 1972, p.138.

[52] Magnifico, G., op.cit., pp.74—5.

[53] During the period 1958 to 1972 the ratio of capital formation has increased from 21% to 24,3%.

[54] Van Ginderachter, J., 'Economic integration and regional imbalance', *Tijdschrift voor Economie en Management,* no.1, 1975, pp.54—5.

[55] Frey, L., op.cit.

[56] Frey, L., op.cit., p.134.

[57] Jürgensen, H., 'The regional impact of port investment and its consideration in port investment policy', in Regul, R. (ed.), *The Future of European Ports,* Bruges, 1971. See also Klaassen, L.H. and Vanhove, N., 'Macro-economic evaluation of port investments', in Regul, R. (ed.), op.cit.

7 Objectives and strategies of regional economic policy in EEC countries

Regional economic policy has three pillars: objectives, strategies, and instruments. In the present chapter we pay attention to the first two of these; instruments will be dealt with in the next two chapters.

The subjects of this chapter are spread over three major sections. In the first section we pay attention to three points: (a) the factors influencing the fixing of the objectives, (b) the evolution of the objectives and strategies, and (c) the present objectives of regional policy in EEC member countries. The criteria for selecting the regions to be assisted will be dealt with in the second section. The third section deals with the strategy of regional development. A special point will be made of the link between regional development and different types of growth poles.

The objectives of regional economic policy

Preliminary remarks

The objectives of regional policy are largely determined by the prevailing problems. In chapter 1 and chapter 2 we considered many types of regional problems. In underdeveloped regions the main aim is to build up an industrial or tertiary structure in a predominantly agricultural economy. In stranded regions, where the basic problem is an industrial structure dominated by old and declining industries, the aim of the policy may be defined as the adaptation or conversion of the region's economy to reduce the level of unemployment and increase income per head.

The objectives are also determined by an amalgam of political, social, and economic pressures. Here we refer to the first chapter and to the excellent contribution of M.C. MacLennan[1] that forms the backbone of this section.

For an active regional policy, the costs of letting certain regions decline or leave them underdeveloped must be compared with what it would cost in infrastructure and incentives to develop them. The outcome of the comparison depends on the weights the government attaches to certain objectives of social and economic policy. If the government accepts the social right of its citizens to live, and to be sure of a job, in their own region, it will not conduct a regional policy that aims at the optimum allocation of resources all over the country.

In the 1960s, the problems of underdeveloped or stranded regions were in many countries considered in the context of government policies aimed at achieving the maximum rate of growth of national output consistent with price stability and a balance of external payments. To that end, policies to develop poor regions or redevelop lagging regions were judged by the criterion of their effect on the national growth rate: are they likely to increase that rate within a reasonable period or will they rather reduce it by channelling resources to locations where they will be used less efficiently? [2]   Following that train of thought, M.C. MacLennan states: 'If this criterion is not satisfied then regional development will not be justified in terms of strictly economic costs. The authorities will then have to decide whether there are social and political factors important enough, to offset the reduction of national growth which regional development will produce'. [3]

Evolution of objectives and strategies

Since 1950 the objectives as well as the strategies of regional development have changed very much. Originally regional policy was regarded as a rescue operation for certain areas, often very small areas, justified on social rather than on economic grounds. Although in the United Kingdom the Barlow report stressed the need to diversify a region's industrial structure and encourage self-sustained growth, unemployment was the criterion of backwardness. The Dutch Government started with very small problem areas; they were chosen on the basis of unemployment rates. In France, too, a large number of small areas predominated; 26 'zones critiques' were qualified as problem regions in 1955, to be supplemented later by 'zones spéciales de conversion'.

In many countries the areas qualifying for help as 'problem areas' were too small to support a labour market of some consequence; applying 'rate of unemployment' as the main criterion meant, moreover, that the areas picked were often the ones with the least chances of development. Indeed, such a regional policy based on the criterion of local unemployment encourages the disregard of economic costs and development worthiness, and is apt to come into conflict with policies aimed at stimulating regional and national growth. In the late 1950s and early 1960s the interdependence of regional and national policies came to be recognised; in that same period economic rather than social motivations for regional policy came to the fore (see chapter 1). The criterion of growth was introduced into the regional policy of almost all European countries, and there was a renewed emphasis on the rational use of resources.

In 1958 the Dutch Government started to put the emphasis on development centres instead of the industrialisation centres on which attention had been focussed in the period between 1951 and 1958; thus it gave evidence of a more dynamic approach and of the intention to take account of growth potentials.[4]

In France the criterion of growth was introduced in the beginning of the 1960s. The Fourth National Plan, covering the period 1961—65, was the first plan explicitly to tackle the regional aspects of economic development. In it, a general distinction was made between the less developed regions of Western France, where a vigorous policy of stimulation (entraînement) was required to increase income, and the industrial regions of the North and East where a less intensive policy of 'assistance' (accompagnement) was to be applied. The French were also conscious of the loss of potential output which could result from expensive attempts to industrialise the West (the situation has changed since) and the imposition of excessive restrictions on the growth of the Paris region.[5] In this period the 21 regions became administrative units (since 1972 there have been 22 regions) and in 1963 a famous new institution, DATAR (Délégation à l'Aménagement du Territoire et à l'Action Regionale), was created. DATAR was to be 'an agency of coordination and stimulation' whose task it was 'to prepare and coordinate the information required for governmental decisions in regional planning and action, and to see that the various technical administrations adjust their actions and use the means at their disposal in the light of objectives beyond their respective responsibilities — an interministerial task that requires the authority of the prime minister'.

In the United Kingdom, the 1962 report on the Scottish economy (the Toothill Report) urged that regional policy should concentrate on developing selected areas within the declining regions by means of comprehensive infrastructure programmes and the allocation of newer, technically developed, high productivity, high income industries. The first British plan (1961—66) prepared by the National Economic Development Council in 1963 underlined that approach in the following ways:

1 It stressed the contribution to national growth which could come from the reduction of regional unemployment and the increase in activity rates by encouraging industry to move to the declining regions.
2 Regional development would reduce pressure on the labour markets in the expanding areas.
3 Regional development would obviate the need to impose deflationary measures to reduce the pressure of demand in those regions:

these measures aggravate the problem of the less developed areas (see chapter 1).

4 The alternative policy of encouraging the already considerable migration from the less developed regions was rejected (such a strategy would cost much more in social and economic terms than immigrant workers would contribute to national output.)

During the same period, the thesis of concentration of efforts was widely defended. The leading idea is found in OECD publications, 'The concentration of efforts in order to obtain the best results from limited resources is a fundamental notion of a regional development policy'[6] and in the contribution of MacLennan. 'The increasing attention paid to the cost of regional development, measured in both financial terms and in terms of growth of national output foregone, has resulted in a movement away from policies aimed at aiding all backward regions and towards a concentration on "growth poles"'(see technical and geographical polarisation in chapter 4. 'Following these lines regional development policy ought to aim at attracting particular industries to particular areas of a region and thus create an expanding, self-sustaining, industrial complex which will increase regional and national income. The aim of policy is in fact to stimulate the conditions which have allowed growth to occur in the more prosperous regions'.[7]

According to M.C. MacLennan the economically most important characteristics of the prosperous areas are the economies of scale and the external economies. Creating these in an underdeveloped region require both an industrial policy and an infrastructure policy. Two questions must be answered in view of an industrial policy, namely (1) What are the key industries of the growth pole?, and (2) What are the necessary characteristics of new plants? According to M.C. MacLennan, to fulfil its role successfully 'the plant must be large, achieving economies of scale, providing a sizeable initial boost in employment opportunities and affording the prospect of a reasonably sized market for components manufacturing and service industries, many of whom may be enjoying economies of scale in their existing locations'.[8] Here we refer to the notion of a 'propulsive unit' dealt with in chapter 4. L. Davin in his Liège study emphasises the metal working industries and chemicals.[9] In France, the Citroen plant at Rennes was envisaged as the focal point of a growth pole. A. Tosco concentrates on the mechanical engineering sectors.[10] As we have seen in chapter 4 his idea was to plan a complex based on primary units of such a size that their demand would allow sufficient economies of scale to promote the development of secondary and auxiliary units in sufficient numbers to supply the main needs of the primary inputs (horizontal integration).

MacLennan describes infrastructure policy in the following terms:

A growth area is an area where the prospects for self-sustained growth are most promising and which will act as a focal point for the growth in a wider region and over a period of time induce growth in other parts of the region. Growth area strategy aims at creating in a pre-selected area the necessary conditions for an industrial growth pole . . . The development of a growth area involves a decision to create in advance of industrial development the kind of external economies which normally follow the natural concentration of industry. This requires planned programmes of public investment to provide modern infrastructure services such as roads, ports, water, housing, industrial sites. [11]

MacLennan provides a very good justification of growth area policy: regional development will proceed more quickly and will be achieved at lower cost.

The national economy will benefit since fuller utilisation of resources and the creation of economies of scale and external economies will enable productivity to increase faster than if the resources devoted to creating these favourable conditions had been spread more widely over the region. [12]

The economic justification of growth area policy starts from the need to indicate and create an area where an industrial complex composed of the faster growing industries is likely to establish itself . . . The distinguishing feature of a growth area is that it provides land, labour and other factors on a scale large enough to meet the needs of a few really large firms capable of sparking off multiplier and linkage effects which would not be produced to the same extent by the combined activities of several smaller firms. [13] (See also definition of propulsive unit and forms of polarisation.)

This argument has important policy implications. It suggests that a growth area should be geographically fairly extensive. A commuting radius of up to 25–30 km from a main centre of population and industry would be a feasible labour market area. This radius can be even less in countries with a high population density such as the Benelux countries. The impact on inter-regional transport facilities, housing policy, auxiliary units within a radius of economic utilisation, is evident. A 'growth area' policy can thus be a necessary condition for improving living conditions in a lagging region. The large scale of urban development which it involves can be used to attract the growth industries required by offering them the facilities of a small or medium sized city, as a centre of regional expansion.

In a third phase, during the 1960s, a closer link was laid between regional policy and physical planning goals. In many countries better spreading of the population became a major target. In France, regional policy and physical planning are both incorporated in the notion 'Aménagement du territoire'. The policy, outlined in the Fifth Plan, of developing nine 'métropoles d'équilibre' as provincial counterweights to Paris, aims at reducing some of the costs which continued immigration would create in the Paris region.

The decongestion of London and the Midlands has long been a major preoccupation of the British authorities. In the United Kingdom and in France the social and economic costs (see chapter 8) of urban congestion forced the authorities to think in terms of channelling migration and population growth. That was one of the main reasons for modifying regional policy in the United Kingdom in 1963. Growth areas were indicated and regional planning started. It was a first attempt to relate economic planning to physical and transport planning.

In the mid 1960s the Dutch Government took a step in the same direction, as it became increasingly preoccupied with congestion in the Rimcity. More attention was paid to the link between regional planning and physical planning. This led in the beginning of the 1970s to the introduction of discouragement measures in the Netherlands (see chapter 8). Similar measures were taken in Italy for the same reason. In other European countries decongestion of large urban centres was widely discussed.

The recent relaxation of discouragement measures in all European countries does not herald a new stage; political pressures have forced many governments to be less stringent with the application of control. In a period of economic recession incentives are less effective too.

In recent years regional economic policy has been increasingly incorporated in an overall policy. Policy makers are more and more concerned that the classical approach to regional policy is insufficient to organise the national space; actions must be taken in all fields to accomplish the reorganisation. This is a leading idea in the French Seventh Economic Plan.

After these general considerations, let us now analyse in more detail present objectives in some of the EEC member countries. One preliminary remark is in order. No clear definition of regional objectives is to be expected. Rarely are objectives formulated in quantitative terms, they are sometimes much more a description of existing regional problems and fields of intervention than a well defined formulation of targets.

France [14]

Three major problems dominate French regional policy. The first is the imbalance between the Paris Region and the rest of France. The most innovative sectors are concentrated in the Paris Region. In 1973, out of the 500 largest French firms, 382 had their headquarters in Paris. Furthermore, relative population growth is rapid in that area. The Paris Region represented 16.8 per cent of the French population in 1946, in 1962 the share had increased to 18.2 per cent, and according to the Sixth Plan it was to increase to 19.0 per cent.

The second problem is the decline of employment in agriculture. As we have seen in chapter 2, agriculture constitutes a very important part of total employment in France. Between 1954 and 1974 the employment in agriculture fell by 50 per cent. The decline was very important in the West of France where two-thirds of the agricultural population live. That reveals a second disequilibrium in France between the more developed regions of the East and the problem regions of the West.

These regional problems spring from the complex processes of transformation. That is true of the agricultural sector but also of the industrial sector. The decline of basic industries — especially coal mining, the steel sector, and textiles — gave rise to the problem of stranded areas in France. Employment in the coal mining sector declined by 176,000 jobs between 1957 and 1971. The impact is particularly heavy in the regions Centre, Midi, Nord, and Lorraine.

Regional policy objectives have always been defined in very vague terms. DATAR undertakes actions of all sorts, as is emphasised by R. Prud'homme where he writes: ' . . . it can be said that regional policy was what DATAR did'. [15] O. Guichard in his publication 'Aménager la France' described the objectives of regional planning in the following terms:

> Public order objectives: disequilibria must not be aggravated dangerously; in some regions depopulation would be intolerable. Strategic objectives: we have already mentioned the removal of some defence industries. Social objectives: income disparities between regions must not be too great. The search for parity, more and more required by public opinion, has its limits, however; it should not lead us to welfare policies or to non-economic interventions that would freeze situations . . . Constant restructuring, together with some geographic and social mobility, is indispensable. Cultural objectives: public authorities cannot neglect performing this mission, through, for instance, radio and TV regionalisation;

and the location of colleges and universities. Economic objectives: regional planning must promote better overall economic progress. [16]

Other official documents are no more explicit: the goal setting is indeed very vague and unstable; it results from the two major goals ascribed to regional policy in the Fifth and Sixth Plan: (a) to maximise growth, and (b) to minimise social costs; and those mentioned in the Seventh Plan: (a) to stop the demographic decline of certain rural areas, and (b) to control urban growth. R. Prud'homme comes to the conclusion that the objectives of French regional policy are more easily defined in terms of sectors or of fields of intervention than in terms of broad goals. He then goes on to deal with five domains.[17]

1 Decentralisation of industry and tertiary activities
Four major goals are explicitly or implicitly stated:
(a)   to promote the creation of industrial employment in western, south-western and central France; according to the Sixth Plan, industrial and tertiary employment in these regions has to increase from 75 per cent to 80 per cent of total employment;
(b)   to facilitate the conversion of the North and Lorraine (declining industries); the Sixth Plan aimed at localising in these regions 30 per cent of the national net increase of employment in the mechanics, car construction, and chemical sectors;
(c)   to ease the difficulties of particular cities located in the other regions;
(d)   to restrict the growth of manufacturing industries in the Paris region.

2 Urban growth
Several leading ideas have been developed in this respect, new options being taken at regular intervals:
(a)   the defining of eight equilibrating metropolises (métropoles d'équilibre): Lyon (St.—Etienne), Marseille (Aix), Lille (Roubaix-Tourcoing), Bordeaux, Toulouse, Nantes (St. —Nazaire), Metz-Nancy and Strasbourg.[18]   They were a major commitment of the Fifth Plan, and were regarded as counterweights to the attraction of Paris. Such a policy based on the growth pole theory, was designed to promote the growth of all the large metropolitan areas outside the 'Région Parisienne', as the only realistic means of diverting jobs which would otherwise have been attracted to that region;
(b)   in 1967 a special effort was to be made for the medium sized cities located within a radius of about 100—200 kilometers

from Paris (e.g. Rouen, Troyes, Reims, Le Havre, etc.). This was considered by DATAR a less expensive policy than the creation of new towns;

(c) in 1970 the medium sized towns with 50,000 to 200,000 inhabitants were to be promoted. This was inspired by humanitarian and economic factors. That was once more emphasised in the Seventh Plan: 'The growth of small and medium towns should be faster during the Seventh Plan period than the one observed during the period 1968–75';

(d) the promotion of new towns in the Paris area (1964) and later on (Sixth Plan); plans were developed for new towns elsewhere in France (near Lyon, Lille, Rouen, Marseille);

(e) since the beginning of the 1970s, the promotion of Paris as an international centre has become more and more a policy target.

The conclusion is evident: urban growth is a policy of promoting everyone. It should be recognised, however, that the Seventh Plan advocates controlling the growth of the big centres, and favours small and medium towns.

3 Transportation
DATAR has coordinated and modified the actions of many public agencies working in the field of transport (long term plans for highways, changing priorities of regions, etc.). The Seventh Plan gives priority to the West, the South-West, and the Massif Central as far as the construction of highways and the modernisation of railways and canals are concerned.

4 Rural activities
The development of rural areas took two forms: (a) promotion of industrialisation in western, south-western and central areas of France, and (b) implementation of special programmes of rural renewal in Brittanny and Manche, Limousin-haut, Auvergne, and mountain areas. These programmes aimed at: improvement of communications, investment in education and training, increase of production and productivity in the agricultural sector, and development of industrial and tertiary activities.

5 Environmental protection.

Italy [19]
The main regional problem of Italy springs from the disequilibrium between the South, or Mezzogiorno, and the rest of the country. Many factors are responsible for the persistent dualism. The lack of

integration of the Mezzogiorno arose from natural conditions, peripheral location, social structure and traditions in the South, and, last but not least, national fiscal and foreign trade policies in the second half of the nineteenth century. The unification of Italy has favoured the industrial and commercial development of the North. Certain areas in central and northern Italy (representing about 14 per cent of the population of these parts) also have employment problems or demonstrate a rather low income level and high emigration figures. These problems are, however, relatively small compared to those of the Mezzogiorno.

A third major regional problem in Italy is the urban congestion. Along with the problem of the Mezzogiorno, Italy faces that of overcrowding in a number of large cities (Milan, Turin, Genoa, and Rome).

More than for other countries, in Italy we must make a distinction between different periods of regional policy, all of them, however, concerned with the dualism between the South and the other regions. V. Cao-Pinna distinguishes four periods:

> (a)   the 1947—57 period: tentative reorganisation of the agricultural sector and special public works in the backward areas;
> (b)   the 1957—65 period: promotion of industrialisation in the backward regions;
> (c)   the 1965—70 period: tentative coordination of projects and actions within the framework of national economic planning;
> (d)   the 1970—80 period: a new approach to national economic planning.

The distinction between the periods is to a large extent inspired by four factors: (a) the kind of economic activity to be stimulated, (b) the integration of regional development into national planning, (c) the change in instruments of regional policy, and (d) a number of institutional reforms.

During the first period the more equitable distribution of agricultural revenues was a prime objective; to that end, 700,000 ha of poor land (uncultivated 'latifundia') were expropriated and redistributed to farmers. A second objective was to exploit natural resources better by means of aqueducts, irrigation, etc., and to improve the basic infrastructure of the South; the creation of the Cassa per il Mezzogiorno in 1950 should be seen in that light. It is a government executive agency under the supervision of a Committee of Ministers for the South. Initially, the Cassa was instituted only to execute a ten year programme of extraordinary public works in the South.

Regional development was given a new orientation in 1955 by the 'Vanoni Plan' promoted by Minister Vanoni and carried out by SVIMEZ (Association for the Industrial Development of Southern Italy). It was a national plan for economic development over a period of ten years, but it had a spatial dimension. Two basic aims were: (a) the creation of 4 million jobs, and (b) the elimination of income disparities between the North and the South. The attempt to translate the Vanoni Plan into concrete action failed. Nevertheless, the ideas of Vanoni and of H.B. Chenery were changing the regional approach;[20] they inspired the industrialisation of the South, and constituted new approaches to the problem of economic dualism. Previously, most economists had advocated raising productivity in the agricultural sector or migration from the South to the North. Attempts to get the industrialisation of the South going started in 1957. Many ideas of the Vanoni plan were retained, such as the obligation of public and semi-public enterprises to locate at least 60 per cent of their new investments in the South, and the extension of the financial means of the Cassa. In that period the doctrine of 'polarisation' was introduced. The responsible interministerial committee stipulated that industrialisation efforts had to be concentrated, but efforts of concentration were diluted by local political pressure. Instead of a few growth poles, a large number of industrialisation nodes were created.

In the third stage the government wished to intensify the industrialisation of the South and to improve the coordination between the different departments and regional agencies. To that end regional instruments were intensified and institutional links established between the national planning systems (first national plan 1966—70), and the various agencies responsible for the development of the Mezzogiorno. The reformed interministerial committee for the South set up within the CIPE (Comitato Interministeriale de Programmazione Economica) was charged with the formulation of plans for more than one year. For the first time regional action formed part of a general plan of national economic development. At the same time new ideas or strategies were developed:

(a) to intensify the concentration of growth poles and the implementation there of special and integrated projects (integrated growth poles);
(b) to study the relationship between public intervention (infrastructure and incentives) and direct investments (contrattazione programmata);
(c) to pay more attention to non-material investments such as marketing, research, education, universities, etc.

It was also the first time that quantitative regional targets for the development of the South were incorporated in a National Economic Plan. Unfortunately the targets for the period 1966—70 were not reached.[21]

	Target	Actual performance
Employment in Agriculture		
Italy	− 600,000	−1,273,000
South	− 350,000	− 438,000
rest of the country	− 250,000	− 835,000
Employment in other sectors		
Italy	+ 1,400,000	+ 1,101,000
South	+ 590,000	+ 294,000
rest of the country	+ 810,000	+ 807,000

The new directions of regional policy for the 1970s were laid down in two official documents: the 'Project 80' and the Second National Plan (period 1971−75). Most of the ideas proposed in them were incorporated in a new Act for the South (1971), which was sustained by the acceptance of the national planning system and of administrative decentralisation (1972). At the same time the scope and the mechanism of public intervention in the South changed. The main regional aims presented in the two documents were:

(a) full employment all over the country;
(b) decentralisation of productive activities;
(c) higher quantitative and qualitative standards of social infrastructure;
(d) the design of a more comprehensive and rational space policy (geographical concentration of the nationwide industrial concerns) as a reaction to unplanned polarisation;
(e) redistribution of the urban population among thirty interconnected urban systems, eleven of which situated in the South, to relieve congestion in a number of cities;
(f) giving the South the following shares in GNP and gross industrial product:

	1970	1975	1980
GNP	24.0	24.4	25.7
Gross industrial product	14.4	16.4	19.0

Even the objectives are rather vague at this stage, the scope of public intervention illustrates a willingness to improve the economic position of the South. The new policy adopted for the 1970s finds expression in new policy instruments as well as in the extension of existing measures (see also chapter 8), or, more specifically:

(a) in the shares allotted to the South in the national fund for financing regional economic plans (60 per cent), in investments of public and semi-public companies, investments of public authorities, and in purchases of public goods;
(b) in special projects to be implemented in Southern Italy;[22]
(c) in disincentives in the framework of the decongestion policy;
(d) in additional resources for the Cassa per il Mezzogiorno;
(e) in social security concessions to induce labour intensive industries to locate in the South;
(f) in the authorisation of the CIPE to establish a special credit company for the South to help small and medium sized firms.

Finally, the administrative decentralisation achieved by the creation of new regional authorities may help regional development for financial resources and certain legislative and administrative powers are now given to the regions.

We can conclude that through all four stages it has been the aim of Italian regional policy to decrease the inequality between the Mezzogiorno and North and Central Italy. The stages differ more in the strategies and instruments used to achieve that aim than in the objectives. Industrialisation of the South, integration of the Mezzogiorno in national planning, and the extension of regional incentives and disincentives are the major changes.

United Kingdom [23]

The regional problem of the United Kingdom is not so much one of income disparities as one of a persistent disequilibrium on the labour market. While some regions have high unemployment rates and out-migration, there are other, developed, ones that are suffering labour shortages despite immigration. The problem springs from differences in industrial structure and, to a lesser extent, from differences in natural population increase. Some regions that had specialised in 'old' industries (coal mining, shipbuilding, textiles, steel manufacturing) have suffered an absolute loss of job opportunities and thus become the notorious 'stranded areas'. Continued migration towards the core regions has led to acute congestion problems in the London area and in the Midlands; moreover, conurbation areas are exerting inflationary pressure.

The labour reserve of the United Kingdom, concentrated in the peripheral regions, where the natural increase is great and female activity rates low constitutes a valuable resource in a country where the national labour market is expected to increase by no more than 3 per cent in the

Table 7.1

Labour market characteristics by region in the United Kingdom

Region	Population share		Population Natural increase 1961–71 (x1,000)	Migration per 1,000 population 1971	Unemploy- ment rate 1972	Activity rates, 1968		
	1951	1973				Male and female	Male	Female
South-East	31.1	31.8	99.6	−0.2	2.2	59.7	77.9	43.4
East-Anglia	2.8	3.2	8.4	+7.2	2.9	48.5	64.6	33.1
South-West	6.6	7.1	15.0	+5.9	3.4	47.0	63.5	32.2
East-Midlands	5.9	6.3	22.2	+2.1	3.1	60.2	78.4	42.6
West-Midlands	9.0	9.5	39.8	−0.3	3.6	56.3	74.1	39.3
Yorkshire and Humberside	9.2	8.9	26.5	−1.5	4.2	56.1	74.7	38.8
North-West	13.1	12.4	33.8	−1.7	4.9	58.1	75.9	40.1
North	6.4	6.1	17.3	−3.3	6.4	51.8	70.0	34.8
Wales	5.3	5.1	9.8	−0.1	4.9	47.1	65.6	30.1
Scotland	10.4	9.6	34.3	−6.2	6.5	56.4	74.5	40.4
Northern Ireland	*	*	17.3	−4.3	8.1	48.9	64.0	35.2
United Kingdom	100.0	100.0	324.1		3.9	56.2	74.1	39.8

Sources: G.C. Cameron, op.cit. and OCDE, op.cit.

*Not taken into consideration.

period 1967–81. The figures of Table 7.1 illustrate the regional problems in terms of population, unemployment and activity rates. These regional problems should be placed in the complex national context of a slow growth rate, fundamental changes in the industrial pattern, and a persistent inflationary pressure, and it should be kept in mind that traditional instruments for tackling the inflation have an unequal impact on the different regions.

The nature and the causes of regional problems are well known, but the objectives of British regional policy are vague; traditionally so, for British governments have always preferred open-ended targets. Even after the Economic Planning Boards for the eight planning regions of England and for Scotland, Wales, and Northern Ireland had been set up in 1965, governments remained loth to set quantified targets.

The implicit objectives of British regional policy can be brought under four headings:

1 to reduce unemployment and increase activity rates in the peripheral regions;
2 to slow down migration from the North to the South-East;
3 to diversify the economic structure of the stranded areas;
4 to stop the uncontrolled growth of the conurbation areas in order to reduce social costs and to check inflationary pressure.

These objectives are not so very different from those formulated in the famous Report of the Royal Commission on the Distribution of the Industrial Population (The Barlow Report) published in 1940.[24] This Commission concluded that on strategic, social, and economic grounds, the geographical distribution of population and industry led to serious handicaps, and that government action was required, to be guided by three main objectives:

(a) the redevelopment of congested areas;
(b) the decentralisation of population and industry from the congested areas;
(c) the encouragement of a 'reasonable' balance of industrial development throughout the regions.

One basic merit of the Barlow Report is that it emphasised the close interdependence of physical and economic planning as well as the interrelationship between congested and depressed areas.

The United Kingdom is the country with the longest history of regional policy; it started in 1928 when the government encouraged the movement of labour from the depressed areas to the more prosperous regions. In 1934 a new type of regional policy was started: industry

271

was encouraged to move to depressed regions. In the post war period different regional policies can be distinguished: [25]

(a)   the post war policy up to 1960;
(b)   the regional policy of the period 1960—64;
(c)   the policy of the period from 1964—70;
(d)   the policy of the 1970s.

The new element in post war regional policy as conducted between 1945 and 1960 was the control, by means of Industrial Development Certificates (see chapter 8) of the location of industrial development. It was not practised in the same way throughout that period however: government priorities changed in response to the business cycle, general economic problems, the boom in such traditional industries as coal mining, shipbuilding, and steel industry, which lasted until 1958. There was a tendency to relax regional policy in times of boom, the very times when it was most likely to be effective.

The sharp increase in unemployment in many regions in the late 1950s led to the 1960 Local Employment Act. Development Areas were replaced with Development Districts, but the greatest change was the intensification of regional instruments. The main concern of the government was to provide employment in districts of high unemployment. The motives were social rather than economic and location policy was concentrated on narrowly defined districts rather than larger areas. Later on the social approach lost ground and in the National Economic Development Council's report more emphasis was laid on conditions fostering growth; [26] for the first time attention was paid to the growth point theory; growth points were to be encouraged in larger development areas. It was this report that inspired the Labour Government reforms of the period 1964—70. The major changes were: (a) the introduction of Regional Economic Planning Councils and Regional Economic Planning Boards, and (b) the 1966 Industrial Development Act, which replaced the Development Districts by Development Areas (1966). Later on Special Development Areas (1967) and Intermediate Areas (1969) were introduced. The 1966 Industrial Development Act also introduced radical changes in the field of incentives and disincentives (wage subsidies, investment grants, strict IDC control). According to P.J. Randall, the Special Development Areas are clearly a return to the Development District Concept. For the latter regions the criterion for designation as a Special Development Area was a high rate of unemployment; the potential of such regions for economic growth was disregarded. [27] In the Hunt Report it was recommended to give to seven small regions in the neighbourhood of Development Areas the status of 'intermediate regions' to compensate them for the loss of potential development they suffered because of the incentives offered in Development Areas.

The 1970s policy is not basically different from the policy pursued in the period 1964–70, but the return to power of a Conservative Government in 1970 did bring a number of technical changes. The Special Development Areas and the Intermediate Areas were extended (additional designation of Intermediate Areas). New regional measures were outlined in a White Paper which lead to the 1972 Industry Act.[28] The new system is considerably more generous than the old one, emphasis being laid on the modernisation and extension of existing firms within the problem areas. The mere attraction of new projects to assisted areas had failed to bring relief to Development Areas, and so the toolbox of regional policy was reorganised in two ways. First, the 1972 Industry Act no longer reserves grants for projects that provide employment; henceforth modernisations are also subsidised if the work force is kept at par and the 'building infrastructure' improved. Secondly, the grants will also be available to firms already located in Development Areas as well as in the Special Development Areas, on the same conditions as to firms from outside.

Growth point philosophy is another feature of the new regional machinery. This philosophy is not new; it was already mentioned in the Barlow Report and was a strategic element during the previous period of regional policy. The question can be raised whether growth pole policy is compatible with the definition of Development Areas and if it does not discriminate in favour of growth points.

Germany [29]
Equal living conditions in all parts of the country is one of the aspirations laid down in the Constitution of the Federal Republic of Germany; this general target was recast in a more specific form in the 1965 Federal Spatial Planning Law of which Art. 2 stipulates: 'In regions in which the living conditions in their totality are significantly lagging behind the federal average, or in which such lags are to be anticipated, the general economic and social conditions as well as the cultural facilities shall be improved'. It should be emphasised that in Germany income disparities and disequilibria in the employment balance are not of the same magnitude as in many other European countries. Neither does Germany face the conurbation problems of the United Kingdom, France, and Italy. Germany has twenty-four conurbation zones of population (Verdichtungsräume), but they are far smaller than such zones in England or France. Moreover, these population centres are spread evenly across the whole territory, a factor of the utmost importance for regional policy strategy. All German Länder have also been able to profit from a generally high growth rate, which has stimulated German

firms to move to regions where labour was available. The movement started in the late 1950s. Nevertheless, there are regional problems in West Germany. About 20 million Germans live in, for Germany, poor economic regions or areas with a deficient structure. In 1971 in these regions the income *per capita* was about one-third below the national average, a situation that does not satisfy the principles of the Basic Law of the FRG.

The less developed regions, or stranded regions, can be classified in three groups:

> the 'Zonenrandgebiet', an approximately forty kilometer wide strip of land along the East German and Czechoslovakian borders and along the Baltic Sea in the North. This area suffers from the interruption of traditional trade relationships;
> the agricultural regions (in Schleswig-Holstein, Niedersachsen, and Bayern);
> the stranded regions like the coal basins in the Ruhr area and the Saar.

Germany's regional policy springs from two preoccupations. First, the governmental authorities consider it their task to create, and guarantee to all citizens of the country, equal chances in life. Secondly, they want to mobilise all regional development potentials in the pursuit of national economic growth.

German regional policy further operates on two levels, encompassing both spatial planning and regional economic development, each with their own goals. The major objectives of the 'Raumordnungspolitik' — spatial planning — are the improvement of living conditions in rural and depressed areas and the correction of socially unhealthy patterns of spatial settlement, particularly in urban and industrial agglomerations, by controlling the spread of people and infrastructure. The concept of 'Raumordnung' refers to 'spatial organisation' as well as to 'spatial orderliness', two ideas that are, of course, related.

The 1965 Federal Spatial Planning Law indicated the necessity of consultation and coordination between the federal and state governments in matters concerning spatial planning problems. In 1967, therefore, the State and Federal Intergovernmental Cabinet Commission for Spatial Planning (MKRO) was established. The Federal Spatial Planning Law identifies, apart from the Eastern border zone, two categories of regions as its principal targets:

> In the first category are areas where the overall living conditions are significantly below the federal average, or where such a situation is to be anticipated. In order to reduce differentials in living

conditions the states were asked to specify for their respective areas of jurisdiction central places within acceptable distances to all inhabitants, and to assist in the development of adequate infrastructure services for such central places. Subsequently, MKRO prescribed a four-level hierarchial central place scheme for criteria for the selection of central places and their appropriate infrastructure facilities. The second category includes areas in which the concentration of employment and residences has reached a level which could endanger healty spatial living and working conditions as well as balanced economic and social structures [30]

In 1968 MKRO identified twenty-four such Verdichtungsräume; they represent 45.5 per cent of the total population and 6.8 per cent of the territory.

The goals of regional economic policy are more limited in scope than the broad spatial planning goals. According to G. Krumme, there are four motives behind the German Government's regional policy: '(a) the mandate of the German Constitution to guarantee equal living conditions; (b) the necessity to create an optimal economic structure in order to ensure that unused and underutilised factors of production are being mobilised for economic growth; (c) the task of facilitating adjustment processes which result from structural problems in already developed regions; and (d) the problems of Germany's division and the related separation of an integrated economic unit (economic assistance for Berlin and the Zonenrandgebiet)'.[31] The major aim of regional economic policy in Germany is to set up the best regional economic structure and to see that all potential resources are used. Regional policy must attempt to increase the economic capacity of regions with a weak structure, and to offer better employment prospects and better wages.

Since 1969 the alleviation of regional problems has been a joint task of state and federal governments. This does not mean that regional policy did not exist before. The support of depressed regions started in 1952 as an emergency measure (rescue operation). The subsequent changes in terminology reflect some of the changes in regional policy objectives during the 1950s and the 1960s (from emergency areas to rehabilitation areas to expansion areas). The policy towards the Zonenrandgebiet started in 1953. Worth mentioning is also the effort made towards deliberate spatial bundling of federal support in selected centres. In 1959 the 'development programme for central places in rural, structurally weak areas' was introduced. Present regional policy objectives and strategies are incorporated in the famous 'Regional Action Programme', introduced in 1969. In 1971, the twenty-one action regions covered about 33 per cent of the population and 58 per cent of the territory (West Berlin excluded).[32] Each action

programme contains the employment objectives and the level of anticipated expenditure. Their main characteristic is coordinated and spatially concentrated assistance. The focuses for concentration are the
'gewerbliche Schwerpunkte' or the industrial development centres. In
1972 no fewer than 312 Schwerpunkte were selected; their minimum
population size was fixed at 20,000 inhabitants. These growth poles are
of four different types; for each type a different grant rate is applied in
function of the urgency of the needs. In contrast to practice in the
United Kingdom, regional assistance is practically entirely oriented
towards Schwerpunkte within each of the programme regions, and the
employment objectives are quantified.

The Netherlands [33]
Dutch regional policy also started as a rescue operation; during the
period 1951—59 it aimed at combating regional structural unemployment in nine problem areas. In 1959 the policy became less social and
more economic. During the second stage, from 1959 to 1969, the
objectives changed greatly. In addition to the combating of regional
structural unemployment, much attention was paid to a better dispersion of economic activities and population. Overconcentration in the
Rimcity (Amsterdam — The Hague — Rotterdam — Utrecht) became a
concern of first priority. According to the spatial planning programme
prepared during the 1960s, the aims were:

1 to check the strong out-migration of population which threatened to drain the economic and social life of peripheral areas;
2 to avoid excessive income differences among regions; and
3 to avoid excessive congestion in concentrated areas.

Problem areas were replaced by Development Areas, within which
development nuclei were designated. Only towns that had good chances
of attracting new economic activities were eligible. However, as in the
case of Germany, too many poles were selected.

In a third phase, which started in 1969, the structural unemployment
in some regions remains the government's primary concern. The
Netherlands were still confronted with a labour surplus in the North
(agricultural area) and a conversion problem in Limburg. But at the
same time more and more emphasis was given to the dispersion of
industry and economic activities. The latter objective was explicitly
stated in a bill purporting to limit investments in congested areas by a
selective procedure (see chapter 8). To enforce the new policy, a
number of other targets were set and measures introduced.

1 In a Memorandum on the North of the country, it was stated

that 'attention should be drawn to the location of industries with very capital intensive production processes'.[34]   This was a reaction to the fact that the industrial moves to the Development Areas did not create sufficient jobs for skilled labour.

2 The dispersion of government institutions to the North and to South Limburg was advocated.

3 The creation of one urban agglomeration in North-Groningen as a counter-magnet to the Rimcity was suggested.

Belgium [35]

To get a proper idea of the regional problem in Belgium we must separate the North (Flanders) from the South (Wallonie). Both parts of Belgium comprise areas of high unemployment and/or relative low income.

The regional problem of the North springs from various causes. Certain areas, such as Westhoek in West Flanders, the Kempen, and Limburg, suffer from a structural unemployment problem due to an insufficient industrial tradition and/or high increase of active population. Other regions are confronted with declining employment opportunities in such traditional sectors as textiles, leather, and coal mining; West and East Flanders (textiles) and Limburg (coal mining) are cases in point. The province of Limburg is now the area within Flanders with the greatest employment problem and the lowest income level.

In Wallonie the regional problem also has two different causes. The South of Belgium has a very old industrial structure (coal mining, steel, etc.) and lacks of industrial initiative; the combination has provoked persistently high unemployment figures. The conversion problem is typical of the provinces of Liege and Hainaut. The province of Luxembourg has, like Limburg, a relatively low income level and suffers, moreover, from its peripheral situation in relation to the rest of Belgium.

Regional policy was introduced in Belgium in 1959; its objectives were never clearly defined. According to the criteria retained in the legislation, there are two regional policy targets: combating underemployment (due to unemployment, commuting, declining activities, or more general deficits in the employment balance), and reducing regional differences in income level. A third objective can be added: the regional authorities have always tried to diversify the industrial structure of stranded areas.

As in most other countries the objectives are open-ended. It should be emphasised that the Provincial Economic Councils (at present the Regional Development Authorities) on several occasions made efforts to quantify the objectives, or at least the employment objective. Such efforts were also made in the study 'The development of the Flemish economy in the international perspective', carried out for the

Commission of the European Communities and the Belgian State.[36]

Denmark

Denmark, too, knows its regional problems, though less pronounced than those in other EEC countries. There are two aspects to regional disequilibrium in Denmark: high unemployment figures in the rural areas, and concentrated growth in the urban centres, particularly in Copenhagen. The rural areas, principally in the North West of Jutland, in spite of a sizeable emigration have unemployment rates which are three times the national average. Two figures aptly illustrate the concentration phenomenon: the Sjaelland region accounts for about 50 per cent of industrial employment and about 55 per cent of tertiary employment.

The fisheries on the West Coast of Jutland and above all on the Faroe Islands and Greenland, constitute a special regional problem; other activities — agriculture in Jutland, sheep breeding on the Faroes, mining in Greenland — develop but slowly in those parts.

Objectives of regional policy are very loosely formulated in Denmark; back in 1958 the main purpose was to combat unemployment. Regional policy was started in earnest in 1967 with the designation of development areas, the main targets being to decrease regional disparities as to job opportunities, and to stop the out-migration from rural areas. The 1967 and 1972 laws bid for development of industry and other economic activities in the country's less favoured regions, in order to enable the people there to enjoy a fair share of the country's economic, social, and cultural progress.

Ireland

Ireland is a special case within the EEC. The economy of this country is far below the EEC level (see chapter 2) and there is a marked out-migration problem. The annual rate (per 1,000 inhabitants) of out-migration amounted to 5.7 per thousand in the periods 1961—66 and 3.7 per thousand during the period 1966—71. Only the East region (Dublin) escaped out-migration, which brings us immediately to the large difference between the Dublin region and the rest of the country.

	Population 1971	Economic structure 1971 Employment in major sectors as a percentage of total labour employment		
		Agriculture	Industry	Services
East region	1,062,000	6.2	38.1	55.7
Ireland	2,978,000	26.4	34.9	38.7

In such a situation the first concern of the Irish Government is evidently the industrialisation of the whole country and the increase of the country's share in international trade. Attention is paid to the needs of the least developed regions, but it is not an exclusive concern; that means that in Ireland, more than in any other country, regional policy has national significance. Although the first measures were taken in 1952, the objectives must be derived from the 1969 Industrial Development Act and a number of new measures proclaimed in 1972. The regional aims and strategies can be summarised in five points:

1 In the framework of regional policy the country is divided into three areas:
   (a) designated areas in the West (55.9 per cent of the territory and 32.5 per cent of the population;
   (b) the Dublin regions;
   (c) the rest of Ireland.
2 The Industrial Development Authority has the task of distributing new activities all over the country, but that does not imply correcting any too high concentrations. This illustrates that regional development is one component of the Industrial Development Authority's industrialisation task.
3 The urban structure of the country is to strengthen so as to create a counterweight to the attraction of Dublin; special measures are taken to stimulate the expansion of Cork, the Limerick-Shannon -Ennis zone, Waterford, Galway, Dundalk, Drogheda, Sligo, and Athlone.
4 The growth of Dublin must be kept within the limits of the natural increase of its population (no restrictive measures are taken to control the size of Dublin).
5 A goal closely linked with the previous ones is that of keeping people in their home areas. It is the Irish Government's policy to support and encourage the use of the Gaelic language in the Gaeltacht, the part of Ireland where it is still spoken; to that end the government aims at giving those who live there a chance to find remunerative employment and to enjoy a reasonable standard of living.

Unlike in most other countries, the employment target is quantified in Ireland: the Industrial Development Authority fixed for each planning region a quantified employment target for the period 1973—77.

Criteria for the selection of regions
to be assisted

The previous section not only indicates the objectives of regional policy in each individual country but gives also an idea of what problem areas are. Problem areas are not by definition 'assisted regions'. There is in practice a large overlap between regions with socio-economic problems and areas to be assisted. The extent to which this overlap is justified can be a point of discussion; we have the impression that on more than one occasion areas without problems have received assistance. In all EEC countries the assisted areas cover a large portion of the territory and of population (see Map 7.1); the figures in Table 7.2 are illustrative in that respect. Only in the Netherlands is the population share rather low.

Table 7.2
The percentage of population and territory covered by the
assisted regions in the EEC (a)

	Assisted regions	Percentage of population	Percentage of territory
France (b)	Zones for investment grants (4 categories)	31	47
Italy (c)	Mezzogiorno and assisted areas of the North and Centre	54(43)	86(37)
United Kingdom	Development Areas, Special Development Areas, Intermediate Areas, and Derelict Land Clearance Areas	44	66
Germany (d)	Regions covered by a Regional Action Program	38	59
Netherlands (e)	Development zones	16	26
Belgium	Development zones	33	28
Denmark (f)	Development zones	31	56
Ireland (g)	Designated areas	31(100)	56(100)
EEC		41	61

(a) Source: Internal EEC document, 1975.
(b) Excluding areas which benefit only from tax exemptions.
(c) The corresponding figures for the Mezzorgiorno alone are 43 per cent and 37 per cent.

Table 7.2 continued:

(d) West Berlin included.
(e) Development poles outside development zones are not included.
(f) Greenland excluded.
(g) Incentives are given to industry and services throughout the territory; *vis-à-vis* the rest of the Community they have the effect of regional aids.

It is rather surprising that the assisted regions in the EEC should represent 41 per cent of the population and 61 per cent of the territory; one can hardly speak of a discriminatory policy in favour of a limited number of regions to be developed. That brings us at once to the question how development areas are selected. Study of the legislation and of official documents of the individual countries, and of comments on them, leads to two conclusions: (a) in most countries there is no systematic approach, and (b) all kinds of groups are exerting pressure to extend the incentive systems to new areas. The absence of any systematic approach does not mean a lack of criteria. Numerous are the criteria that are meant to objectify the selection: *per capita* income, unemployment rate, evolution of population, out-migration, share of agriculture in total active population or local employment, number of jobs per 1,000 inhabitants, long distance commuting, actual or imminent decline of important economic activities, industrial structure, slow economic growth, abnormally low standard of living, actual and future imbalance of employment, distance from a big city, etc. The enumeration gives rise to two remarks. First, most of the indicators are not independent factors but have obvious mutual repercussions. Secondly, most if not all of these factors are in fact negative socio-economic factors. Seldom is a locational advantage or the development worthiness of a region considered. We agree that more attention is paid to economic potential in the selection of growth poles within the designated areas than to the selection of assisted regions.

To avoid the problem of interdependence between factors, we are in favour of two basic criteria: (a) the present and expected situation of the employment balance, and (b) the income level. Possibly migration should be added as a third factor.[37] In the employment balance several factors are integrated: evolution of active population, labour reserve due to low activity rates, disguised unemployment, unemployment, commuting, increase or decrease of employment possibilities in existing firms. Two situations should be taken into account: the present and the medium term situation. Forecasting an employment balance for longer than five years ahead is a useless and risky operation.

Map 7.2: Regions in which the European Regional Development Fund can intervene (1978) (omitting overseas areas)

The following table presents in a schematic way the different items to be considered; in fact, separate tables like this should be drawn up for each level of skill.

Present employment balance situation (year t)	— Supply of labour in the region —Possible surplus of job opportunities <--- or ---> e.g. immigration	Demand for labour in the region Possible deficit of job opportunities composed of — unemployment — disguised unemployment — long distance commuting — labour reserve due to low activity rates
Medium term employment balance (year T+5)	— Present deficit of job opportunities — Autonomous increase of labour	— Present surplus of job opportunities — Autonomous increase of demand for labour
	Surplus <--- or --->	Deficit

A few years ago an interesting effort was made in Germany to delimit the development areas according to objective criteria, defining them as units of economic activity instead of political or geographical units. The actual or potential weakness of each region is derived from three major criteria: (a) labour potential (labour surplus based on a present and a forecast employment balance); (b) income level (wage level, income per active inhabitant); and (c) infrastructural situation (highways, railways, energy supply, schools, medical services, etc.).

For each of the 170 German regional labour markets index values of the three criteria were fixed, weighted and added up. The weighting system is based on the following coefficients: potential labour: 1; income: 1; and infrastructure: 0.5. In this way a classification of the regions according to priority is achieved. In a second stage two further criteria: labour density (number of non-agricultural jobs as a percentage of total active population), and the number of inhabitants, were used to identify the centres of the labour markets qualifying as growth poles within the labour market areas. Only towns of a certain size possess a labour market large enough to justify the location of several firms of varied size and specialisation. [38]

The selection of criteria to delimit development areas is, of course, not unrelated to the particular situation within each country and the targets of regional economic policy. Indeed, the German system just described is quite suitable for analysing the labour market situation in Western Germany and defining regional objectives for that country.

If it is not easy to select objective criteria for identifying problem areas, far more difficult is it to integrate factors that indicate a region's economic potential. There are many such factors. The employment balance is an important location factor; the social and economic resistance that could be involved by measures to enhance a region's economic potential could well be even more important. Indeed such a policy could cost the government the support of other regions.[39]

In an attempt we made a few years ago, we proposed the following criteria for the selection of a limited number of regions that should help to boost the national growth rate:

(a) there should be a sufficiently large centre which could be the basis of a take off;
(b) growth must be possible at reasonable cost;
(c) the amenities of life and external economies must be better than in other problem regions;
(d) the economic structure must provide good starting points for a further growth;

in addition, the group of regions had to be sufficiently spread over the country.

The strategy of regional development

Regional economic policy is usually presented under two headings: (a) objectives, and (b) instruments. A third, equally important, aspect is, however, the strategy of regional development, that is, the path that should be followed to realise the objectives with the support of the available instruments.

There are several aspects to a strategy of regional development:

(a) the preparation of regional development plans;
(b) the role of regional development authorities;
(c) the choice of the regions to be assisted;
(d) the option of concentrated or non-concentrated efforts within the designated areas;
(e) the choice of the centres to be developed;
(f) the option with respect to the deconcentration of congested areas;

(g)   the economic activities which must be given priority;

(h)   the decentralisation of power to the regions.

There are no uniform solutions to the problems encountered with each of these aspects of development strategy; there are many factors that intervene:

(a)   the objectives of national economic policy;

(b)   the objectives of regional policy;

(c)   political considerations and the influence of pressure groups;

(d)   the degree of development of the country considered;

(e)   the density of population in the regions;

(f)   the distribution of large cities about the country;

(g)   the type of regional problems;

(h)   the economic structure of the regions;

(i)   the existence of conurbation areas and their geographical situation within the country;

(j)   the size of the country.

The aspects and influencing factors enumerated show us how complicated the strategy of regional development is. Yet we believe that national governments should pay more explicit attention to their development strategy, which now is often only implicit.

The first section of this chapter repeatedly refers to strategic elements, such as growth poles, development axes, 'métropoles d'équilibre', propulsive units, deconcentration of institutions, sectors to be promoted. It is highly interesting to compare regional development in France, Germany, United Kingdom, and the Netherlands from the strategic point of view.

In this section it is not our intention to analyse the subject in depth from the theoretical point of view or to explain the strategy followed in the EEC countries. We restrict ourselves to a limited number of aspects: (a) how many regions should be promoted? (b) what is the relationship between growth pole theory and regional development? (c) how big should a centre be? (d) what kind of investment and activities should be promoted? (e) what is the role of a regional development agency?

To present these matters in a lively manner we shall illustrate them with practical examples derived from the regional policy of EEC countries.

How many regions should be promoted?

From the second section of this chapter the impression may have been gained that the number of regions to be promoted is very large. We have already pointed out why there are so many problem regions in each country. Regional underdevelopment is a relative notion and in the last two decades people in developed countries have become extremely sensitive to income disparities or unequal job opportunities. From the economic point of view it is desirable for a government to stimulate economic development in a limited number of regions, what with scarce capital resources to finance regional development and the high level needed to assure a self sustained growth process. For developing countries another argument in favour of regional concentration can be added. In most developing countries people who are skilled enough to elaborate and properly implement regional plans are scarce.[41] The scarcity of capital and skilled staff for regional promotion and the complete lack of external economies in the areas to be assisted are arguments for restricting the number of regions to be promoted in developing countries even more than in developed ones.

The relation between growth pole theory
and regional development

The theory of growth poles was analysed in chapter 4. On page 260 of the present chapter we referred to the link between this theory and regional development, a link that is clearly recognised by J.H.P. Paelinck as he states: ' . . . the theory of polarisation is a conditional theory (théorie conditionelle) of regional growth; it has a special value in that it clearly indicates the conditions under which accelerated regional development can occur'.[42] In that sense the theory of growth poles is a strategic conception.[43]

In applying the growth pole concept to regional policy, two elements should be distinguished. The first concerns the definition of 'growth pole' as (a) a functional relationship in an abstract space; (b) a geographical concentration of activities, and (c) a functional polarisation in an economic space (localised functional growth pole, see definitions in chapter 4). The second element concerns the type of depressed regions: (a) the problem regions close to strong regions; (b) stranded regions, and (c) peripheral problem regions. According to K. Allen the pressured regions may also be counted among the depressed areas.[44] The combination of these elements allows a number of general policy rules to be fixed.

First, the growth pole in its purely functional conception, as it was developed by F. Perroux, is not useful for any regional policy. F. Perroux intended to provide a development theory and not a workable method for regional growth.[45]

Secondly, a growth pole, in the sense of a growth centre ('nucleus', Schwerpunkt'), is a workable concept in a strategy for less developed areas that are not too far removed from a developed region or large city.

In the Benelux countries and in Germany, the situation is like that. In Germany, to quote P. Wäldchen,[47] the large towns are historically dispersed such that all development areas are within 200 to 250 km from large industrial centres; in the Benelux, where everything is on a smaller scale, the distances are smaller. With large centres near, population density high, and the infrastructure network adequate, new projects can be attracted to problem areas even if there are no auxiliary, subsidiary, and intermediate companies in the growth nuclei themselves. In the growth poles, income polarisation and psychological polarisation can be expected, but intersectoral relations tend to be established in a larger space. That explains why for instance in Flanders not much technical polarisation can be observed within a radius of 30 km.[46] Indeed, for development areas at a relatively short distance, industrial growth poles seem less suitable than so-called secondary centres, or central places. [47] The size of the nuclei, which is variable, will be discussed in the next sub-section.

Thirdly, in a stranded area, where the basic problem is the extinction of former propulsive units, it may be good strategy to concentrate activities either in the old nucleus or in a new one.

Fourthly, the geographical conception of growth poles may be the one to use with success in peripheral regions, far from a core centre or core region. In that case, the growth centre should have a certain minimum size. Actually for this type of region we would plead the combined of functional and geographical version of a growth pole repeatedly referred to in chapter 4 by the name of 'localised functional growth pole'; the method proposed by A. Tosco to develop Southern Italy is based on that concept. A few points of the theoretical approach may be recalled in that connection. Before a firm decides to start a new activity in a growth pole, it will compare its requirements with what the growth pole has to offer in the way of inputs, labour market, and socio-cultural amenities.[48] Once the new project is operative, it will make the local input structure more diversified and stimulate the amenities of life; thus a cumulative growth process is set going.

In the context of the fourth policy rule given above four remarks are in order:

1 in peripheral regions, regional actions should be concentrated in a small number of centres; the size of the pole is important too;
2 the growth of the pole cannot be based exclusively on relations between firms; economic overhead capital and social overhead capital, to use the terminology of N. Hansen, are essential;
3 although sector bundles are important, they cannot be the only starting point; a harbour, a big industrial project, a university, can

also incite polarisation processes;

4 lastly, the development worthiness of a region should be considered. If an isolated problem area has no centre of 50,000 inhabitants provided with a minimum of amenities, local initiative, and a good economic structure, or, if development should entail high costs, a solution must be found outside the region. [49]

Growth pole theory is not only a strategic conception for the development of depressed areas, it can also be usefully applied for restricting the growth of conurbations and spreading growth among medium sized and larger cities. In that respect the policy of 'métropoles d'équilibre' in France and the role of growth centres in pressured regions as overspill and interception centres (in the terminology of K. Allen[50]) may be cited.

Let us first take K. Allen's ideas. A number of countries are confronted with the problem of achieving the greatest possible reduction of pressure in the congested conurbations at a given cost. Overspill population can be either spread over a larger number of centres or concentrated in a few (large) centres. If the overspill population is not large, if there is no spare infrastructure in the receiving towns, and if these are not short of labour, K. Allen argues that it is economically preferable to concentrate the overspill in a few large centres. That is not only inevitable, but also desirable as far as it brings about two other advantages. '. . . first, that a large concentration away from the main conurbation is likely to take proportionally more pressure off this conurbation than would be the case if the overspill was spread. Secondly, a large concentration may allow economies of scale in the provision of infrastructure'. [51] A further argument for concentrating overspill in centres rather than spreading it, is that large centres are likely to be more stable than smaller ones because of the prospects of greater diversification.

In concentrated regions, growth centres may also act as 'interception centres'. K. Allen describes the relevant strategy in the following terms: 'It is to surround the major conurbation with selected centres, normally based on existing fairly large settlements, which will intercept the flow of population into the major conurbation, relieving it therefore of the pressures which would otherwise occur'.[52] These interception centres should be sufficiently large to be able to provide most of the services and facilities of the major centre.

In the British and French conception of urban planning and in the framework of decongestion policy, new towns were planned and constructed. They could be, among other things, interception centres.

The experience of several years has not been positive for various reasons: (a) new towns are a physical planning device. They are designed to appeal to people who already live in urban areas and are attached to them. (b) The construction of new towns is a very costly operation. (c) Location decisions for new towns are not made so as to maximise their chances for industrial development. (d) The population is not positive, or is in any case hesitant, in its attitude towards the artificial character of a new town (repetitive and monotonous in terms of physical design). These four factors are the main reason why in the last few years more attention has been paid to the extension of existing medium sized towns within a radius of 100 to 200 km from congested areas. N. Hansen's thesis supports such a policy: '. . . a more realistic approach to the problem of rechanneling migration streams might be to build on existing external economies in growing cities . . . '.[53]

One obvious question is what the size of overspill and interception centres should be; we return to this point in the next sub-section. Overspill centres and interception centres are theoretical notions frequently used in French regional policy; a 'métropole d'équilibre' is equivalent to an overspill centre, and several medium sized towns within 100 to 200 km of Paris act as interception centres (see page 263).[54] N. Hansen, writing about cities in the Paris Basin,[55] remarks:

> In particular, it is necessary to define as soon as possible the policy which should be pursued concerning the organisation of cities circling Paris at a distance of some hundred kilometres. These urban centres — Amiens, Rouen, Chartres, Orléans, Troyes and Reims — should become key sites for the economic development and urbanisation of the Paris Basin. In addition, policy in this regard should be established in terms of the principal transportation axes which follow the valleys of the Seine and the Oise, and to a lesser degree, the Marne and Yonne'.

While the British discourage new activities near large towns, the French system actually promotes the cities that circle the conurbation.

The policy of the 'métropoles d'équilibre' is a major topic of the French Fifth Plan. To check the growth of Paris, urban growth has to be oriented towards alternative locations; at the same time the idea has been conceived to develop a few provincial agglomerations into growth poles that should stimulate their own spheres of influence. That strategic idea has been inspired by many French authors, among them not only the obvious one, F. Perroux and J. Boudeville, but also P. Bauchet and F. Bloch-Lainé. P. Bauchet argued that all French citizens should be assured of having basic administrative, social, health, and educational activities which come under the responsibility of public authorities, at a reasonable distance from their homes. 'Experience shows that these functions attract and reinforce one another in the same centre, while developing badly in isolation'.[56] When there are no major provincial centres providing such services, people will demand them in Paris; 'the transfer of these activities — business headquarters, study laboratories, insurance, publishing — empties the provinces of managers and other leaders and overcrowds the capital'. Planning authorities have attempted to establish an urban hierarchy in terms of functions performed by urban centres. In that context F. Bloch-Lainé states: 'The whole of the territory is polarised by an urban network . . . This hierarchical system constitutes the "armature urbaine". Because it governs the distribution of population and activities; it can be one of the essential elements in a long run strategy of "aménagement du territoire"'.[57]

The eight 'métropoles d'équilibre' defined in the Fifth Plan were, in a European context, rather large cities; in comparison to cities of a similar size in other European countries, however, they show pronounced deficiencies in the field of cultural activities, commerce, banking and finance (the eight 'métropoles' taken together have a financial importance which equals about one-tenth of that of the Paris region), educatson and research, headquarter function (French métropoles are rarely headquarters of national administration and private companies), and equipment in services. To make them into a counterweight to Paris, the eight 'métropoles d'équilibre' received priority as far as public investment in culture, research, higher education, specialised hospital equipment, administration, and transportation is concerned. The essence of the 'métropoles d'équilibre' is not to have a large population but to perform certain functions.[58] They were designated to provide a balance to Paris and to stimulate the region where they are situated.

It was to be expected that the new policy would provoke much opposition. There was not only political pressure but there were also theoretical objections. N. Hansen made a synthesis of the criticism, and found that three objections are very often made. The first is that concentrated development of the 'métropoles d'équilibre' would drain the surrounding regions as Paris has drained France as a whole, the extreme consequences being the transformation of the countryside into a desert. The second objection against this policy is a corollary of the first. On several occasions F. Gravier has warned against the creation of external diseconomies;[59] it is feared that the proliferation of tertiary activities will in turn induce industrial activities to settle in the new agglomerations. Here we return to Aydalot's thesis (see chapter 4) that the propulsive industry is not a cause of polarisation but rather an effect of it. The third objection against the 'métropoles' is related to the high growth rate of smaller cities, which creates additional needs; a spreading of investment would be of more general benefit. Another weighty argument is that of the growing public hostility to large cities with over 500,000 inhabitants. Population increase, though, is not an explicit aim of the policy, it may well be an implicit consequence.

These objections seem to draw too black and white a picture. Drainage of surrounding regions and congestion in the 'métropoles' were never aims of the new policy. The Fifth Plan stressed the need to define more carefully the hierarchic urban structure of France. The 'métropole' cannot be seen in isolation from its region; it rather complements the rest of the region's urban pyramid. Towns at the base of the pyramid can be given priority with regard to industry, while the 'métropole d'équilibre' may be given priority as far as education, research, and deconcentration of administration is concerned.

In the French Sixth Plan (1971—75) the conception of 'métropoles d'équilibre' was maintained but completed with a few new orientations: [60]

1 the promotion of medium sized cities in order to realise semi-concentration of population and economic activities. A consideration which inspired this new attitude is the desire to preserve and to exhance the environment (conditions de vie);
2 in the 'métropoles d'équilibre' the French Government tries to ameliorate the environmental as well as the technical conditions of economic development, by replacing radial concentric urbanisation, with development along axes. The idea is to draw population to the axes and to the large capacity traffic infrastructure; in practice the two will coincide. Masterplans to realise this new orientation have been prepared for, among others:
the valley of the Seine;
Dunkerque-Lille-Valenciennes;
Lyon-St. -Etienne-Grenoble;
Marseille-Aix-en-Provence-Fos.

We believe that the French policy of 'métropoles d'équilibre' has its merits. It is a valuable conception, which must be seen in the context of the French urban pattern and within an urban hierarchy. It is true that the policy of 'métropoles d'équilibre' cannot be applied uniformly in the whole country. The position of Lyon in Rhône-Alps cannot be compared with that of Nantes in the West, a distinction that was not sufficiently realised from the start. The system can only work, however, if the authorities responsible for regional matters have sufficient power and instruments to realise the conception.

How big should a centre be?

As we have seen on page 286, growth centre strategy has been instituted in numerous industrial countries during the last three decades. In most cases growth pole theory was developed in the sense of growth centre policy (see Germany, Netherlands, Ireland, France, and to a certain extent Italy). The definition given by N. Hansen illustrates quite well the aim of the national governments, although he envisages applying it in vast, less developed regions at a great distance from large centres; 'A growth pole is an urban centre of economic activity which can achieve self-sustaining growth to the point that growth is diffused outward into the pole region and eventually beyond into the less developed region of the nation'. [61] According to N. Hansen growth centre policy should be based on unbalanced growth, favouring urban places which are intermediate to congested areas on the one hand and lagging areas on the other. It should also concentrate on growth centres as poles of attraction for commuters and migrants. Thus, concentrated investment in growth poles would help to develop lagging regions by making scale and agglomeration economies available to them; moreover, they would attract migrants who would otherwise go to large congested urban areas.

We admit that the German and Dutch outlooks are slightly different from the French one. Owing to the geographical structure in both countries, smaller places tend to be selected as growth centres. The geographical pattern is important, but the activities we want to attract should also be considered: propulsive tertiary activities are more demanding in terms of city size than basic industrial activities. The same is true of interception centres.

The above consideration already suggest how difficult it is to give general rules for the selection of growth centres, especially as regards their size. Let us concentrate our analysis on the development of lagging regions at a great distance from developed regions. The problem then is not so much what is the optimum size for a centre, as what is the minimum size required to provide the range of services needed by people and firms, and what is the impact of size on growth potentials. We refer for this problem and the problems to be treated below to chapter 5. N. Hansen paid full attention to these problems. His analysis and the authors he quotes suggest that the city size offering the best chances of regional development in lagging regions lies between 100,000 and 250,000 inhabitants. [62] This is also the thesis of K. Allen and L.H. Klaassen. [63] L.H. Klaassen and N. Hansen mentioned a second condition: that priority should be given to centres that are growing fairly fast, for the simple reason that such places are demonstrating their ability to create new jobs. Yet there may also be cities which, though not growing so fast, may have real growth potential.

B. Berry has found that the necessary conditions for self-sustaining growth seem satisfied in centres with a population above 250,000, and he suggests that the greatest pay off in terms of increasing employment and reducing unemployment would be achieved by using the public treasury to enable centres close to that size to achieve self-sustaining growth rather than sinking resources into much smaller places.[64]

W. Thompson suggests that, when the population of an urban area reaches a critical size of around 250,000, structural characteristics, such as industrial diversification, political power, huge fixed investments, a rich local market, and a steady supply of industrial leadership will virtually ensure its continued growth.[65]

E.A.G. Robinson reports:

> The general sense of our discussion was that the minimum size of growth points that experience had shown to be successful was nearer to a population of 100,000 than to one of 10,000 and that even 100,000 was more likely to be an underestimate than an overestimate. It must be large enough to provide efficiently the main services of education, medical facilities, banking, shopping facilities ... Above all it must be large enough both to provide an efficient infrastructure of public utility services, and to permit the early and progressive growth of external economies for its local industries. [66]

In his contribution 'Efficient regional resource allocation and growth centre policy' N. Hansen states:

> Such tools (public overhead capital) have been applied to promote economic growth in rural areas and small towns but they have been not only economically inefficient, but largely ineffective too. To be sure, there may be some sites in rural areas with promising industrial potential, but the most efficient use of public funds would be to encourage the growth of medium size cities, especially those which have given some real evidence of growth characteristics.[67]

In a more recent contribution he is more precise as far as the size is concerned:

> In general, then, the evidence supports the proponents of growth spurt threshold, but suggest that the threshold tends to be in the 150,000 to 200,000 range, somewhat lower than the usual estimate. However, there is no evidence of automatic self-sustained growth following the spurt.

Large cities should not be considered; even if they exist, they have reached or passed their optimum size. Here N. Hansen's thesis is very formal:

> . . . though it is agreed that small towns rarely make viable growth centres, the intermediate sized city often does have the necessary conditions . . . There is evidence for believing that self-sustained growth is more easy to maintain in a city of 200,000 than in smaller places. On the other hand, external diseconomies may make expansion of alternative locations desirable from an opportunity cost viewpoint after a city passes the 750,000 mark. [68]

All this is proof of the inter-relationship between the growth pole concept, economic growth, and urbanisation.

In the framework of this section K. Allen's analysis is particularly interesting. [69] Starting from the objective of realising the fastest rate of regional growth at a given national cost, he raises the question whether a growth centre policy is likely to ensure faster regional growth and/ or whether it is likely to be the cheaper policy (for instance in terms of infrastructure). According to K. Allen large cities offer to industry the evident advantage of attracting more industry and of fast growth, mainly owing to external economies. These economies are due to: (a) proximity to suppliers and markets (see horizontal integration); (b) the possibility of a larger and more diversified labour market; and (c) the greater possibility of finding services for both people and industry (education, hospitals, maintenance and repair services, etc.). His conclusion is that the larger the centre, the greater the external economies. But in chapter 5 we have seen that the social costs involved in a city are not independent from its size. K. Allen analysed the relationship between social costs and city size. He examined three main costs: (a) the costs of providing infrastructure in towns of various sizes, (b) the management costs of these towns, and (c) other social costs imposed upon people (e.g. travel to work). He comes to the conclusion that the composite average cost curve covering infrastructure costs, management costs, and travel costs, tends to rise only slowly between towns with populations of about 30,000 and 250,000. Next he converts the composite average cost curve into a net cost curve — net of the benefits which people gain by living in towns of various sizes (net average social cost curve). Two conclusions are relevant to our argument. The author first states:

> It can be argued, and this is the line that we intend to pursue, that when the cost curve is made net of these benefits then the resultant curve is flatter than the simple cost curve as far as the slightly higher infrastructure costs and higher travel costs at the upper population range of 250,000 will to some extent be offset by the satisfaction gained from the facilities available in the large towns. There are a number of personal services which are highly desirable

and only likely to be found at higher population levels.[70]

The second conclusion is related to the question whether a net average social cost curve would ever turn upwards to any degree and at what population; it reads: '. . . above 250,000 it may be that the additional costs are in excess of the additional personal benefits and our net average social cost curve rises much faster than previously'.[71] The conclusion that can be reached from these two findings is that the optimum size is a range between 30,000 and 250,000.

A very important point to be dealt with now is the probability that industrial needs are satisfied in centres of various size. We mentioned above that the larger a centre is, the more attractive it is likely to be for industry. This brings K. Allen to a very important conclusion:

> If this is the case, and given a fairly flat net average social cost curve, then the benefits for industry arising out of population size would encourage one to try for the upper end of our range of 30,000—250,000 and perhaps even above, though it seems likely, most external economies having already been secured at the higher level, that the additional benefits for industry would be offset by the higher additional personal social costs like travel and infrastructure.[72]

The author remarks that it is quite possible that the size of growth centres (100,000 to 250,000 inhabitants) which satisfies the objective of achieving the fastest rate of growth at given national cost, is not acceptable. Then the objective must be changed. A modified objective might be the fastest regional growth at given national cost compatible with an acceptable balance within the region. The obvious question is then: 'Is there a minimum size below which it is unwise to fall?' K. Allen argues that the minimum is probably somewhere around 30,000 inhabitants, basing his statement on (a) the infrastructure cost curve, (b) the need for the provision of basic services to industry, (c) the need for a reasonably large and diversified labour market, and (d) the need for a labour reserve which is not likely to be completely exhausted with the settlement of a new project. He stresses that the figure of 30,000 is very much a minimum. With such a size it is highly unlikely that a firm finds suppliers of materials and semi-finished manufactured goods on the spot. Moreover, centres of 30,000 inhabitants are unlikely to be found in sparsely populated areas. In that case a growth centre must be created. K. Allen calls that an 'active' or 'initiating' policy opposed to a 'passive' or 'reinforcing' policy. In the latter case development is concentrated in existing centres. Growth centre creation is an attempt to build up a centre from a small size to a population level beyond the threshold of about 30,000. The closer to the threshold the centre is, the easier it will be for that centre to develop. He offers one alternative that brings us back to the concept of the localised functional growth pole.

> Easier perhaps, and capable of taking even a small centre well beyond the threshold, would be to make use of an inter-related industry complex. This would involve a planned simultaneous build-up, in the centre, of a group of firms which depend upon each other for supplies and markets and to plan the complex so that there are sufficient component firms and of sufficient size to gain adequate economies of scale to make them competitive outside the region. These complexes are not all easy to plan or implement, though the benefits from a successful complex, particularly in the circumstances above, could be very great.[73]

We are very doubtful, however, about the possibility of realising a localised functional growth pole in a relatively small centre. There is one more consideration in K. Allen's study worth mentioning. In the long run the need for larger settlements seems to increase. Four factors point in that direction: (a) infrastructure is becoming increasingly indivisible and sophisticated; (b) industry is becoming more and more specialised and less vertically integrated, making greater demands on services and other suppliers; (c) there will be a greater need in the future to secure development in the depressed regions; that can only be done if the beneficial aspects of larger conurbations are simulated in the lagging regions; (d) proximity will remain an important location factor.

What kind of instruments and activities should be promoted?

In this section we want to make two basic points. The first is related to growth centres. It is not sufficient to select a number of rapidly growing cities of intermediate size. The objective of growth centres in vast lagging regions is to stimulate employment, the basic problems of these regions being, indeed, spare labour resources and low income. For that reason education and training programmes in less developed regions should be geared to employment opportunities in growth centres. Investment in human resources (human capital) is essential. It has been proved that among the factors which contribute to economic growth the quality of the human input ranks very high.[74]

Very important also are the trend in industry towards less vertical integration and more specialisation, and the increasing demand for services and other suppliers. Much attention must therefore be paid in the centres to:

1 local amenities in the field of education, medical services, recreation, housing, etc.;
2 training and retraining of the labour force;
3 the creation of a large and differentiated labour market;
4 the existence of auxiliary, subsidiary, and intermediate firms (see localised functional growth pole);
5 the provision of industrial sites fully equipped with good connections to the regional and national infrastructure.

Our second point concerns the kind of activities to be attracted. Here we refer first of all to what was said in the context of growth pole theory and the attraction model, stressing, however, that the strategy and the content of regional policy towards a region must be adapted to: (a) the economic structure, (b) the population structure, and (c) the natural vocation of the region. Too often only industry is considered in a potential growth pattern. In certain regions the improvement of the agricultural structure and the promotion of complementary activities merit much more attention than they are getting. In other regions tourism can be promoted; it is frequently a vehicle for regional development. The income level *per capita* in tourist regions is very often higher than in industrial regions. Moreover, it must be emphasised that agriculture and tourism can prosper without the existence of a large centre. Other tertiary activities than tourism may also be considered. It is true that most services are linked to industry and/or population size; as such they are not basic activities. But within the gamut of service activities there are some that can be used as propulsive units in regional development, such as: harbour activities, universities, research institutions, national defence, medical institutions on the higher level, government agencies, insurance companies, etc. A recent OECD document defends the thesis that services are an essential source of economic development and not simply a secondary result of the growth of the primary and secondary sectors.[75]

From what has been said in the present and other chapters of this book it must be clear that services other than those mentioned above, play an important role in regional development. Centralisation of public and private services in growth centres should therefore be recommended. A number of countries are taking measures to have a more direct control of the growth of services in lagging regions (see next chapter).

The role of regional development agencies

A strategic element in the development of any region is the existence of a regional development agency (authority). The development of a lagging region cannot be managed from London, Paris, Brussels, or Rome. Why not? In the first place a government authority sitting in a capital city does not have the same interest in a region's development as the people who live there. There is a lack of motivation. In the second place a regional development authority situated in the lagging region knows much more of, and is more sensitive to, the needs, problems, and chances of the region than a centralised administration. Therefore we look upon a regional development authority not only as an instrument of regional policy (see next chapter), but also as an element of the over-all development strategy.[76]

The role of a regional development authority can be played on five levels:

1 Research. It seems unthinkable to promote a region without a profound knowledge of the region itself. What are the economic forces, the economic potential, the socio-economic deficiencies, the needs of the region? Moreover this knowledge must be placed in the context of general economic development and the evolution of the different economic sectors and subsectors. A regional development authority should not only have a basic knowledge of a region, but should also be able to provide at any moment infor-mation about all sorts of things. Sometimes the agency may be charged with market research for a particular sector (e.g. tourism); to that end it should have a study office or study department.

2 Strategy. On the basis of all such information, the authority is able to develop a strategy for the medium term and the long term. What part of the region should be given priority, what centres can be promoted, what activities should be attracted, etc.?

3 Promotion. Promotion is, of course, an expression that can cover many items, and in regional development it certainly does. It is here that the field work starts, work that calls for the ambi-tion and the dynamism of the general manager of a large concern. The daily tasks are: (a) to assist existing firms either in their expan-sion or in dealing with their problems of all kinds (technical, finan-cial, infrastructural, etc.); (b) to advise the public and private sectors; (c) to attract new projects; (d) to stimulate the improve-ment of general economic infrastructure; (e) to promote sub-contracting ('bourse de sous-traitance'); (f) to provide information to industry, social organisations, schools, and the local population, through press, radio, television, conferences, newsletters, guided visits, articles, and possibly, the agency's own review. It should be stressed that the information service is extremely important in regional development.

4 Coordination. Many national departments, far more than two

decades ago, are involved in regional development. Quite often more than ten government agencies are involved in the implementation of one project. The formal administrative procedure is incompatible with regional development, so a regional development agency should fulfil the role of coordinator in order to shorten the procedure period and to increase the chances of a project to be implemented.

Moreover, regional growth is strongly inter-related with physical planning, housing, education, environment, and coordination is essential there, too.

For the frontier regions, coordination is necessary, not only within the region or between national and/or provincial departments, but also with the region(s) on the other side of the international border.

5 Implementation. This function includes first and foremost the creation of regional infrastructure such as industrial sites, ready built factories, other economic overheads, housing, etc. to sustain the regional development. A regional agency may be financially responsible (with its own equity capital), and/or work with the funds from the central government. Another function may be the participation in investment projects or even the creation of firms in the competitive and non-competitive sectors. In Belgium the Regional Development Authorities are charged by law with that investment function.

On account of the inter-relationship between regional development and physical planning, a regional development authority may be charged with the preparation of physical planning documents (detailed plans, master plans, district plans, and regional plans).

The above list of functions shows that a dynamic regional development agency has a catalysing role in regional development. Without such an agency it is impossible to accomplish maximum growth on the regional level. A regional development agency should not act purely as a body of public administration, but as a promotion institution, and should be run like a business concern.

Notes

[1] MacLennan, M.C., *Regional Development Policies for Backward Regions*, in *Regional disequilibrium in Europe*, Brussels, 1968.
[2] Ibid., p.45.
[3] Ibid., p.45.
[4] Vanhove, N., *De doelmatigheid van het regionaal-ekonomisch*

beleid in Nederland, 1962, p.15.   Vanhove, N., 'Quelques considérations concernant l'efficience de la politique d'économie régionale
pratiquée en Belgique et aux Pays Bas', in *L'efficacité des mesures de
politique économique régionale, Actes du VI Colloque annuel, de
l'Association de Science Régionale de Langue Française,* 1967, pp.172—
212.
[5] MacLennan, M.C., op.cit., pp.47—8.
[6] OCDE, *Le facteur régional dans le développement économique.
Politique suivies dans quinze pays industrialisés de l'OCDE,* Paris, 1970.
[7] MacLennan, M.C., op.cit., p.48.
[8] MacLennan, M.C., op.cit., p.49.
[9] Davin, L.E., Degeer, L. and Paelinck, J., *Dynamique économique
de la région Liégeoise,* Liège, 1959.
[10] Tosco, A., *Etude pour la création d'un pôle industriel de développement en Italie méridionale,* op.cit.
[11] MacLennan, M.C., op.cit., pp.49—50.
[12] MacLennan, M.C., op.cit., p.51.
[13] Ibid., p.57.
[14] OCDE, *Politique de l'aménagement du territoire et du développement régional de la France,* Paris, 1973. OCDE, *Les problèmes et les
politiques de développement régional dans les pays de l'OCDE,* vol.I,
Paris,1976. OCDE, *Les politiques régionales — Perspectives régionales,*
Paris,1977. Prud'homme, R., 'Regional economic policy in France', in
Hansen, N. (ed.), *Public Policy and Regional Economic Development.
The Experience of Nine Western Countries,* Cambridge, 1974. Hansen,
N.M., *French Regional Planning,* Edinburgh, 1968. Gravier, J.F., *Décentralisation et progrès technique,* Paris, 1954. Gravier, J.F., *Paris et le
désert Français,* Paris, 1958. Monod, J., 'Région parisienne, bassin
parisien et aménagement du territoire', *Revue juridique et économique
du Sud-Ouest,* no.3, 1970. Zangl, P., *Regionalpolitische Zielsetzungen
und Strategien in Frankreich,* Köln, 1974. Allen, K. and MacLennan,
M.C., *Regional Problems and Policies in Italy and France,* London,
1970. Guichard, O., *Aménager la France,* Paris, 1965. Commissariat
général du Plan, 'Aménagement du territoire et du Cadre de vie',
Préparation au VIIième Plan, Documentation française, Paris 1976.
[15] Prud'homme, R., op.cit., p.41.
[16] Guichard, O., op.cit., p.25.
[17] Prud'homme, R., op.cit., pp.42—6.
[18] For policy purposes, however, the 8 'métropoles' are in most cases
more broadly defined than single cities. The reason is that certain
polynuclear urban areas are beginning to appear.
[19] See OECD publications, op.cit. See also Cao-Pinna, V., 'Regional
policy in Italy', in Hansen, N. (ed.), op.cit. Holland, S.K., 'Regional
underdevelopment in a developed economy: the Italian case', in

Regional Studies, no.2, 1971. Mountjoy, A.B., *The Mezzogiorno,* Oxford, 1973. Allen, K. and MacLennan, op.cit.. Lutz, V., *Italy: a study in economic development,* Oxford, 1962.

[20] Chenery, H.B., *Politiche di sviluppo per l'Italia meridionale,* Rome, 1962 (SVIMEZ).

[21] Cao-Pinna, V., op.cit., p.170.

[22] Cao-Pinna, V., op.cit., p.173.

[23] See OECD publications. See also: Cameron, G.C., 'Regional economic policy in the United Kingdom', in Hansen, N. (ed.), op.cit. Brown, A.J., op.cit. McCrone, G., op.cit. The Hunt Report, op.cit. Lind, H., *Regional Policy in Britain and the Six,* London, 1970. Wilton, T., 'The British regional policy in the European context', *The Banker,* February 1973. Hallett, G., 'British regional problems and policies', in Hallett, G., Randall, P. and West, E.G., *Regional Policy for Ever?,* London, 1973. Randall, P., 'The history of British regional policy', in Hallett, G., Randall, P. and West, E.G., op.cit. Chisholm, M. and Manners, G., *Spatial Policy Problems of the British Economy,* Cambridge, 1971. Tress, R.C., 'The next stage in regional policy', in *The Three Banks Review,* March 1969.

[24] Barlow, L. (Chairman), 'Report of the Royal Commission on the Distribution of the Industrial Population', HMSO, January 1940.

[25] Randall, P.J., op.cit.

[26] NEDC, 'Conditions favourable to faster growth', HMSO, 1963.

[27] Randall, P.J., op.cit., p.38.

[28] Industrial and Regional Development, HMSO, 1972.

[29] OECD publications, op.cit. OECD, *Salient Features of Regional Development Policy in Germany,* Paris, 1968. Krumme, G., 'Regional policies in West Germany', in Hansen, N. (ed.), op.cit.

[30] Krumme, G., op.cit., p.119.

[31] Krumme, G., op.cit., p.116. Gesetz über die Gemeinschaftsaufgabe *Verbesserung der regionalen Wirtschaftsstruktur,* vom 6 Oktober 1969.

[32] Rahmenplan der Gemeinschaftsaufgabe *Verbesserung der regionalen Wirtschaftsstruktur,* Bonn¡ 1971.

[33] See OECD publication, op.cit. Hendriks, A.J., 'Regional policy in the Netherlands', in Hansen, N. (ed.), op.cit. Klaassen, L.H., *Het regionale industrialisatiebeleid in Nederland,* Rotterdam, 1962. Klaassen, L.H., *Regionale economie en regionaal-ekonomische politiek in Nederland,* Rotterdam, 1968.

[34] Hendriks, A.J., op.cit., p.195.

[35] Vandermotten, C., 'La politique du territoire en Belgique. Objectifs, instruments et coûts', *Cahiers économiques de Bruxelles,* no.62, 1974.

[36] Vanhove, N., *The Development of Flemish Economy in the Inter-*

national Perspective — synthesis and options of policy, Brussels, 1973.
[37] See Vanhove, N., op.cit., pp.56—61.
[38] OECD, op.cit., p.167.
[39] Hilhorst, J.G.M., *Regional Planning — a systems approach,* Rotterdam, 1971, p.78.
[40] Klaassen, L.H., *Regionale economie en regionaal-ekonomische politiek in Nederland,* op.cit., p.13.
[41] See Hilhorst, J.G.M., op.cit., p.79.
[42] Paelinck, J.H.P., 'La théorie du développement régional polarisé', *Cahiers de l'ISEA,* March 1965, p.47.
[43] Vanneste, O., 'Het groeipoolkoncept als strategisch element in het regionaal beleid', *Liber Amicorum Prof. Dr. G. Eyskens,* Leuven, 1975, p.536.
[44] Allen, K., 'Growth centres and growth centre policy', Warne, E.J.D., *Regional Policy in Efta,* Geneva, 1971.
[45] See also Klemmer, P., 'Die Theorie der Entwicklungspole — strategisches Konzept für die regionale Wirtschaftspolitik', *Raumforschung und Raumordnung,* June 1972.
[46] Vanhove, N., op.cit.
[47] Wäldchen, P., 'Die Studie Bari-Tarente und die Methode der industriellen Schwerpunkte', *Informationen,* 3.10.1966, p.628.
[48] See also Klemmer, P., op.cit., p.106.
[49] Klaassen, L.H., *Growth Poles. An Economic View,* op.cit., p.39.
[50] Allen, K., op.cit., p.103.
[51] Allen, K., op.cit., p.105.
[52] Ibid., p.107.
[53] Hansen, N., *Rural Poverty and the Urban Crisis,* p.252. See also Hansen, N., *A growth centre strategy for the United States,* Discussion paper, Programme on the role of growth centres in regional economic development, Kentucky, 1969.
[54] Hansen, N., *French regional planning,* op.cit., chapter 10.
[55] Ibid., p.234.
[56] Bauchet, P., 'La compatibilité économique régionale et son usage', *Economie Appliquée,* January 1961.
[57] Bloch-Lainé, F., 'Justification des choix', *Urbanisme,* no.89, 1965, p.6.
[58] Guichard, O., op.cit., p.69.
[59] Gravier, J.F., *L'Aménagement du territoire et l'avenir des régions françaises,* Paris, 1964.
[60] Rousselot, 'L'Aménagement du territoire et la régionalisation du VIieme Plan', *Politique de l'aménagement du territoire et du développement régional de la France,* EOCD, Paris, 1973.
[61] Hansen, N., 'Criteria for a growth centre policy', in Kuklinski, A., *Growth Poles and Growth Centres in Regional Planning,* The Hague,

1972, p.103.

[62] Hansen, N., 'Efficient regional resource allocation and growth centre policy', Paelinck, J.H.P. (ed.), *Programming for Europe's Collective Needs*, Amsterdam, 1970.

[63] Allen, K., 'Growth centres and growth centre policy', op.cit. See also Klaassen, L.H., *Regionale economie en regionale ekonomische politiek in Nederland*, op.cit., pp.13—14.

[64] Berry, B.J.L., 'Spatial organization and levels of welfare', Paper presented to the Economic Development Administration Research Conference, Washington, 1967.

[65] Thompson, W.R., *A Preface to Urban Economics*, Baltimore, 1965, p.24.

[66] Robinson, E.A.G., 'Introduction', in Robinson, E.A.G. (ed.), *Backward Areas in Advanced Countries*, New York, 1969.

[67] Hansen, N., *Efficient Regional Resource Allocation and Growth Centre Policy*, op.cit., p.73.

[68] Hansen, N., *Criteria for a Growth Centre Policy*, op.cit., pp.119—20. See also Hansen, N., *Rural Poverty and the Urban Crisis*, op.cit., chapter 10.

[69] Allen, K., op.cit.

[70] Allen, K., op.cit., p.94.

[71] Ibid., p.95.

[72] Ibid., p.96.

[73] Allen, K., op.cit., p.100.

[74] Denison, E.G., *Why Growth Rates Differ*, Washington, 1967.

[75] OECD, *La politique régionale et le secteur des services*, Paris, 1978, p.13.

[76] Vanhove, N., 'De rol van een welvaartsorgaan in de regionale ekonomische expansie — Het voorbeeld van West-Vlaanderen', *De Gewesten in Europa, Bulletin*, no.2, 1970.

8 Instruments of regional economic policy in EEC countries

To realise the objectives of regional policy a wide variety of instruments has been created. It can be said that the national authorities have been very imaginative in that respect.

In this chapter we are dealing more particularly with the instruments used on the national level. These national instruments can be categorised as follows: infrastructure aids, financial incentives, disincentives, decentralisation of government offices, regional allocation of public investment and public orders and, finally, regional development agencies. We could add migration and mobility policy, but that category is treated in a separate chapter. Each of the categories is composed of several specific instruments, as will be demonstrated in this chapter.

This chapter is divided into three sections. The first analyses the different categories of instruments just mentioned. In the second section we deal with the function, advantages and disadvantages of particular instruments. The third concerns macro-evaluation methods of regional economic policy instruments.

It should be emphasised that most instruments of economic policy and also those of more general policy, have a regional impact. In this study we limit ourselves to regional instruments with explicit regional economic aims.

Categories of instruments

In the introduction to this chapter we have distinguished six different categories of instruments; in this section we shall analyse them one by one.

Infrastructure aids

One of the main handicaps of a problem region is very often a lack of basic infrastructure. A region becomes underdeveloped by a long process. Backwardness leads to less political power and insufficient financial means; an infrastructural lag usually follows. To remedy this handicap and reverse the situation, medium and long term infrastructure programmes are needed. We do not hesitate to say that in the long run infrastructure aids are the most important regional economic instrument.

Infrastructure aids can be grouped as follows according to their level of spatial impact:

1 infrastructure on the level of individual firms: industrial estates, ready built factories, link roads, equipment of industrial sites;
2 local infrastructure: training centres, housing, social, medical, and cultural infrastructure;
3 regional infrastructure: general transport network (roads, canals, railways, airports, harbours), decentralisation of institutions, universities, water supply, purification stations, power stations.

The above short lists immediately show the great variety of infrastructure aids. They are not restricted to purely economic infrastructure but cover social, medical, and cultural infrastructure as well. That is to be expected in view of the present role of external economies as location factors. The high costs involved in social, medical, and cultural infrastructure are an argument for concentration in a limited number of development centres.

A very important infrastructure instrument is the industrial site or the industrial estate. The British were the first to use this instrument. At present no regional development plan can be conceived without one or more industrial sites. They are also an essential element in physical planning. The quantitative need for industrial sites can be calculated rather easily from the situation on the labour market, the demand for industrial labour, and site coefficients per group of economic activities.

Another special type of infrastructure is housing. Housing programmes should be incorporated in any regional development plan, but in practice the responsible authorities do not sufficiently integrate their housing policy in the regional development programmes.

In the light of growth pole theory, also social infrastructural elements, such as universities, technical institutes of higher education, or research institutes can be considered propulsive units (unités motrices) of a growth pole. There are many cases where the role of a university in regional development is evident. Its impact can take different forms: income polarisation, technical information and exchange, innovation, applied research and, last but not least, upgrading programmes for staff people, managers, and employees. The Faculty of Science of the University of Grenoble, for example, had a very positive impact on the development of the electronics industry in that region.[1] Training and retraining centres are an essential element of regional development in underdeveloped and stranded regions. Indeed the quality of labour is one of the criteria in the location decision. In less developed regions the level of technical education is already lower than in other regions, while the population does not have an industrial tradition. The role of training and retraining becomes more important as the present trend towards specialisation and automatisation leads to higher professional requirements, but it is very difficult, if not impossible, to prepare a local labour force for all kinds of technical requirements. Therefore in most countries grants are provided to firms for the upgrading of their employees. In that case the firms take over the function of training centres.

For the regional authorities and politicians of development regions infrastructure aid concerns in the first place transport infrastructure: roads, highways, railways, canals, airports, docks, and pipelines.[2] Good transport infrastructure is a necessary condition for regional development. A very good example of the development of transport infrastructure in the regional framework is to be found in the French Seventh Plan. The objectives with respect to highways, roads, railways, and canals are quite well defined. In many cases new transport infrastructure works have become the propulsive force in the regional development process. In this context 'axes of development' and 'investment polarisation' are interesting concepts. By axes of development L.E. Davin, L. Degeer, and J.H.P. Paelinck mean: ' . . . all auxiliary infrastructures which favour a flexible functioning of the industrial complex studied and particularly the flows of goods'.[3] Investment polarisation takes place when a harbour, a highway, an industrial site form the base of a process of technical polarisation.[4] Examples of investment polarisation are the Nieuwe Waterweg in Rotterdam, the Albert Canal in Belgium, and port areas such as Antwerp, Dunkirk, Fos, Bari-Torante-Brindisi, etc. On the other hand, E.H. Van de Poll and J.A. Bourdrez provide historical examples from which we can learn that insufficient adaptation of infrastructure to present needs acts as a brake on regional development.[5]

The results of any improvement of transport infrastructure can be classified in three groups:

1 shorter connection, due to a more direct link;
2 faster connection, due to greater capacity or better quality;
3 the possibility of using a more modern form of transport (canals for push convoys, pipeline transport, accessibility of a port for large ships, etc.).

In many cases the above mentioned results can be achieved together. What they mean for the economy of a region becomes clear when they are translated into factors of economic significance:

(a) speedier and/or shorter transport means a reduced use of factors of production (labour, car park, etc.);
(b) better transport infrastructure very often leads to faster and

more frequent supply to firms and thus to lower storage costs and a supply of raw materials of better quality;

(c) faster traffic saves business time;
(d) better highways, for example, enlarge the markets;
(e) better infrastructure makes for greater safety;
(f) better infrastructure enables firms to give a more reliable service.

In fact, improved infrastructure saves costs all round, and therefore makes a region more attractive to firms and individuals.

Very often the remark is made that transport costs do not represent a high percentage of the total production costs and therefore are not an important location factor. That is a very dangerous thesis, for several reasons. First, the situation varies widely according to industrial sector or subsector; secondly, transport costs may be very important in proportion to profits, and, lastly, transport costs are among the few production costs which a firm can influence by the choice of the place of settlement.

So far we have put the emphasis on the infrastructure required for industrial development; we were agreed that transport infrastructure, housing, medical, social, and cultural infrastructure do have a general positive impact on the development of trade and tertiary activities. But apart from that there are some special elements of infrastructure that are of particular importance to the development of certain regions. To regional economies largely based on agriculture, irrigation or drainage works, water supply works, a produce market, etc., can be vital, because they reduce costs, increase production, or improve the marketing of farm products. To those European regions that have a vocation for tourism; they can be made more attractive by man made infrastructure such as yacht ports, recreational facilities and beach equipment.

Financial aids or incentives

The range of financial incentives to regional development is wide; all sorts of grants, interest rebates, credit facilities, and taxation allowances are provided to attract new projects and/or stimulate the expansion of existing firms. They are related either to labour or to capital, and vary geographically.

Financial instruments are used to stimulate economic development in problem regions; that is the general motivation. The specific reasons for introducing certain incentives become clear when we look at their functions.

The function of incentives

An incentive is given to compensate a region for what it lacks in economic attraction, because it has no, or not enough, skilled labour or social amenities, or fails in external economies, owing to high communication costs, absence of an industrial tradition, low productivity, or duplication of management in branch companies. Naturally, the financial impact of a handicap or handicaps is difficult to measure, the more so because such handicaps differ from sector to sector and from firm to firm. Sometimes it is possible to use specific aids to compensate for specific deficiencies; financing a training programme when workers are lacking in skill is a very good example. But the trouble is that most problem regions suffer from several handicaps at the same time.

During the last two decades financial aids to compensate for all kinds of deficiencies were increasingly introduced in all European countries, thus acquiring a new, second, function, namely that of guaranteeing 'international competitiveness' by attracting new investment projects.

A third function is the procuration of financial means; loans may be introduced to procure financial means to certain firms. Sometimes financial aid is given as an 'aide de démarrage', as a means to get going, that is to say, to help problem regions adapt their industrial structure to new economic and technical conditions.

Specific financial instruments may be introduced to discourage non-productive activities (tax allowances) or concentrate firms in a limited number of centres (location premiums).

Mostly, financial incentives fulfil more than one purpose, for instance compensation, financing, and physical planning purposes.

The variety of financial aids is due not only to their different functions but also to other factors; we may mention in that respect:

(a) type of problem region (e.g. stranded region versus agricultural region);

(b) objectives of the regional policy of a country;

(c) role of the financial incentive;

(d) structure of the banking system in the different countries;

(e) size of firms;

(f) infrastructure provisions and geographical situation (for example reduction in transport tariffs);

(g) degree of willingness to attract sound projects (for example tax allowances);

(h) linked aids to compensate for specific deficiencies;

(i) economic situation of a country, and, last but not least,

(j) political pressure.

Analysis of incentives

We shall try to give, on the basis of some OECD studies, a study recently carried out for the European Commission, and a few other publications, a general survey of the financial aids applied in the countries of the EEC.[6]   The terms on which aid is given and the size of the amounts involved are established by national legislation, and measures may be suspended according to the economic situation. In fact, the application of financial instruments of regional policy is continually being changed, amended, and developed. We shall not, therefore, go into details here. Table 8.1 groups the financial instruments used in regional policy into 23 categories, and shows their application in the countries of the European Community. Some categories comprise several instruments. We have indicated the instruments applied in a country by A, a country's major regional instruments are, however, indicated by [A]. Instruments applied indiscriminately to the whole country have been disregarded, though it is not always easy to make a distinction between regional and national application. A number of instruments to be dealt with under another heading — for instance equity participation (allocation of public companies), disincentives, ready built factories, and industrial sites at reduced prices — are also included in the table.

What are the main conclusions to be derived from this synoptical table?

1 In all EEC countries financial and fiscal instruments are applied in great variety.

2 The main financial incentives are capital grants, soft loan schemes, and accelerated depreciation allowances. Capital grants in the wide sense are used in all EEC countries as an instrument of regional policy; in seven out of the eight countries considered they feature as the main instruments. Soft loan schemes are also used in all countries; in five countries they are applied as a basic instrument. Accelerated depreciation allowances belong to the arsenal of regional policy instruments in seven EEC countries; in four countries they are considered a major instrument. A working paper of the Commission of European Communities of 1976 gives an idea of the magnitude and the structure of direct regional aids (excluding infrastructural aids, sectoral aids, and a whole series of minor instruments). Its findings are summarised in Table 8.2. We doubt that the information from different countries is entirely comparable as far as the content and the classification by type of aid is concerned; nevertheless the figures give a good idea of the importance of the direct aid system.

For some countries, notably the Netherlands and the United Kingdom, Tables 8.1 and 8.2 do not quite correspond as far as the

Table 8.1

Financial incentives applied in the framework of regional economic policy in the countries of the EEC*

Category	Belgium	Denmark	Germany	France	Ireland	Italy	Netherlands	United Kingdom
1. Capital grants (investment grants & investment allowances)								
– buildings	[A]	[A]	[A]	[A]	[A]	[A]	[A]	[A]
– equipment	[A]	[A]	[A]	[A]	[A]	[A]	[A]	[A]
– working capital	–	A	–	–	A	–	–	–
– rationalisation & reorganisation	–	–	A	–	A	A	–	A
2. Ready built factories	–	A	–	–	A	–	–	A
3. Ready built factories & industrial sites at reduced prices (including factory rent concessions)	A	[A]	–	[A]	A	A	A	A
4. Soft loans schemes (interest rebates and/or concessionary loans)	[A]	[A]	[A]	A	A	[A]	A	[A]
5. Credit facilities								
– medium and long term credit banks	–	–	–	–	–	A	–	–
– loans with state guarantee	A	A	A	–	A	–	A	–
6. Labour grants (employment premium)	A	–	–	A	A	–	–	[A]**
7. Tax exemption								
– accelerated depreciation allowance	A	–	[A]	[A]	[A]	A	[A]	A
·· or special depreciation allowance								
– from profits	–	–	A	A	A	[A]	–	–

	C1	C2	C3	C4	C5	C6	C7	C8	C9
– from income	A	—	—	A	—	[A]	—	—	—
– export profit tax relief	—	—	—	—	—	—	—	—	—
– from consumption of energy (oil, natural gas)	—	—	—	—	A	—	A	—	—
– other tax exemptions (business tax exemptions, local registration fees, turnover tax, property income)	—	—	—	—	[A]	A	—	A	A
8. Training (very often applied nation-wide)	—	—	A	A	A	A	A	A	A
9. Transfer premiums									
– decentralisation indemnity & decentralisation allowances	—	A	A	—	A	—	—	—	—
– decentralisation grant for artisanal subcontractors	—	A	—	—	A	—	—	—	A
10. Incentives to incite labour to leave problem regions	—	—	—	—	—	—	—	—	—
11. Incentives to incite labour to move to problem regions	A	—	—	A	A	—	—	A	A
12. Capital removal grants or allowances for the relocation of firms	A	A	A	A	—	A	A	A	A
13. Equity participation	—	—	A	—	A	A	—	A	A
14. Reduction of public utility tariffs									
– transport	—	—	—	—	A	—	A	—	A
– electricity	—	—	—	A	—	—	A	—	—
15. Preferential regime for public tender	—	—	—	A	—	—	A	—	A

16. Regional allocation of public orders (government expenditure)	—	—	—	A	—	A	—	—	A
17. Regional allocation of public investment	—	—	—	—	—	A	—	—	—
18. Social security concessions	—	—	—	—	—	[A]	—	—	—
19. Marketing assistance to firms	—	—	—	—	—	A	—	—	—
20. Location controls (disincentives included)									
– location tax (levies)	—	—	[A]	—	—	A	A	—	—
– building licence	—	—	[A]	—	—	—	A	—	[A]
– notifications in respect of new industrial buildings, installations and offices	—	—	—	—	—	A	A	—	—
21. Deconcentration of administration, consultancy & data processing activities (research activities grant included)	—	—	A	—	—	—	A	—	A
22. Redistribution of fiscal receipts	—	A	—	—	—	—	—	—	—
23. Artisanal schemes	—	—	A	—	—	—	—	—	—

312

Table 8.2

Direct regional aids in the EEC countries, 1974

Type	Belgium	Denmark	Germany (excluding West Berlin)	France	Ireland	Italy	Luxembourg	Netherlands	United Kingdom	EEC
Capital subventions	24.9	36.2	65.8	55.1	42.5	22.4	44.0	100.0	63.6	45.8
Interest allowance & aid in loans at reduced rates	63.2	47.8	—	0.4	—	13.9	2.4	—	..	8.0
Employment premiums & social security concessions	—	6.1	—	—	15.2	51.8	—	—	30.6	30.8
Fiscal exemptions	8.5	—	34.2	34.9	37.7	11.9	38.6	—	—	12.7
Aid for purchase of industrial land & buildings	1.8	9.9	—	9.6	4.6	—	15.0	—	5.8	2.7
Cost of state guarantees granted for security of loans	1.8	—	—	—	—	—	—	—	—	0.1
Total	100.0	100.0	100.0	100.0	100.0	100.0	100.0	100.0	100.0	100.0
Million UA	116.7	8.7	435.8	124.0	114.2	1,148.8	4.3	21.1	1,037.7	3,015.8
% of GDP	0.28	0.04	0.14	0.06	2.15	0.96	0.25	0.05	0.68	0.33*

Source: EEC Working paper, 1976.

* The GDP of West Berlin is included.

major instruments are concerned; we believe that Table 8.1. represents the reality better.

3 Ready built factories and price reductions on buildings and industrial sites are important instruments in Denmark, France, and the United Kingdom.

4 Location controls are characteristic of France, the United Kingdom, the Netherlands and Italy.

5 A number of countries each emphasise one particular instrument, such as:
— United Kingdom: labour grants;
— France: local business-tax concessions;
— Ireland: export-profits tax relief;
— Italy: social security concessions.

These are very general features of the financial incentives (disincentives) applied in the EEC countries; a more profound comparison must be based on the real content of each instrument. Such a comparison was made by K. Allen in the above-mentioned study, which covers seven aspects: [8]

1 *Discretion:* discretion on the part of the authorities to decide whether or not to award, and to decide the rate of award. Discretion enables the award to be tailored to the needs of the regions and the applicant. It avoids inefficient use of public finance. There are two drawbacks to a discretionary system. First, it significantly reduces the visibility of the incentives on offer. Industrialists are unsure whether or not they will receive an award and what its level will be. Second, it may lengthen the time required by administrators to make award decisions. K. Allen therefore states that simplicity and predictability are essential requirements for regional incentives;

2 *Coverage:* eligibility for regional incentives is assessed by activity and project type. In terms of activity coverage regional incentives are very similar throughout the EEC countries, being concentrated on manufacturing. Only France, Ireland, and the United Kingdom have regional incentive schemes aimed specifically at the service sector in the problem regions. There is, furthermore, a general lack of specified discrimination along industrial and sectoral lines. Project type eligibility is fairly similar among the various incentives and countries. New projects are eligible in all countries, and extensions are also widely covered. Similar conditions hold for reorganisation and modernisation projects;

3 *Eligible expenditure:* eligible items and eligible forms of expenditure must be considered. Buildings are an eligible item in all schemes, and plants and machinery are so in most cases. The major items excluded in

most schemes are vehicles, low value items, 'short life' items, stocks, and working capital. As many firms in problem regions will have to have larger stocks, K. Allen pleads for taking a more generous view towards working capital. The eligibility of replacement investment is a point of discussion. Another aspect of eligibility from the eligible systems: cash payment, phased payments, hire purchase, and leasing. For most countries and most incentives, assets purchased under hire purchase and leasing arrangements are not generally eligible. There is, however, little reason to discriminate against these forms of finance; incentives should be awarded to projects that are financed in that way;

4 *Tax treatment:* a major factor which influences the relationship between nominal and effective values of incentives is their tax treatment. Taxing of incentives is widespread in the EEC countries. It can be direct (taxable profits) or indirect (for tax purposes, any grants received must be left out of account in the depreciation of aided assets). Major exceptions are the investment allowance in the Federal Republic of Germany, the regional development grant in the United Kingdom, and the capital grant in Italy. It should be remarked that the extent to which incentives are actually taxed depends also on whether firms make taxable profits;

5 *Timing and phasing of awards:* another factor which can lower the effective value of incentives is the timing and phasing of awards;

6 *Integration:* additivity of incentives, cumulativeness, and the relationship between regional incentives and national incentive schemes. Incentives frequently are not additive and where they are combined, the award of one may detract from the value of another. Furthermore, most countries have systems for limiting total public contributions. One of the most serious problems concerns the integration of incentive with non-incentive aspects of regional policy (e.g. infrastructure policy) and with national policies, incentive or not (for example the closing of railway lines, and sectoral policies);

7 *Changeability of policy:* monitoring of firms and projects to which aid has been granted, and evaluation. Many firms see the changes in policy in the course of time as a major shortcoming of the system of regional incentives, the more so as the aid is taken into account in investment and location decisions. In most countries the monitoring of firms and projects to which regional incentives have been granted is limited, for various reasons. Moreover, the effectiveness of schemes is not always evaluated.

Comparison of the values of incentives given in EEC countries

K. Allen has made an interesting comparison of incentive values in EEC countries, expressed in three standard valuation denominators: [9] initial capital costs, annual capital costs, and value added.

While we are considering the effective subsidy value of the maximum combination of incentives in the top priority region of each of the EEC countries, K. Allen bases his calculations on each country's major regional financial incentives; the forced simplification does not appear to influence the overall results. The method applied by K. Allen in the European Regional Policy Project is a development of the net present value approach used by the EEC. It comprises two stages: (a) the calculation of the effective percentage subsidy associated with each of the major regional incentives, involving the calculation of the cash value of each incentive discounted to a net present value, tax treatment, delays in payment and eligible items being taken into account; (b) translation of the above reductions in factor prices into equivalent reductions in annual factor costs.

In the first stage the major possible steps of the calculation scheme are:

(a) the calculation of the nominal subsidy or the estimation of net grant equivalent percentage (e.g. interest rebates) and corresponding net present value;
(b) the move from nominal to effective subsidy;
(c) the move from approved capital to total expenditure (investment), or, for loans at reduced interest, the move from effective subsidy as a percentage of loan levels to effective subsidy as a percentage of project capital costs.

To calculate the net grant equivalent of a concessionary loan and its net present value we need to know: (a) the period of the loan, (b) the period of grace, (c) the interest free periods, (d) the level of interest rate subsidy, (e) the repayment systems, and (f) the appropriated discount rate.

To move from nominal to effective subsidy we must take into account two main factors: taxation, and administrative delays in the payment of the subsidy (e.g. timing and phasing of the payment of a grant).

The influence of both factors can be demonstrated with the application of the regional employment premium (REP).[10] In the Special Development Areas the REP amounted to 3.9 per cent of labour costs in 1976. With taxation taken into account (on the assumption that profits were being made), the percentage became 2.3; the effective subsidy as a percentage of total labour costs post tax and delays was reduced to 2.2 per cent.

In the second stage the reductions in relevant factor prices are translated into annual capital costs or value added. The total annual capital charge is the sum of the depreciation charge and interest cost. They are related to initial investment costs by the formula:

$$N = \frac{Cr(1+r)^n}{(1+r)^n - 1}$$

in which

N	=	annual capital charge;
C	=	initial investment cost;
r	=	discount rate;
n	=	asset life.

The use of this formula requires that assumptions are made about asset lives and the capital cost mix (land, buildings, plant, vehicles, and working capital). The calculation of the reduction in annual capital costs due to financial incentives proceeds in three steps:

1 Calculation of total annual capital costs. To get the annual capital costs it is sufficient to weight the annual capital cost factor $[r(1+r)^n/(1+r)^n - 1]$ of each capital item with the corresponding share of the asset mix; in fact initial capital costs are thus annuitised.
2 Calculation of the total annual subsidy value. In this step the incentives received towards the capital costs are also put on an annual basis. A major problem here is the lifetime over which the subsidies should be spread; it depends on whether or not replacement will be subsidised. Once those elements are known it is not difficult to calculate the annual subsidy factors $[r(1+r)^n/(1+r)^n - 1]$. Given these, the total annual subsidy value associated with any given incentive is calculated by multiplying the effective percentage subsidy value (see first stage) by the portion of total capital costs covered by the incentive and then by the appropriate annual subsidy factor (transforming the results to an annual basis).
3 Reduction in annual capital costs due to incentives. The annual subsidy value (step 2) is expressed as a percentage of the annual capital cost figure (step 1).

The third incentive denominator referred to above, value added, is very important in connection with the impact of incentives on competition. To move from the annual capital costs denominator to the value added one, a key value for the labour to capital ratio needs to be fixed.

317

In the approach for the United Kingdom a ratio of 3 to 1 was applied.

The results of the calculation methods described are given in Table 8.3. The table presents the effective subsidy value of the maximum combination of incentives in the top priority region of each EEC country. Despite the fact that Table 8.3 includes neither the tax relief on export profits in Ireland nor the tax and social security concessions in Italy, the top group of incentives in the EEC is made up of the Italian and Irish packages. It should be emphasised that the percentages for Italy relate only to small projects; the incentive value of the combination of capital grants and national soft loans is much lower for large and very large projects. Italy and Ireland are also the countries of the Community with the gravest regional problems.

To interpret correctly the relative impact of the effective subsidies it should be taken into account that the French local business tax concession is not included in the French incentive package of Table 8.3, so that the French subsidies are underestimated.

According to K. Allen's results, in all EEC countries except Ireland and Italy the incentive packages are far less valuable outside the top priority problem regions than within them. A few examples can illustrate this. The effective percentage subsidy is 3.3 per cent of value added in the intermediate areas of the Netherlands, 3 per cent in non-Zonenrandgebiet in Germany, 2.7 per cent in the French Award Zone 2, and 1.6 per cent in the French Award Zone 3. Another interesting result of the Allen study is the effective value per individual incentive. Capital grants are the most important element of the incentive package in all EEC countries, ranging from 2.7 per cent of value added in Luxembourg to 8.9 per cent in Italy. Soft loans or interest rebates are ranging from 0.9 to 3.2 per cent of value added, and accelerated depreciation allowances from 0.6 to 2.0 per cent of value added.

Discouragement measures

The over concentration of economic activities in certain regions or a pronounced disequilibrium between core regions and less developed regions have led some countries to introduce discouragement measures, not to conflict with financial incentives but to complement them.

The whole system of controls and disincentives aims at restricting investment in regions that are already developed or even overdeveloped. Its implementation forms a further link between the goals of physical planning and regional economic policy.[11] [12]

From Table 8.1, which includes discouragement measures, we can see that they are applied in four EEC countries, and that they count among the major instruments in the United Kingdom and France. The Italian and Dutch parliaments recently adopted laws to limit growth in certain

Table 8.3

The effective subsidies based on maximum rates and maximum incentive combinations by top priority region in each EEC country

Country	Main problem region	Incentive combinations	Effective percentage subsidies		
			Initial capital costs	Annual capital costs	Value added
Belgium	Development zones	Capital grant, interest subsidy, accelerated depreciation	11.3	10.1	3.3
Denmark	Special development regions	Company soft loan, investment grant	15.4	13.8	5.2
France	Award Zone 1	Regional development grant, special depreciation allowance	13.5	12.2	3.7
Germany	Zonenrandgebiet	Investment allowance, investment grant, special depreciation allowance	18.2	15.5	5.3
Ireland	Designated areas	Industrial development grant, investment allowance	34.7	32.1	10.0
Italy	Mezzogiorno	Capital grant, national soft loan	46.3	41.7	12.1
Luxembourg	–	Capital grant, tax concession	7.8	7.1	2.7
Netherlands	Development areas	Investment premium, accelerated depreciation	15.9	13.7	4.9
United Kingdom*	Special development areas	Regional development grant, interest relief grant	21.5	21.7	4.8

* For the United Kingdom the 'annual capital cost' percentage is higher than the 'initial capital costs' because that item-related replacement is subsidised as part of the regional development grant scheme.
Source: K. Allen, op.cit. p.228.

areas, but in neither are they fully operative yet. A few years ago the need for special decongestion measures was an object of public discussion in Germany and Denmark.[13] The United Kingdom was the first country to introduce disincentive measures; since 1948 British regional policy has controlled the location of industry. In that year the Industrial Development Certificate (IDC) system was introduced, which since then has been modified several times. At present any firm wishing to create industrial floor space (new building or extension) covering more than 1,100 square metres in the South East Economic Planning Region or more than 1,400 square metres in all other regions outside the Development or Special Development Areas has to get an IDC from the Department of Industry. In 1965 the control system was extended to offices, and Office Development Permits (ODP) from the Department of the Environment are now required for all office developments in the South East and in London exceeding 900 square metres.

The two control systems have different aims, however; while the IDC system was set up for the purpose of transferring investments from developed to development areas, thus reducing labour market pressure in the South and the Midlands by shifting employment opportunities to the North, the specific aim of the ODP system is to relieve congestion in and around London. It can be refused if the company could reasonably be expected to set up its production in an assisted area, and/or is likely to add appreciably to the pressure in an area where labour is in short supply.

In the system of controls the onus of proof rests upon the company, which must show that its long run efficiency and/or its export competitiveness would suffer if it were diverted to a development or intermediate area. Proposals to erect offices are judged by the criterion whether or not the development 'would enhance London's prospects as an international financial and commercial centre'.[15]

Compared with British development controls, the scope of the French measures is somewhat wider. It is concerned firstly with relieving congestion in the Paris region (including five cantons of the Oise department) and secondly with transferring investment to the development regions. The most important control is the building permit of the 'Ministère de l'Aménagement du Territoire'. It was introduced in 1955 and at present is involved in any development in the Paris regions which creates new or extends existing floor space beyond 1,500 m^2 for industrial developments, 1,000 m^2 for offices and 5,000 m^2 for warehouse floor space. The system is enforced fairly stringently, but cannot prevent an investor from setting up just outside the Paris region.[16]
Since 1955 the building permit instrument has been given a larger field of application. Regional policy makers were provided with a powerful tool by a 1961 law which specified that building permits could, and

even should, be denied to projects working 'against regional policy'. To make sure that regional policy objectives would be taken into consideration, at least in the case of large projects, it was decided in 1964 that DATAR approval would be necessary for industrial constructions of more than 2,000 m^2.[17] If relocation of a project to the assisted regions or to other regions outside the Paris region appears impossible, the building permit is used to ensure that a location within the Région Parisienne conforms to the location priorities in that region (for instance since 1970 in new towns). During the period 1955—76 the annual refusal rate varied between 5 and 33 per cent in terms of floor space, and between 4 and 25 per cent in number of projects.

In order to help bring about a balance in the Paris region itself, a special tax is levied on industrial and office development in most parts of the region. This is a once and for all tax which is payable for the construction of every square metre of industrial and office floor space. At present, the rate of tax ('redevance') for industrial floor space varies between 0 and 150 FF/m^2 and for office floor space between 0 and 400 FF/m^2. This variable rate favours certain areas of the Région Parisienne.

A third discouragement measure in France is the special transport tax levied in Paris and in three adjacent areas. It takes the form of a payroll tax of about 2.0 per cent of gross wages on all firms employing more than nine persons. The transport tax is intended to raise revenue to cover the deficits of the Paris bus and underground system and the French railway company. It is at the same time an attempt to make firms pay part of the real costs of their being in the Paris region and as a disincentive against investing in that area.

As we have noticed in Table 8.1, the French Government also offers a range of incentives to encourage firms already located in the Paris area to move out (a decentralisation grant, a service sector grant, assistance to workers who move to follow their firm out of the Paris area, and, finally, tax incentives are available to investors in the development regions leaving the Paris and Lyon areas).

The Italian policy, like the British, aims mainly at diverting investment to the development areas. The 1971 law gives the Italian Government powers of administrative control over major investment decisions. [18] There is an obligation for private corporations with assets over 5 billion lire and for public or semi public companies to submit their investment programmes to the Minister of the Budget and Economic Planning. This obligation also holds for any company planning to create new industrial plants or to expand existing ones if the investment exceeds 7 billion lire. The CIPE (Comitato Interministeriale de Programmazione Economica) is entitled to express a negative opinion if the projects increase congestion in certain areas or if new investments are not directed to areas where there is an abundance of unemployed manpower. Those going against the regulations have to pay 25 per cent of the amount of the investment to the tax authorities. Moreover, public administrations will not license or authorise the implementation of investment programmes about which the CIPE has pronounced a negative opinion.[19]

The Netherlands is the fourth EEC country to apply discouragement measures. In February 1974 the Selective Investment Regulation (SIR) Bill became law; it came into force in October 1975. The Regulation applies mainly to the West (the entire provinces of North Holland, South Holland, and Utrecht, except a few areas), and is intended to slow down to some extent the establishment and extension of industries and of more or less related activities such as offices. In this congested area the Regulation is designed as a policy instrument to deal with problems of congestion and overheating in this congested area. Because it came into force during a period of economic crisis, it has not been enforced stringently. Three instruments were foreseen: a special licence, a congestion tax, and a notification duty. Within the SIR area outside Rijnmond a special licence used to be required for all building projects costing over 3 million guilders and open air installations of over 15 million guilders; that rule is now inoperative. In the Rijnmond area the building licence is operational but the ceilings are lower, 1 and 5 million guilders respectively. The licences, issued by the Ministry of Economic Affairs, were to be refused only on considerations in connection with the concentration of activities and of population in the West or with the economic structure or the conditions of the labour market in that area. The congestion tax introduced by the law of 1975 originally imposed on buildings in the Rijnmond area, and on open air facilities in the whole Western part of the country. Ten per cent tax had to be paid on the cost of buildings (industrial buildings, installations, and offices, new constructions as well as extensions) in excess of 250,000 guilders, and 3 per cent on the cost of open air facilities (oil refineries for instance) in excess of 2 million guilders. Very soon, because of the economic crisis, the rates were reduced, and many derogations, exemptions, and exceptions put into practice. By mid 1976 the tax was suspended. In the Memorandum on Regional Social Economic Policy 1977–80 the Selective Investment Regulation is maintained but without the congestion tax. The present situation is very far removed from that envisaged in the original bill, in which the tax was the main controlling instrument (100 per cent on buildings and 12.5 per cent on open air installations).

The third SIR control instrument is the compulsory notification of intended building projects. Every project in the SIR area outside Rijnmond that involves an investment of more than 1 million guilders or

5 million for open air installations) must be reported to the Ministry of Economic Affairs. The Ministers of Economic Affairs and Physical Planning can decide that a Selective Investment Regulation licence is required for the investment project in question. A notification can ultimately lead to the refusal of a building licence.

Decentralisation of government offices

Centralisation of government offices is a major cause of congestion in certain areas, and their decentralisation not only makes for decongestion but may also help to create external economies in assisted regions. Two EEC countries are stimulating the decentralisation of government offices: the United Kingdom and the Netherlands. The new Southern regional organisations in Italy may also be considered in this context.

In the United Kingdom government offices have been dispersed, especially away from central London, and the claims of the Development Areas have been increasingly met in relocation decisions. Since the end of the War one-third of dispersed government jobs have gone to assisted areas.[20]

In the Netherlands efforts have been and are being made to disperse government offices to more peripheral parts of the country, in particular to the North and to South Limburg. At least one urban agglomeration in the North is supposed to grow to such an extent that it can serve as a counter magnet to the Rimcity; the city of Groningen has been selected for that function.[21]

Regional allocation of public
investment and government orders

Quite another method of direct public intervention for the sake of regional development is the establishment of public companies. It is particularly effective when regional policy calls for a certain industry to be started, either to found a new growth centre or to make a location attractive to other industries by filling a gap in the regional economy. In Italy it is one of the main instruments available to the government to tackle regional problems; the two state holding companies, IRI and ENI, have been instructed to invest a large proportion of their resources in the South.[22] According to the recommendations of 'Project 80' the share of the South in investments in public and semi-public enterprise has been raised from 60 per cent to 80 per cent for the period up to 1980, and that in total investments from 40 to 60 per cent. It is a little harder to find nationalised industries in the United Kingdom used to boost regional employment, but the government's decision to allow the British Steel Corporation to build a new steel producing complex on

Maplin Sands in the South East, and the Corporation's subsequent choice of a site in the Teeside development area, can be seen as an example of deliberate regional bias.[23]

A government may also favour development areas through its purchasing policy, giving priority to contractors there if they can compete with bidders from non-development areas. In the United Kingdom two schemes are in operation, a general one and a special one. In the general scheme, firms in development areas are given every opportunity to tender for public contracts from the government, public bodies, and nationalised industries. Where price, quality, delivery, and other considerations are equal, the development area firm is given preference. In the special scheme, government purchasing departments review the initial competitive tenders and if not at least 25 per cent is awarded to bidders from development areas, an offer is made to the first unsuccessful bidder in the development area. Provided the overall cost of the project is not increased, an amount up to 25 per cent of the overall purchase can be awarded to this bidder. If he refuses the offer, the next lowest price tender is offered a contract, and so on.[24]

In Italy provisions assure the South a 40 per cent share of the investment programmed by public administrations and 30 per cent of the value of each contract for current purchases of industrial goods. Similar stipulations are made with respect to national funds for restructuring industrial and commercial companies and for the expansion of research activities.[25]

Regional development agencies

In chapter 7 we described the role of a regional development authority, the major task of which is the economic promotion of the region in which it is operating. As we have seen, promotion can take different forms, such as: (a) keeping a permanent inventory of resources and needs; (b) providing assistance to existing firms; (c) providing marketing assistance to firms; (d) attracting new projects to the region; (e) a production unit run by the authority itself and/or infrastructure projects carried out by the authority; (f) informing the local population; (g) defending the interests of the region on the national level; (h) coordinating regional and/or national agencies; (i) preparing physical planning studies.

Examples of regional development authorities are the 'Economisch-technologische Instituten (ETI's)'in the Netherlands, the 'Regional Development Authorities' in Belgium (GOM's and SDR's), the DATAR-OREAM in France and the Cassa per il Mezzogiorno in Italy,[26] of which the latter two are the best known. DATAR (Délégation à l'Aménagement du Territoire et à l'Action Régionale) was created in 1963 and placed under the direct authority of the prime minister. As the founding decree puts it DATAR was to be 'an agency of coordination and stimulation' (see chapter 7). But DATAR is really a national agency, one that governs the French regional policy. It derives its influence and power from (a) the high quality of its staff, (b) the money it can distribute (through FIAT — Fonds d'Interventions pour l'Aménagement du Territoire), and (c) the political influence and importance of its leaders. Officially, DATAR has no responsibility for setting goals; that is the task of the Planning Commission.[27] DATAR has its headquarters in Paris, but has created, in each of the major urban areas, planning commissions (Organisations Régionales d'Etudes des Aires Métropolitaines or OREAM) to study the problems of these areas extensively and develop master plans that serve as vehicles for DATAR ideas.

The Cassa per il Mezzogiorno in Italy was created in 1950 as an executive body under the control of a Committee of Ministers for the South. In 1972 new southern regional administrations were created, which took over a number of the Cassa's functions. Although no longer responsible for the projects now under the authority of the regional administrations, the Cassa is still responsible for the diffusion of the industrialisation process through the construction of infrastructure, the training of skilled staff, the provision of marketing assistance to entrepreneurs, etc.

Advantages and disadvantages
of some regional instruments

In the first section of this chapter we analysed a variety of regional policy instruments. The range of financial incentives was found to be extremely wide, and we tried to explain why. In this second part we pay attention to the function, advantages and disadvantages of a number of regional policy instruments. Such an evaluation of instruments must be too general; each incentive can in fact be applied in many different ways: for example capital grants may be given only for new plants for for extensions as well, a tax exemption may take the form of accelerated depreciation allowances or of regionally differentiated corporation taxes, and so on.

Investment grants

In all but one EEC country grants count as the most important financial incentive. A system of grants is credited with several advantages. For one thing it is simple and transparent; benefits can be calculated easily and quickly, and have a direct bearing on the decision where to place new investments. For another, cash grants are very practical for covering the extra costs involved in a new establishment for the first few years after the move or settlement, and circumvent the criticism of encouraging long term inefficiency. Furthermore, grants are supposed to facilitate a project's financing, which is notably important for small and medium sized firms. Indeed, a cash investment grant contributes directly to a firm's liquidity. Another, if controversial, advantage of a system of grants is that it helps to attract industries of advanced technology. But the system also has some well known drawbacks:

1 the grant system is very expensive to the exchequer;
2 the financial responsibility of the government agencies is greater than with an interest rebate system (valuation system);
3 there are spread effects in the form of inflationary pressure on other regions;[28]
4 to receive grants is sometimes felt as slightly humiliating, as a slur on industrial efficiency (such feelings are often illogical);
5 grants for regional development represent a bias towards capital intensive projects and favour over mechanisation.[29]

The bias towards capital intensive projects is by far the most important point of criticism levelled at capital grants, the argument being that employment should be stimulated because a balanced labour market is the main objective of most regional policies. We have to treat the latter objections very carefully, asking ourselves if there is an alternative in view of the economic function of the EEC in the world economic order and with a view to long term solutions for problem areas. Now regional economic policy, if it is to further the long term economic viability of problem regions, will have to make local industry more efficient. As to the impact of a project on employment, the indirect effects should be taken into account; every sector needs inputs from other sectors (see chapter 1), and to calculate what that means in terms of employment, we need to know the employment multiplier by sector. Unfortunately, this multiplier tends to differ from region to region.

An argument often heard is that the more capital intensive industries are also the more progressive, faster growing, or higher wage industries, so that it should be good for problem areas to attract them by preference. However, A.J. Brown points out that in the United Kingdom there was no significant rank correlation between capital intensity and percentage growth of employment in the period 1961–69,[30] and the Hunt Committee report showed the rate of employment growth tends to be higher in development areas than elsewhere for all industries except those with very low capital intensity and those already largely concentrated in development areas.[31]

According to A.J. Brown there is no clear relation either between high earnings and high capital intensity.[32]

To keep the costs to the exchequer within bounds and limit the bias towards capital intensive projects a ceiling can be set for the level of 'automatic assistance', that is, financial assistance that follows indiscriminately if a company settles in a problem area. In the West Central Scotland Plan it is pointed out in that respect that with automatic assistance capital grants may be given to companies that even without inducement would have invested in a problem region, and that with capital grants a great deal of assistance may be given to projects that create few jobs. In both cases it may be difficult to justify the spending of public money by the employment created. The likelihood of such unfortunate outcomes can be reduced, however, even with automatic incentives, by defining ceilings referring to both the size and the capital intensity of projects.[33] Some countries have introduced ceilings, mostly with respect to the size of the project. The Italian Government, which had long sought for ways to develop small and medium sized firms in the South, in its law of 1976 discriminates clearly between small, medium sized, and large projects.

Soft loan systems

Soft loans are in fact closely related to capital grants and it is fairly easy to calculate their grant equivalent. In some countries investors have a choice between a grant and interest rebates. The soft loan system has one major advantage: projects are financially evaluated by a private or public credit institution, which gives the public agency more security about the efficient use of public money. Another advantage could be that it is not necessary to mobilise a large amount of capital in the initial stage. The disadvantages of soft loans are very similar to those of investment grants; in addition, they are less transparent and their benefits are not so easy and quick to evaluate.

Tax exemptions

Most tax exemptions (accelerated depreciation allowance, regionally differentiated profit tax, etc.) have one major advantage: they inspire efficiency. The more profitable a project, the greater the bonus. Because the subsidy depends on the firm's viability, waste of public funds is avoided. Another, far less important, advantage is that allowances are not felt to be degrading the assisted region. A regionally differentiated corporation tax could reduce the bias in favour of capital intensive projects, by being factor neutral for multi-plant companies with all their establishments in assisted regions, and having a labour bias for those that have plants both inside and outside such regions; the latter companies would thus be encouraged to move their labour intensive processes to problem regions. One preliminary condition must be made, though: a firm's profits should be attributed to its individual plants in proportion to their share in the firm's total employment;[34] as long as that condition is not fulfilled, there is no way to decide in what region multi-plant (and, for that matter, multinational) companies are operating as far as taxes are concerned.

Tax exemptions as incentives have also drawbacks. For one thing, many projects in assisted regions have no immediate prospects of profit for the first few years of operation, nor are present profits always a dependable criterion for a firm's long term performance. For another, and that is more serious, the incentive value is low, for companies are apt to ignore tax when computing profitability, while no project can be considered free of risks.

C. Clark suggests the introduction of a regional pay roll taxes and rebates scheme.[35] Rates should be fixed, in consideration of the extent of local and zonal congestion and the local labour situation. Clark's suggestion is closely related to the Regional Employment Premium System (REP) (see below). Such a policy would not only relieve the regional problem in its twin forms of congested areas and declining areas, it would also make a contribution to the macro-economic policy of full employment without inflation, by bringing idle resources into use, and by taking the pressure off resources in the prosperous areas.

Regional employment premium or labour subsidies

The REP was introduced in the United Kingdom in 1967; the exchequer was to contribute towards the labour costs of all firms in manufacturing industry and the REP was therefore not directly related to expansion. [36] This system was introduced for several reasons:

(a) it implies no discrimination against existing firms;
(b) it gives special encouragement to labour intensive types of industry;
(c) it cuts regional production costs and so has the positive effects of a regional devaluation without the negative ones (no higher import prices);
(d) it minimises the spreading of effects to other regions;
(e) it incorporates an income transfer from rich to poor regions.

The REP is in fact an application of the Keynesian techniques of economic management on the regional level in that it aims to achieve a better balance between aggregate demand and resources available. The purpose of the inducements is to attract development to locations where resources are available, and this can be achieved by influencing the costs of operating in those locations. If the REP is passed on in lower prices, it will boost regional aggregate demand by enabling more regional production to be sold in competition with the output of other areas. Output should be able to expand without producing either inflationary or balance of payments pressure.

The efficacy of the REP depends on the condition that the premium is not simply absorbed by higher wages or profits but leads to a reduction in prices. However, one cannot expect the full effect of the REP to be passed on in a reduction in prices. Labour may successfully bargain for higher wage rates. If the REP is absorbed in increased wages, the effect on employment can be calculated via the regional multiplier. Profits of firms, especially those facing little competition, may also rise. Higher profits do not *per se* have a negative effect: they can lead to higher investment on the part of the firms already in the region. Still, the main effect of the REP should be price reductions and expansion of production, and whether or not they materialise depends not only on the attitude of trade unions and employers but also on the locational advantages and external economies of the region.[37]

Detailed analyses of likely effects of the REP were carried out by A. J. Brown and the Hunt Committee.[38]

The REP has very often been criticised, mainly because it is a very expensive form of incentive. To keep public outlays in check it would be wise to limit the REP to basic activities, or even to the exporting sector alone, for in that case the devaluation effect and the spreading effects to other regions can be kept at a minimum. The problem is how to carry through in practice the distinction between basic and non-basic activities.

The second objection raised concerns the relatively small impact of the REP in the United Kingdom. In 1975 it represented 5.0 per cent of the earnings of male workers and 4.4 per cent of those of female workers, which is not more than about 3.5 per cent in terms of value added. The same remark can be made about other incentives (see Table 8.3). However, REP is just one element of a whole package of financial measures.

Apart from these two points of criticism the question has been raised if REP is an effective form of subsidy in relation to its cost. Moreover, from the administrator's point of view the scheme is too legalistic. The criticism that it is a 'blanket subsidy', not tailored to the needs of individual firms, applies to other regional incentives as well: none of them operates at the margin.

In spite of criticism, the British Government considers the REP a useful counterbalance to the more selective elements in the regional incentive package, and the recipients' attitude is also positive. For Moore and Rhodes 'the major conclusion is that about half the business firms receiving REP believe that their labour force is higher than it would have been without REP'.[39] Not surprisingly, the Unions' attitude to REP is also favourable.

On the other hand, the EEC takes rather a negative view of the REP; it does not fit in with the Commission's system of measuring regional aid. Aids which cannot be gauged by the EEC criterion are termed 'opaque', and also the REP, being an ongoing subsidy unrelated to any particular investment, is so qualified. The reasoning is open to criticism, for the present value after tax can be calculated and expressed as a percentage of annual capital costs.[40] Mindful of the dangers of any measure which distorts competition, the EEC Commission prefers aid to go towards capital rather than operating costs and to be selective rather than automatic. In 1973 C. Thomson, former commissioner, stated that 'the feeling in the Commission so far has been that the difficulty about operational assistance is that it tends to turn into a long term, permanent subsidy and then, within Community terms, leads to a permanent distortion of competition; whereas the advantage of aid given in the form of direct help to investment — if it is given wisely — is that it has the best chance of promoting long term self-sustaining growth'. It must be said that the attitude of the Commission towards 'opaque aids' changed after the completion of the UK 'renegotiation'. In view of the calculation scheme of K. Allen there are good reasons to take a more positive attitude towards the REP.

The above considerations concerning the REP hold also, of course, for concessions on social security contributions, one of the main incentives of regional economic policy in Italy (costing 542 billion lire in 1975). Social security contributions are high in Italy, substantially higher than elsewhere in the EEC. A system of partial relief from social security charges was first introduced in 1968, on a temporary basis, in favour of industry locating in the Mezzogiorno. The system has changed very often since it was introduced and at present it is very complicated. It is temporary and certain laws can be applied only to additional jobs created. The concessions represent 18.5 to 28.5 per cent of the relevant wage bill net of overtime. Since the concession, unlike the REP in the United Kingdom, is in percentage terms, expenditure continues to grow with rising wages. The 1976 budget of the Instituto Nazionale per la Previdenza Soziale provided for rebates of 699 billion lire. They are regarded less as a positive attraction than as a means of compensating investors for the higher costs of training the industrial labour force in the South.

Transport cost subsidy

A transport cost subsidy is a typical regional instrument to compensate for a well defined handicap; this is a really positive characteristic of the measure. For a transport subsidy to be unambiguously beneficial to the region and to misallocate national resources as little as possible, it needs to have the following characteristics:

(a)   it should only be for trade to and from the region;
(b)   exports from the region should be subsidised only to the extent that exports are at a transport disadvantage compared with competitors outside the region;
(c)   imports should be subsidised only to the extent to which their price is higher in the region because of transport costs. [41]

There are several drawbacks to this instrument, the most serious being that it takes no account of the 'development worthiness' of a region. The bureaucracy needed for its effectuation is a disadvantage too. And what exactly are 'normal' transportation costs? The instrument is also one sided; after all, transportation costs are not the only costs that vary from one location to another, and remote places that involve high transportation costs may well offset them by cheap labour.

Industrial sites and advance factories

In all problem regions high quality industrial sites are offered at reduced prices to attract new firms. From a macro point of view, industrial sites are a powerful instrument in physical planning. Provision of factories was first used in the United Kingdom to encourage firms to move to assisted areas. They are either advance or custom built and are to let or for sale. Most government factories are rented. Although rents are at the current market value it is generally conceded that they tend to be below the full commercial rent in Development Areas. The incentive value of a government factory lies in its being available very quickly and at a cheap rate and in the fact that an investor by reducing the investor's investment costs, leaves him more money as working capital.

IDC's and other building licence controls

On page 318 we saw that various discouragement measures are being applied throughout the EEC. They cannot be reduced to a common denominator, but fall into two main groups: control by licence (such as the Industrial Development Certificate — IDC — in the United Kingdom and the building licence in France) and levies; in this section we shall consider only the former group.

To evaluate the licence control systems a further division must be made between systems concerned with transferring investment from developed to development regions, such as the IDC scheme, and systems like that of the ODP in the United Kingdom and the building licence in France, which aim at solving the congestion problem. The French licence system also contributes to the decentralisation of activities to lagging regions, but tends to encourage a ring of new developments just outside the licence controlled area.

Restricting ourselves to licence systems within the range of regional economic policy, we must start from the reality that wherever licence control is operated, it is combined with financial incentives. Licences have various advantages. For one thing it does not involve a lot of public money — the exchequer's argument —, and lower the amount of incentive financing needed to move new projects or expansions to assisted regions; in France, incentive measures and controls are complementary. For another thing, licence control, by imposing constraints on entrepreneurial behaviour, and drawing attention to financial incentives, force companies to examine alternative locations. The very fact that entrepreneurs have to discuss their projects with government agencies can make them wise to regional policy in general and incentive systems in particular.

Thirdly, licence control makes it possible for an agency for regional development to enter into negotiations with large national and international companies about package deals, allowing them for example to build additional floor space or a new plant in a controlled area provided they realise another new plant in a problem area. Such bargaining has enabled DATAR in France to relocate certain activities. Including both the government's control policy and the applicant's location requirements in the bargaining gives a better chance of relocation in the areas designated by the government than the mere refusal to locate in control areas, which leave entrepreneurs still free to choose locations other than those preferred by the government.[42] The French location contracts for very large companies and financial institutions are typical results of bargaining, allowing these companies and institutions to modernise existing establishments in the Paris region and ameliorate their working conditions.

Fourthly, as an administrative control licences enable the government to act selectively and flexibly, treating each case according to its merits and varying stringency with the economic cycle.

A final advantage is that through a licence system a direct relationship is created between the regional policy of a country and its physical planning policy.

Various objections have been raised to the system of building licences.

It is argued, firstly, that there is no guarantee that being refused a licence to build in a control area, firms will go and set up their plant in a problem region; the project may be cancelled altogether, as the investor may decide to expand his business abroad. Or the plant may be set up in a problem region at considerable loss of efficiency;[43] and thus at economic cost to the nation. However, it seems that the impact of IDC's in terms of employment cost has not been alarming. According to G.C. Cameron, data from the Department of Trade and Industry show that in the two most rigidly controlled areas, the South East and the Midlands, the employment that is not realised in control areas through the refusal of IDC's amounts to an average of 20 to 30 per cent of the employment associated with all applications submitted; moreover, the IDC system has been relaxed since 1971. Most refused projects go ahead in other parts of non-assisted areas; only 5 per cent of all projects are abandoned or realised outside the United Kingdom.[44][45] In France, both the companies involved and the public sector agree that very few potential jobs are lost as a result of the licence system. French medium sized and large firms tend to take a positive attitude towards the control system, but most small firms are of a different opinion. According to DATAR there is no evidence of a multinational company taking its project out of France after a refusal.

It has been argued that formal figures about lost employment are incomplete, because manufacturers who wish to expand their establishments may be discouraged at the informal stage of enquiring and never tender a formal application to the controlling ministry. A.J. Brown asserts that this kind of loss of potential growth has been very slight indeed.[46]

The effectiveness of IDC's was recently evaluated carefully and with an eye for detail in the analysis by B. Nicol and G. Wehrmann;[47] they come to the conclusion that mere formal refusal to build or expand in one region does little to divert activities to assisted regions. During the period 1950—71 only 9 per cent of the projects formally refused or 25 per cent in terms of employment, were subsequently realised in assisted areas. If other government preferred areas (for example new towns) are considered as well, the project diversion becomes 18 per cent, and the employment diversion about 35 per cent. These are rather low percentages, and not consistent with the objective. However, as B. Nicol and G. Wehrmann point out, by counting the behaviour of companies after a formal refusal, the diversion effect is underestimated, for within the range of IDC policy, the government can yield other tools, such as informal refusal, offers of package deals, warning letters, notice of expected refusal, to stimulate the desired diversion; the authors estimate that such control components account for a further diversion of 32 per cent in terms of employment. That figure does not account for the diversion effect accomplished by supplying information about the labour market, industrial sites, and other features of problem regions, and about the incentives available to those who decide to settle there.

All things considered it would be wrong to conclude that licence control has been an insignificant factor in the movement of manufacturing firms to development areas; two multiple regression analyses, which later sections (page 347) prove the contrary.[48] Moore and Rhodes state: 'The IDC controls have been the cornerstone of regional policy in that they have been the most effective regional policy instrument'.

On the other hand, it cannot be denied that the system has caused additional costs to the companies involved; those to be quoted here are taken from B. Nicol and G. Wehrmann.

Costs associated with approval are: (a) costs associated with modified plans (for instance less floor space); (b) costs associated with package deals; (c) conditions on the subsequent use of vacated premises.

Costs associated with refusal or other forms of discouragement are:

(a) projects abandoned and projects relocated abroad. IDC control has caused 13 per cent of the projects to be abandoned and 1 per cent to be moved abroad after their formal refusal; the authors have no information on the extent to which projects were abandoned or moved elsewhere from other features of control, such as informal or expected refusal. The authors A. Farhi, C. Lemaître, and R. Schmitges consider the French control system less deterrent than the English one.[50] The job loss ratio, i.e. the total number of jobs actually created divided by the total number of jobs that could have been created without the control system, was 0.85 to 0.87 for the period 1959—64, and 0.93 to 0.95 for the period 1969—73. Of course, the alternative location possibilities in France (Bassin Parisien and new towns) and England (new towns) are not identical, and neither the effect of steering through bargaining nor the stringency of application in the two countries are very well comparable. In fact, it is not easy to evaluate the efficacy of the licence system in France;

(b) costs associated with forced relocation in assisted areas. Additional costs often mentioned are transportation, operating, and duplicated (for instance management) costs; but it is also admitted by some firms that the additional costs are offset by financial incentives;

(c) the costs ensuing from the unstability of branch plant economies as sources of employment; this is contested by H.W. Atkins, however.[51]

A second objection to building licence schemes is that governments are not the best judges of plant location. There is, however, no clear evidence of a loss of efficiency by moving to other regions and, furthermore, firms only consider the private costs of their decisions and not the social costs that may result from them (see chapter 1 and chapter 5). [52] We must not forget that there are incentives to compensate for part of the costs of setting up projects and that long term operating costs may well be lower in assisted regions. The control system may also tap idle resources and reduce inflationary pressure. This is the 'overheating argument' which is operated as the rationale for IDC policy. As far as effects on the nation as a whole are concerned, B. Nicol and G. Wehrmann state:

> IDC policy has obviously led to benefits for the assisted areas by diverting projects to these areas, thereby improving their employment situation. We are unable to conduct the appropriate cost side of the calculation to find whether the control has resulted in a net resource gain or loss, overall. Theoretical arguments can be used to show that the control can achieve a net resource gain effect whenever it creates diversion to the assisted areas or constrains the behaviour of others in the 'overheated' areas. This argument only applies in expansionary periods; we therefore require details of its effects in recessions to determine whether a net gain results, in practice, over the cycle. [53]

Another drawback, less frequently suggested, is that, because controls apply only to new construction, they may induce entrepreneurs to put new equipment in old buildings, which would be inefficient as it tends to 'lock in' the industrial pattern of an area, excluding competition from new industries and new firms. [54] Actually, this drawback falls into the category of 'costs associated with refusal'.

Furthermore, it is alleged that with licence control it is hardly possible to discriminate between activities linked with existing industries, and therefore desirable for a region, and activities without such links. Still, in the United Kingdom as well as in France a project's mobility is assessed by its links to the location named in the licence application. A claim that is perhaps more to the point is that the control system inhibits the process of structural diversification in some controlled areas. It can do so both by frustrating the expansion of indigenous firms and by preventing or restricting the location of new plants. But in the United Kingdom the large majority of applications have always been approved and in times of recession the control has always been relaxed. Perhaps the relaxation comes too late, but then we are in a vicious circle.

Finally, it has been claimed that the time involved in getting all the permits required for establishing a plant in a controlled region (as in the Dutch system) diminishes the attractiveness of that region. We must be aware that certain projects can be realised only in well-defined areas (e.g. Rijnmond).

Other discouragement measures

So far, we have analysed only control by means of building licences; there are, however, other instruments. A variety of congestion taxes have been introduced; though their purpose is evident, their efficiency may be less so. Indeed, as an instrument of inter-regional steering of projects they have several deficiencies.[55] First, the burden of taxes imposed on the industrial and tertiary sector within an agglomeration are likely to be passed on to consumers in and outside that agglomeration; because the price elasticity of the demand for the products of these sectors is often low, the taxation may well have inflationary effects. Secondly, a congestion tax does not allow for flexible and selective, case by case treatment. Thirdly, because taxes are paid after the investment, it is difficult to bargain for location agreements, a drawback that could be remedied by compulsory notification of intended projects, Fourthly, congestion taxes do not constitute an active instrument, for they leave the final decision to move or not to move to the firm.

Two final remarks about discouragement measures should be made. The first is that the stringency with which such measures are applied depends largely on the business cycle. In the United Kingdom and France, and also in the Netherlands and Italy, restrictive policies have been relaxed in response to the new and ominous phenomenon of industries fleeing from the cities. We may wonder to what extent the new phenomenon is due to political pressure; anyhow, licence control is not the factor most responsible for the de-industrialisation of inner areas or conurbations; non-controlled agglomerations are facing the same problems.

Our second remark is that it seems impossible to design a system by which the same standards are applied to all countries or conurbations. There are too many factors to be considered, such as the industrial structure, the tertiary and quaternary functions, and the way agglomerations are spread across the territory. It should be emphasised that in practice the French control system has been operated to some extent as a selective instrument designed to promote high level functions in the Paris region while decentralising 'banal' activities to the assisted and other regions.

The question has been raised on several occasions whether incentives should be preferred to controls. To answer that question, many factors should be taken into account, such as the objectives of regional policy, the business cycle, the degree of congestion. However, the considerations of the present section suggest that it is not necessary to make a choice, a suggestion that is confirmed by A.J. Brown's statement: 'The best generalisation one can make is, perhaps, that industrial development certificates and incentives have acted together to produce effects greater than the sum of those that would have been produced by each of the two instruments operated as they were, in the absence of the other'. [56] The British and French control systems demonstrated indeed the need for a package deal of push and pull instruments, if a regional policy effect is to be achieved.

In this section we have dealt with the eight most important instruments of regional policy. There are a few others which are purely compensative or have obvious motives. One other instrument, which is not applied in any EEC country, deserves perhaps to be analysed in some detail, namely a regionally differentiated value added system. There are probably two reasons why it is not applied in the EEC. The first is that in all forms it entails immense administrative problems, for example as far as multi-plant companies are concerned. The second is that such a system, and in particular a tax levied on the principle of origin, would face opposition from the EEC Commission.

Macro-economic evaluation methods of regional economic policy instruments

It is not the main purpose of this section to evaluate the effectiveness of individual instruments; the results of regional policy are never due to one instrument alone. After discussing in the preceding section various regional instruments we shall now present a few methods — applied or not — to analyse the efficiency and the effectiveness of regional policy.

What exactly is efficiency? According to G.C. Cameron the word has two meanings[58] in respect to regional policy. The first refers to the maximisation of growth in real GNP, probably with a long term perspective in mind. The second concerns the use of public resources in such a way that the goals of regional policy are achieved; it might imply a criterion like the minimum of social costs to achieve a given quantity of regional goals. We should like a third and a fourth meaning, the third being connected with the result of the policy; has the regional product, or the employment level, of assisted regions been higher with than without regional instruments; has the policy achieved its objectives? (Unfortunately the objectives are all too often formulated in vague terms.) How the evolution of income disparities can be analysed by region has been explained in chapter 2. Finally, efficiency of regional policy can also be taken to mean that its benefits are shown to exceed its costs in a cost-benefit analysis, without regard to the maximisation of GNP in the country concerned.

The four meanings are not totally independent from one another. The first meaning, maximisation of GNP growth, is partially associated with the economic motives of regional policy, but social, political, and environmental arguments have to be taken into account as well in the motivation of regional policy. In considering G.C. Cameron's second interpretation, analysis of the individual instruments such as we pursued in the first and more particularly in the second section of this chapter, may be relevant. In this section we are concerned specifically with the third and fourth meanings of efficiency, and we shall present some methods to measure it and some evaluation results.

Cost-benefit approach

The cost-benefit approach is the appropriate method to analyse the efficiency of regional economic policy with respect to a specific assisted region. To find out what items are relevant the following scheme may be useful; it distinguishes four levels of costs and benefits (see Table 8.4).

It is very difficult to make a cost-benefit analysis of regional policy measures. As with any cost-benefit analysis it must be admitted that some non-economic costs and benefits and some intangibles cannot be measured, but even apart from that, the data required are in most cases not available for a sufficiently long period. Moreover, to each item the 'with and without' principle has to be applied, which implies a distinction between diverted, autonomous, and subsidy created investment that is very difficult to make.

In our approach all pure transfer transactions, such as direct taxation, reduction of unemployment relief, increase of social security contributions, are neglected, precisely the group of benefits on which L. Needleman mainly based his approach.[59]   B. Moore and J. Rhodes, in an attempt to estimate the impact of regional economic policy on the accounts of the public sector, defined the cost to the exchequer as follows:

> . . . net exchequer cost of regional policy is a compound of the following items (a) initial exchequer outlays on regional incentives, (b) net of any directly recoverable items, (c) net of the change in tax yield necessary to maintain the pressure of demand in fully employed areas, and (d) net of changes in tax revenue resulting from increased employment, output and income brought about by regional policy.[60]

To our knowledge no such cost-benefit analysis ex post has yet been completed; C. Blake's theoretical approach and two recent publications of Moore and Rhodes are along the indicated lines, however.[61] [62]

Blake's approach is mainly concerned with indiscriminate regional subsidies to capital, paid in three different situations:

(a) on subsidy diverted projects; similar investment would otherwise have been made elsewhere;

(b) on autonomous projects; the same investment would have been made even without subsidies;

(c) on subsidy created projects; all or part of the investment would not have been made without the subsidy.

The author considers five headings under which costs and benefits may be expected to arise:

(a) What are the capital outlays directly attributable to the subsidy? In the autonomous case these costs do not occur. In the subsidy created case the entire resource cost of investment is attributable to subsidy. In the subsidy diverted case only those costs which are incurred as a result of selecting the alternative location are attributable to subsidy.

(b) Second, there are gains from the employment of otherwise idle resources in the assisted regions (labour and under utilised plant). In the subsidy created case, the extent of the gain is the difference between market price and shadow price for all labour employed. With the subsidy diverted case, it is the relatively greater extent of this difference in the host region as compared to alternative locations.

(c) In the subsidy diverted case there may be relocation economies and diseconomies (e.g. differences in labour quality). At the same time the investment may increase or decrease external economies or diseconomies. It may carry with it external benefits which accrue to other firms.

(d) In the subsidy diverted case, relocation towards an assisted region may reduce congestion costs in other areas.

(e) Finally, the benefits from the attraction of foreign capital or through the retention of domestic capital that otherwise would have been invested abroad.

The costs and benefits under these headings can be found in Table 8.4.

B. Moore and J. Rhodes analyse the economic implications of regional policy (period 1963—70) in a different way. They start from the idea that any regional policy has an impact in both development and

Table 8.4

Possible items of a cost-benefit analysis concerning regional economic policy with respect to one particular region

Level	Costs	Benefits
The firm's (government) level	C1 (a) infrastructural incentives (b) financial incentives (c) administrative costs of the policy	B1 (a) repayment of rents (e.g. factory rents) and loans (b) lower (higher) construction costs
Unpaid level	C2 (a) possible environmental costs (b) negative effects on agriculture (c) lower efficiency of private firms (d) relocation diseconomies	B2 (a) employment of idle resources (additional income created) (b) decrease of inflationary pressure (c) relocation economies (d) balance of payments effects (quasi-devaluation) (e) avoidance of social and psychological costs of migration (f) sociological and political effects (g) attraction of foreign capital
Underpayment level	C3 (a) employment costs of unemployed labour in the regional infrastructure works (negative cost)	B3 (a) reduction of congestion costs (b) savings on social infrastructure
Side effects	C4 (a) negative effects on competitive firms	B4 (a) positive effects on complementary firms (e.g. savings via improvement of the external economies of existing firms) (b) secondary benefits (multiplier effect)

non-development regions.[63] They calculate the effects of regional policy on employment inside and outside assisted regions before and after restoring the pressure of demand in the fully employed areas. Their approach is represented in Table 8.5. They make a distinction between employment change in fully employed and in Development Areas of the United Kingdom.

Table 8.5
The effects of regional policy on employment inside and outside Development Areas before and after restoring the pressure of demand in the fully employed areas. United Kingdom, period 1963–70

| | | Employment change in (000s) | |
		Fully employed areas	Development Areas
	(1) Before restoring pressure of demand		
(a)	Income effects of initial exchequer outlays (inc. multiplier effects) Average for the period	+ 25	+ 9
(b)	Income effects deriving from the increase in employment and profits. Average for the period	+ 25	+ 9
(c)	Employment creation in and diversion to DAs (inc. multiplier effects)	−195	+260
	Sub total	−145	+278
	(2) After restoring pressure of demand		
(a)	Employment generated by government expenditure associated with migration.	− 20	+ 14
(b)	Total increase in employment required to restore pressure of demand	+131	+ 33
	Total employment change	− 34	+325

Source: Moore, B. and Rhodes, J., op.cit., p.191.

The total effect of the regional policy of the United Kingdom on employment in the whole country during the period 1963–70 is an increase of 291,000; in a second attempt based on other migration assumptions, the total increase of employment amounts to 254,000. The corresponding additional output is estimated at approximately 1 per cent of GDP.

The overall conclusion with respect to economic and exchequer implications is very positive and may have policy consequences:

> Normally changes in government expenditures are viewed in rela-
> tion to the expected claim they make on scarce labour resources.
> We maintain that government expenditures on regional policy
> should not be seen as making such a claim on resources. This is
> because, unlike most other forms of public expenditure, they bring
> about an increase in the overall utilisation of labour resources (i.e.
> an increase in productive potential) which is beneficial to the whole
> economy in terms of increased employment and output. Further,
> in no sense is there a cost associated with these regional policy
> expenditures. Expenditures on regional policy should not be
> regarded as competing with other public or private expenditures
> and do not require sacrifices either in terms of public expenditures
> and therefore increases in regional policy expenditure or in terms
> of higher taxation. On the contrary, all regions enjoy an increase
> in real disposable income because real output is higher and general
> taxation is lower (or public expenditure higher) than would have
> been the case in the absence of regional policy.[64]

Multiple regression approach
based on autonomous factors

In this approach the actual growth of income or employment is compared with the expected growth of income or employment based on
autonomous factors. In the first place an equation must be found which
explains the growth of income and employment by region. In the Dutch
case, it was tried to explain the employment growth in the seventy-eight
economic areas of the Netherlands during the period 1950—60 from the
following factors: labour reserve (A), wage level (L), degree of industrialisation in the beginning of the period (I), and the share of growing
industries (S).[65]

If the basic equation based on the autonomous factors contributes
sufficiently to the explanation of the employment growth, one can
proceed with the second phase.

Let us suppose that the basic equation takes the following form:

$$Y^* = a_0 + a_1 A + a_2 L + a_3 I + a_4 S \qquad (8.1)$$

where Y^* is the calculated percentage growth of employment or industrial employment during the period considered.

By this formula, the growth of employment in each of the assisted
regions can be computed. The efficiency of the regional policy can be

computed. The efficiency of the regional policy can be derived from the residuals, i.e. the difference between the actual (Y) and the calculated or estimated (Y*) values of Y. If the basic equation does not adequately explain Y in the assisted regions (only in the case of positive residuals: $Y - Y^* > 0$), that may be an indication that employment would not have attained the actual growth of employment without an active regional policy. From the difference between Y and Y* the additional employment due to regional policy can be calculated.

The application of this method to the Dutch case during the period 1950—60 led to the following results:

$$Y^* = 7.687 \text{ A} - 12.780 \text{ L} + 0.136 \text{ I} + 0.013 \text{ S} + 49.38 \qquad (8.2)$$
$$(1.321) \qquad (5.138) \qquad (0.145) \qquad (0.130)$$

in which:

Y*	=	the calculated relative growth of industrial employment per area during the period 1950—60;
A	=	the average labour reserve per area during the period 1950—60;
S	=	the share of the chemical and metal industry in total employment, average of the years 1950 and 1960;
I	=	the degree of industrialisation in 1950;
L	=	the average income per taxpayer in industry in 1955.

The correlation coefficient amounted to $R = 0.822$ but only the factors A and L were really significant.

The multiplier regression analysis based only on the factors A and L gave the following result:

$$Y^* = 7.613 \text{ A} - 10.178 \text{ L} + 43.80 \quad R = 0.815 \qquad (8.3)$$
$$(1.300) \qquad (3.857)$$

Both factors were highly significant. The regression coefficients of A and L were, respectively, 5.9 and 2.6 times the corresponding standard error. The degree of influence of the explanatory factors on the dependent factor was equal to:

$$a_1 \, \sigma_A = 847.0 \ (209)$$

$$a_2 \, \sigma_L = 406.1 \ (100) \ (\text{influence of L} = 100)$$

The ratio between the influence of the first exogenous factor and that of the second one is 2 to 1. In Graph 8.1 the difference between

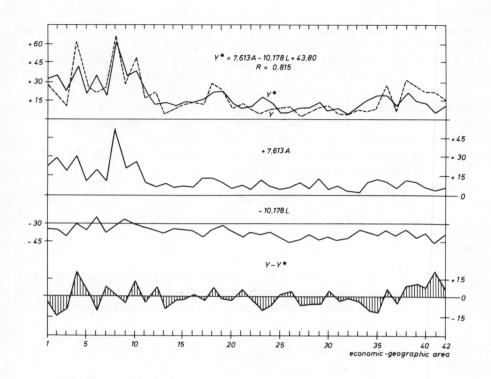

Graph 8.1: The observed (Y) and calculated (Y*) relative growth of industrial employment per economic geographic area, period 1950—60.

the contribution of the two factors to the explanation of industrial growth per area (42 economic geographic areas) is also very clear. Apart from this graph, we have the observed (Y) and calculated (Y*) growth per area. These two autonomous independent factors, however, failed to explain adequately the growth of industrial employment in the Dutch problem area. On an average the observed employment in the assisted regions, during the period 1950—60, was about 50 per cent higher than the calculated one. This is an indication that in most problem regions the regional economic policy of the Netherlands resulted in a growth of employment which would not have been reached without regional incentives. We admit that this approach may call for some reservations. The relevant labour market may be wider than the economic geographic area to which it belongs and there may be other significant explanatory factors. We doubt, however, that such remarks can change the overall conclusion that Dutch regional policy has led to significant

344

results during the period 1950—60.

A study similar to the foregoing was performed by the Netherlands Economic Institute.[66] [67] (See also chapter 2.) As a basis for the study a multi-regional model was used consisting of seven structural equations, one of which relates to investments. In that equation investments are a function of expected profits. In the migration equation the volume of migration is a function of regional wage differentials and the attractiveness of a region. Further equations relate to supply of and demand for labour and *per capita* regional income. The reduced form equations are derived from the structural equations. The most relevant reduced form equation, that for the development of employment, was tested for thirty regions in the Northern provinces of the Netherlands. The result for the period 1960—67 was (t—values in brackets):

$$\frac{\Delta E}{E} = -4.12 + 0.40\ (\frac{\Delta D}{D-n}) - 0.21\ \Sigma S_L + 10.67\ \frac{\Sigma \Delta P}{\Sigma P} + 10.13\ G$$

$$(0.07) \qquad (0.12) \qquad (4.68) \qquad (1.93)$$

$$(R = 0.90) \qquad (8.4)$$

in which:

$\frac{\Delta E}{E}$ = percentage growth of employment between 1960 and 1967;

$(\frac{\Delta D}{D-n})$ = total percentage growth of population from 1951 to 1960;

ΣS_L = percentage share of employment in agriculture in total employment in neighbouring regions in 1960;

G = policy variable.

$\frac{\Sigma \Delta P}{\Sigma P}$ = average annual percentage natural increase in the population of neighbouring areas (1960—65).

The policy variable is a complex dummy variable with as components:

1 financial assistance;
2 special investments in infrastructure (ports, motor roads);
3 special service activities (large hospitals, for example);
4 special regional functions.

An area gets one point, half a point or no point according to the degree to which the area meets the criterion. Thus, the minimum number of points is 0, the maximum 4.

It appears that the constant in the equation is negative, which implies a negative autonomous development of employment in the North. The size of the coefficient of $\left(\frac{\Delta D}{D-h}\right)$ is interesting. This coefficient represents the influence of past population development on present development. Its size corresponds to the participation rate in the North (40 per cent). It shows that the pressure on the expansion of employment equals the increase of the working population. The impulses of the neighbouring regions are represented by the factors ΣS_L and $\frac{\Sigma \Delta P}{\Sigma P}$.

The pressure of the agricultural regions as an indicator of the economic structure appears to be negative, as expected. The influence of the annual increase of the population in neighbouring regions is clearly positive. The final conclusion drawn in the study is that the contribution of the policy variable to the increase in employment in the past is about 35 per cent.

A modified shift-share analysis

A modified shift-share analysis was applied by B. Moore and J. Rhodes to analyse the effects of British regional economic policy during the period 1960—71.[68] The basic idea of the method used by these authors is again to compare a hypothetical position (expected growth), net of any differential structural effects,[69] with what actually 'happened'; the field of application is the whole of Development Areas in the United Kingdom. The essence of the method is the elimination of differences in regional growth rates that spring from differences in industrial structure. The elimination of differential effects is achieved by comparing for each industry the annual growth rates of the Development Areas with those of the United Kingdom as a whole. To that end, the national growth rates of each industry for each year of the period considered were applied cumulatively to the corresponding employment figures of the Development Areas of the base year (1963, or the year in which regional policy was strengthened).[70] The series thus prepared represents what would have happened to industrial employment in the Development Areas if it had grown according to national growth rates. Comparison of this series with the figures of actual employment in those areas, yields their differential growth effect in respect of national growth, undistorted by structural differences.[71] B. Moore and J. Rhodes found that by 1971 manufacturing employment was 12 per cent above what could have been expected without an active regional policy[72] and that by 1970, investment in manufacturing industry had risen to 30 per cent higher than the expectation under a continued passive regional policy throughout the 1960s.

The main point of criticism against this shift-share procedure is that no explanatory factors are taken into account, so that we cannot be sure if the observed differences are due to regional policy or to autonomous factors, for example the labour reserve. The authors, recognising the problem, bring supporting the alleged identification of a regional policy effect with various points of evidence, three of which are mentioned below:

(a)   each Development Area shows a positive difference between actual and expected employment and investment;
(b)   the employment increase in the Midlands and the South East fell below that corresponding with national movements, a pattern that points towards regional policy succeeding in diverting manufacturing activity from prosperous regions to Development Areas;
(c)   the divergence between actual and expected employment was not increasing nearly as much in non-manufacturing industries.

Admittedly these points are convincing to a degree, but the developments they refer to could have been the result of one and the same autonomous factor.

Sometimes it is argued that the assisted areas of the United Kingdom offer marginal location. If that were so, relatively high closure rates could be expected there, and plants in Development Areas would be the first to lay off workers in a period of economic recession. For neither is there any evidence in the United Kingdom;[73] unfortunately the United Kingdom is the only country for which data on that score are available.

The effect of regional policy on the
movement of manufacturing industry
in the United Kingdom

A few years ago two papers were published to demonstrate the effect of regional economic policy in the United Kingdom on the movement of manufacturing firms to Development Areas, one paper representing another piece of research by Moore and Rhodes, the other prepared by B. Ashcroft and J. Taylor.[74] Both analyses were designed to estimate the impact of regional policy instruments on the number of firms moving into Development Areas;[75] to that end they made use of a regression model, evaluating the efficiency of regional policy in the sense of cost benefit effectiveness.

Moore and Rhodes define a move ' . . . as an opening in a new location of a new manufacturing establishment, the origin of which is in some other location'.[76] Four explanatory factors for the number of such moves are taken into consideration: three regional policy instruments and the overall pressure of demand. The latter is a cyclical factor accounting for the shortages of factory space and labour in the development regions during the upswing of the trade cycle. The basic equation is:

$$MDA_t = a_1 + a_2 MU_t + a_3 II_{t-1} + a_4 IDC_{t-1} + a_5 REP_{t-1} \quad (8.5)$$

where:

MDA_t	=	number of moves to British Development Areas in year t;
MU	=	male unemployment rate as an indicator of the overall pressure of demand;
II_{t-1}	=	present value of investment incentives per £100 expenditure in the preceding year;
IDC_{t-1}	=	official IDC refusals (measured in terms of the firms' expectation of the employment involved) in the Midlands and South East regions expressed as a percentage of refusals plus approvals in these regions in the preceding year;
REP_{t-1}	=	regional employment premium in the preceding year; index of real value, REP.

The application yielded the following result:

$$MDA_t = 29.69 - 7.97\ MU_t + 2.01\ II_{t-1} + 2.05\ IDC_{t-1} + 52.67\ REP_{t-1}$$
$$(4.28) \quad (1.81) \quad\quad (5.52) \quad\quad (5.76) \quad\quad\quad (4,79)$$
$$(8.6)$$

The figures in parentheses are t—ratios. The overall result is very positive. About 90.0 per cent of the variation in MDA is explained by the four explanatory factors, with all policy variables significant.

The assessment of the relative impact of the different policy instruments proves that IDC control has been the most effective regional policy instrument. Starting from the basic equation it is not difficult to estimate the average annual number of moves to Development Areas. For the period 1960—71 the average annual numbers of moves to development areas generated by individual regional policy instruments are: [77]

Policy instrument	Number of years in operation	Annual number of moves
IDC policy	12	45
Investment incentives	8	36
REP	4	40
MU	12	11

Although they agree that both incentives and controls had a significant influence on the movement of manufacturing industry, B. Ashcroft and J. Taylor believe that the approach of Moore and Rhodes and the research work done by A. Beacham and W.T. Osborn overestimate the effect of regional policy on industrial movement.[78] B. Ashcroft and J. Taylor distinguish three related models of industrial movement: (a) a pressure of demand model, (b) an investment demand model, and (c) a generation distribution model.[79]

The pressure of demand model is the one suggested by Moore and Rhodes:

$$MDA = f \, (PD, RP)$$

where:

MDA	=	the movement of industry to the Development Areas;
PD	=	the pressure of demand;
RP	=	a measure of the effect of regional policy on the movement of industry to Development Areas.

Industrial movement to problem regions depends upon the general level of business activity. When the capacity ceiling is achieved (for example labour becoming scarce) firms will tend to look towards other regions.

The investment demand model takes other factors into consideration. Industrial moves are associated with the expansion of a firm's capacity. A decision to move is a component of the decision to invest; in other words pressure of demand is not the only factor which has an influence on movement. The main reason for movement being expansion of output, moves may be explained by a model of investment. The authors take a modified capital stock adjustment model:

$$I_t = g \, (\Delta Y_t, S_{t-1}, I_{t-1}) \qquad (8.7)$$

where:

I	=	manufacturing investment;

$$\Delta Y = \text{change in manufacturing output;}$$
$$S = \text{spare capacity in manufacturing sector.}$$

To allow for the effect of regional policy on the movement of industry to Development Areas, we obtain:

$$MDA_t = h \, (\Delta Y_t, S_{t-1}, I_{t-1}, RP_t) \qquad (8.8)$$

In this equation pressure of demand affects moves in two ways: indirectly through its effect on investment and directly through the pressure on resources in the development regions.

Investment activity affects total industrial movement in the whole economy rather than its regional distribution. Accordingly, the authors believe that in addition to an investment demand model a model is required to account for both the generation and the distribution of industrial movement. It means that the investment demand model is more appropriate for explaining the generation of industrial movement than its geographical direction. The share of Development Areas in total movement will depend upon their attractiveness (A) relative to other locations. Therefore, two additional equations are introduced:

$$M_t = i \, (\Delta Y_t, S_{t-1}, I_{t-1}, RP_t) \qquad (8.9)$$

$$\frac{MDA}{M} = j \, (A) \qquad (8.10)$$

where:

M = total movement (and not movement to DAs);
A = attraction of DA locations to other locations (rate of unemployment in the DAs relative to the rate in South East regions).

It is evident that regional policy instruments have an impact on the generation as well as on the distribution of industrial movement. As we have seen on page 333, firms prevented from expanding on the spot through location controls do not necessarily move to an assisted region. 'The potential effect of incentives and controls on the regional distribution of industrial movement is similar to their effect in total movement; mobile plant will be attracted towards the region offering financial incentives; and controls on industrial development in non-development areas will divert mobile plant to the "Development Areas"'.[79]

The two main conclusions of Ashcroft and Taylor, based on their empirical analysis (14 multiple regression equations) are:[80]

(a) 'Our "best estimate" of the effect of regional policy on industrial movement is that over 40 per cent of the moves to Development Areas are a direct result of regional policy, raising the number of moves by about 500. Converting these moves into jobs ... we estimate these moves to have led to a direct increase of around 90,000 jobs in the manufacturing sector of the Development Areas. This is not an insignificant achievement, though it is substantially less than the policy effect estimated in previous research work'.

(b) 'Industrial location controls and capital subsidies both had a substantial effect on the movement of industry, location controls inducing an increase in total movement and capital subsidies inducing a greater proportion of movers to locate in the Development Areas and Special Development Areas'.

The difference between Moore and Rhodes on the one hand and Ashcroft and Taylor on the other, as far as the regional policy effect on MDA is concerned, is due to two factors. First, the male unemployment rate is a poor measure of the pressure of demand. Secondly, the pressure of demand model is incomplete.

In the framework of this study we cannot deal with all the macro-economic evaluations that have been performed; indeed other authors have made valuable contributions in that respect.[81] We should like to make three closing remarks, however. The first is that more macro-evaluations of regional economic policy are commendable. So far most research has been oriented to individual instruments and the implementation of partial objectives rather than to the efficiency of a package of incentives and disincentives. Secondly, the most valuable contributions in the framework of policy assessment were made by British and, to a lesser extent, Dutch authors. That is not surprising: the British school is very advanced in the study of the economic motivation of regional economic policy. Thirdly, the existing evaluations are to a large extent related to our third meaning of regional policy efficiency: what is the difference between regional employment or income with and without regional economic policy?

Notes

[1]   CEE, *Rapports de groupes d'experts sur la politique régionale dans la Communauté Economique Européenne*, Brussels, 1964, p.294.
[2]   Council of Europe, *Effects of transport infrastructure on regional development. The economic impact of the Severn Bridge — a case study*, Strasbourg, 1973. Charles River Associates, *The Role of Transportation*

on *Regional Economic Development*, 1971, see chapter 3: 'Empirical appraisal of the role of transportation in regional growth: past and future'. Plassard, F., *Impact des investissements infrastructurels des transports sur le développement régional*, European seminar of the ministers of transport, Paris, 1977.

[3]   Davin, L.E., Degeer, L., and Paelinck, J.H.P., op.cit., p.83.

[4]   Davin, L.E., 'Les conditions de croissance des économies régionales dans les pays développés', *Théorie de politique de l'expansion régionale*, Brussels, 1961, pp 21-2.

[5]   Van de Poll, E.H., and Bourdrez, J.A., 'Infrastructuur, en regionale ontwikkeling', Klaassen, L.H. (ed.), *Regionale economie*, Groningen, 1972.

[6]   OCDE, *Les problèmes et les politiques de développement régional dans les pays de l'OCDE*, vol.I and vol.II, Paris, 1976. OCDE, *Réévaluation des politiques régionales dan les pays de l'OCDE*, Paris, 1974. OCDE, *Les politiques régionales. Perspectives actuelles*, Paris, 1977. Allen, K., *Regional incentives in the European Community. A comparative study*, Internationales Institut für Management und Verwaltung, Berlin, 1978. EEC, 'Report on the regional problems in the enlarged Community', op.cit. Konings, M., 'La politique régionale', *Cahiers économiques de Bruxelles*, no.52, 1971. Hansen, N., *Public Policy and Regional Economic Development. The Experience of Nine Western Countries*, Cambridge, 1974.

[7]   Luxembourg is not included in table 1.

[8]   Allen, K., op.cit.

[9]   Allen, K., op.cit.

[10] Yuill, D., *A Valuation of Regional Incentives in Great Britain*, Allen, K., *European Regional Policy Project*, op.cit.

[11] See chapter 1 and chapter 8.

[12] Publications on discouragement measures are: Jarrett, R.J., 'Disincentives: the other side of regional development policy', *Journal of Common Market Studies*, June 1975. OCDE, *Les mesures restrictives de politique régionale*, Paris, 1977. Wettman, R., *Deglomeration policy in the EEC — a comparative study*, International Institute of Management, Berlin, 1978. Nicol, B. and Wehrmann, G., *Deglomeration Policy in Great Britain*, vol.I and II, Berlin, 1978. Farhi, A., Lemaître, C. and Schmitges, R., *Deglomeration Policy in France — La procédure d'Agrément*, Berlin, 1978. Fleck, W., Fritsch, M. and Wettmann, R., *Transferability of Regional Control Policies*, Berlin, 1978. Van Duijn, J., *Deglomeration Policy in the Netherlands*, Berlin, 1978. Hansen, N. (ed.), *Public Policy and Regional Economic Development*, op.cit. The Hunt Committee, *The Intermediate Areas*, HMSO, 1969.

[13] Jarrett, R.J., op.cit., p.379. See also Fleck, W., Fritsch, M. and

Wettmann, R., op.cit., vol.II.

[14] The new spatial problems in Britain due to the current recession have forced the government to give the inner areas of London and Birmingham second priority after the assisted regions as areas to which mobile projects should be steered through IDC control (see *Policy for Inner Cities,* HMSO, June 1977).

[15] Cameron, G.C., *Regional Economic Policy in the United Kingdom,* Hansen, N. (ed.), *Public policy* . . . , op.cit., p.85.

[16] Jarrett, R.J., op.cit., p.32. The 'agrément' was also applied to the Lyon region during the period 1967—70.

[17] Prud'homme, R., 'Regional economic policy in France', Hansen, N. (ed.), *Public Policy,* op.cit., p.55.

[18] Law for the South, Act of 6.10.1971.

[19] Cao-Pinna, V., 'Regional policy in Italy', Hansen, N. (ed.), *Public Policy,* op.cit., p.174.

[20] Cameron, G.C., op.cit., p.88.

[21] Hendriks, A.J., 'Regional policy in the Netherlands', Hansen, N. (ed.), *Public Policy,* op.cit., p.196.

[22] Cao-Pinna, V., op.cit., p.174.

[23] Cameron, G.C., op.cit., p.88.

[24] Cameron, G.C., op.cit., p.87.

[25] Cao-Pinna, V., op.cit., p.174.

[26] Initially the Cassa was only to execute a ten year programme of extraordinary public works in the Mezzogiorno in addition to those currently executed by central government departments.

[27] Prud'homme, R., op.cit., p.40. See also Dischamps, J.L., 'Rôle et moyens d'action des pouvoirs publics, semi-publics et des institutions prévues dans l'aménagement du territoire en France', *Revue d'Economie Politique,* no.3 and 4, 1972.

[28] McCrone, G., op.cit., p.192.

[29] The excessive mechanisation argument is mentioned with respect to the forestry industry in Sweden. See Anderson, A.E., 'Regional economic policy: problems, analysis and political experiments in Sweden', Hansen, N. (ed.), *Public Finance . . . ,* p.211.

[30] Brown, A.J., op.cit., p.313.

[31] The Hunt Committee, op.cit., appendix J.

[32] Brown, A.J., op.cit., p.313.

[33] West-Central Scotland Plan, Glasgow, 1974, p.245.

[34] West-Central Scotland Plan, op.cit., pp.384—5.

[35] Clark, C., 'Industrial location and economic potential', *Lloyd's Bank Review,* 1966, no.82, pp.1—17.

[36] The premium was paid using the Selective Employment Tax machinery. Under the Selective Employment Tax an employer in manufacturing industry was able to claim back the full value of the tax paid on

his employee plus a minimum labour grant per worker per week. The use of this system was determined by technical feasibility and administrative costs.

[37] McCrone, G., op.cit., p.193.

[38] Brown, A.J., *The Green Paper on the Development Areas, National Institute Economic Review,* May 1967, pp.26—33. See also Brown, A.J., *The Framework of Regional Economics in the United Kingdom,* op.cit., pp.308—9. The Hunt Committee, op.cit.

[39] Moore, B. and Rhodes, J., 'A quantitative analysis of the effects of the Regional Employment Premium and other regional policy instruments', Whiting, A. (ed.), *The Economics of Industrial Subsidies,* London, 1976, p.215.

[40] Yuill, D., op.cit., p.166.

[41] West-Central Scotland Plan, op.cit., p.379.

[42] See Prud'homme, R., op.cit., p.55. See also Farhi, A., Lemaître, C. and Schmitges, R., op.cit., p.65.

[43] McCrone, G., op.cit., pp.189—90.

[44] Cameron, G.C., op.cit., p.94.

[45] The rate of mortality is not more than the one often found among projects for which IDC's have already been obtained. See Brown, A.J., op.cit., p.303.

[46] Brown, A.J., op.cit., p.303.

[47] Nicol, B. and Wehrmann, op.cit., chapter 4.

[48] Moore, B. and Rhodes, J., 'Regional economic policy and the movement of manufacturing firms to Development Areas', *Economica,* February 1976, p.25. Ashcroft, B. and Taylor, J., 'The movement of manufacturing industry and the effect of regional policy', *Oxford Economic Papers,* March 1977.

[49] Nicol, B. and Wehrmann, op.cit., pp.81—93.

[50] Fahri, A., Lemaître, C. and Schmitges, R., op.cit., section 4.

[51] Atkins, H.W., 'Employment change in branch and parent manufacturing plants in the UK, 1966—71', *Trade and Industry,* 30 August 1973.

[52] Luttrell, W.F., *Factory Location and Industrial Movement,* vol.I and vol.II, London, 1962.

[53] Nicol, B. and Wehrmann, op.cit., p.103.

[54] Balassa, B., 'Regional policies and the environment in the European Common Market', *Weltwirtschaftliches Archiv,* vol.3, 1973, p.410.

[55] Fleck, W., Fritsch, M., and Wettmann, R., op.cit., pp.9—13.

[56] Brown, A.J., op.cit., p.316.

[57] West-Central Scotland Plan, op.cit., p.380.

[58] Cameron, G.C., 'Regional economic policy in the United Kingdom', Sant, M. (ed.), *Regional Policy and Planning for Europe,* op.cit., p.2.

[59] Needleman, L., op.cit.

[60] Moore, B. and Rhodes, J., 'The economic and exchequer implications of British regional economic policy', Vaizey, J. (ed.), *Economic Sovereignty and Regional Policy,* London, 1976.

[61] Blake, C., 'The gains from regional policy', Wolfe, J.N., *Cost-Benefit and Cost Effectiveness,* London, 1973.

[62] See also Moore, B. and Rhodes, J., 'The effects of regional economic policy in the United Kingdom', Sant, M. (ed.), op.cit., pp.53—4. See also Moore, B. and Rhodes, J., *The Economic and Exchequer Implications of British Regional Economic Policy,* op.cit.

[63] Regional policy will affect the pressure of demand in the fully employed regions. 'There will be a dual effect on the pressure of demand in fully employed areas — firstly a diversion (substitution effect which reduces the pressure of demand on account of a diversion of demand to Development Areas; and secondly an income effect on account of the payment of financial incentives which, by increasing incomes and expenditure, increases demand in fully employed areas and the Development Areas'. See Moore, B. and Rhodes, J., op.cit., p.82.

[64] Moore, B. and Rhodes, J., op.cit., p.93.

[65] Vanhove, N., *De doelmatigheid van het regionaal-ekonomisch beleid in Nederland,* Gent, 1962.

[66] NEI, *Kampen en Zwolle na tien jaar stimulering,* Rotterdam, 1972.

[67] Paelinck, J.H.P., 'Techniques of regional plan formulation: problems of inter-regional consistency', Dunham, D., and Hilhorst, J. (eds), *Issues in Regional Planning,* The Hague, 1971.

[68] Moore, B. and Rhodes, J., 'Evaluating the effects of British regional economic policy', *The Economic Journal,* March 1973, p.93.

[69] See also Brown, A.J., op.cit., chapter 6. Weeden, R., 'Regional rates of growth of employment: an analysis of variance treatment', *National Institute of Economics and Social Research, Regional Papers,* no.3, 1974. Buck, T.W. and Atkins, H.W., 'The impact of British regional policies on employment growth', *Oxford Economic Papers,* no.1, 1976.

[70] In fact B. Moore and J. Rhodes use a standardisation technique which can be described as shift-share analysis applied to pairs of adjacent years 1951—71, but with regional weights held constant at 1963.

[71] National industrial growth rates and those in the Development Areas are indeed applied to the same industrial structure.

[72] In another publication but based on the same method, Moore and Rhodes estimated the number of jobs attributable to the regional policy. They estimated that in the period 1960—72 regional policy created about 250,000 — 300,000 jobs (this includes the effect on shipbuilding and metal manufacturing industries, together with an estimate of the multiplier effects on the non-manufacturing sector). See Moore, B. and Rhodes, J., 'The effects of Regional Economic Policy in the United Kingdom', Sant, M. (ed.)., op.cit., p.48. In the same contribution these

authors give eleven reasons why regional policy in the United Kingdom has not been more successful.

[73] Cameron, G.C., *Regional Policy in the United Kingdom,* op.cit., p. 31.

[74] Moore, B. and Rhodes, J., *Regional Economic Policy and the Movement of Manufacturing Firms to Development Areas,* op.cit., 1976. Ashcroft, B. and Taylor, J., *The Movement of Manufacturing Industry and the Effect of Regional Policy,* op.cit.

[75] It is evident that there is a positive impact on employment; the lags in employment buildup in new factories take a long time.

[76] Moore, B. and Rhodes, J., op.cit., p.17.

[77] To estimate the effect of individual policy instruments, the estimated coefficients in each policy variable are simply multiplied by the actual value of the variable for the year during which the policy instrument was in operation.

[78] Beacham, A. and Osborn, W.T., 'The movement of manufacturing industry', *Regional Studies,* no.4, 1970.

[79] Ashcroft, B. and Taylor, J., op.cit., p.89.

[80] Ibid., pp.98—9.

[81] See Paelinck, J.H.P., 'Hoe doelmatig kan regionaal en sectorieel beleid zijn?', *Bedrijfseconomische signalementen,* Leiden, 1973. Prud'-homme, R., 'Critique de la politique d'aménagement du territoire', *Revue d'Economie Politique,* no.6, 1974. Dessant, J.W. and Smart, R., 'Evaluating the effects of regional economic policy: a critique', *Regional Studies,* vol.II, 1977.

9 Mobility and migration

Introduction

In the previous chapter we have considered six categories of instruments of regional policy: infrastructure aids, financial incentives, regional allocation of public investment, regional development agencies, decentralisation of government offices, and location control. In this chapter we will pay special attention to the instruments the public authorities use in their mobility and migration policies, and to the links these policies have with regional policy.

By its measures of mobility policy, a government will seek to increase the general mobility of labour and capital, that is more specifically, to make workers and entrepreneurs react more quickly and more extensively to regional differences in employment income, thus adjusting themselves more fully to changed conditions in the economy. Migration policy tries, by a scheme of incentives and renumerations, to stimulate people and industries to make the moves that serve national targets of equal welfare distribution and the balanced development of regions.[1] Both policies have close links, therefore, with regional policy, links that will have to be kept in mind in studying governments' measures to increase and stimulate the mobility and migration of workers and entrepreneurs within the framework of the more general development policies pursued in the countries under observation.

Motives behind inter-regional migration

There are many factors that are either stimulating or hampering inter-regional migration. Some of them are:

    A   *Economic factors*
    1   Differences in job opportunities between regions (unemployment, labour shortage, qualification of labour);
    2   Differences in income level (income ratios);
    3   Cost of moving.

    B   *Social factors*
    1   Marriage;
    2   Retirement;
    3   Family relationships;

4   Degree of schooling.

C   *Psychological factors*
1   'Alienation'; this factor represents partly the costs of moving, partly the lack of knowledge about conditions in the other region, and partly the different 'environment' in the new region, which is experienced as more alien according as the distance from the home region to the region of destination is greater.
2   Psychical costs. [2] People are often reluctant to leave family surroundings.

D   *Other factors*
1   Difference in climate;
2   Difference in religion;
3   Difference in language, etc.

Migration models

During the last two decades many migration models were elaborated; we shall discuss only four of them here.

The model of M.J. Greenwood [3]

The objective of the study of M.J. Greenwood was to estimate the importance of a number of factors that influenced interstate migration in the USA during the period 1955–60. Several variables were chosen which could reasonably be expected to explain the movements which occurred.

Each of the 48 contiguous states was chosen as a destination, and gross migration from each of the other states to any one of them was analysed. Multiple regression analysis was used on the data, and two steps of relationships were estimated, one excluding the migrant stock variable and one including it.

The assumed relationships were:

$$M_{ij} = f\,(D_{ij},\ Y_{ji},\ E_i,\ U_i,\ U_j,\ R_{ji},\ T_{ji},\ \text{Random errors}) \qquad (9.1)$$

$$M_{ij} = f\,(D_{ij},\ Y_{ji},\ E_i,\ E_j,\ U_i,\ U_j,\ R_{ji},\ T_{ji},\ MS_{ij},\ \text{Random errors}) \ (9.2)$$

in which

M_{ij} =   the dependent variable is the number of persons, five

years of age and over, residing in state j in 1960 who
resided in state i in 1955, divided by the total number of
persons of five years of age and over who resided in
state i in 1955 and in another state in 1960.

D_{ij} = 1955 highway mileage between the principal city of
state i and that of state j.

Y_{ji} = median 1959 money income of males living in state j in
1960 divided by the median 1959 money income of
males living in state i in 1960.

E_i = median number of years of school completed by residents of state i, 25 years of age and over, 1960.

E_j = median number of years of school completed by residents of state j, 25 years of age and over, 1960.

U_i = proportion of the civilian labour force unemployed in
state i during approximately the first week of April 1960.

U_j = proportion of the civilian labour force unemployed in
state j during approximately the first week of April 1960.

R_{ji} = proportion of population living in urban areas of state j
divided by the proportion of population living in urban
areas of state i in 1960.

T_{ji} = mean yearly temperature in the principal city of state j
divided by the mean yearly temperature in the principal
city of state i.

MS_{ij} = number of persons born in state i and living in state j,
1950.

Table 9.1 contains estimates of the equations (9.1) and (9.2) in logarithmic form; one includes migrant stock as an independent variable, the other does not.

Where the migrant stock variable does not appear, each of the parameter estimates is highly significant; where the migrant stock variable does appear, all of the parameter estimates but two (Y_{ji} and U_j) are highly significant.

The coefficients of Y_{ji} and U_j fail to be significant at the 10 per cent level.

The results of the regression analysis carried out on the basis of equation (9.2) indicate that the parameter estimate of the migrant stock variable is positive and highly significant. In terms of its contribution to R^2, the migrant stock is the most important variable.

These results clearly show that persons have a strong tendency to migrate to states to which other natives of their region migrated previously (better information, psychological factors).

Although the evidence on this point is impressive, there is still enough reason to doubt that the migrant stock factor is, indeed, an

Table 9.1
Gross interstate population migration, 1955—60:
logarithmic regression coefficients (β) and t-ratios (t)

Independent variables			Eq. 9.1		Eq. 9.2
D_{ij}	β:	—	.897	—	.300
	t:	—	27.55	—	11.21
Y_{ji}			.540		.160
			2.99		1.27
E_i			2.555		3.401
			8.72		16.60
E_j			1.490	—	.622
			5.06	—	2.95
U_i			.612		.705
			5.09		8.44
U_j			.620	—	.057
			5.15	—	.66
R_{ji}			.669		.771
			4.54		7.52
T_{ji}			1.872		.903
			9.49		6.49
MS_{ij}			—		.521
			—		42.06
R^2			.41		.72

important factor. It could very easily be shown that if a set of factors (excluding migrant stock) determines migration flows between regions, the very same factors also determine the building up of the stock. So then the stock is introduced into the migration equation, the result may be very satisfactory from a statistical point of view, but theoretically the approach becomes rather shaky because the same explaining factor has been used twice, once in a direct way and once in an indirect way, in one and the same equation. In fact, the improvement in the regression results obtained by introducing the migrant stock variable does not tell us anything about the importance of this variable in the explanation of migration flows. It could be considerable, but the intercorrelation prevents us from estimating it.

L.H. Klaassen and P. Drewe assume that three groups of factors play a role in explaining the flow of migration from one region i to another region j.

1 Social relations between the regions i and j

In principle the maximum number of such relations between the two regions equals the product of the two population sizes of both regions. In practice the number of relations probably does not increase proportionally with that of possible relations. It is assumed that the actual number increases proportionally to a power a ($0 < a < 1$) of the number of possible relations, and that migration is proportional to the number of actual relations.

2 Income ratio between the region i and the region j

Although not only the income factor but also the employment factor might play a role, the authors neglect the employment factor, assuming for simplicity's sake that the income factor represents both. In reality, areas with higher income are usually also the areas with lower unemployment.

3 The psychological factor distance

Expressing these factors in a simple formula, we may write:

$$M_{ij} = a_o P_i^a P_j^a \left(\frac{Y_j}{Y_i}\right)^\beta e^{-\Upsilon A_{ij}} \qquad (9.3)$$

in which

M_{ij}	=	number of people migrating in a given period from region i to region j;
$P_i, P_j,$	=	population of the regions i and j;
Y_i, Y_j	=	average income in regions i and j;
A_{ij}	=	distance between i and j.

For the flow of people migrating from region j to region i we write:

$$M_{ji} = a_o P_i^a P_j^a \left(\frac{Y_i}{Y_j}\right)^\beta e^{-\Upsilon A_{ji}} \qquad (9.4)$$

If we assume that $A_{ij} = A_{ji}$, the ratio between the numbers of people migrating from region i to j and from j to i is given by

$$\frac{M_{ij}}{M_{ji}} = (\frac{Y_i}{Y_j})^{2\beta} \qquad (9.5)$$

We may draw from this simple analysis the following important conclusions:

1 The results of surveys in which migrants are asked to state their motives for migration may be used only to trace the factors determining *gross* migration. No conclusions may be drawn from these surveys regarding the variables determining net migration.

2 Motives derived from surveys give insufficient information about the decision making process of the migrant, unless to each motive an average weight is attached. Such weights could be found by statistical analysis of the survey results. In the above formulas these weights are expressed by the exponents attached to the variables.

3 The influence of income on net migration is considerably larger than on gross migration, the coefficient of the income ratio in equation (9.3) being twice as large as that in (9.1) and (9.2).

Lack of data on regional incomes prevented the authors from testing their model. Instead they tested what they call a parsimonious migration model of inter-regional migration.

$$M_{ij} = a_0 \; E_j^{a_1} \; L_i^{a_2} \; e^{-a_3 D_{ij}} \qquad (9.6)$$

or
$$\log M_{ij} = \log a_0 + a_1 \log E_j + a_2 \log L_i - a_3 D_{ij} \qquad (9.7)$$

The magnitude of migration flows from region i to region j is directly related to the total number of non-agricultural jobs in j (E_j: destination) and to the total labour force in i (L_i: origin), and negatively related to the distance between origin and destination.

L.H. Klaassen and P. Drewe applied this parsimonious migration model to data for France, Great Britain, the Netherlands, and Sweden during 1960—68 (see Table 9.2).

The conclusions to be drawn from both models is that a variety of factors seem to be responsible for the inter-regional migration flows. The second model possesses an interesting feature in the different distance influences for differently sized countries. The influence of distance is obviously largest for the Netherlands, the smallest country of the four, and lowest in Sweden, the largest of the four. Influences of

Table 9.2
Results of the testing of the model for four European countries
Klaassen—Drewe

Variable		Intercept, regression and multiple correlation coefficient	Standard error of regression coefficient and of estimate	Partial correlation coefficient
$\log a_o$	F	−4.94		
	GB	−4.53		
	NL	−1.46		
	S	−2.96		
$\log E_j$	F	1.00*	.05	.51
	GB	.86*	.10	.54
	NL	.59*	.04	.53
	S	.83*	.05	.50
$\log L_i$	F	1.06*	.06	.46
	GB	.93*	.11	.50
	NL	.61*	.05	.50
	S	.77	.06	.39
D_{ij}	F	−0.0023*	−.00014	−.39
	GB	−0.0023*	−.00043	−.40
	NL	−0.0090*	−.00042	−.84
	S	−0.0014	−.00009	−.53
R	F	.83**	.28	
	GB	.87*	.20	
	NL	.96*	.15	
	S	.79**	.28	

* Significantly different from zero at a level of confidence <.001
**Significantly different from zero at .05 level of confidence.

intermediate size appear in France and Great Britain. This indicates that a regional policy trying to develop areas at a given distance from a developed area might be considerably more difficult in the Netherlands, where distance friction is high compared to Sweden or even France and Great Britain.

The J.A.M. Heijke—L.H. Klaassen study

A third study, carried out at the Netherlands Economic Institute by Heijke and Klaassen,[5] concentrated on explaining the migration flows

Table 9.3

Foreigners working or staying in a number of Western European countries, by country of origin, 1969

Countries of origin	Austria (only workers) on 1 August 1969 [a]	France on 1 January 1969 [a]	Western Germany on 1 September 1969 [b]	Switzerland on 1 January 1969 [a]	Belgium on 1 October 1969 [a]	Netherlands on 1 July 1968 [c]	Sweden (only workers) on 1 January 1969 [a]
Greece	275	10,885	271,300	8,000	13,760	2,300	5,940
Italy	860	632,080	514,600	522,600	176,250	14,500	5,325
Portugal	—	367,425	37,500	2,200	4,435	3,100[d]	680
Spain	170	667,610	206,900	87,700	47,745	18,300	3,185
Yugoslavia	48,105	43,340	331,600	16,100	3,415	2,400	14,015
Turkey	8,060	7,160	322,400	7,800	11,335	13,500	1,785
Algeria	—	562,000	3,300	—	3,460	—	155
Morocco	—	119,520	9,100	—	20,980	12,800	470
Tunisia	—	73,260	3,100	—	1,290	100[d]	135
Subtotal Mediterranean area	57,470	2,483,250	1,699,800	644,465	282,670	67,000	31,690
Other countries of origin	10,310	516,750[e]	681,300	288,675	172,935[f]	137,000[g]	107,000[h]
Total immigrants	67,780	3,000,000[i]	2,381,100	933,140[j]	455,605	204,000	138,690
Population countries of destination (in millions)	7.4	50.3	60.8	6.2	9.6	12.7	8.0
Immigrants from Mediterranean area as a percentage of the population	0.8	4.9	2.8	10.5	2.9	0.5	0.4
Total no. of immigrants as percentage of population	0.9	6.0	3.9	15.2	4.7	1.6[k]	1.7

Table 9.3 continued:

Notes:

a)   Source: *Migration Today*, no.14, Geneva 1970.
b)   Source: *Wirtschaft und Statistik*, August 1972.
c)   Source: *Statistisch Zakboek*, CBS, 1969.
d)   NEI's own calculations based on CBS data end of 1967 and end of 1972 concerning the number of foreigners present and migration balances in intermediate years.
e)   Among whom approximately 131,000 Poles, appr. 250,000 Africans (including 60,000 from Senegal, Mali and Mauretania), 35,000 North and South Americans and West Indians.
f)   Among whom 3,175 Zairese (Kinsjasa).
g)   Exclusive of Surinamese, Antillians (35,000) and Moluccans (25,000).
h)   Among whom 19,000 Danes, 75,000 Finns and 13,000 Norwegians.
i)   Exclusive of 129,858 seasonal workers (including 119,301 Spaniards, 3,110 Portuguese, 2,408 Italians, 2,079 Moroccans).
j)   Exclusive of seasonal workers (114,081 in August 1968 and 14,233 in December 1968) and frontier workers (63,062).
k)   Inclusive of Surinamese, Antillians, and Moluccans this percentage becomes 2.1.

of foreign workers from the Mediterranean countries to Western Europe. It was the first study to consider a psychological (or social) barrier, viz. the degree of kinship between languages of the country of origin and the country of destination. In this study two groups of countries are considered, viz. the immigration countries: Austria (A), France (F), West Germany (D), Switzerland (CH), Belgium (B), the Netherlands (NL), and Sweden (S); the relevant emigration countries (the Mediterranean countries): Greece (GR), Italy (I), Portugal (P), Spain (E), Yugoslavia (YU), Turkey (TR), Algeria (DZ), Morocco (MA), and Tunisia (TU).

The data on which the analysis is based are presented in Table 9.3. It appears from this table that the data base, if not so homogeneous as one would wish, is still sufficiently complete for the analysis. The figures relate to the year 1969.[6] We quote from the study:[7]

Two remarks should be made before the results of the analysis are presented. The first is that only migration from Mediterranean countries towards Western European countries was taken into consideration; as the migration flows in the opposite direction are negligible, their inclusion did not seem opportune.

The second is that, because incomes in Mediterranean countries and the Western European countries differ considerably, an income difference factor (ΔW_{ji}) was added to the variables used in the analysis of migration and mobility in the four European countries (see model Klaassen-Drewe). The other variables have been defined similarly to those in the latter analysis.

Two equations were tested. In the first the influence of distance was expressed, as in the European analysis, as an exponential function, in the second as a power function, which means that in the statistical test applied to the natural logarithm of the number of migrants, the explaining factor in the first test was D_{ij}, in the second $\ln D_{ij}$.

The results were (t-values in brackets):

$$\ln M_{ij} = \underset{(3.57)}{0.68 \ln \Delta W_{ji}} + \underset{(6.10)}{1.46 \ln E_j} + \underset{(4.44)}{1.22 \ln L_i} - \underset{(4.71)}{0.002 D_{ij}} - \underset{(3.11)}{5.61}$$

$$R_c^2 = 0.648 \ (9.8)$$

and

$$\ln M_{ij} = \underset{(3.76)}{0.72 \ln \Delta W_{ji}} + \underset{(6.69)}{1.59 \ln E_j} + \underset{(4.31)}{1.17 \ln L_i} - \underset{(5.00)}{2.69 \ln D_{ij}} + \underset{(2.80)}{11.07}$$

$$R_c^2 = 0.661 \ (9.9)$$

R_c^2 is the corrected value of the coefficient of determination.

The results do not differ much for the two approaches. Neither the regression coefficients nor the t-values or correlation coefficients differ significantly.

Using the first equation (9.8) as a basis for comparison with the results of the inter-regional migration analysis for the four Western European countries, we find some significant facts.

1 Income differences between Mediterranean countries and Western European countries do play a role but their contribution to the explanation of the variance in migration is modest.
2 The influence of push and pull factors is considerably greater for people from Mediterranean countries than for migrants from any of the European countries. In other words, they are much more sensitive to the pressure of the population at home and the pull of jobs available elsewhere.

3 The influence of distance in Mediterranean countries is comparable to that in Great Britain and France; it is stronger than that in Sweden, but quite a bit weaker than that in the Netherlands.

4 General mobility in Mediterranean countries as expressed by the logarithm of the constant in the equation is lower than that in the Netherlands and also below the average of the four European countries; it is considerably higher than the figure for Great Britain and France and comes actually close to that for Sweden (-6.81).

A study of the residuals suggests additional systematic factors that influence the flows of migrants between the two groups of countries. One hypothesis is that religion plays a role, so that, for instance, migrants from Spain, Portugal and Italy would preferably go to the Roman Catholic countries: Austria, France and Belgium. The hypothesis was tested, and the outcome was negative. The hypothesis that language differences might be significant was the next one to be tested, with much more promising results.

For the language test, the immigration countries were divided into three groups, viz.

1 France as a French-speaking country, and Belgium, where French is one of the two main languages; even in its Flemish provinces the inhabitants have a considerable knowledge of French.

2 Switzerland as a multi-lingual country.

3 Austria, Germany, the Netherlands, and Sweden, where · Germanic languages are spoken.

The emigration countries were also divided into three groups, viz.

(a) Algeria, Morocco, and Tunisia as countries with French as important second language;

(b) Spain, Italy, and Portugal as countries where other Latin languages are spoken;

(c) Greece, Turkey, and Yugoslavia as countries where neither Germanic nor Latin languages are spoken.

The residuals per country group are presented in Table 9.4.

The first conclusion that may be drawn from the table is that the sum of the residuals for each group of emigration countries is relatively small compared to the residuals for each group of immigration countries separately. That means that there are hardly any significant differences between groups of countries as far as

Table 9.4
Residuals per country group

Destination	Origin	DZ MA TU	E I P	GR TR YU	Total
F, B		+ 6.7	+ 3.9	− 2.7	+ 7.9
CH		−	+ 2.8	+ 1.6	+ 4.4
A, D, NL, S		− 8.8	− 5.0	+ 1.5	−12.3
Total		− 2.1	+ 1.7	+ 0.4	0

their total migration is concerned.

A second conclusion is that there seems to be a strong preference for the Germanic countries, with Switzerland taking an intermediary position.

One explanation for this preference could be the distribution of language groups among immigration and emigration countries. The countries with French as important second language (DZ, MA, and TU) show considerable positive preference for migration to France and Belgium and a strong negative preference for the Germanic countries. The same, but to a lesser extent, holds for the other Latin languages speaking countries (E, I, and P), where we find positive preference for France, Belgium and Switzerland (possibly also due to the fact that in Switzerland also Italian is spoken) and a negative preference for the Germanic countries.

The remaining group of countries, whose languages have no direct kinship with either Latin or Germanic tongues and who therefore can be considered to have a free choice, show a slight preference for the Germanic countries.

The results confirm the expectation that language barriers are an important element of psychological distance, and affect migration behaviour significantly.

Indeed, further analysis in that direction might well prove fruitful. On the whole it seems that in migration analyses, more attention should be given to social and cultural factors, and in particular to language differences, than has been so far.

In a recent study[8] Bartels and Ter Welle present the results of a migration study performed within the framework of a labour market study for the three Northern Provinces of the Netherlands (Drenthe, Friesland, and Groningen). The interesting feature of their study is that they computed migration equations for different educational groups of the population separately for migration towards the Northern provinces and from these provinces. The explaining variable used in log-linear functions are

> 1 for migration towards the Northern provinces (30 observations) the variables physical distance, active working population, and percentage of one family houses in the total housing stock as a measure for the attractiveness of the residential environment;
> 2 for migration from the Northern provinces the variables physical distance, active working population, attractiveness of the physical environment (measured as a weight average of the areas with different types of natural land uses), and the unemployment ratio.

The conclusions drawn from the study are:

> 1 The influence of the distance variable was similar in the two cases.
> 2 The constant in the equation (general mobility) increases in both cases with the educational level of the migrants.
> 3 The flows towards the North show a stronger relation with the residential indicator than with the employment indicator. Moreover, the first influence increases with the educational level, the second decreases.
> 4 The flows from the North show a strong relation with the employment variable (about equal for all educational levels).
> 5 The influence of the factor quality of the physical natural environment is smaller, increases over time, and is positively correlated with the educational level.

Mobility policy and migration policy

The general purpose of mobility policy is to make people react faster to stimulants that are likely to improve their social economic position, as well as to avoid as much as possible errors both of the first and the second order. This means that it is tried to avoid migration in cases where it would not be justified and to avoid non-migration in cases where emigration would be justified.

It follows that, in the terms of the first model of L.H. Klaassen and P. Drewe, the object of a mobility policy is to influence the value of the coefficients in the equation explaining the level of migration. More precisely (a) to increase the positive value of the income elasticity and (b) to decrease the negative value of the distance coefficient. A migration policy tries to influence the variables determining the migration flows given the value of the coefficients.

For a person considering migration from i to region j three elements play a role:

(a) the advantages and disadvantages of staying in region i;
(b) the advantages and disadvantages of working and living in region j;
(c) the cost involved in moving from region i to region j.

In this context the basic elements of a mobility policy are:

1 Improvement of the general educational level, particularly in regions where this level is below average. A higher educational level will not only directly increase the knowledge about other regions but will also contribute to the quality of the judgements about prospects elsewhere.
2 Improvement of information on specific prospects in expanding regions. Measures in this respect might range from simple written information about future job opportunities and vacancies to information evenings and informative journeys to these regions. It has been shown that lack of information about other regions is one of the main obstacles to migration and also one of the causes of unjustified migration.

In order to reconcile the decision to migrate with national targets of regional balanced growth or in order to make private economic decisions match national economic goals, three major groups of instruments are used in migration policy.

(a) Improvement of the skills of potential migrants and adjustments of these to the need in expanding regions.
(b) Financial assistance in the costs of moving.
(c) Housing programmes in the receiving regions to facilitate the move to these regions. The point is important because expanding regions are usually regions with a considerable housing deficit so that the conditions in which immigrants have to live at least for the first year or so are usually rather primitive.

Mobility policy, migration policy and regional policy

In order to study the relationships, let us start from a simple labour market model developed by L.H. Klaassen and P. Drewe.

$$\frac{\Delta L_s}{L_s} = N + \frac{M}{L_s} \qquad (9.10)$$

The increase of labour supply in a given region equals the natural net increase (N) plus the migration rate (M) (net migration)

$$\frac{M}{L_s} = a\,\frac{Y - \overline{Y}}{Y} - a\,G_1 \qquad (9.11)$$

The rate of net migration depends on the deviation of the average real income of region from the national average as well as on the relative size of government support to migrants recalculated on an annual basis ($G_1 = \frac{S_1}{Y}$, in which S_1 is the absolute amount of support also calculated on an annual basis).

$$\frac{\Delta L_d}{L_d} = -\beta\,\frac{Y - \overline{Y}}{Y} + \beta\,G_c + E \qquad (9.12)$$

This equation concerns the demand equation for labour. It says that the increase in labour demand depends on the deviation of the wage rate, the government subsidy to locating and extending industries (G_c, recalculated on annual basis per worker employed), and the autonomous rate of growth of labour demand in the region (E).

$$\frac{\Delta L_d}{L_d} = \frac{\Delta L_s}{L_s} \qquad (9.13)$$

Equation (9.13) is an equilibrium and states that the relative increase in demand equals the relative increase in supply.

In the equations (9.11) and (9.12) the coefficients a and β represent the mobility of labour and capital.

> a represents the degree to which workers react to financial incentives;
> β represents the degree to which industries react to differences in wages;
> a policy that tries to influence the value of a is a *labour mobility*

policy;
a policy that tries to influence the value of β is a *capital mobility policy*;
a policy using G_l as an instrument to influence migration of workers is called a *migration policy;*
a policy using G_c as an instrument to influence the migration of capital is called a *regional industrialisation policy*.

The model solved for the exogenous variables, leads to four equations:

$$\frac{Y - \overline{Y}}{Y} = \frac{1}{a+\beta} (E - N) + \frac{a}{a+\beta} G_1 + \frac{\beta}{a+\beta} G_c \qquad (9.14)$$

$$\frac{M}{L_s} = \frac{a}{a+\beta} (E - N) + \frac{a\beta}{a+\beta} (G_c - G_l) \qquad (9.15)$$

$$\frac{\Delta L_d}{L_d} = \frac{\Delta L_s}{L_s} = \frac{a}{a+\beta} E + \frac{\beta}{a+\beta} N + \frac{a\beta}{a+\beta} (G_c - G_l) \qquad \begin{array}{c}(9.16)\\ \text{and}\\ (9.17)\end{array}$$

Equation (9.14) shows how the income level of the region is influenced by the differences between the autonomous growth rate of the demand for labour and the natural rate of increase of the working population as well as by the subsidies on labour and capital. The influence of the first factor is decreasing with increasing mobility of labour and capital. The effect of the migration policy increases with labour mobility while the effect of the regional policy increases with capital mobility.

From equation (9.15) it appears that the capital subsidy *counteracts* the labour subsidy as far as migration is concerned.

It appears, then, that if migration policy and regional policy are carried out simultaneously, their effects cumulate as far as regional income is concerned but compensate each other as far as migration and labour demand are concerned (see equation (9.16)).

Considering more specifically migration policy, i.e. the use of G_l as an instrument variable and stating that equalisation of regional incomes is the goal to be pursued, we come to the following conclusions.

1 The effect of a migration policy in a region with a relatively low income level is more favourable as the mobility of the population in the region is greater.
2 A simultaneous regional policy contributes to the effect of

migration policy as far as income is concerned.

The first statement implies that high mobility is a condition *sine qua non* for a successful migration policy. The major instrument to increase the effectiveness of migration policy is a mobility policy. If mobility cannot be raised at short notice (which seems very likely) for the region under consideration, a *regional policy* might be more effective.

Some remarks seem to be in place here:

1 The foregoing gives an answer to the question to what extent a regional industrialisation policy and a migration policy could be combined in order to reach given targets.

2 The measures taken within the framework of a regional industrialisation policy to stimulate the growth of certain underdeveloped regions may not be taken independently of the 'development worthiness' of the region (in the labour model represented by the possibility of raising E). If the potential industrial development of a region is promising, the job should be brought to the people; if it is not, the people should be brought to places where the jobs are.

3 The basis of such a policy is the designation of growth poles in places where a sound potential basis for future development is present. That implies a decision about which areas shall be out-migration areas.

Workers to the work or work to the workers?

The question raised at the end of the preceding section centres around an old discussion point, viz. should jobs be created in areas where there is an oversupply of labour, or should this oversupply of labour be stimulated to leave the area and migrate to areas where there is an oversupply of jobs. Different writers think differently about this problem. There are in fact two schools:

A. *The 'workers to the work' school*[9]

One of the most important arguments mentioned in favour of bringing the 'worker to the work' is that businessmen usually select very carefully the optimum location for their plant and, if influenced by government policy (or mere pressure) to move, would be forced into a situation of lower profitability of their firm, which would decrease economic growth. As long as one relies on labour mobility such costs will not occur because there is no interference with the location decisions of entrepreneurs. In addition it is argued that labour mobility should be promoted anyway as it is a necessary condition for economic growth (see H.W. Richardson and E.G. West).[10] Apart from this positive argument, the negative argument is used that a policy to influence capital migration will always encourage inefficiency, as subsidies will have to be paid out also to firms that would expand or locate in less prosperous areas anyway, even without subsidy. The larger their number is, the greater the inefficiency of the policy.

The settling of industry in the selected growth centres is stimulated by financial assistance to industries moving to those centres, while the out-migration of labour from the areas that are not stimulated is facilitated by the measures taken in the framework of the geographic labour mobility policy. Whenever out-migration from an area starts, the younger and most active people will leave the area and consequently the prospects for its development will, in the long run, become poorer. Consequently, if the young and skilled are important for future growth, emigration of this group should not be excessive in comparison to the natural growth of their number. This seems to be an important argument against the reasoning of the 'workers to the work' school.

B. *'Work to the workers' school*[11]

The counterarguments used by this school are:
Intervention in private location decisions of firms does not necessarily reduce national economic growth, for a variety of reasons:

> 1 The first reason is that many industries are footloose anyway, which by definition means that the financial outcome of their operations is independent of their location.
> 2 Firms do not necessarily select optimum sites. This argument is rather weak. If it were true, the policy of the government should be to assist firms in finding ways to choose a better location and not to force them in another direction which from a strict business point is concerned with social costs rather than with private costs, it could from that point of view be justified to push the firm towards less prosperous regions. There are three specific sources of divergence between social costs and private costs:
> (a) Congestion costs: these are only considered by firms as far as they bear on private costs (not so evident for the United Kingdom – see G.C. Cameron, op.cit.).
> (b) Costs of social infrastructure: firms do not fully consider the costs imposed on the community by the necessity of providing additional social infrastructure (most social services are provided through general taxation). The marginal costs of providing

additional social infrastructure might be low in less prosperous regions because of underutilisation of social capital there. It seems that this argument remains weak until proof is presented that the quality of the social infrastructure in both cases is the same.

(c)   The final argument is a cultural one: migration of labour could reduce inter-regional cultural variation, which could be considered a social cost.

3 A third group of reasons is that in general labour migration is socially undesirable and economically inefficient.

(a)   The body of this group of arguments is that migration has a depressing effect on the economy of the donor region and an expansionary effect on the host region. Multiplier effects (see chapter 1) work negatively in the donor region and positively in the host region. The additional investments needed in the expanding region might moreover tend to aggrevate the regional problems by adding to the demand for labour in the regions already suffering from excess demand and subtracting from the demand for labour in regions already faced with excess supply.

(b)   As far as the quality of labour is concerned it may be expected that the younger and more enterprising groups of the population tend to be the more mobile so that existing differences in quality of labour supply will become even worse as a result of the move of workers.

(c)   A final argument is that labour migration could add to the inflationary pressures in the prosperous regions (see chapter 1).

Government action to influence geographical labour mobility: migration subsidy or not?

Considering the migration policy in Sweden, the Netherlands, France, and the United Kingdom, we can underline two important points concerning the nature of this policy.

(a)   Policies are focused on migration and not on mobility (Sweden is to a certain extent an exception).
(b)   Policies are only concerned with the migration of the unemployed and key workers between certain well-defined regions.

The migration policy is a servant of general economic goals (the case of Sweden during the 1960s)

Sweden's policy for encouraging labour mobility was particularly noteworthy. Despite relatively full employment, employment declines in forestry and agriculture have resulted in high unemployment in some areas of the country against labour shortages in others. In response the government has established a comprehensive programme to assist unemployed workers in lagging areas in moving to areas where labour is in short supply and acquiring skills that are marketable in the latter areas. Financial assistance includes travel and moving expense allowances, family allowances, starting allowances, and special settlement payments to induce people to move from lagging regions. Workers who are unemployed, or who are likely to become unemployed, are informed of job opportunities in other areas by the Employment Service. Frequently Employment Service officials from areas where labour is short visit areas where there is a surplus to describe the opportunities available.[12]

The characteristics can be summarised as follows.

1 It is felt that full employment and economic growth should be the major targets of national policy and that migration policy should assist in reaching these general goals.[13]

2 Regional policy in Sweden was considered a complement to migration policy, which is also a mobility policy, rather than the other way around.

One of the main reasons for the Swedish approach was the fact that urban areas in Sweden were considerably smaller than those in many other countries (France, Great Britain, the Netherlands); the consequence was that movements to the main urban areas in Sweden were also subsidised. Meanwhile, the policy has changed. In 1965, the political catch phrase in regional policy was changed from 'men to jobs' to 'jobs to men'.[14]

A few remarks should be made here.

1 During the period 1950—65 mobility measures were not sufficient to reduce regional disparities in potential employment. But the use of mainly capital subsidising means in regional policy during the period 1965—71 has been disappointing also. The regional variation in employment, which was reduced during the period 1950—65, increased in the period 1965—71.

2 The problems of the metropolitan areas were considered to be excessively rapid expansion, leading to congestion, air pollution, noise, and other environmental problems.

Migration policy is a servant of regional policy
(see the case of France, the Netherlands, Great Britain)

The present migration policy in the Netherlands, the United Kingdom and France is dictated by the objective of the regional development policy.

The Netherlands
Migration policy has changed in the course of the post war period from a policy that tried to eliminate the labour surpluses in some specific areas in the Eastern and Northern parts of the country by emigration to any other developing region, into a policy aiming at a general equilibrium in the distribution of both economic activities and population over the country. This change in the targets of the policy resulted from the idea that too heavy a concentration in the urbanised Western part of the country would not only be too costly from an economic point of view but would also influence unfavourably the living conditions in this part of the country. A shift of the (additional) population to the more developed Northern and Eastern parts of the country would not only improve the position of these areas but would simultaneously avoid further concentration in the already congested urbanised Western parts. Instruments to be used in reaching these goals are, on the one hand, restrictive measures for further growth in the West, and financial and other assistance to new and expanding firms in the selected development areas in the country. Additionally, the migration policy was introduced to assist this movement of industries and population by giving different sorts of financial assistance to key workers moving with factories into the development areas as well as to the unemployed moving into these areas (see Table 9.5).

Table 9.5
Goals of Dutch migration and regional policy

Goals	Migration policy		
	Assistance to unemployed non-key workers	Assistance to key workers	Regional policy
Balanced distribution of economic activity	.	+	+
Balanced distribution of population	.	+	+
Provision of employment for the structurally unemployed	+	+	+

+ = assistance provided; . = no assistance provided.

It appears that the goals of the policy assistance to key workers emigrating with their firm from the Rimcity are identical to those of the regional policy. As far as the assistance to unemployed non-key workers is concerned, the direct goal is to offer to the structurally unemployed the possibility of employment in a development area.

There is one point that deserves particular attention. It is not clear why assistance to the unemployed is limited to those going to development nuclei in development areas only and why the assistance is given to the unemployed only.

France
Regional policy in France is directed at decentralisation from the Paris area and migration policy is adjusted to this goal by subsidisation of key workers moving with their firm from Paris as well as unemployed workers moving to designated development areas outside the Paris region.

It follows from the foregoing that the situation in France is basically not very different from that in the Netherlands. Here also the decentralisation policy which aims at preventing further excessive growth of the Paris region as well as promoting growth of other regions in France basically determine the structure of the schemes for migration.

If we compare the Dutch and the French programmes we get the scheme as in Table 9.6.

Table 9.6
Dutch and French mobility aid programmes

from	to	Rest of the country (designated areas)			
		Employed		Unemployed	
		Key	Non-key	Key	Non-key
Paris (Rimcity)		+	.	+	+
Rest of country		.	.	+	+

+ = assistance provided; . = no assistance provided.

United Kingdom
In Great Britain the migration policy is influenced to a very considerable extent by the regional policy. If we put the goals of the British migration and regional policies in a table we would get one identical to that for the Netherlands.

Three schemes are in operation in Great Britain:

(a) *The Resettlement Transfer Scheme.* This assists unemployed workers and those about to be involved in redundancy who have poor employment prospects in their home area to move to jobs in another *development area,* either for the purpose of permanent resettlement in the new area or temporarily until work is available to them in their home area.

(b) *The Key Workers' Scheme.* This scheme assists *employed workers* who transfer either permanently or temporarily to key posts in establishments which their employers are setting up in development areas (also in intermediate areas).

(c) *The Nucleus Labour Force Scheme.* This assists *unemployed workers* recruited in areas of high unemployment who are temporarily transferred to their new employers' factory for training.

The foregoing presentation leads us to a number of remarks.

1 The basic problem in the United Kingdom, France and the Netherlands is really that the social costs of the larger cities to which migration is not stimulated are not charged to the inhabitants of these cities and consequently a considerable gap might exist between these costs and the level of local income out of taxation.

Moving to a large city for a worker implies a number of advantages (higher wages, higher level of amenities) but the tax rate is not higher. If therefore, the government claims that social costs exceed the level of taxation in the cities this is not recognised by the worker as long as the gap between taxes and social costs persists. Measures on the fringe of this problem, such as the exclusion of the conurbation areas in migration policy do not touch the heart of the problems. They do not make the conurbation areas less attractive, they only make other areas somewhat less unattractive.

2 So far no specific benefit-cost studies on migration have been made in the four countries considered.[15]

3 It should be noted that the policy of subsidising the costs of transferring *key workers* moving with their employers to a development area has its *main influence on the mobility of capital.* At the first sight it would appear to be an encouragement to labour mobility but the main effect is to increase the capital inflow to less prosperous regions by reducing one of the problems associated with relocation of firms.[16]

4 Removal of market imperfections causing immobility as an instrument of labour mobility.

(a) National wage bargaining systems prevent regional income differentials reflecting fully regional unemployment differentials. A system of local wage bargaining would permit the market mechanisms to work more freely.

(b)   Inadequate information constitutes another market imperfection (see above). The role of   the government is clear in this respect: to publicise nationally opportunities for investment in regions where labour is the abundant factor and opportunities for employment in regions where capital is abundant.

Notes

[1]   Klaassen, L.H. and Drewe, P., *Migration Policy in Europe*, 1973.
[2]   See also Sjaastad, L.A., 'The costs and returns of human migration', in Richardson, H.W. (ed.), *Regional Economics: a Reader*, op.cit.
[3]   Greenwood, M.J., 'An analysis of the determinants of geographic labour mobility in the United States', *The Review of Economics and Statistics*, no.2, 1969.
[4]   Klaassen, L.H. and Drewe, P., op.cit.
[5]   Heijke, J.A.M. and Klaassen, L.H., *Human reactions to spatial diversity. Mobility in regional labour markets*, NEI/FEES, 1977/14. Compare also: Heijke, J.A.M., *Gastarbeid en economische structuur*, NEI, Rotterdam, 1977. Report prepared for the Working Group Migration of the State Committee Population Problems (The Hague, Netherlands).
[6]   It may be remarked here that the data collected by J.A.M. Heijke are in fact unique and as far as the authors know, the first more or less complete set of data on mediterranean workers in Western Europe.
[7]   Heijke, J.A.M. and Klaassen, L.H., op.cit., page 6 ff.
[8]   Bartels, C.P.A. and Ter Welle, J., 'Een analyse van de migratie van beroepsbeoefenaren uit en naar het Noorden per opleidingsniveau', *Economisch Statistische Berichten*, no.3166, 1978.
[9]   Stilwell, F.J.B., *Regional Economic Policy*, 1972, pp.42–7.
[10] Richardson, H.W. and West, E.G., 'Must we always take work to the workers?', *Lloyds Bank Review*, January 1964.
[11] See also Cameron, G.C., *Regional Economic Policy in the United Kingdom*, op.cit., p.25.
[12] See Hansen, N., *Rural Poverty and the Urban Crisis*, chapter 11, p. 273.
[13] See Andersson, A., 'Regional economic policy: problems, analysis and political experiments in Sweden', in Hansen, N. (ed.), op.cit. chapter VII.
[14] Ibid., p.206.
[15] See Klaassen, L.H. and Drewe, P., op.cit., chapter 3, Cost-benefit analysis in migration.

[16] Stilwell, F.J.B., op.cit., pp.46–7.

10 Regional economic policy on the Community level

The Treaty of Rome

In the Treaty of Rome of 25 March 1957, there is no special chapter dealing with regional policy at the EEC level. There are, however, implicit and explicit references in the Treaty to regional problems.

Implicit references

The implicit references are to be found in the preamble of the Treaty of Rome and in article 2. The preamble leaves no doubt: 'Anxious to strengthen the unity of their economies and to ensure their harmonious development by reducing both the differences existing between the various regions and the backwardness of the less favoured regions'.

Article 2 of the Treaty, which stipulates the mission of the Community, also underlines harmonious development: 'The Community shall have as its task, by establishing a Common Market and progressively approximating the economic policies of Member States, to promote throughout the Community a harmonious development of economic activities, a continuous and balanced expansion, an increase in stability, an accelerated raising of the standard of living and closer relations between the States belonging to it'.

Furthermore one can remark, as was shown in chapter 6, that the fundamental objectives of the Treaty imply a regional policy at the Community level. We cannot imagine a realisation of the objectives of article 3 without a regional policy.

It must also be clear that the common policies have regional effects, but, conversely, the common policies can be an instrument of regional policy at the Community level (see further). Another implicit reference is to be found in the Protocol concerning Italy. This Protocol implies a protection of the Mezzogiorno (see Treaty of Rome — Protocols and Conventions).

In the Treaty of Rome there are, however, explicit references to regional problems, and even a number of Community instruments are given.

A number of articles referring to agricultural, social, and transport policy imply regional preoccupation (see article 39 Par. 2a, article 42a, article 49d, and article 75 Par.3). Structural adaptations must take regional realities into account.

Article 39 Par. 2a: 'In working out the common agricultural policy and the special methods for its application, account shall be taken of the particular character of agricultural activity, which results from the social structure of agriculture and from structural and natural disparities between the various agricultural regions'.

Article 42: 'The Council may in particular authorise the granting of aid: (a) for the protection of enterprises handicapped by structural or natural conditions; (b) within the framework of economic development programmes'.

Article 49d says that in the framework of the measures for free movement of workers, there may not be 'serious threats to the standard of living and level of employment in the various regions and industries'.

Article 75 Par.3: 'By way of derogation from the procedure provided for in paragraph 1, where the application of provisions concerning the principles of the regulatory system for transport would be liable to have a serious effect on the standard of living and on employment in certain areas and on the operation of transport facilities, they shall be laid down by the Council acting unanimously. In so doing, the Council shall take into account the need for adaptation to the economic development which will result from establishing the Common Market'.

Typical 'regional' articles of the Treaty are article 80 Par.2, article 82, article 93 Par.2c, and article 92 Par.3a and c. They are all related to aid systems or regional policies applied in a number of particular cases.

Article 80 Par.2 says, that in respect of transport operations within the Community: ' . . . taking account in particular of the requirements of an appropriate regional economic policy, the needs of underdeveloped areas and the problems of areas seriously affected by political circumstances on the one hand, and of the effects of such rates and conditions on competition between the different modes of transport on the other'.

Article 82: 'The provisions of this Title shall not form an obstacle to the application of measures taken in the Federal Republic of Germany to the extent that such measures are required in order to compensate for the economic disadvantages caused by the division of Germany to the economy of certain areas of the Federal Republic affect by that division'.

Article 92 Par.2c: 'The following shall be compatible with the Common Market: . . . aid granted to the economy of certain areas of the Federal Republic of Germany affected by the division of Germany, in so far as such aid is required in order to compensate for the economic disadvantages caused by that division'.

Article 92 Par.3: 'The following may be considered to be compatible with the Common Market: (a) aid to promote the economic development of areas where the standard of living is abnormally low or where there is serious underemployment; (b) aid to promote the execution of an important project of Common European interest or to remedy a serious disturbance in the economy of a Member State; (c) aid to facilitate the development of certain economic activities or of certain economic areas, where such aid does not adversely affect trading conditions to an extent contrary to the common interest'.

Later on it was stipulated that incentives should be: (a) selective, (b) temporary, (c) degressive, and (d) exceptional. A country could only contribute to investment costs and not to running costs. In practice, however, most of these principles were never respected.

Methods and instruments designed
to encourage regional policy

Three articles should be mentioned in this respect, namely 123, 128, and 130. Article 123 concerning the European Social Fund is, however, very vague. '. . . it shall have the task of rendering the employment of workers easier and of increasing their geographical and occupational mobility within the Community'. From the outset there was a built-in advantage for Italy in the distribution of the European Social Fund.

When this Social Fund was reformed in 1971 it included a more precise commitment to give differential assistance to regions with employment problems. Article 128 relative to a common policy of occupational training stipulates: 'The Council shall . . . lay down general principles for implementing a common vocational training policy capable of contributing to the harmonious development both of the national economies and of the common market'.

The most powerful instrument in the Treaty is the European Investment Bank. Article 130 stipulates: ' . . . the Bank shall, operating on a non-profit making basis, grant loans and give guarantees which facilitate the financing of the following projects in all sectors of the economy: (a) projects for developing less developed regions; (b) projects for modernising or converting undertakings or for developing fresh activities called for by the progressive establishment of the common market, where these projects are of such size or nature that they cannot be entirely financed by the various means available in the individual Member States'.

When the Spaak Committee was drafting the Treaty of Rome, it discussed the potential role of the EEC in regional development and even considered the creating of a regional fund. Eventually however, it opted for the establishment of the European Investment Bank.

The regional articles and the methods and instruments designed to encourage regional policy together with article 56 of the Treaty of Paris (ECSC) concerning readaptation and reconversion (the coal crisis in 1958 and the necessary reorganisations of the steel sector in 1960 provoked a modification of article 56), are the basis of regional actions at the Community level.

Regional economic policy on the EEC level takes shape

EEC regional policy as such was shaped in the 1960s and the beginning of the 1970s. In fact regional economic policy on the Community level was formed step by step: the Community became more aware of regional disparities, the national governments developed their own regional policies, and the elaboration of certain common policies was not possible without more EEC impact on the regional level.

In this context a number of conferences, documents and decisions at Community level must be mentioned.

(a)   The 'Conférence sur les économies régionales' held in Brussels in 1961 emphasised a number of regional problems, especially serious disparities.[1] This conference was convened by the Commission, and led after four years' gestation to the presentation to the Council of its first memorandum on regional policy on 11 May 1965.

(b)   In 1962 a contract was concluded by the Commission for a study about the creation of an industrial development pole in Southern Italy. The report, which has become famous, was published in 1966.[2]

(c)   An important document was the 'Rapports des groupes d'experts sur la politique régionale dans la CEE' published in 1964.[3] Three reports were prepared, dealing respectively with:
     the objectives of regional policy in the EEC;
     the adaptation of the stranded regions;
     the instruments of regional policy.

(d)   Following the decision of the Council of 15.4.1964, regional policy was integrated in medium term economic policy. The first medium term programme (1966–70), approved by the Council in 1967, contained one chapter dealing with regional policy.[4]

(e)   Meanwhile the Commission had published its first report on regional policy in the EEC. It was submitted to the Council in May 1965.[5] The report was based on the conclusion of the three groups of experts. The Commission stressed in these 'Premières Communications' the necessity of a coordinated action by the regional authorities on the national and the European level via the elaboration of regional development programmes.

(f)   In 1968 a Directorate General for regional policy was created. In fact it was a fusion of the former administrative units of the EEC Commission and of the High Authority preoccupied with the regional problems. In mid 1968 Jean Rey, President of the Commission, proclaimed in a speech to the European Parliament: 'Regional policy in the Community should be as the heart is in the human body . . . and should aim to reanimate human life in the regions which have been denied it'. [6]

(g)   A very important step forward was the proposal for a Council Regulation submitted by the Commission to the Council on 17 October 1969: 'Proposition de décision relative à l'organisation des moyens d'action de la Communauté en matière de développement régional'.[7] The introduction of the customs union and the implementation of economic and monetary union required growing Community responsibility for regional development. It was in order to respond to that need that the Commission submitted its proposal, based on article 235 of the EEC Treaty, and designed to furnish the Community with the appropriate instrument. It met with only lukewarm response from most governments and has never been implemented. Furthermore, it was criticised for its timidity and its failure to identify clear policy objectives. Nevertheless, its main ideas provided the basis for the proposals made in 1973 (i.e. Regional Development Fund and Committee for Regional Policy).
    The essential elements of the 1969 proposal were:

> 1 indication of the regions to be developed in the framework of the general objectives of the Treaty (the functioning of a Common Market and rapprochement of the economic policies);
> 2 the need for regional development programmes;
> 3 the creation of a Permanent Committee of regional development (Member States and Commission);

4 the provision of appropriate financial aids to stimulate the rea-
lisation of the development programmes,
Regional Development Rebate Fund (Fonds de bonification);
System of guarantee for regional development.

The debate in regional policy was prompted by two other factors.
The first was an economic one. In the late 1960s there were made a
series of proposals on the establishment of an economic and monetary
union. We refer in the first place to the Werner Report. The economic
debate on the Werner Report suggested that the continuance of severe
regional imbalances would prejudice the attainment of the European
Monetary Union . . . A second factor which animated the debate was
the enlargement of the Communities. This immediately added to the
regional problems of the EEC by including further areas that were by
any criterion impoverished.

(h)   The Third Medium Term Economic Policy Programme, adopted
by the Council on 8 February 1971 insisted on two main points: [8]
a better coordination of national regional policies and the necessity
that the national policies take into account Community preoccupations. That would be realised in the framework of infrastructure
policy, sectoral policy, and aid systems;
the balanced development of the Community requires that the
responsibility of the Member States should be supplemented by
Community responsibility for a number of regional problems of
common interest.
On the occasion of the Agreement of 9 February 1971, it was also
decided to introduce regional policy priorities. The points to be given
priority were:

1 problems posed by the considerable backwardness of certain
large, less developed peripheral regions;
2 difficulties that may result directly from Community integration,
for example in frontier regions;
3 the regional impact of the principal common policies (and
especially of the Common Agricultural Policy) which must be
coordinated with a regional policy aimed at promoting economically healthy activities in the regions affected by the trend in agriculture;
4 problems posed by changes appreciably affecting the economic
potential of certain regions, in particular as a result of the decline
of a dominant economic activity in the region.

(i)   In its resolution of 22 March 1971 on the establishment by stages of economic and monetary union, the Council and the Representatives of the Governments of the Member States recognised the role of and the need for a common regional policy in the following terms: [9] 'In order to bring about a satisfactory growth rate, full employment, and stability within the Community, to correct structural and regional imbalance therein . . . the Council and the Representatives of the Governments of the Member States express their political will to introduce during the next ten years, an economic and monetary union' and decided among other things, that the principles laid down by them should apply to

> the structural and regional measures called for in the context of a Community policy possessing appropriate means, so that these, too, may contribute to the balanced development of the Community, in particular with a view to solving the most important problems . . . In order to achieve these objectives, the Council and the Representatives of the Member States have agreed to initiate, as from 1 January 1971, a number of measures to be carried out during a first phase lasting three years . . . In order to reduce, by taking action in the regional and structural sphere, any tensions which might jeopardise the timely achievement of economic and monetary union, the Council shall decide, on a proposal of the Commission, on the measures required to provide an initial solution to the most urgent problems, due account being taken of the guidelines laid down by the Third Medium-term Economic Policy Programme, in particular by making available to the Community the appropriate means under the Treaties currently in force'.

(j) The Council resolution concerning new guidelines for the Common Agricultural Policy, adopted on 25 March 1971, provided, in the chapter devoted to the concerted development of the Common Agricultural Policy and of the other common policies, that

> rapid progress must be achieved with other Community policies, especially as regards economic and monetary union, regional policy and social policy. Progress in these spheres would substantially contribute to the achievement of agricultural reform. In particular, the Council agrees that Member States and the Community will set up a system of incentives to regional development, encouraging the creation of jobs, notably in regions with surplus farming population'.

(k) In a memorandum to the Council of 28 May 1971, the Commission made two proposals for regulations on common measures of regional policy in the priority agricultural regions. [10] [11] They were meant to provide the means necessary to start solving the problems of economic development of regions where farmers who have become redundant must be transferred to other branches of economic activity. These were the regions where economic activity was largely focused on agriculture, where agricultural productivity was lowest, and where modernisation of structures would involve large scale redeployment of labour. Instead of acquiescing in migration of the population towards already overcrowded areas, the Community must encourage investments in regions where growth points should be created. Such action would also help to improve the living conditions of the population in accordance with the Preamble to the Treaty of Rome, which specifies this as an objective of the Community.

The Commission had to demarcate the priority agricultural regions for which the proposed measures are intended, on the basis of the following criteria:

percentage of the working population employed in agriculture above the Community average;
gross domestic product *per capita* at factor costs below the Community average;
percentage of the working population employed in industry below the Community average.

The Commission proposed two types of measures:

1 Measures for conversion in the form of premiums, granted by the Community, of 1,500 units of account (u.a.) per job created and filled by a farmer or a direct descendant of a farmer leaving agriculture. An amount of 250 million u.a. for five years would be earmarked for this purpose from the Guidance Section of the European Agricultural Guidance and Guarantee Fund.
2 Financial measures for regional development consisting of a reduction of not more than three points, for a period of twelve years, of the interest (Regional Development Rebate Fund) on directly productive investments or on infrastructures in the priority regions as specified in the Third Medium term Economic Policy Programme.

(1)   The first intervention of the EEC in the context of the coordination of financial aids was the Council regulation of 20 October 1971.[12] This regulation is important not only because it is the first regulation concerning EEC regional economic policy, but also because it is a step forward to avoid 'risques de surenchères' (risks of overbidding). This regulation was extended to the three new member states in 1973 (from 1 July 1973). The general regional aid systems were revised in 1975; in fact the revision was an extension of the regulation to all the regions of

the Community. The content of the regulation and the revised regional aid systems are dealt with on page 410 of this chapter.

In the background to these interventions there were three principal factors. First, since the realisation of the customs union, the number of aids for regional purposes had been increasing very fast. This phenomenon is important as the impact on competition becomes greater with the abolition of trade barriers. Secondly, to avoid the risks of overbidding, a pragmatic method was proposed to the member countries in 1968, referring to article 92 and article 93 of the Treaty. A system whereby the national governments would give prior notification of regional aids to the Commission was foreseen. Because this pragmatic method was not successful, the regulation of 1971 became the only alternative. It aimed to judge and to coordinate the aids applied in the different countries of the Community. It fixes the main principles according to which the Commission will judge incentives in order to avoid the risks of overbidding. Thirdly, the Commission's intention was to limit the amount of aid that could be given to the already affluent regions, precisely in order to encourage more investments in the poorer regions of the EEC. It does not mean in reality that the risk of overbidding is fully avoided.

(m) The resolution of the Council of 22 March 1971 expressed a political engagement to start with a real regional economic policy on the Community level. The resolution reads: 'In order to undertake without delay measures in the regional or structural field which are necessary to the ultimate achievement of economic and monetary union the Council agrees in principle that:

from 1972 onwards the EAGGF may be used for measures to foster regional development;
a Regional Development Fund be set up or any other system that will provide the requisite Community resources for regional development'.[13]

(n) The Conference of the Heads of State or Government, held in Paris from 19 to 21 October 1972, established the Community regional policy, alongside economic and monetary union, as an essential factor in the strengthening of the Community. For the first time the new members of the Community had the opportunity of discussing policy priorities. In the final communication of the Conference, we find an important passage concerning regional policy. The ways and means of the action to be taken were specified as follows:

1 'The Heads of State or Government agreed that a high priority should be given to the aim to correcting in the Community, the

structural and regional imbalances which might affect the realisation of economic and monetary union.

2 The Heads of State or Government invite the Commission to prepare without delay a report analysing the regional problems which arise in the enlarged Community and to put forward appropriate proposals.

3 From now on they undertake to coordinate their regional policies.

4 Desirous of directing that effort towards finding a Community solution to regional problems, they invite the Community institutions to create a Regional Development Fund. This will be set up before 31 December 1973, and will be financed, from the beginning of the second phase of economic and monetary union, from the Community's own resources. Intervention by the Fund in coordination with national aids should permit, progressively with the realisation of economic and monetary union, the correction of the main regional imbalances in the enlarged Community and particularly those resulting from the preponderance of agriculture and from industrial change and structural underemployment'.

The content of the statement made it appear that the main battle had been won; regional policy had secured the support of the most senior political leaders.

(o) The Commission has carried out this mandate. On 3 May 1973 it adopted a document entitled 'Report on regional problems in the enlarged Community'. It was called the Thomson Report.[14] The report deals with the psychological, ecological, and economic reasons for the Community's regional policy, regional imbalances, the main features of the policy to be pursued, the operation of the Regional Development Fund and the coordination of national policies.

The Commission laid before the Council on 25 July 1973 the draft for a decision establishing a Committee for Regional Development. This Committee is to facilitate the coordination of regional policy by member states. At the same time the Commission presented to the Council a proposal for a regulation establishing a European Regional Development Fund.[15] [16]

For the purpose of identifying the regions eligible for assistance from the Regional Development Fund, the Commission submitted to the Council a proposal setting out more detailed criteria and provided a list of the names of the beneficiary regions.[17] [18]

In October 1973 the proposition of the Commission to the Council of 28 May 1971, whereby the Guidance Section of the EAGGF would contribute to the costs of creating non-agricultural jobs in a number of priority agricultural regions in the Community, was maintained.

The Commission drafted a proposal for a Regulation of the Council relating to the list of priority agricultural regions and areas provided for in the Regulation (EEC) on the financing by the Guidance Section of the European Agricultural Guidance and Guarantee Fund of projects falling within the framework of development programmes in priority agricultural regions.

The final negotiations were very difficult and no agreement could be reached to make the Regional Development Fund operational before 1 January 1974. The main reasons were: (a) substantial differences of opinion on the main principles persisted among the nine. The most demanding countries were Britain, Ireland, and Italy. The greatest reservations came from Germany, the chief paymaster. The British and the Germans dominated the negotiations over the Fund; (b) the debate was complicated by the Yom Kippur War and the oil embargo of the Arab oil producers; (c) the turbulence in the international monetary system and the economic recession of the 1970s; and finally (d) the abandonment of the Commitment to Economic and Monetary Union in the foreseeable future deprived the Commission of one of its trump cards in the argument for the rapid establishment of the Regional Development Fund.

The political change in the United Kingdom in 1974 led to further delay. The new Labour Government promised to renegotiate the terms of British accession to the EEC. Furthermore the new Labour Government was not so enthusiastic toward Community intervention in the regional field.

By the end of 1974 the Irish and Italians threatened not to attend the Summit to be held in Paris in December. They agreed to attend if and only if the other governments would give an immediate and firm commitment to set up the Regional Development Fund. For a good description of the negotiations we refer to Helen Wallace's publication.[19]

(p) At the Summit meeting on 9 and 10 December 1974 in Paris, an operational decision was reached with respect to the European Regional Development Fund. In accordance with this decision the European Regional Fund, whose purpose was to be to correct the main regional imbalances within the Community resulting from a predominance of agriculture, industrial change, and structural underemployment, was to be set up for a three-year trial period beginning on 1 January 1975. For this period the Fund was to have at its disposal 1,300 million u.a. (300 million u.a. for the first year and 500 million u.a. for each of the following years). Of this 1,300 million u.a., 150 million u.a. will be drawn from unused appropriations to the Guidance Section of the European Agricultural Guidance and Guarantee Fund.

The resources of the Fund were to be shared out as follows: 1.5 per cent for Belgium, 1.3 per cent for Denmark, 15 per cent for France, 6.4 per cent for F.R. of West Germany, 6 per cent for Ireland, 40 per cent for Italy, 0.1 per cent for Luxembourg, 1.7 per cent for the Netherlands and 28 per cent for the United Kingdom.

Ireland, however, was also to receive 6 million u.a., this sum to be deducted from the share of the other member states, with the exception of Italy.[20]

What the Paris Summit of October 1972 had promised to be an impressive target for the newly enlarged Community ended up as the hesitant creation of a modest fund. The original proposal would have allocated 3,000 million u.a. The ESC advocated 5,000 million u.a. in July 1973.

One fence remained to be cleared: the authorisation by the European Parliament of the supplementary budget to finance the Fund.

(q)   The year 1975 was to a certain extent an important year for harmonised regional development within the EEC and a further step towards European integration. The European Regional Development Fund was established in March and the Regional Policy Committee was set up in July.[21]

(r)   Before the end of the trial period on 3 June 1977, the Commission submitted to the Council a communication and a number of proposals. This was in accordance with the Fund regulations stating that the Commission was to submit to the Council in the course of 1977 proposals concerning the future of Community regional policy.[22]

The Commission felt that Community Regional Policy needed to be reviewed as the economic and social background of the policy had fundamentally altered.

> The economic crisis has accentuated existing regional problems and, at the same time, has generated new ones. The crisis and the gradual emergence of a new international division of labour are involving the Community's economy in a far-reaching restructuring process, thereby giving rise to new sources of regional disequilibrium. In addition, it is clear that decisions in other areas of Community policy may have repercussions at regional level. Accordingly, what is needed is an overall concept for a Community regional policy that is endowed with appropriate instrument and pursues two major objectives: reduction of existing regional disequilibria and prevention of fresh disequilibria.

The motives for regional economic policy on the Community level

In the first chapter we dealt with the motives for regional economic policy on the national level. These motives remain valid on the Community level. But besides these national motives, a number of specifically Community arguments should be mentioned.

General EEC issues

With reference to the first section of this chapter, the first motive for a regional economic policy is to be found in the Treaty: namely the need for 'a continuous and balanced expansion'. Continuous expansion has been achieved; balanced expansion has been lacking. The Thomson Report has indicated this target as a human and moral requirement of the first importance. In this respect two points were emphasised in the Thomson Report.

> (a)   No community could maintain itself nor have a meaning for the peoples which belong to it so long as some have very different standards of living and have cause to doubt the common will of all to help each Member to better the conditions of its people.
> (b)   Furthermore, if capital is not moved towards the less developed regions in order to enable labour to find employment in conditions which are comparable to those existing in the regions of greater development, workers will not have a real choice on which the free circulation of labour in the Community can be based. [23]

The risk of overbid

Free competition is a leading principle in the integration process (see the first section of this chapter). The Commission has to legitimise the regional aids of the States. 'The Commission shall, together with Member States, constantly examine all systems of aids existing in those States. It shall propose to the latter any appropriate measure required by the progressive development or by the functioning of the Common Market' (see Art.93 Par.1). There is only one exception which concerns regions of the Federal Republic of Germany affected by the division of Germany, to the extent that such aids are necessary in order to compensate for the economic disadvantages caused by division.

Since the creation of the EEC, regional policies have remained largely in national hands and in each country the national aid systems have been extended for two reasons: first, with the elimination of tariffs and export subsidies, member countries' governments have increasingly applied measures of regional assistance; secondly, with the extension of aids, these measures have become instruments of competition among national firms and means of attracting foreign investments.[24]

The pragmatic approach of coordination of the regional aid systems, as it was developed during the 1960s, did not work (see page 390 of this chapter). There were two disadvantages to prior notifications by national governments to the Commission. In the first place, it is very difficult to compare aids. Furthermore there is a risk of compromise between member countries to the detriment of spatial rationality.

An attempt to avoid a risk of overbid has been made in 1969.[25] However, it was only in 1971 that a real step forward was made with the regulations of 20 October concerning the coordination of aids granted in the framework of regional policy in the central regions of the EEC.

The efforts made in the framework of aid systems are only one element of the necessary coordination of national approaches. A complete coordination would cover all phases of a policy making: formulation of objectives, development of strategies, and the use of instruments. Can a Community Regional Policy be effective in the hands of the national governments? Later we shall see that even the Regional Development Fund is, after all, largely based on national objectives, strategies, and instruments.

A pre-condition for the realisation of
a monetary and economic union

Although we emphasised in the first chapter the relationship between regional disequilibria (or, more generally, structural disparities) and inflationary pressure in the different countries, and dealt in chapter 6 with the impact of a customs union and a monetary union on regional disparities, it seems necessary to pay particular attention to one of the main elements of the background to the Community regional policy.

The basic idea of the Treaty is that there should be a single internal market; it is an area organised according to the principles of a market economy with free movement of factors of production and abolition of discrimination in the interest of free competition. Competition policy and the aim of a single internal market form the basis, let us say the general infrastructure, for all economic, social, and political considerations. In his address to the European Parliament, H. von der Groeben, a former member of the Commission, stressed that competition is not a target in itself and that competition regulations are not sufficient to solve all problems. It is necessary to have a common economic and monetary policy. H. von der Groeben went even further by suggesting that good regulation of competition and coordination of general economic and monetary policy are not sufficient to guarantee the development of the Common Market. The structural differences in the individual countries are not only detrimental to the inhabitants and from the general economic viewpoint, but such disequilibria are a danger for the development of the Common Market. The unequal evolution of costs and prices is not only due to differences in economic policy. Unequal inflationary pressures are also due to structural disparities. Therefore it is necessary to eliminate regional and structural disparities to such an extent that a real start can be made with a common economic policy.[26]

The general relationship demonstrates the necessity of a regional and structural policy in the Community.

According to J. van Ginderachter, the specific justification of a regional policy on the Community level is its contribution in the first phase, to a good functioning of the Common Market and, later on, to the economic and monetary union. He very clearly describes this specific justification of the regional economic policy.[27] Therefore we quote his argumentation.

> Already, in its first general report in 1958, the Commission drew attention to the necessity of a Community regional policy to ensure the good functioning of a common market between countries with very different economic structures (sectoral and regional) and to realise, in the long run, a well balanced economic expansion. If a country in a common market, where goods circulate freely without customs duties, returns a persistent deficit on its balance of payments because its economic structure (sectoral or regional) is not adapted to integration, it can adjust its rate of exchange. This is probably the least expensive means of strengthening the competitive position of its economy. So far as the regional structures of a country do not adapt themselves — spontaneously or as a result of public interventions — to an integrated common market, the effectiveness of the latter is not much endangered if the fixed rates of exchange are adjusted at regular intervals. On the contrary, if this situation continued it would finally result in the exclusion of development regions from the common market, either by a mass emigration of its population to more developed centres or by the constitution in these areas of a closed economy, not integrated in the Common Market, and with very low productivity and income. The customs union would continue to work correctly between countries, but its integration radius would be reduced. Since the EEC concerns the whole territory of the Community this would be an argument for Community intervention. While proceeding to adaptations of exchange rates, the Member States have in fact considerably strengthened their regional policy interventions during the last decade, so that the relative *status quo* of the

development areas in the Community could be maintained.

The situation becomes quite different when the Community passes the customs union stage to become an economic and monetary union of which one of the main objectives is to create a European currency by 31 December 1980 or, with technically almost the same effect, to fix mutual and immutable rates of exchange between the currencies of the Member States. A monetary union facilitates the intra-community exchanges of goods and capital and consequently the interpenetration of the economies, which in turn permits a better utilisation of the economies of scale and specialisation between countries and areas of the Community. However, this monetary union implies that the economic structures of the countries forming the union adapt themselves in such a way as to make, according to the given rate of exchange, their economies sufficiently competitive with respect to those of the other countries as not to provoke a constant deficit on their balances of payments. Actually, being no longer allowed to adapt its parity, a Member State in difficulty will be forced to take measures with an equivalent effect incompatible with the economic and monetary union or even with the Common Market (e.g. quantitative restrictions or import duties). Consequently the formation of the monetary union requires an effective policy of structural adaptation, particularly as far as the regions are concerned. No regional policy means no economic and monetary union, and vice versa. The debate between 'monetarists' and 'structuralists' becomes pointless to the extent that progress must be realised simultaneously in the monetary and economic areas and that progress in the monetary area conditions progress in the economic area, and vice versa.

The regional policy should be all the more vigorous the wider is the gap between developed and developing areas within a country. It should be a Community policy for two reasons: on the one hand to ensure by means of an appropriate coordination that the public interventions attack in the first place the regional imbalances that might affect the realisation of the economic and monetary union; on the other hand to help Member States that, in view of their economic situation, are unable to bear themselves the financial costs of the regional policy needed to meet Community necessities. From a strictly economic point of view, then, the Community's financial contribution with respect to regional policy must not *a priori* concern all the Member States of the EEC.

Yet this Community is not only economic or mercantile; it is also social and political. So runs the argument of Community solidarity in favour of development areas identified by comparison with a Community average. All the countries of the Community have such areas but some have more than others. That is why all the Community countries must be able to benefit from the European Fund for regional development according to the volume and the gravity of their regional problems and not according to the principle of 'juste retour'.

In this context the question arises why the problem of regional imbalance is predominant among necessary structural adaptations. In fact the differences between countries are due as much to sectoral structures (agriculture, industry, commerce, and services) and company structures (size, dynamism) as to regional structures. The answer to this question is relatively simple. In a market economy there is a high correlation between regions, sectors, and highly productive companies, and vice versa; in the strong regions the greater part of the sectors and the greater part of the companies have a high labour and capital productivity and vice versa. This probably depends on the equipment of the regions, the pattern of existing economic activities and external economies. These are precisely the elements that the public authorities try to influence in a market economy. Consequently, one should not be surprised that in the context of structural imbalances the public authorities pay great attention to regional imbalances.

The realisation of other common policies

Regional economic policy is a precondition not only for the achievement of a monetary and economic union. A number of other common policies could be realised more easily and much faster if they were sufficiently linked to a programme of regional policy.

In its advice on the Commission's proposal of 17.10.1969[28] the Social and Economic Committee emphasised the widespread need for regional economic policy.[29] In this advice the realisation of policies occupies a central position. Therefore we cite the Committee's general observations in extenso.

A coordination of the regional policies of the Member Countries of the European Community and a Community action are necessary to:
1) realise with success the objectives mentioned in the Treaty (article 2), namely a harmonious development of economic activities in the whole Community (a continuous and balanced expansion), and also an accelerated raising of the standard of living;
2) to draw up the national programmes according to Community objectives;

3) to reduce the disparities in the development of the various regions that have still been observed after 12 years of Common Market;

4) to promote in the middle long run the progressive harmonisation of conjunctural and economic policies and of monetary and social policies;

5) to realise or to continue the common policies provided in the Treaty (e.g. in the energy, transport and agricultural sector);

6) to prevent or to abolish the distortion of competition resulting from a 'race' for aid systems between the Member States and to harmonise their regional promotion measures.

Moreover, the necessity of an efficient Community regional policy proceeds not only from:

— the implication inherent in the reorganisation of the agricultural sector;
— confirmation that disparities between advanced areas and less favoured areas are growing;
— the degenerating situation in the unfavoured areas or in the regions with declining or stagnating development;
— social-economic difficulties and problems concerning public health arising in congested areas;

but also from the necessity:
— to correct the bad utilisation of resources and the distortions that result too frequently from the regional policies adopted by the Member States;
— to orient the regional policies pursued in each country so that they are attuned to the common policies concerning economy, social affairs, energy, agriculture, transport, industry, science, etc.

The Committee is well aware of the fact that the regional policy at Community level can only interfere in a progressive way. However, in order to guarantee in the long run a harmonious and balanced development of the Community, national programmes should be oriented according to Community objectives. The Commission's proposal must therefore be completed by a Community conception based on the ideas of the future structure of the Community and on the criteria adopted by the different Member States for the realisation of their own regional policy; in this way the Community regional policy will constitute more than the simple summing up of national regional policies and it will be integrated in the concept of an overall structural order.

In addition, a coordination of regional policies is made all the more necessary by the fact that national regional policies have so far not always been drawn up according to the principles agreed and accepted by the Member States as laid down in the first communication of the Commission concerning regional policy, and in the first medium term programme.

In general the 'Proposed Council Decision concerning the organisation of the Community's means of taking action in the matter of regional development' (Proposition de décision du Conseil relative à l'organisation de moyens d'action de la Communauté en matière de développement régional) can be considered as an effort of the Community authorities to coordinate in a first period the national regional policies on Community level. The Committee welcomes this project as a first measure on the way to the achievement of a Community regional policy. The Community should take all useful initiatives to realise this concept.

To meet the impact of the integration process
and the new international division of labour

A further motive for a regional economic policy on the Community level is to be found in the unequal impact of the integration process on the different regions of the Community. In chapter 6 we come to the conclusion that the integration process must lead to an increase of the existing disparities. This is fully recognised in the recently published new guidelines for a Community regional policy:

> . . . the progressive establishment of the Common Market had not achieved the positive results expected in terms of a better distribution of economic activity throughout Community territory. On the contrary, the prosperity of the richer regions increased while regions with less-advanced economies encountered increasing difficulty in integrating themselves into the growing market. This was largely a consequence of the way in which the EEC Treaty was conceived and implemented, with the emphasis mainly on the abolition of barriers to trade. The sustained growth of the Community economy over this period clearly had positive results, even in the less favoured regions, but it contributed equally to hiding the persistent imbalances which had existed before the establishment of the Common Market.[30]

This argument was already to be found in the Community decision on regional policy adopted in 1975.

In the same document the Commission argues further:

Economic and social trends in recent years have made the situation even more complicated and worrying. Since 1973 the effects of the economic crisis and the increased cost of raw materials have led to a slower growth rate and less inclination to invest.

In an economy whose growth rate has so declined, the development of the weaker regions is seriously affected, and the persistence of regional imbalances even threatens the proper functioning of the Common Market itself. Indeed, not only do the less developed regions fail to integrate fully within the Community, but the problems to which they give rise become an increasingly heavy burden on national economies and thus increase the pressure on the public authorities concerned to refuse the constraints inherent in the mechanism of Community integration. It is, moreover, an illusion to hope for the convergence of Member States' economies so long as regional problems continue to weigh so heavily on certain economies.

Furthermore the new international division of labour now gradually emerging, is imposing major structural changes on the Community economy, so creating new sources of regional imbalance.

In the light of this situation, Community regional policy must become more ambitious than in the past. Even in a period of sustained growth, the assistance given to the least-favoured regions did not make a sufficient contribution to the reduction of regional differences. As well as an increased effort to improve the working of the Common Market, a comprehensive policy of structural change is necessary. This should help both the regions that were insufficiently developed even before the creation of the Common Market and regions either experiencing or vulnerable to the difficulties of restructuring and redevelopment.

It follows from this situation that Community regional policy must be strengthened and its field of application expanded. This is not only desireable; it is now one of the conditions of continuing European economic integration.[31]

The objectives of the regional policy in the EEC

Since the creation of the EEC the objectives of regional policy on the Community level have been formulated and published several times in official documents.

Objectives stated in the 'First Communication of the
Commission on Regional Economic Policy in the EEC'[32]

Reduction of welfare disparities
'The regional policy must contribute to the correction of the excessive
income disparities between the regions, without systematically trying to
equalise regional incomes and without artificially restricting the growth
of the most developed regions'.

Priority must be given to: (a) regions with low income level and (b)
regions with readaptation difficulties.

Development according to growth potentialities
'The regional policy has to develop the regions, taking into account
their natural vocation and present potential resources, and should favour
specialisation in those activities able to withstand competition. In this
way, the people of the different regions will be able to play an active
role in the growth of their region, and benefit from the best employment
conditions and a higher welfare level'.

Specialisation according to growth potentialities may lead to a mono-
structure. We must consider the economic vocation of each of the
regions taking into account that the influence of primary location factors is diminishing.

Better utilisation of factors in production and reduction of social costs
in the big agglomerations

Potential incompatibility between the optimal distribution of factors of
production and other objectives
'In exceptional cases, a certain incompatibility may be seen between an
optimal repartition of factors of production and other objectives. The
priority must be given to a regional action which contributes in the most
efficient way to the growth of the national and community economy;
but other necessary measures must be taken, on the social level, to
remedy difficulties that an action justified on economic grounds cannot
reduce'.

The objectives stated in the Commission's proposal
to the Council, 17.10.1969[33]

The formulation of objectives in this document is also very vague. A
distinction can be made between objectives of any policy on the national level (see chapter 1 and chapter 7) and the specific targets of regional
policy on the Community level. The latter can be summarised as
follows:

1 to meet the consequences of the creation of a common market. We refer here to what we stated in chapter 6;

2 to make the realisation of common policies less difficult by making the regional structure less heterogeneous;

3 to regularly confront and coordinate regional policy with other economic policies;

4 to coordinate the existing policies in the different member countries;[34]

5 to respond to existing and expected social and economic mutations:

the development of the tertiary sector;

changes in the qualifications required of the labour force induced by structural changes;

changes in the transport system (e.g. the new vocation of maritime regions);

the concentration of population and the need to avoid excesses thereof;

6 to elaborate a conception of a global 'aménagement du territoire'.

There can be no long term value in the reduction of regional disparities unless the new regional structures have been conceived as part of a global community structure corresponding to future economic, technological and social necessities.

Analysis of these objectives gives rise to doubt that it is correct to use the term 'objectives'. They are, rather, a mixture of the content of the regional policy and 'open-ended' targets.

In the Thomson Report the term 'objectives' is no longer used. Instead the Commission formulated a number of guidelines that are, after all, more indicative than the foregoing general targets.

The guidelines for a Community regional policy stated in the Thomson Report[35]

1) Community regional policy cannot be a substitute for the national regional policies which Member States have been conducting for many years. It must complement them with the aim of reducing the main disparities across the Community. The role of Community regional policy will progressively increase as the Community increases and improves its instruments of intervention, together with the coordination of national regional policies which will be undertaken in the light of the varying extent of regional problems.

2) Since overconcentration of economic activity in some regions is

a major social and economic problem, the Community should seek agreement between the Member States on common policies to reduce concentration in the congested regions.

3) Community regional policy requires not only new incentives and disincentives but coordination of the various common policies and financial instruments which exist at Community level with a view to their improved utilisation for regional objectives.

4) It will also be essential to achieve the real coordination of national regional policies. This is a role for the Regional Development Committee.

5) The principal vehicle for mobilising Community resources as a complement to actions of the Regional Development Fund. The assistance of the Fund should be presently carried out in the Member States and should be devoted entirely to the medium and long term development of less developed and declining regions within the Member States, with the aim of bringing about self-sustaining growth.

6) The Regional Development Fund must be of sufficient size to contribute effectively to meeting the target set by the Heads of State or of Government who gave a 'high priority' to the reduction of structural and regional imbalances in the Community which might affect the achievement of European Economic and Monetary Union.

7) The Fund will have to concentrate its expenditure very largely in those regions which are the most in need in relation to the Community as a whole. In other words there must be standards to ensure that the means available to the Fund are used in a manner quite independent of any criterion of juste retour, and which reflect the size and urgency of the regional problems facing the Community.

8) The main regional imbalances within the enlarged Community are found in 'areas whose problems arise from the preponderance of agriculture, from industrial change and structural underemployment'.

Aims stated in the framework
of the new guidelines [36]

It cannot be denied that the formulation of aims in the framework of the new guidelines are also very general:

To reduce existing regional problems which appear both in regions traditionally less developed and in those involved in a process of industrial or agricultural reconversion.

To prevent new regional imbalances arising from the change in

404

world economic structures or from measures adapted by the Community within the framework of its own policies.

As far as the tasks required of the Community and the Member States are concerned:

1 They involve the permanent analysis and assessment of trends in regional economies throughout the whole Community, territory, principally, through not only in the field of employment, to assess the range and nature of the regional imbalances affecting the integration process at Community level.

2 They require that Community policies and financial instruments, structural and other, are used in a coherent and convergent way, if their consequences may, at one or another, have a regional impact.

3 There must be coordination of the regional policies of Member States, both mutually and in relation to Community aims.

4 There is the question of a policy on financial assistance (Regional Fund); on the one hand, this takes the form of support for national regional policies, and on the other it must be a catalyst in working out and applying specific development and reconversion measures at Community level.

The strategy of regional development

An analysis of Commission documents reveals albeit in a general way, a number of strategies.

The first strategic element is to be found in the identification of the priority regions. They can be classified in four groups:

(a) the underdeveloped peripheral regions;
(b) the agricultural regions;
(c) the stranded regions;
(d) the frontier regions.

Although the EEC has on several occasions emphasised the priority regions, its influence has been only indirect. Up to now the allocation of the Regional Development Fund has been entirely based on the nationally recognised problem regions.

The recognition in the Commission document 'Community regional policy — New guidelines' of four types of regional problems will not very much change the above mentioned classification.

The New European Regional Development Fund has to cope with four types of problems:

(a)   the underdevelopment of a number of regions, which, despite sustained efforts, still lie well behind, and which will require massive Community aid for a long time to come; (Mezzogiorno, Ireland, Northern Ireland, Greenland);

(b)   the industrial or agricultural changes, which have appeared in the last quarter of a century in numerous regions of the Community, and which necessitate measures of development and reconversion to which the Community must contribute, but certainly for a shorter time and in a less intensive way than in (a);

(c)   the current or expected problems caused in some regions by the change in world economic structures or by existing or future Community policies and calling for a Community contribution each time the effects reach a certain scale;

(d)   the special problems of frontier regions.

The Commission can, however, refuse the application of the Fund and even intervene as far as the acceptance of national assisted regions is concerned. In 1972 the Commission objected to a number of Belgian problem regions, on the basis of its regulation of October 1971.

Account being taken of the part of the Community that is covered by the so-called priority regions, this first aspect of the strategy is losing much of its power (see chapter 7).

The new guidelines of June 1977 do not change very much the existing procedure and leave untouched a major handicap to an effective Community policy towards regional problems.

The influence of the Commission with respect to the priority regions and the formulation of objectives may increase once the general development programmes are available and form a basis for action. According to article 6 of the Fund Regulation these programmes had to be prepared before the end of 1977. They could be a first step in establishing an objective criterion for the identification of the problem regions to be developed.

The Third Annual Report on the activity of the ERDF states:

Regional development programmes provide the reference framework for Fund activity. Projects financed from the Fund have to fall within that framework, so as to ensure coherence between national measures of regional development and the Community's effort. Moreover, in addition to their importance in relation to the Fund, the programmes will form the basic means of ensuring better coordination of national regional policies.

It was a task of the Regional Policy Committee to study technical methods for the drafting of regional development programmes so as to arrive at a common approach to the concept of a regional policy programme.[38] In 1975 the Regional Policy Committee adopted an outline of what the regional development programmes should contain.[39]

Regional development programmes in the sense of the EEC regulations are in principle concerned with regions qualifying for ERDF contributions. Member States should prepare a programme for each region or group of regions, taking particular account of the institutional framework and the statistics available.

Regional development programmes should have five chapters:

1 *Economic and social analysis*

The purpose is a proper economic analysis and not a simple statistical description. The analysis should reveal the main regional problems and their causes. This analysis, performed with the help of the relevant statistics that are available, should cover the following subjects:

(a) main aspects of past economic and social development;
(b) principal imbalances besetting the region, and their causes;
(c) effects of past corrective actions;
(d) development possibilities and conditions, including bottlenecks;
(e) probable economic and social development during the programme period provided no new factors intervene, to the extent that it is possible to foresee developments with a minimum degree of assurance.

2 *Development objectives*

In this chapter, the outline of regional development programmes should go beyond a simple indication of broad aims such as raising the standard of living, creating jobs, reducing unemployment or migration, etc. The development targets of the region must be more clearly specified and, as far as possible, quantified, at least in so far as certain basic elements are concerned. Where it proves impossible for sufficiently important practical reasons to quantify a development target, or targets, a sufficiently detailed specification, if relevant in qualitative terms, of the aim or aims could be given instead.

The most basic elements to define are:

(a) the level of employment and, where possible, the number of jobs to be created or maintained;
(b) the effects sought on different economic activities and income of the region;
(c) the provision of infrastructure.

The objectives indicated should not, therefore, take the form of an inventory of regional needs or aspirations; instead they should make up a coherent whole on the national level. There is question here of real targets, comprising practically relevant priorities for the medium term, and which regions can reasonably achieve in the given situation with the means available.

3 *Measures for development*

In this chapter the programmes should give details of the development measures envisaged in order to attain the objectives indicated.
   Of essential concern are:

> (a)   direct regional policy measures in the strict sense such as aids, disincentives, decentralising public services, financial equalisation systems between regions, etc.;
> (b)   investment in infrastructure (economic and social) for regional development purposes.

4 *Financial resources*

5 *Implementing the programme*

This chapter is to indicate where the responsibility rests for implementing the whole or part of the programmes. The tasks allotted to each agency or institution should be clearly stated and details should be given of the administrative methods employed to ensure consistency between the different parts of the programme.

   All the programmes for all the regions eligible for Fund assistance were sent to the Commission before the end of 1977. The Third Annual Report on the activity of the ERDF gives a summary of the submitted regional development programmes.
   One other strategic aspect of EEC regional policy, albeit a general one, is the fact that according to the Commission the Community regional policy cannot be a substitute for the national regional policies. The Community policy is only a complement. This is a very important decision. The new proposal to split the Fund into two sections, one on the basis of pre-established national quotas and another not involving national quotas, does not change the prevailing guiding principle. The new proposal became a definite Council decision in February 1979 (Council Regulation no.214/79).
   The fact that the Community regional policy is only a complement to the national regional policies, makes it very difficult for the Commission to set up its own strategy with respect to priority regions, the choice of

growth poles or growth centres, and the concentration of efforts, three very important elements of any regional development strategy. They are to be found neither in the existing documents nor the EEC regulations. Even the regional development programmes need not refer to them.

Traditional instruments of
EEC regional policy

As we have seen in previous sections, the greatest responsibility and effort for regional policy rest so far largely in the hands of the national governments. This necessitates the coordination of the national instruments. In addition to the national interventions, the Community has at its disposal a number of instruments of its own such as the European Investment Bank, the Guidance section of the EAGGF, the articles 54 and 56 of the Treaty of Paris and the Social Fund. They are the traditional Community instruments. The new instruments, the Regional Development Fund and the Regional Policy Committee, will be dealt with in the following section.

The coordination of national
financial instruments

The coordination of the national financial instruments is regulated by the General Regional Aid Systems. [40] These systems are based on the first resolution of 20 October 1971 concerning the coordination of regional policy aids in the central regions of the EEC. They were later extended to the new member states (see the communications of the Commission to the Council of 27 June 1973 and of 26 February 1975).

On 21 December 1978 the Commission informed the Member States of the principles which, in accordance with the powers vested in the Commission by Articles 92 et seq. of the EEC Treaty, it will apply to regional aid systems already in force or to be established in the regions of the Community.

When the principles of coordination were defined in 1971 and when they were subsequently completed when the Community was enlarged in 1973, the need to put an end to outbidding in state aids was felt to be most urgent in the most developed regions of the Community. Nevertheless it was, even then, specified that an appropriate solution should be formulated to take account of the specific problems posed in each of the other regions. The coordination has four principal aspects which form one whole: (a) ceilings of aid intensity, (b) transparency, (c) regional specificity, and (d) the sectoral repercussions of regional aids.

In the latest communication of the Commission on regional aid systems, a number of new elements were introduced. The principles of coordination have been partly redefined and the methods for their implementation have been amended and supplemented. These new elements are taken into account in this section.

The common method of evaluation had hitherto fixed investment as the sole denominator in considering the transparency of aids and aid systems. Account being taken of the employment situation in the various regions of the Community and the emphasis which some Member States wish to give to the creation of jobs in their regional aid scheme, an alternative denominator expressed in European units of account (EUA) per job created by the investment is being introduced into the principles of coordination. In addition the methods for measuring aids are being supplemented as a result of the studies of measurability. The technical studies have also led to the adoption of an ex-post system of measurement in situations where the regional aid systems of a Member State include both aids which can and aids which cannot be measured in advance (e.g. tax concessions). All aids which have maximum intensities that can be expressed in investment or jobs created can now be coordinated.

For the first time a method of coordinating aids with respect to the transfer of an establishment is introduced. However, the Commission still has, in principle, reservations as to the compatibility of operating aids. The Commission will specify, before the end of a three-year period, the circumstances, if any, in which it might consider operating aids to be compatible.

(a) *Ceilings.* The ceilings of aid intensity are differentiated according to the nature and the gravity of regional problems. The maximum level of intervention are fixed in terms of net grant equivalent, calculated according to a common evaluation procedure. [41] The net grant equivalents are expressed either as a percentage of initial investment or in EUA per job created by the initial investment. Different groups of regions with different ceilings are provided for.

Group 1: No maximum; this is the case for Greenland.

Group 2: The alternative ceilings for this group are: (a) 75 per cent net grant equivalent of initial investment applying to aids linked and fixed in direct relation to initial investment or jobs created, or (b) a net grant equivalent of 13,000 EUA per job created by the initial investment. In addition, as from 1 January 1981, for projects with an initial investment exceeding three million EUA, no more than a further 25 per cent net grant equivalent of initial investment or a net grant equivalent of 4,500

EUA per job created by the initial investment can be paid in other aids, to be spread over a minimum of five years.

These ceilings apply to Ireland, Mezzogiorno, Northern Ireland, West Berlin, and the French Overseas Departments.

Group 3: The alternative ceilings are 30 per cent net grant equivalent of initial investment or a net grant equivalent of 5,500 EUA per job created by the initial investment. The latter may not exceed 40 per cent net grant equivalent of initial investment. These ceilings apply to:
— that part of French territory which has received industrial development grants (primes de développement industriel);
— the aided areas in the Italian regions of Friuli-Venezia-Giulia, Trentino-Alto-Adige, Valle d'Aoste, Lazio, Toscana, Umbria, and Veneto, insofar as these regions are not included in the Mezzogiorno;
— the other assisted areas of the United Kingdom (with the exception of areas classified as Intermediate Areas).

Group 4: The ceilings in net grant equivalent are fixed at 25 per cent of initial investment or 4,500 EUA per job created by initial investment. The latter may not exceed 30 per cent net grant equivalent of initial investment. The following regions belong to this group:
— 'Zonenrandgebiet' in West Germany (regions along the frontier with East Germany);
— Danish aided areas (the special development area in the north of Denmark, and the islands of Bornhalm, Aerø, Samsø and Langeland).

Group 5: In the other assisted regions the ceilings are fixed at 20 per cent net grant equivalent of initial investment or a net grant equivalent of 3,500 EUA per job created by the initial investment (the latter may not exceed 25 per cent net grant equivalent of initial investment). For these regions the trend should as far as possible be towards a reduction in the level of aids.

Group 6: No intervention.

Derogations from the intensity ceilings may be granted by the Commission provided that the necessary justification is communicated in advance in accordance with the procedure provided for in article 93 of the Treaty establishing the European Economic Community. The Commission will periodically supply the Council with a list of any such derogations. [42] The level of all ceilings will be revised at the end of a three-year period.

(b) *Transparency of aid.* An essential condition for the coordination and appreciation of general aid systems is their transparency. Transparency depends on many factors. An aid is transparent or measurable when the new common evaluation method can be applied, and when all factors necessary for the application of the method are known, as well as the criteria for application and the terms of cumulation.

(c) *Regional specification.* The principle of regional specification implies a differentiation of the intensity of the aid according to the kind, the intensity, and the urgency of the regional problem. According to the latest communication of the Commission on regional aid systems, regional specificity will be implemented on the principle:
— that regional aids do not cover the whole national territory, i.e. general aids may not be granted under the heading of regional aids;
— that general aid regions clearly specify, either in geographical terms or by quantitative criteria, the limits of aided regions or, within these, the limits of aided areas;
— that, except in the case of growth points, regional aids are not granted in a pin point manner, i.e. isolated geographical points having virtually no influence on the development of a region;
— that where problems which are different in kind, intensity, or urgency occur, the aid intensity needs to be adapted accordingly;
— that the graduation and variation of rates of aid across different areas and regions is clearly indicated.

(d) *Sectoral specificity.* Sectoral specificity of aids is required for two reasons. Firstly, the lack of sectoral specificity in general regional aid systems makes their assessment difficult because of the problems that the sectoral repercussions of these aids may pose at the Community level. Secondly, when investment benefits from a sectoral aid on a regionally differentiated basis, a regional aid may be given only insofar as, when the regional aid and the regional component of other types of aid are cumulated, the above mentioned ceilings are not exceeded.

The European Investment Bank

The European Investment Bank (EIB) began operations in 1959. According to article 130 of the Treaty of Rome, the Bank is a development fund, whose task is to contribute to the balanced and smooth development of the Common Market. For that purpose, the Bank shall, by granting loans and guarantees on a non-profit making basis, facilitate the financing of projects for developing less developed regions. [43] [44]

The EIB does not have power of initiative in regional policy, but is only a body which may participate in the financing of such a policy.

The Bank statutorily enjoys a large degree of autonomy and in particular independence from the EEC Commission. The relationship between these two institutions is currently being reviewed by an interdepartmental committee of the Commission.[45]

Three principles guide the selection of projects to be financed: (a) concentration on propulsive units (e.g. the steel and cement complex in Tarente), (b) minimum dimensions of the project (there is a minimum limit to loans; this is a disadvantage for small and medium size firms unless they present a project as a group,[46] and (c) only investment may be taken into account. Urban infrastructure projects not directly linked to economic development, such as schools, houses, hospitals, are not eligible.

The advantages of the EIB loans are several. In the first place they provide financial means for certain projects which have difficulty in raising funds elsewhere. Secondly, all loans of the Bank are guaranteed. [47] Thirdly, EIB finances most of its loans by borrowing on the international market in the countries where interest rates are lowest. If it offers lower interest rates than other sources of finance, it is because it has borrowed cheaply itself and not because it is subsidising interest rates. There is, however, a real danger for borrowers in weak currency countries. EIB loans can be paid in individual currencies but the Bank usually lends in a cocktail of currencies, and borrowers in weak currency countries can expect the real value of their debt to rise if their currency exchange rate depreciates. That is why the EIB has found it hard to persuade private industry in Britain to borrow from it.[48] Fourthly, the Bank is instrumental in channelling back capital exported from certain less developed regions. One can imagine that people in South Italy seek security for their savings abroad. Via the Bank, that money can return to Southern Italy. Fifthly, the rate of interest applied to loans to borrowers in the member countries is independent of riskiness, of the location of the project, and of the statute of the borrower (remunerativeness of the project is, however, a condition) being calculated according to the time period covered and the composition of the basket of currencies in which the loan is provided. The loan can also be provided in one currency. Lastly, since most of the cash goes to the poorer countries, it also helps to finance balance of payments deficits.

A number of conditions limit the intervention of the Bank. The first is quite normal; the rule of remunerativeness must be applied to any project. The second condition is related to the function of the EIB. The Bank will intervene only if there are difficulties of finance, without challenging the normal banking structure. Thirdly, the intervention of the Bank is complementary. The share of the Bank is limited to 50 per cent. Fourthly, the Bank must operate at the prevailing rates of interest on capital markets. The Member States may, however, give rebates on the interest payable on EIB loans, provided these comply with competition law. Lastly, the Bank cannot participate in a project and requires the normal securities.

The resources of the Bank are twofold. The Bank has its own resources and borrows on the international capital markets. The Bank can also obtain a small amount of additional capital from special interest bearing loans granted by member states. At the end of 1976 the subscripted capital by member states was 3,544 million u.a. of which 556,8 million u.a. called capital. [49] The total resources (comprising paid-up capital, the statutory and other reserves, and borrowings) amounted to 5,587.1 million u.a. The main resources are bond issues. The Bank issues bonds and places them on international capital markets. There is no constraint on the issue of bonds although the statutes require that loans granted by the Bank shall not exceed 250 per cent of its authorised capital. During the period 1961—77 the Bank borrowed 6,152 million u.a. on the capital markets. [50]

Table 10.1 gives a breakdown of the financing by the Bank by type of operation and location of investment project. Table 10.2 shows a breakdown of the financing by economic policy objective.

What can we learn from both tables? First, the Bank is operational mainly in the Member States. Secondly, the especially large share of outstanding loans to Italy and, since 1973, also to the United Kingdom, reflects the original purpose of the Bank. The Bank is applying the criteria of backwardness and underemployment in its selection procedure. Looking at the breakdown by economic policy objectives, Italy and the United Kingdom represent 68.5 per cent of the financing with a regional development objective. [51]

The sectoral breakdown of the financing shows that most of the Bank's support of regional development takes the form of finance for infrastructure development. During the period 1958—77 infrastructure represented 66.9 per cent of EIB financing within the Community; 33.1 per cent went to projects in agriculture, industry and services.

Intervention in the framework
of the Treaty of Paris

Interventions in the framework of the Treaty of Paris, establishing the European Coal and Steel Community (ECSC) fall into three different categories: (a) participation in studies and research, (b) readaptation of workers, and (c) reconversion.

Studies and research
At the request of the national governments, the ECSC has financed or participated in studies and research concerning the creation of new

Table 10.1
Financing by the EIB during the period 1958–77 —
breakdown by type of operation and location of investment project*

	Number	Amount (mln u.a.)	%	%
Ordinary operations in the EEC				
Belgium	9	112.0	1.5	
Denmark	24	85.9	1.2	
Germany (FR)	73	793.5	10.7	
France	109	1,449.3	19.6	
Ireland	21	243.8	3.3	
Italy	320	3,039.3	41.0	
Luxemburg	3	9.0	0.1	
Netherlands	9	105.2	1.4	
United Kingdom	77	1,458.3	19.7	
Other (outside the Community, article 18)	6	110.5	1.5	
Total	651	7,406.8	100.0	87.1
Ordinary operations outside the Community	88	571.0		6.7
Special operations	113	527.8		6.2
Grand total	852	8,505.6**		100.0

* A summary of financing provided over such a long period should be interpreted cautiously; data for successive years are affected by price movements and exchange rate variations occurring between 1958 and 1977.

** The corresponding investment amounted to about 47 billion u.a. at 31.12.1977 (at prices of 1977).

Source: EIB.

Table 10.2
Financing by the EIB provided within the Community during the period 1958—77 — breakdown by economic policy objective

Objective	Million u.a	%	
*Regional development**	5,523.0	100.0	
Belgium	75.1		1.4
Denmark	55.6		1.0
Germany (FR)	366.4		6.6
France	922.8		16.7
Ireland	243.8		4.4
Italy	2,579.0		46.7
Luxemburg	4.0		0.1
Netherlands	70.5		1.3
United Kingdom	1,205.8		21.8
*Common interest to several Members***	2,964	100.0	
Energy	1,864.8		62.9
Transport	706.7		23.9
Other	392.5		13.2
Deduction to allow for duplication in the case of financing justified on the basis of both objectives	−1,080.2		
Total	7,406.8		

* Article 103(a) and (b) of the Treaty of Rome.
**Article 130(c) of the Treaty of Rome.

Source: EIB.

activities to re-employ redundant workers. This item is not to be neglected. In 1978 ECSC budget 41 million European Units of Account (EUA) is allowed for grants for study and research.

Readaptation

In 1960, when the transitional provisions expired, it was clear that the coal and steel sectors were experiencing structural difficulties of a persistent kind. Article 56 was therefore extended to allow the financing of readaptation and reconversion operations made necessary by changes in the conditions of the market.

Pursuant to article 56, 2b, at the request of the national government and provided it pays 50 per cent of the charges, the Commission can grant non-repayable aid to contribute to the retraining and resettlement or rehousing of workers and the maintenance, for a limited period, of wages of workers in the coal and steel sectors.

During the period 1976–77 the Community paid 50.1 million EUA for readaptation: 38,200 workers were involved. During the period 1964–75 credits for 265.0 million u.a. were provided for readaptation; 563,540 workers could profit from this system.

Reconversion

Article 54 of the Treaty permits the Commission to facilitate the carrying out of investment programmes in the coal and steel industries 'by granting loans to undertakings or by guaranteeing other loans which they may contract'. These loans are normally granted under the prevailing conditions of the capital market.

Under article 56, 2a, of the Treaty the Commission may

> facilitate, in the manner laid down in Article 54, either in the industries within its jurisdiction or, with the assent of the Council, in any other industry, the financing of such programmes as it may approve for the creation of new and economically sound activities or for the conversion of existing undertakings capable of reabsorbing the redundant workers into productive employment.

Article 56, 2a may be involved when profound changes in market conditions for the coal and steel industry should compel some companies permanently to discontinue, curtail, or change their activities (see Table 10.3).

The facilities provided under the term of article 56, 2a are of a supplementary nature and are generally subject to more favourable conditions than those obtaining on the capital market, i.e. in particular, a lower rate of interest.

The loans and/or guarantees can be obtained at the request of the

Table 10.3
Loans granted under article 56, 2a of the ECSC Treaty, 1961—77

	Number of loans granted	Amount in million EUA
Belgium	12	36,67
Denmark	—	—
Germany (FR)	62	126,58
France	53	221,09
Ireland	1	2,00
Italy	19	79,32
Luxemburg	—	—
Netherlands	38	46,82
United Kingdom	12	109,95
Community	197	622,43

national governments but without any financial obligations of the latter. Two conditions must be met by beneficiary firms: (a) they must provide re-employment for workers dismissed by the coal and steel industry and (b) they must be engaged in new activities (or extensions) that are safe.

The European Social Fund

Strictly speaking, the European Social Fund in its original form did not represent a proper means for regional policy. Article 123 of the Treaty of Rome states:

> In order to improve employment opportunities for workers in the common market and contribute thereby to raising the standard of living, a European Social Fund is hereby established in accordance with the provisions set out below: it shall have the task of rendering the employment of workers easier and of creating their geographical and occupational mobility within the Community.

To achieve these aims, article 125 provides that:

> On application by a Member State the Fund shall, within the

framework of the rules provided for in article 127, meet 50 per cent of the expenditure after the entry into force of this Treaty by that State or by a body governed by public law for the purpose of:

(a) ensuring productive re-employment of workers by means of:
  —vocational retraining;
  —resettlement allowances;

(b) granting aid for the benefit of workers whose employment is reduced or temporarily suspended, in whole or in part, as a result of the conversion of an undertaking to other production, in order that they may retain the same wage level pending their full re-employment.

The assistance of the Fund is granted, in the case of retraining and rehousing, upon the demand of the Member State concerned when the recipient worker has been re-employed in his new trade or location for a period of six months. In the case of reconversion, the member Government is requested to present in advance a project for the enterprise concerned; if the Commission approves the project, payment from the Fund will be made to workers once they have completed six months' employment with the reconverted enterprise. [52]

As the Birkelbach Report stated, the retraining and resettlement support provided by the Fund has benefited backward areas only in as far as it has stimulated the migration of workers and eased congestion on the labour market. In fact the objective was a social and not a regional one. As long as the regional problem is one of unemployment (the original idea), the social objective of the Fund would contribute at the same time to a solution of the regional problem. But we have seen that the regional problem is much larger. In its original form the European Social Fund was not an instrument of regional policy.

In view of the many weaknesses of the Social Fund (e.g. unemployment before action and re-employment before payments), proposals were made during the 1960s to reform it and to make it useful for regional purposes. The Elsner report on the Commission's proposals of 1965—66 for increasing the effectiveness of the Social Fund noted that the conditions for which the Fund was set up (unemployment and the threat to jobs in industries suffering from increased competition in the Common Market) had been largely replaced with a situation of shortage of labour. Therefore the Fund should provide for the constant adaptation of skills to new technological conditions. [53]

The reform of the Fund in 1971 [54] must also be seen in the context of the growing interest in regional policy and industrial policy in the EEC.

P. Lemerle in 1970 described very well the need for reform:

Conceived during a period in which considerable unemployment in certain Member States was the major preoccupation, the interventions (of the Social Fund) were originally aimed exclusively at the elimination of unemployment. Since that time, the economic and social situation has evolved considerably; at present the fundamental problem for the Community is that of under-employment and potential unemployment, or, more generally, that the qualitative structure of the active population is maladapted to the needs of a rapidly changing production system. The Fund, being subject to rigid regulations, cannot possibly adapt its interventions to the newly arisen employment problems.

In effect, the economic development of the Community is more and more characterised by extensive structural changes which entail and accelerate the growing interdependence of the economies of the Member States, the intensification of competition and the demands made by technological development. The repercussions of this development on employment are so important that the adaptation of the labour force, which constitutes the principal obstacle to the development of industry and of the economy in general, can be considered to be one of the capital problems with which the Community is going to be faced.

Furthermore, the realisation of the customs union and the progressive adoption of common policies influence the economic life of the Member States ever more clearly and directly; as a result, the Common Market and Community policies, orientations and actions are increasingly at the origin of the restructuring process.[55]

In 1971 the reform of the European Social Fund took definite form. [56] Two types of intervention were distinguished. First, the Social Fund can intervene when the employment situation is affected by Community policies (article 4). Secondly, the Social Fund may intervene when in certain regions, in certain sectors, or in certain groups of firms, the labour market is affected by difficulties which do not follow directly from decisions taken by the Council related to Common policies, but which result indireclty from the functioning of the Common Market or are harmful to a harmonious development of the Community (article 5). In the latter type of intervention, aid may be given in the case of the elimination of unemployment, the elimination of under-employment, the training of high skilled labour, the integration of handicapped persons, older workers, women, and young workers.[57]

The Social Fund intervenes at the request of the national authorities. The maximum contribution of the Social Fund is, however, limited to 50 per cent of the cost of each project. In 1978 the percentage was increased to 55 per cent for a few areas, such as Mezzogiorno, Ireland, and Greenland.

The Council regulation of 10 November 1971 describes as the kind of activities that can profit from the aid system of the Social Fund (see article 3), those aiming:

to facilitate the retraining of persons;
to facilitate resettlement of persons;
to maintain a given income level during a certain period;
to ameliorate information concerning the labour market;
to eliminate hindrances to the access of certain groups of workers to the labour market;
to promote the best possible employment conditions in the less developed regions.

Although the new European Social Fund contains many elements of great importance to regional development (training, retraining, resettlement aids, etc.) it is in practice not a very strong instrument of EEC regional policy. Even after the creation of the European Regional Development Fund the link between the Social Fund and regional policy was loose. The regional development programmes offer a new opportunity of integrating the Social Fund as an essential instrument of regional policy. It should be recognised that in 1977 some 73 per cent of Social Fund grants, which amounted to 877 million EUA, went to less favoured regions.

The European Agricultural Guidance
and Guarantee Fund (EAGGF)

The link between the EAGGF and EEC regional policy is in the first place indirect. The agricultural regions of the EEC are frequently the problem areas. Both the Guarantee and the Guidance Sections of the Fund have improved living conditions in these problem regions. The Guarantee Section is improving the income levels (price policy). This is not to say that the impact is sufficient to raise agricultural earnings to the level of those in other sectors.

It was felt that the Guidance Section should impinge upon the cause of low productivity. The Guidance Section administers Community Funds for the partial financing of projects whose purpose is the modernisation of the structures of agricultural production and marketing. The fact that the richer agricultural regions presented more projects to the Fund than the poorer ones, created a bias in the operation of the guidance section in favour of the richer agricultural regions. (This bias also exists with respect to the Guarantee Section). The regional impact of the Guidance Section also depends on the type of farming.

Efforts were made to link regional policy and the EAGGF more directly. A first attempt was the 'Regulation No. 17/1964' of the Council. Article 15 of that Regulation stated that: 'Projects benefit from priority assistance by the Fund when they form part of an overall group of measures for the promotion of the harmonious development of the general economy of the region where such projects will be carried out'. The procedure sought to give greater rationality to the choice of projects receiving Guidance Section finance. There was unfortunately no obligation for a development plan. When the programmes were published, however, there was no agreement between the Member States about the amount of investment in the fields which the programmes specified.[58]

In the second section of this chapter we referred to the Commission's proposals of 28 May 1971 for a regional policy concerning the priority agricultural regions of the Community. These proposals were never accepted. They were meant to provide the means needed to start solving the problems of economic development of regions where redundant farmers must be transferred to other branches of economic activity.

In these proposals the link with the Guidance Section was indirect but not without importance. The ratio of the source of income to the number of employed persons gives a good idea of the structural situation of agriculture in a region. Structural policy measures aim to influence the nominator and/or the denominator of this ratio. Modernisation of structures involves large scale re-employment of labour. Instead of acquiescing in migration of unemployed labour towards overcrowded areas, the Commission was in favour of creating and/or stimulating growth points in the agricultural regions.

The Summit of December 1974 brought a new direct link between the Guidance Section and the European regional policy; 150 million u.a. were transferred from the Guidance Section of the EAGGF to the Regional Development Fund. (They were appropriations held in reserve by the Guidance Section.)

The Regional Fund itself can be used for the financing of rural infrastructure projects in hill farming and in certain less favoured regions. [59] [60]

Regional development studies

Each year the Commission helps to finance a number of studies in the regional field. Very often the Commission takes the initiative. These studies cover very different aspects of the regional policy in the EEC, such as harmonised employment statistics, the efficiency of instruments of regional policy, deconcentration measures in member countries, the

development of particular regions, etc. To be financed by the Commission, studies must have a Community dimension or be related to the
Community regional policy. A number of studies are also undertaken
in the framework of the Treaty of Paris.

The European Regional
Development Fund (ERDF)

The Structure of the Fund

The European Regional Development Fund was established in 1975 and
that was without doubt an important milestone on the road towards
economic integration in Europe. For the first time since 1958, the
Community decided on specific measures designed to help reduce its
regional disparities. However the Fund is not to be confused with
Community regional policy. It is but one instrument of that policy, if,
for the present, one of the most important.

According to article 1 of the new Council Regulation, the Fund is
intended to correct the principal regional imbalances within the Community resulting in particular from agricultural preponderance, industrial
change, and structural underemployment.

The Commission is responsible for administering the Fund. The
Fund is assisted by two committees on which national officials sit: the
Regional Policy Committee and the Fund Committee. We return to the
Regional Policy Committee in another section. The Fund Committee's
principal task is to formulate opinions on the Commission's draft
decision to grant aid from the Fund.

At the Paris Summit Conference of December 1974 an ERDF of
1,300 million units of account was agreed upon for the period 1975–77.
This amount included 150 million u.a. from the Guidance Section of
the EAGGF (see previous section). The Summit allocated the most
important shares of the Fund to those countries which have the most
serious regional problems in terms of both size and intensity.[61] The
Member States have drawing rights as follows: [62]

	Quota 1975—77	Quota 1978—80	% popu- lation	Ratio quota/pop.
Belgium	1.5	1.4	3.8	39.5
Denmark	1.3	1.2	2.0	65.0
France	15.0	16.9	20.2	74.3
Ireland	6.0	6.5	1.2	500.0
Italy	40.0	39.4	21.3	190.5
Luxemburg	0.1	0.1	0.1	100.0
Netherlands	1.7	1.6	5.2	32.7
Germany (FR)	6.4	6.0	24.1	26.6
United Kingdom	28.0	27.0	22.1	126.7

For the period 1978—80 the Council agreed to increase the Fund to 1,850 million European units of account (EUA) of which 5 per cent for the non-quota section.[63]   However, the Fund is no longer an obligatory expenditure. It should be recalled that in 1975 Parliament and the Council agreed that Fund expenditures after 1977 would rank as non-obligatory. The amount retained in the budget for 1978 amounts to 581 million EUA. This represents a net increase on former years if it is taken into account that the Fund is expressed in new units of account. It means a very high increase for Italy, the United Kingdom and Ireland.[64]

The quota section will provide support for (measures supporting) regional policy measures adopted by the Member States. This section is subject to a distribution of appropriations on the basis of pre-established national quotas. In addition to the quota section the renewed Fund contains a non-quota section for the assistance of specific regional development measures. The Commission originally proposed to the Council a Fund of 750 million EUA with 650 million to continue the existing Fund and 100 million for specific Community measures (non-quota section). For the latter an interest rebate scheme within the Fund was proposed. The intention was to create a system of interest, rebates for certain EIB and ECSC loans and, where appropriate, for other loans granted by the European Communities.[65] The interest rebate scheme never became operative. Instead, the non-quota part will be used to finance specific actions. According to article 13 of the renewed Fund, the Fund may participate in financing specific Community regional development measures:

— either linked with Community policies and with measures adopted by the Community in order to take better account of their regional dimension or to reduce their regional consequences;

— or, in exceptional cases, intended to meet the structural consequences of particularly serious occurrences in certain regions or areas with a view to replacing jobs lost and creating the necessary infrastructures for that purpose (see problem type 3 page 406).

For the first time a real regional impact assessment system (i.e. to assess the impact on regions of Community policies) is introduced. This is a net improvement in regional policy at Community level. As Community policies gradually develop, such specific actions will become a more and more important part of the ERDF's task.

Via the non-quota section, the Commission is taking the initiative in regional matters:

> In the specific actions, the Community will be expressing its own responsibility for correcting regional imbalances. These actions are primarily regional policy measures intended to supplement or to strengthen the application of other Community policies, or to correct any adverse regional effects they may have. The geographical scope of these actions depends on the location of the industries at which Community policies are directed and the relative intensity of regional problems. Consequently there are no grounds for an *a priori* distribution between Member States of ERDF resources available for this purpose. [67]

The intervention of the ERDF

According to article 3 of the Fund regulation, the regions which may benefit from the Fund are limited to the aided regions established by Member States in applying their systems of regional aids and to which State aids are granted which qualify for Fund assistance. This implies that the choice of the problem areas to be assisted on the European level is so far entirely in the hands of the Member States. Of course the Commission must give its agreement to the definition of the national problem areas. The power of the Commission is, however, very restricted.

The non-quota section of the Fund could be applied in other regions provided that the Member State concerned also give assistance.

The Fund may intervene in three categories of investment individually exceeding 50,000 EUA:

> (a)   investment in infrastructure which can contribute to the development of the region in which it is located provided that it is justified by regional development programmes (maximum 70 per cent of the quota section); formerly it was restricted to infrastructure directly linked to productive investments;
> (b)   investments which are directly productive, both in the manufacturing and service sectors. Service activities qualifying for

assistance shall be those concerned with tourism and those which have a choice of location. Such activities should have a direct impact on the development of the region and in the level of employment. Investments in industrial, handicraft, or service activities qualify for assistance if at least ten new jobs are created or existing jobs are maintained;

(c) investments in infrastructure which are covered in article 3 of the Council Directive on mountain and hill farming and farming in certain less favoured areas.[68]

One important remark should be made. Directly productive investment and investments in infrastructure may benefit from the Fund's assistance only if they fall within the framework of a regional development programme, the implementation of which is such as to contribute to the correction of the main regional imbalance within the Community. These imbalances are likely to prejudice the proper working of the Common Market and the convergence of the Member States' economies with a view, in particular, to the attainment of economic and monetary union.

The extent of the Fund's contribution is, however, limited:

(a) in respect to investments in infrastructure, the limit is 30 per cent of the expenditure incurred by public authorities when the investment is less than 10 million EUA, and from 10 per cent to a maximum of 30 per cent for investments of not less than 10 million EUA. However, for projects which are of particular interest for the development of the regions in which they are located the maximum rate may be 40 per cent;

(b) in respect of investments in manufacturing and tourism, the limit is 20 per cent of the investment cost without, however, exceeding 50 per cent of the aid accorded to each investment by public authorities under a system of regional aids, such contributions being limited, moreover, to that part of the investment which does not exceed 100,000 EUA per job created and 50,000 EUA per job maintained.

In the case of services, by way of derogation, the Fund's contribution may exceed 20 per cent of the investment cost, provided that the amount does not exceed 10,000 EUA per job created or maintained, or 50 per cent of the national aids.

The State aids to be taken into consideration in this connection are grants, interest rebates or their equivalent where loans at reduced rates of interest are concerned, whether these aids are linked to the investment or to the number of jobs created. These aids may include aids paid to undertakings in connection with the transfer of workers.

Complementary character of Fund
activity and national measures

In order to speed up structural improvement and job creation, the
Community resources made available through the Fund must be additional to what the Member States would have been able to make available from their own resources if the Fund had not existed. The regulation expresses this by saying that ' . . . the Fund's assistance should not
lead Member States to reduce their own regional development efforts
but should complement these efforts'. [69]

As far as investments in industry and the service sector are concerned
the principle of 'additionality' can be applied in two ways. In the first
place the Fund assistance can be added on top of the aid granted to an
individual investment by the national authorities (possibility of 'topping
up'); secondly, the financial resources deriving from the Fund can be
added globally to the Member States' expenditure on regional development, thus enabling them to speed up and increase their efforts in this
field. [70]

There are two arguments against the application of 'topping up'.
First, it implies a discrimination in favour of the relatively small number
of investors whose projects can be awarded a Fund grant. Secondly, but
far more important, it carries the danger of unfair competition. For
these two reasons the Commission would not wish to see 'topping up'
become general practice, though in certain circumstances it might be
used to provide an extra marginal incentive to attract selected investments to the regions facing the greatest disadvantage.

The Fund's activity in the
first period: 1975—77 [71]

During the period 1975—77, 1,300 million units of account were distributed in accordance with the quota system of the Fund. In total 4,747
projects were accepted (representing a total investment of 11,711 million u.a.) of which 1,604 (33.4 per cent) were related to manufacturing
and service activities. In terms of aid granted the major part went to
infrastructure projects. The 1,604 projects related to direct investment
totalise a grant of only 452,66 million u.a. or 34.8 per cent of the total
Fund (see Table 10.4).

The relative importance of infrastructure is characteristic of each
country taken individually. Only Ireland and West Germany show a
different distribution for industry and infrastructure.

In relation to infrastructure the most important types of investment

Table 10.4

Aid granted (in million u.a.) in the framework of the ERDF, 1975–77

	Industrial handicraft and service activities		Infrastructure		Rural infrastructure		Total		
	Number of projects	Aid	Number of projects	Aid	Number of projects	Aid	Number of projects	Total investment	Aid*
Belgium	16	3.67	94	14.11	1	1.55	111	158.78	19.33
Denmark	27	2.40	108	14.47	–	–	135	144.24	16.76
France	385	72.78	234	116.68	6	3.88	625	1,761.22	193.32
Ireland	84	39.43	149	34.19	34	11.10	267	633.61	83.83
Italy	323	146.28	165	333.74	704	40.41	1,192	3,452.49	520.00
Luxemburg	–	–	2	1.29	–	–	2	7.36	1.29
Netherlands	–	–	16	21.91	–	–	16	179.56	21.91
Germany (FR)	426	34.38	244	37.84	–	–	670	1,205.05	71.98
United Kingdom	343	153.72	1,323	211.49	64	8.71	1,730	4,038.73	360.89
Total	1,604	452.66	2,335	785.72	809	65.65	4,747	11,711.04	1,289.31

* Less decommitals.

Source: ERDF, Third Annual Report, 1978.

assisted are industrial estates, road infrastructure designed to service industrial estates, telephone networks, advance factories, port developments, and production aid and distribution of electricity.

As we have seen above, the first regulation states that regions eligible for Fund assistance shall be limited to those regions aided by Member States under their own systems of regional aid. This implies a real danger of insufficient concentration of effort. In practice, however, priority was given to investments located in national priority areas (see Second and Third Annual Report, ERDF):

— in Denmark, 77 per cent of Fund assistance went to Greenland;
— in Germany, about two-thirds of assistance went to Berlin, to the Zonenrandgebiet and to first priority development poles qualifying for 20 per cent aid;
— in Italy, more than 90 per cent of Fund assistance went to the Mezzogiorni;
— in France, more than 80 per cent of Fund assistance went to regions in the West and South-West, to Corsica and to the Overseas Departments;
— in the United Kingdom, about 85 per cent of assistance went to projects located in priority areas such as Northern Ireland, Special Development Areas, and Development Areas;
— in the Netherlands 58 per cent of Fund assistance went to the North;
— Ireland is one of the five areas recognised as having priority in the Commission's 'Guidelines on Regional Policy'. The other areas are Mezzogiorno (Italy), Northern Ireland, Greenland, and French Overseas Departments.

The Regional Policy Committee [72]

The creation of a Regional Policy Committee was entirely inspired by the idea of, and the willingness to, facilitate Community coordination of Member States' regional policies.

The Committee's task is to examine, at the request of the Council or of the Commission, or on its own initiative, problems relating to regional development, the progress made or to be made towards solving them, and regional policy measures needed to further the achievement of the Community's regional objectives. The Regional Policy Committee studies in particular:

(a) the aims, means, methods and experience of Member States in the field of regional policy, taking account of the Community's other policies;
(b) on a continuing and comprehensive basis, economic and social trends in the various regions of the Community;

429

(c)   technical methods for drafting regional development programmes so as to arrive at a common approach to the concept of a regional policy programme;

(d)   the development programmes presented by Member States, particularly in respect of the regions referred to in article 3 of Council Regulations (EEC) No.724/75 setting up a European Regional Development Fund;

(e)   the financial resources which Member States and the Community propose to provide for regional development over a period of years;

(f)   the impact of Community financial instruments in regional terms;

(g)   investment trends in the regions of the Community and the coordinated implementation of Community measures, together with measures by Member States, with a view to facilitating the implementation of programmes;

(h)   systems of aid which are regional in purpose or effect;

(i)   disincentive measures in regions with a heavy concentration of economic activity;

(j)   the promotion of better information services for both public and private investors in regional development.[73]

The Committee is requested to deliver every two years an opinion on the preliminary draft of the report prepared by the Commission on social and economic trends in the regions of the Community. This is a net improvement introduced by the new ERDF.

The coordination of national policies is, in our opinion, the main task of the Regional Policy Committee. One has to avoid certain actions in the regional field which would neutralise similar actions of other countries. Differences between national regional aid systems are more important than the absolute amount of aid given. What should be given for projects in the Mezzogiorno if a rich region in Germany, were to receive a grant equivalent of 20 per cent? In that context the ERDF, in spite of its limited size in comparison to the national aid systems, has more significance than is normally recognised.

The common policies

In chapter 6 we underlined the possible impact of a number of common policies on the regional disparities within the Community.[74] The fear of a possible negative influence can also be perceived in the Commission's proposal relative to the renewed Regional Development Fund. The non-quota section of the Fund has as its main function to correct regional imbalances caused by the application of Community policies (regional impact assessment).

The relationship between regional policy and other Common policies can also take the opposite form in that the realisation of certain common policies can contribute to a weakening of regional disparities or to a partial solution of the problem of certain regions.

The most striking fields of positive linkage between a Common policy and regional development are to be found in: (a) agricultural policy, (b) transport policy, (c) energy policy, (d) social policy, (e) environmental policy, (f) commercial policy, and (g) the integration of the regional dimension into medium term economic policy programming.

On many occasions in this study, we have demonstrated the role of particular common policies as instruments of a Community regional policy. In this section we limit ourselves to the role of a few common policies.

A first common policy which may be very helpful to regional development is transport policy. There are many aspects, of which rates and conditions are one. In the Treaty there are a number of derogations in favour of less developed regions. The neutrality of rates and conditions in the frontier regions is another aspect. Differences in transport conditions can influence the location of firms in the regions on either side of a common border.[75] We are personally not very much in favour of price falsification in favour of less developed regions.

A more positive contribution of transport policy to regional development is to be found in the implementation of infrastructure programmes such as the creation of European axes connecting peripheral regions to the central regions of the Community, maritime projects, etc. They belong to the category of measures which are directed at raising competitiveness at large in a backward region without disturbing competition.

Energy policy demonstrates two similar aspects: (a) the price of energy in the less developed regions, and (b) the location of energy sources. Today we are much more free in the location of energy sources than we were a few decades ago. Here we refer to natural gas, oil and nuclear energy. A natural gas import harbour or an oil refinery must be considered a propulsive unit of a growth pole.

We are rather doubtful about the positive contribution of commercial policy to regional development. Instruments of regional policy, on the contrary, fall within the definition of non-tariff distorsions of international competition. More important is the question of the extent to which commercial policy is detrimental to problem regions. Many backward regions are in direct competition with imports from third countries. A liberal commercial policy may then run counter to the immediate interests of the least prosperous regions.

Very important also is the integration of the regional dimension into medium term economic policy programming. By including regional policy in medium term economic policy programming, the Commission hoped to ensure that overall economic policies would take account of regional needs and also that regional policy would benefit from being considered not in isolation but in a global context.

Notes

[1] CEE, *Documents de la Conférence sur les Economies Régionales*, Brussels, 1961, 2 volumes.
[2] CEE, 'Etude pour la création d'un pôle industriel de développement en Italie méridionale'; *Série économie et finances*, no.5, Brussels, 1966, 2 volumes.
[3] CEE, *Rapports de groupes d'experts sur la politique régionale dans la CEE*, Brussels, 1964, 3 volumes.
[4] O.J., no. 10/79, of 25.4.1967.
[5] CEE, *Première communication de la Commission sur la politique régionale dans la CEE*, June 1965. See also G. Bersani, 'Rapport sur la première communication de la Commission de la CEE sur la politique régionale dans la CEE', *Parlement Européen, Doc.*, 58, 23.5.1966.
[6] European Parliament, of 15.5.1968.
[7] CEE, Doc. Com. (69) 950, Brussels, 15.10.1969. O.J., no. C152 of 28.11.1969. See also O.J., no. C108/2 of 26.8.1970. 'Avis du Comité Economique et Social sur une proposition de décision du Conseil relative à l'organisation de moyens d'action de la Communauté en matière de développement régional'.
[8] O.J., L49, of 1.3.1971.
[9] O.J. no. C28, of 27.3.1971.
[10] See O.J., no. C90, of 11.8.1971. 'Proposition de règlement du Conseil concernant le financement par le Fonds Européen d'Orientation et de Garantie Agricole, section orientation, de projets s'inscrivant dans le cadre d'opérations de développement dans les régions agricoles prioritaires'. 'Proposition de règlement du Conseil relatif au Fonds Européen de bonifications d'interêts pour le développement régional'.
[11] The regions that could benefit from the proposed Regional Development Fund were not only the priority agricultural regions. However the Commission considered that during this period the money should mainly be used for development of the priority agricultural regions.
[12] O.J., no. C111, of 4.11.1971: 'Première résolution du 20 octobre 1971 des représentants des Etats membres, réunis au sein du Conseil concernant les régimes généraux d'aides à finalité régionale'. See also O.J., no. L73, of 27.3.1972. See also the proposal of the Commission to

the Council extending the principles of the regulation of 1973 to the new member states (Doc. Com. (73), 1110 of 27.6.1973.

[13] O.J., no.C38, of 18.4.1972.

[14] EEC, 'Report on the regional problems in the enlarged Community', Brussels, 1973.

[15] EEC, Com. (73) 1170, of 25.7.1973 and O.J. C86 of 16.10.1973, 'Proposal for a Council Regulation establishing a European Regional Development Fund'.

[16] EEC, Com. (73) 1171, of 25.7.1973 and O.J., C86 of 16.10.1973.

[17] EEC, Com. (73) 1751, of 10.10.1973, 'Proposal for a Council Regulation on the list of regions and areas referred to in the Regulations (EEC) establishing a European Regional Development Fund'.

[18] EEC, Com. (73) 1750 of 10.10.1973.

[19] Wallace, H., 'The establishment of the Regional Development Fund: Common Policy or Pork Barrel', in Wallace, H., Wallace, W. and Webb, C. (eds), *Policy Making in the European Communities*, London, 1977. See also Talbot, R.B., *The European Community's Regional Fund*, Oxford, 1977.

[20] EEC, 'Eighth General Report on the Activities of the European Communities in 1974'.

[21] O.J., no.L.73, of 21.3.1975. Regulation (EEC), no.724/75 of the Council of 18 March 1975 establishing a European Regional Development Fund. Regulation (EEC), no.725/75 of the Council of 18 March 1975 on the transfer to the European Regional Development Fund of 150 million units of account out of the appropriations held in reserve by the Guidance Section of the European Guidance and Guarantee Fund. Council decision of 18 March setting up a Regional Policy Committee. Financial Regulation of 18 March 1975 supplementing the financial Regulation of 25 April 1973 applicable to the general budget of the European Communities. Council decision of 18 March 1975 to apply Regulation (EEC) no.724/75 establishing a European Regional Development Fund to the French Overseas Departments.

[22] EEC, 'Guidelines for Community Regional Policy, *Bulletin of European Communities*, Supplement, 2/77. Proposal for Council Decision amending Council Decision 75/185/EEC of 18 March 1975, setting up a Regional Policy Committee. Proposal for Council Regulation amending Regulation (EEC) no. 724/75 of 18 March 1975 establishing a European Regional Development Fund. Proposal for a Council Regulation establishing an interest rebate scheme within the European Regional Development Fund.

[23] EEC, 'Report on the regional problems in the enlarged Community', op.cit., p.4.

[24] Balassa, B., 'Regional policies and the environment in the European Common Market', *Weltwirtschaftliches Archiv,* 1973, vol.3, p.407.

[25] EEC, 'Pour une politique régionale dans la Communauté', Proposition de décision du conseil relative à l'organisation de moyens d'action de la Communauté en matière de développement régional), 1969.

[26] Von der Groeben, H., 'Lignes directrices de la politique régionale de la Communauté', *European Parliament*, 6 May 1969 (see O.J. no. 114, 1969).

[27] Van Ginderachter, J., *La politique régionale de la Communauté, Justifications, modalités et propositions*, op.cit., p.469.

[28] EEC, 'Proposition de décision du Conseil relative à l'organisation de moyens d'action de la Communauté en matière de développement régional', op.cit.

[29] O.J., no. C108 of 26.10.1970.

[30] EEC, 'Community regional policy — new guidelines', *Bulletin of the European Communities*, Supplement 2, 1977, p.6.

[31] EEC, 'Community regional policy — new guidelines', op.cit., p.6.

[32] EEC, 'Première communication de la Commission sur la politique régionale dans la Communauté Economique Européenne', Brussels, 11.5.1965, op.cit.

[33] EEC, 'Pour une politique régionale dans la Communauté', Brussels, 1969. See also O.J., no. C108 of 26.8.1970 (Advice of the Social and Economic Committee), pp 13-14.

[34] See also Maillet, P., Hipp, G., Krijnse-Locker, H. and Sunnen, R., *L'Economie de la Communauté*, Brussels, 1968.

[35] EEC, 'Report on the regional problems in the enlarged Community' op.cit., pp 12-14.

[36] EEC, 'Community regional policy — new guidelines', op.cit.

[37] See article 3 of the Fund regulation of 18 March 1975. 'Regions and areas which may benefit from the Fund shall be limited to those aided areas established by Member States in applying their systems of regional aids and in which State aids are granted which qualify for Fund assistance. When aid from the Fund is granted, priority shall be given to investments in national priority areas, taking account of the principles for the coordination at Community level of regional aids'.

[38] See also article 2 of the Council decision of 18 March 1975 setting up a Regional Policy Committee.

[39] O.J., no. C69 of 24.3.1976, 'Outlines for regional development programmes'.

During the printing period of the book a number of documents were published by the Commission concerning the regional development programmes.

The Commission has adopted an opinion on regional development programmes submitted by the Member States, together with a series of recommendations concerning the coordination of national and community regional policies. These indicative programmes concern the 75 regions and zones where the ERDF provides assistance, and cover 55 per cent of the area and 38 per cent of the population of the Community. The Commission considers that improvements will have to be made to the programmes before they can fulfil the tasks outlined below. The Commission proposes a number of improvements.

The programmes have three main aims:

— to provide the framework for examining applications for grants from the ERDF;
— to enable the Commission to define priority areas for Fund activity;
— to become the basis for the coordination of the Member States and Community regional policies.

See: EEC, 'Regional development programmes', Brussels, 1979; O.J., no. L 143/7 of 12.6.1979, 'Commission opinion of 23 May 1979 on the regional development programmes'; O.J., no. L 143/9 of 12.6.1979, 'Commission recommendation of 23 May 1979 to the Member States on the regional development programmes'.

[40] EEC, 'General Regional Aid Systems', Communication of the Commission to the Council of 26 February 1975. EEC, Communication of the Commission on regional aid systems, O.J., no. C31 of 3.2.1979.

[41] O.J., no. C111 of 4.11.1971. See also O.J., no. C31 of 3.2.1979.

[42] It was announced that the ceilings will be re-examined before the end of 1977 taking account of experience gained of the evolution of regional situations and changes in aid systems and in relation to the problems of the combination of regional and sectoral aids.

[43] The Bank also has other targets which are not related to less developed regions; see art. 130 of the Treaty.

[44] Menais, G.P., *La Banque Européenne d'Investissement*, Paris, 1968. See also Flockston, Ch., *Community Regional Policy*, P.E.P., 1970. Woolley, P.K., 'The European Investment Bank', *Three Banks Review*, no.1, 1975. Dupont, C., 'Die Europäische Investitionsbank', Regional Wirtschaftspolitik und Agrarstrukturpolitik in der Europäischen Wirtschaftsgemeinschaft', Schriftenreihe des Gustav-Strasemann-Institutes e.v. für europäische Bildungs — und Informationsarbeit, no.3. 'La Banque Européenne d'Investissement', Centre de Recherches Européennes, Lausanne, 1977. Harrop, J., 'The European Investment Bank', *National Westminster Bank Quarterly Review*, May 1978. EEC, European Investment Bank, 1958-78, Brussels, 1978.

[45] Bank loans can be subsidised from the Regional Development Fund.

[46] P.K. Woolley emphasises the provision of global loans as a worthwhile evolution. These loans go to financial institutions which, subject to Bank ratification in every case, make subloans to relatively small companies usually for projects that are of benefit to regional develop-

ment. It is typically the smaller companies that find difficulty in raising funds at a reasonable rate of interest or even at all.

[47] In most cases the loans are guaranteed by Member States.

[48] *The Economist*, 28.2.1976. Certain countries are opposed to the proposal that the Commission should bear the exchange rate risks. This is considered to be encouraging bad monetary policy in weak currency countries. The UK Treasury guarantee to the public sector against exchange rate risks. At the end of 1977 this guarantee against the risks of exchange rate losses was extended to the private sector as well.

[49] The interest payments foregone on the capital sum contributed by each member country amount to a tax and constitute the transfer element in the Bank's operations.

[50] In this amount 187.8 million u.a. takes form of participations by third parties in EIB loands.

[51] During the period 1958-76 80 per cent of loans provided to Italy were used for projects in Mezzogiorno (cfr BEI, Informations, no.11, 1977).

[52] Flockston, Ch., op.cit., p.41.

[53] Ibid., p.42.

[54] O.J., L 28 of 4.2.1971.

[55] Lemerle, P.N., 'Le Fonds Social Européen', *Reflets et perspectives de la vie économique*, no.2, 1970, pp 119-20.

[56] O.J., no. L 28 of 4.2.1971, 'Décision du Conseil de ler fevrier 1971 concernant la réforme du Fonds Social Européen'. O.J., no L 249 of 10.11.1971, 'Règlement (CEE) no 2396/71 du Conseil du 8.11.1971, portant application du Conseil du 1.2.1971, concernant la réforme du Fonds Social Européen'.

[57] Concerning the distribution of credits between the two types of interventions, an agreement by the Ministers was reached that at least 50 per cent of the interventions would be available for actions of the second type. Later on, when the common policies would become more effective, interventions of the first type would become more important.

[58] Flockston, Ch., op.cit., p.45.

[59] O.J., no.L128, of 19.5.1975, 'Council Directive of 28 April 1975, on mountain and hill farming in certain less favoured areas.

[60] The new ERDF can also be used for such rural infrastructure projects.

[61] A sum of six million units of account was granted to Ireland, which was deducted from the share of other Member States, with the exception of Italy.

[62] From 1978 onwards the share of France increased with 2 per cent to be used in the overseas departments.

[63] 580 million EUA for 1978, 620 million EUA for 1979 and 650 million EUA for 1980. The new European Unit of Account (EUA)

which has been in use since 1.1.1978 is based upon a weighted average of the nine national currencies, its value varies therefore from day to day. The former unit of account (u.a.), used until 31.12.1977, had a fixed value in relation to national currencies. At the exchange rate operative on 1.1.1978, 1 EUA = 1.34 u.a. See also O.J., L35 of 9.2.1979 (Council Regulation EEC no. 214/79). See also O.J., C36 of 9.2.1979. The European Parliament proposed to increase the budget for 1979 to 1,100 million EUA. Finally the Council agreed on a budget of 945 million EUA.

[64] The Regional Development Fund 1975–77 equals about 1,000 new units of account (EUA). Taking into account the average rate of inflation during the trial period, the real increase of the ERDF is about 20 per cent.

[65] The use of Community loans as regional instrument was proposed in 1977 (see New Guidelines, p.13).

[66] EEC, 'Community regional policy – new guidelines', op.cit., p.11.

[67] The Commission is taking the initiative but the national States will have a financial obligation (joint venture.). (A Council Regulation is announced).

[68] O.J., no.L128, of 19.5.1975, 'Council Directive of 28 April 1975, on mountain and hill farming in certain less favoured areas'.

[69] See preamble to the regulation.

[70] In the case that topping-up is not applied art.18 of the new Fund Regulation becomes important.

[71] EEC, 'European Regional Development Fund', *Third Annual Report*, 1977.

[72] O.J., L73, of 21.3.1975, 'Council decision of 18 March 1975, setting up a Regional Policy Committee.

[73] O.J., L73 of 21.3.1975.

[74] See also Cairncross, A., Giersch, H., Lamfalussy, A., Petrilli, G. and Uri, P., *Economic Policy for the European Community*, chapter 3, pp 81-3.

[75] Röper, B., 'Regionalpolitik für EWG-Binnengrenzgebiet, insbesondere für das Aachener Grenzgebiet', *Beitrage zur Regionalpolitik*, Berlin, 1968.

11 A new basis for regional policy on the Community level

Introduction

In chapter 2 we analysed the disparities in population density, economic structure, employment, and income between the regions of the Community, and found them quite important, much greater indeed than the regional disparities in the United States. The analysis of their evolution revealed that in most countries and in the EEC as a whole the disparities decreased in the course of the period 1960—70 thanks to the redistribution of people and income. It seems, however, that as far as income is concerned, the progress made towards a more even distribution was undone in the 1970s owing to unstable exchange rates; indeed, the regional disparity in income is now even greater than when the integration process started; the evolution of income differences in the EEC by country in the period 1960—76 represented in the figures of Table 11.1 leaves no doubt on that score.

Table 11.1
Income differences based on gross domestic product per head,
1960—76 (current prices and exchange levels, EEC = 100)

Country	1960	1965	1970	1975	1976
Belgium	106	102	107	121	127
Denmark	112	123	129	135	144
Germany (FR)	112	113	124	132	136
France	113	117	113	121	121
Ireland	55	55	54	48	47
Italy	60	65	70	60	56
Luxembourg	141	118	127	117	121
Netherlands	83	89	99	113	119
United Kingdom	118	106	89	78	72
EEC	100	100	100	100	100

Calculations based on EEC data

The figures form no reason to doubt the efficiency of the regional policy of the individual countries, but it is an indication that a better balance between the regions of a country or of the EEC is not a medium term target, nor even an objective to be realised in one generation's time. It is also a false hope that it would be feasible to achieve relative equality within a range of 20 per cent around the average; as A. Cairncross et al. put it: 'To achieve results it is necessary to show perseverance over a long period with policies that are bound to be costly and may be slow to show results. The most common mistakes are to underestimate the size of the problem and to look for swift solutions'.[1] There is a sad lack of realism with respect to the time horizon of regional development.

Difficult though it may be to bring about an even distribution of employment and income among regions, national governments and EEC authorities should continue and intensify their efforts to that effect. There are arguments in favour of national regional policy — we discussed them in chapter 1 — which are also valid for regional policy on the level of the EEC. Additional arguments for the latter were analysed in chapter 10. An active regional policy is indeed required

(a) to effectualise a dynamic growth policy;
(b) for political, social, environmental and general economic reasons;
(c) due to fundamental changes in the economic and social structure;
(d) to realise a monetary and economic union;
(e) to realise certain common policies;
(f) to achieve a fundamental objective of the Treaty of Rome, 'a continuous and balanced expansion'; a continuous expansion has been achieved, but not a balanced expansion.

A direct or indirect approach?

As we have seen in chapter 10, regional economic policy is still largely in the hands of national governments. A few figures may illustrate that. The direct national aid given by national governments for the development of ERDF regions amounted to 3,184 million units of account in 1975. This amount does not include the resources allocated to infrastructure for regional development. For the three-year period 1975—77 the total amount of the ERDF for industrial and service investments as well as infrastructure investments was not more than 1,300 million units of account. Of course we should also take into account the other EEC instruments,[2] but that would not change the thesis that regional economic policy is largely a national matter. The question should be raised whether a direct or an indirect approach is best for the regions of the Community. With a direct approach regional economic policy is in the hands of the Community institutions, while with an indirect approach it remains the responsibility of the member states. Arguments in favour of a direct or Community approach are given by G. Magnifico and A. Cairncross et al.

G. Magnifico gives three reasons why it would be a mistake to leave regional policy entirely in national hands.

> The first is that in the absence of central control there is a real danger that regions will compete with one another in offering incentives to attract industry, the net result of which will be to increase industrial profits without achieving any systematic effect in steering industry toward the less prosperous regions . . . The second reason is that fiscal transfers constitute one of the most powerful factors tending to maintain income within a region of an economic and monetary union which experiences a decline in demand for its output. As countries lose the opportunity of compensating for a decline in demand by altering the exchange rate, they will require the Community's fiscal powers to be exercised in a way that acts as a substitute. A third reason is that the decrease in the regional multiplier will make an injection of central funds more essential. [3]

We find two more arguments in the contribution of A. Cairncross et al.

> The need for Community action arises in part because the formation of the Community, and the adoption of policies aimed at promoting economic integration, was bound to have unequal effects on different regions. Some regions gain substantially from improved market opportunities through trade liberalisation. On the other hand, other regions may gain little or even lose because of the opening of local markets to more intense competition. Regions cannot count on the kind of reciprocal advantage from free trade that national economies enjoy thanks to their ability to adjust, if necessary, the exchange rate of their currency. A common policy is necessary in order to deal with the regional impact of economic integration and to help individual regions to make the structural adjustments which it induces or accelerates. Solidarity in sharing the burdens of integration which, like the benefits, are unequally distributed is a condition for the survival of the Community. This must include a continuous scrutiny of the regional policies adopted in member countries in order to assess their impact on the progress of backward regions in other member countries — particularly on those which have to overcome the greatest obstacles to catch up

with the rest of the Community.

A further reason applies to the less prosperous members of the European Community who lack the necessary resources to deal adequately with their regional problems. The backward regions in these countries are often strongholds of separatist movements; and it is in the common interest of the Community as a whole to discourage the forces of disintegration by offering additional help for the development of such regions.[4]

Neither G. Magnifico nor A. Cairncross et al. pleaded the pure direct approach; they both want the Community to have responsibilities in addition to those of the individual countries.

In favour of the national approach plead the better knowledge national governments have of regional problems, and the heavier interest they are bound to have in these problems. They are also most motivated to use their own resources to the full and to assist the areas that have fallen behind the rest of the country. Moreover, a decentralised approach, with largely autonomous regional development authorities, is desirable, for regional development implies more than dealing out financial aid, as we have seen in chapters 7 and 8.

However, the arguments for the direct approach and for a regional policy on the EEC level put forward in chapter 10 are strong enough not to leave regional policy entirely to national governments. The best approach, and the one that has been adopted by the Commission, seems to be a combination of the direct and indirect methods (see the Thomson Report of 1973).

Community regional policy cannot be a substitute for the national regional policies which Member States have been conducting for many years. It must complement them with the aim of reducing the main disparities across the Community. For this reason the effectiveness of the Community's policy will also depend on the close cooperation of Member States: the activities of Member States in the regional field, whether economic, social or cultural, in fact form an indispensable basis for the mobilisation of financial resources for regional development. The role of Community regional policy will progressively increase as the Community increases and improves its instruments of intervention, together with the coordination of national regional policies which will be undertaken in the light of the varying extent of regional problems.[5]

EEC coordination as a support
to the direct approach

Regional policy on the Community level is not only a matter of financial resources; it is also to a large extent a question of coordinating national regional policies. The necessity of coordination was stressed in chapter 10. If the Commission has sufficient power and is willing to demand that each government respect the rules of the game, its impact on regional matters can be much greater than it seems to be from the financial resources available. [6]   Unfortunately the rules of the game are not always respected and up to 1977 the ERDF was not a real instrument of Community regional policy. To date the Regional Fund has provided not inconsiderable support to the regional policies of the Member States; the same is true of the other EEC instruments. But the right of initiative is largely in the hands of national governments or national authorities. The most important modification to which the Council has now agreed lies in the creation of a 'non-quota' section of the Fund; it will be used to finance specific Community actions, undertaken to remedy new regional problems which may arise as a result of economic crises or of certain Community policies. The 'non-quota' portion of the renewed Fund is, however, very small, as we have seen in chapter 10.

In the new phase of the regional policy of the Community the introduction of the 'Regional Impact Assessment' (RIA) is a step forward; it is meant to ensure that when important Community policy is drafted and implemented in other fields, the likely consequences for the regions and, in particular, for regional employment, are automatically taken into account. The Council has also undertaken to heed these effects when deciding on such policies. This would mean that the interests of the regions in question are taken into consideration and that, where appropriate, specific measures are drawn up to ensure both that these policies are fully implemented and that any negative effects on regions will be remedied. It reminds us once of the famous phrase of J. Rey, former President of the Commission of the European Communities: 'Regional policy in the Community should be as the heart is in the human body'.

In the future the efficiency of regional policy in an EEC context will depend to a large extent on the coordination (a) between the national regional policies; (b) between the national policies and the Community policy, and (c) between the Community instruments (regional policy in the framework of the Treaty of Paris, the Social Fund, the European Investment Bank, the Guidance Section of European Agricultural Fund, and the Regional Fund).

For all three levels the regional development programmes dealt with in chapter 10 provide an appropriate framework for coordination. There

are, however, two conditions: a sufficient standardisation of the regional programmes and an upgrading of all programmes to the highest level.

As far as coordination among the national regional policies and
between these and the Community regional policy is concerned, strong
emphasis must be laid on the following points.

1 The definition of the problem regions and their ranking in terms of
priority is a first requisite. Differences in the criteria applied by the
individual members of the EEC may accentuate regional disparities on
the Community level. In this context, we must also repeat what we have
stated in chapter 7: that it is rather surprising to find that the assisted
regions in the EEC represent 41 per cent of the population and 61 per
cent of the territory and that in these circumstances one can hardly speak
of a discriminatory policy in favour of a limited number of regions. We
know that in practice not all regions profit to the same extent from
regional aid systems.

In chapter 7 we mentioned the factors that should be taken into
account in defining the problem areas. This defining will not be easy.
Statistical methods for measuring the elements of a regional problem
still differ considerably among the individual countries. Furthermore,
we agree with K. Allen that there remains a problem of interpretation.
'Social, political and economic factors play a major role in determining
the statistical intensity of a regional problem and without firm and deep
understanding of the individual economies it is difficult to reach anything like a standardised view'.[7] It should be stressed that the problem regions must be defined otherwise on the EEC level than on the
national level.

2 Defining problem regions is a first step; it should be followed by a
selection of regions to be assisted. Two conditions must be fulfilled:
(a) the policy must be concentrated on a limited number of regions, and
(b) priority should be given to those problem regions that have a real
chance of developing.

The first condition is inspired by the fact that in every country and
even more on the Community level, the resources are limited in comparison to the needs. We are aware that for all kind of reasons this condition is not likely to be fulfilled in practice, and yet the effectiveness of
regional policy depends on the direction of our efforts towards sustained
growth.

The second condition implies that in most cases priority should not
be given to a country's least developed regions and that in no case the
whole territory of a country should be selected for assistance. To
achieve a take off a region must have certain locational advantages. It is
to be expected that pressure groups will come into action once more,

and that in the face of their opposition it will be extremely difficult to carry through N. Hansen's excellent idea of supporting first and foremost some 'intermediate areas'. We admit that Hansen's suggestion cannot be applied to all EEC countries, but Italy, Ireland, France, and the United Kingdom might profit from it.

Even if on the national level the principle of selecting a restricted number of priority regions cannot be maintained, EEC policy should certainly be guided by it. We find the same idea expressed in the study 'Economic policy for the European Community — the way forward'.

> What the Community requires are acceptable guidelines for deciding which areas can hope to expand on the basis of aid and which should be given support only as a means of meeting the social cost of adjustment to a limited development ceiling. In the absence of these guidelines the Community's regional policy is in danger of becoming an exercise in chronic subsidisation without bringing about much sustainable growth. There is also a danger, as the European Parliament's regional policy and transport committee has rightly emphasised, that aid will be dispersed on small projects throughout the Community instead of being concentrated on particular areas that would repay assistance. [8]

3 Particular attention must be paid to the strategy of regional development . There is no unique strategy; for each development area a different path must be followed. In chapter 7 we have stressed the necessity of a strategy and tried to define some types; here we will just make a few remarks.

The creation of new centres of attraction in selected development regions at carefully chosen locations is of vital importance. We share the concern of A. Cairncross et al. that the building up of new centres as 'growth points' or 'growth poles' from which expansionary impulses radiate to the surrounding areas is an attractive but politically explosive idea.

> It implies a concentration of regional measures in favour of the centres showing most promise of achieving self-sustained growth. Conversely, it means refusing aid to other areas that lack such promise or confining support for those areas to grants towards moving or commuting to more favoured areas. We do not overlook the fact that the larger backward regions of the Community include more than a few urban centres of cultural and social importance. Any proper regional policy must aim at revitalizing such towns and cities by bringing modern industry to them and preventing their decay through intra-regional migration which is as unacceptable as

emigration to other regions. With this proviso, we think that, in spite of the deliberate discrimination between areas and the political opposition likely to result, a strategy of growth points should be intensively pursued by the Community.[9]

Regional development strategy must also avoid the erection of 'cathedrals in the desert'; auxiliary development around new plants must not be neglected.

We stated above that it is a mistake — and one that is often made — to look for swift solutions in matters of regional policy. Nor, we add here, should miracles be expected from strategies: in most cases at least a decade is needed to test the value of a development strategy adopted for a region.

4 Regional development plans should indicate who is responsible for improving a region's locational development factors, and how the improvement activities are to be timed. That applies not only to economic infrastructure, but also to social, cultural, and medical infrastructure, and to the training and retraining of labour, housing programmes, amelioration of the agricultural structure, attraction of auxiliary firms, etc. Some improvements are clearly related to the traditional EEC instruments (especially the Social Fund and the Guidance Section of EAGGF).

5 Very important is the coordination of financial aids. Some efforts made to that effect were mentioned in chapter 10 (Regional Aid Systems). The ceilings of aid intensity differ according to the nature and gravity of regional problems; in fact, the differences between the systems of national aid are more important than those between the absolute amounts of aid given. According to Table 8.3, which shows the effective subsidies based on maximum rates and maximum incentive combinations for the top priority regions in each EEC country, there are considerable differences among countries, but we doubt that the real differences are like that. National governments are famous for their ingenuity when it comes to attracting interesting projects. It may well be that other financial advantages than those foreseen in regional policy laws are more effective.

We are also doubtful about a second principle that should govern the coordination of national aid systems, that of transparency. Analysis of Table 8.1 shows how little the requirement of transparency of aids and aid systems is respected. Admittedly, an enormous amount of background information is needed for a fair comparison of incentives; the analysis carried out by K. Allen in the European Regional Policy Project proves that. Indeed, apart from such financial incentives as infrastructure aids and the regional allocation of public investments, how can incentives be compared and/or coordinated?

What makes judgement by the Commission even more difficult is the increasing use of sectoral aids for regional purposes. Since the economic depression set in, sectoral aid systems have been intensified in all European countries.

All things considered it is evident that a well developed control system is needed to coordinate financial aids effectively.

6 A special case of coordination concerns the frontier regions on either side of a border. Very often these regions do not need extra efforts so much as the coordination of development programmes and policy instruments to avoid distortions. 'Development programmes for frontier regions generally consider these regions in isolation from the area across the frontier and their economic interdependence is taken into account only in devising measures of policy competition to favour one area over the other'.[11] Economic efficiency calls for joint programmes of infrastructure. In the short run there may be distortions due to different arsenals of financial incentives.

As we stated above, coordination is necessary not only among national policies and between national and Community policies, but also among the institutions which manage the EEC instruments. Coordination was improved by the mutual representation of these institutions in the corresponding working committees. The implementation of regional development programmes offers an excellent occasion to improve this coordination. As far as the coordination of regional instruments is concerned, we should like to go further: we suggest a merging of the Guidance Section of the EAGGF and of a part of the Social Fund with the Regional Development Fund. A similar proposition was made by A. Cairncross et al.; they proposed that the EAGGF be merged with the Social Fund and the ERDF, 'For aid to agriculture is essentially a matter of regional and social policy and it would be a great advantage if agricultural policy came to be regarded as a form of regional policy'.[12]

The FLEUR study as a means towards the creation of consistent regional policy for the territory of the Common Market as a whole

For several years a team of researchers belonging to the Division of Locational Studies at the Netherlands Economic Institute, collected theoretical, methodological, and statistical information about the situation in Western Europe. They were successful in making operational models for all sectors in single countries, and for single sectors or groups of sectors in the whole of Europe.

The experience thus gained led to the conviction that it must be feasible to integrate the sectoral and regional aspects and to develop a model of the locational evolution of all economic activities across all regions of the European Community. The results of the investigations made were brought to the attention of the European Community, and discussions between EEC and NEI representatives on the structure to be given to the study in view of the uses the Commission would want to make of it finally resulted in a study project, which was baptised FLEUR (*Factors of Location in Europe*). Its aim is to explain for the past (1950—60—70) and stimulate for the future (1980—90) the economic development in all programming regions of the European Community of total economic activity split up into some 70 sectors .[13]

Data resulting from the FLEUR study were used in chapter 2 of this book to describe regional disparities in the EEC.[14]

Variables identified

The most important variable is, of course, the measure of 'economic activity', which had to be defined in a way relevant to regional economic policy. As such was selected the number of people employed. 'In view of the location optique of FLEUR every employed individual is assigned to the region in which the usual work is actually carried out, in practice the region in which the establishment that employs the individual is located'.[15]

The data were in principle derived from the national censuses. For 1950, lack of information made it necessary to regroup a number of smaller sectors into one broader sector. Comparisons between 1950 and 1960 had to be based on only 58 industry groups.

For the explanatory variables the description provided by W. Molle and B. van Holst is given below.

The first factor pointed out in all studies for almost all sectors analysed is the presence or nearness of markets for inputs and outputs. Very often firms appear to investigate first of all whether a prospective region of location offers raw material and intermediary products as well as market outlets, after which their final choice of a site within the region is determined by a number of other factors. In view of the regional scale of the study, markets are likely to exert a significant influence.

Another factor often emerging in location studies is transport.

This is not an independent factor, however; its importance just indicates that not only the presence but also the accessibility of markets plays a part in location decisions. This factor is, therefore, the logical complement of the first one.

The third factor generally mentioned is availability, quality, and price of labour. Though perhaps less widely applicable than the previous two, this factor is supposed to exert an influence on a significant number of sectors.

Markets, transport, and labour were the only factors generally mentioned. Close inspection of the diverse other factors indicated in location studies has revealed that some of them, notably in the socio-cultural-educational field, are thought of by many as highly correlated with urbanisation. The regions distinguished show considerable differences in the character and degree of urbanisation, so that inclusion of an urbanisation factor, which would account for a large number of other specific elements, seems justified.

Regional and sectoral policy has a place of its own among the factors of location. It must be included as a factor relevant to the study, for without taking into account the interference of policy measures with the free play of other factors, it is impossible to understand why the effects of those other factors are ofted distorted.

After the identification of the factors that, on the strength of evidence contained in empirical studies, count as being of general relevance to the FLEUR study, their statistical representation had to be decided on.

The quantification of the first factor 'markets' is essentially based on the regional/sectoral employment data. On the hypothesis that the economy of Western Europe is a closed system, for every sector total consumption can be set equal to total production. With the help of output coefficients the parts of final and intermediate markets for the whole of Europe are then determined. Regional final demand for the products of a sector is next approximated by the regionalisation of this Western European total final demand (expressed in employment) on the basis of regional population and gross domestic product figures, and other relevant information. Regional intermediate demand is approximated by combining information on input coefficients and productivity with regional sectoral employment figures.

All necessary statistical information, viz. comparable regional figures on GDP and population, and general information on input-output relations, is now in preparation. Gross domestic product figures are based on the conventions adopted in the framework of the European Regional Accounting Program 1970, to which a large number of official and academic estimates have been adapted. For population, internationally and intertemporally comparable figures have been set up on the basis of a Standard developed for this study, which corresponds largely to the usual residence concept. Input-output information is based on the EEC 1965 detailed tables and on a number of USA tables.

The transport variable has been quantified by establishing a network between the centres of all regions based on the principal road network. Distances on each link of this network have been weighted by the average speed that could be achieved on the type of road that forms the link, in order to obtain average time distances. Sea links that are essential to a complete network between insular and continental regions have been integrated in this system by introducing directly the time that a ferry takes to make the crossing. A shortest-route algorithm was then used to establish the final time distance matrices of each regional centre to all others. [16]

The model

The model that is proposed for the analytical part of the study has two extremely important characteristics, viz. it is inter-industrial as well as inter-regional. The general form of the FLEUR model is presented as

$$\underline{e} = A\underline{e} + B\underline{f} + C\underline{l} + D\underline{u} + E\underline{p} + \epsilon \qquad (11.1)$$

in which

$\underline{e}$	=	employment by region and sector;
$\underline{f}$	=	final demand;
$\underline{l}$	=	labour availability;
$\underline{u}$	=	urbanisation;
$\underline{p}$	=	policy.
A,B,C,D,E	=	matrices of coefficients of location influences.

It may be noted that the employment vectors actually consist of 100 columns of 60 sectoral employment figures superposed at a certain point in time (t + 1) as a function (matrices A to E) of the qualitative importance of the selected location factors in the beginning of the period, during the period or occasionally at the same moment (vectors $\underline{e}$, $\underline{f}$, $\underline{u}$, and $\underline{p}$). [17] This implies that the model is also a dynamic model.

In principle the model proposed is an inter-regional attraction model. Demand and supply effects are taken into account, the interaction between sectors in different regions is accounted for and the secondary

449

factors of location as well as the policy variables have their proper place.

The presentation of the general form of the model does not mean that this form is operational. It gives just a more or less symbolic picture of what the authors have in mind which is, as stated, an inter-regional, intersectoral model with dynamic features. Formulation (11.1) is nothing but the mathematical translation of this general picture. The broad experience with this kind of model obtained through several studies in different sectors and different countries in Europe may give us full confidence that this follow up of the part of the FLEUR study devoted to collection of the statistical data can be performed as efficiently and thoroughly as the first part.

Significance of the FLEUR study

It is the opinion of the authors of this book that the value of the FLEUR study cannot be overestimated; this opinion is based on a number of considerations.

1 So far regional studies in the EEC have been performed almost exclusively for single regions. These were studied in detail. Economic structures were analysed and locational factors studied. Programmes for future development were designed and policy measures proposed. But two things were usually not very well and at least not very systematically treated viz. the influence that the developments in other regions would exert on the region studied and the influences that the region in question would exert on other regions. Neglecting these two influences means that if similar studies were performed for all regions of Western Europe, the chances are negligible that forecasts of future developments and proposed policy measures are consistent with each other. If the statistical material of FLEUR that is now available is used in a model similar to the general model described above, consistency is automatically guaranteed because of the inter-regional character of the model. This feature also implies that regional policy is enabled to develop into an inter-regional policy in which due account is taken of the influences that each region exerts upon other regions.

2 The same reasoning holds in principle for the sectors. The model generates the effects of a development in a given sector on all other sectors in all regions. This implies that sectoral policy also could develop into an intersectoral policy, so that, if particular measures are being contemplated in a given sector, the consequences of these measures for all other sectors can be computed and taken into consideration before the measures are actually taken.

450

3 These facts taken together imply that insight will be gained into the inter-relations between sectoral policy and regional policy and even that a basis will be laid for the integration of these policies, on the EEC level as well as on the national level.

4 Combining the FLEUR model with a population growth and migration model would in principle be not too difficult. Such a combination would be extremely valuable since it could give us a starting point for an integration of regional policy and labour market policy, the FLEUR model treating the demand side of the labour market and the population migration model the supply side.

5 The implicit role played in the model by the quality of the infrastructure forms the basis for a possible integration of infra-structure policy and regional policy. Admittedly, the networks considered are not the dense networks that should be considered in a fully fledged infrastructure study, but they constitute or could constitute the basic European network linking the different EEC regions. The effects of important improvements of this basic net-work on the location of activities could be studied with the help of the model. This, again, would contribute to wider perspectives for infrastructure policy on the EEC level.

6 Finally, the model will allow us to evaluate the efficiency and efficacy of the different instruments used on the regional level. The EEC countries seem to offer ideal opportunities for establish-ing the importance of different instruments used in different countries and regions. It would be difficult to find another group of countries where such a variety of instruments has been used on the regional level as is the case in the EEC. Such knowledge could contribute significantly to our knowledge of regional instruments and the way they affect regional development.

Each of these six reasons would separately justify the further elabora-tion of the FLEUR idea. If the decision is made to go ahead in this dir-ection, an important step will be taken towards a more efficient and certainly more integrated approach to Europe's regional problems.

Community regional policy should consider congested regions

In chapters 1 and 5 we stressed the economic and social costs of con-gestion. To a certain extent the dualism between congested regions and laggard regions has been the thread connecting the different chapters of this book, but we admit that our presentation has been too indiscriminate. In chapter 5 on urban developments, we presented as a new fact to be taken into account the decline of the population in large agglomerations, a phenomenon that among other things provoked an unbalanced spread of employment within these agglomerations. We shall take up that aspect on page 459.

Certain countries have taken measures to check congestion; the interesting initiatives taken to that end by the United Kingdom and France have to some extent been successful (see chapter 8). The Commission, too, is aware of the congestion problem; one of the guidelines given in the Thomson Report for a regional policy to be conducted by the Community refers to congested areas in the following words: 'Since overconcentration of economic activity in some regions is a major social and economic problem which tends to become more and more acute, the Community, as well as giving aid to the poorer regions, should seek agreement between the Member States on common policies to reduce concentration in the congested regions. The Commission will in this matter make appropriate proposals in due time'. [18]

Yet we fail to find in EEC regional policy any measure to control overconcentration. There are several good reasons for considering the congested regions in the context of policy aims and policy instruments. First, from the purely economic, the social and the environmental point of view regional policy can only be efficient if at the same time measures are taken on the one hand to control the extension of conurbations and incentives given on the other to stimulate and accelerate the take off of laggard regions.

Secondly, for a few years now certain countries have been afraid to apply 'negative' measures not only because of the economic crisis but also because they fear that, owing to the economic integration, negative measures would benefit other countries.

Thirdly, central funds are not necessarily allocated for public investment on the basis of needs for regional development. Here we quote once more A. Cairncross et al.

> At the political level, concentrations of electors in the industrial areas have been able to draw the special attention of government to their problems, among them bottlenecks in transport and social infrastructure which make heavy demands on public investment and are forever arising as urban development proceeds. The same kind of distortion in favour of existing urban centres may result from the financing of their deficits on transport services out of the budget of a higher fiscal authority. This too, means that the larger industrial centres are being subsidised by the rest of the country

. . . . Considerations of this kind, and the consequent need to aim at improving efficiency in the regional allocation of public funds, suggest the need for continuous parliamentary scrutiny. But such a scrutiny promises to be efficient only if all regions can compete for the funds on an equal footing within the legislature. We accordingly propose, at Community level, the establishment of a separate house in the European Parliament to represent regional interests. Such a Chamber of Regions might be instituted on a basis similar to the Senate in the United States.[19]

An interesting but far reaching task is set here for the Regional Policy Committee.

A more powerful Regional Development Fund

Although we have already stressed that the power of the Commission in regional matters is not only a function of the magnitude of the ERDF and the traditional instruments, the funds available do not correspond to the enormous task of improving the regional balance in the EEC. The Commission itself has on several occasions proposed that more money be made available for regional purposes. (See also the point of view of the European Parliament).

The Community impact of the ERDF depends also on the division between the quota section and the non-quota section. In the renewed Fund the share of the non-quota section is beyond any doubt too small, which greatly reduces the Commission's initiative in regional matters.

Creation of new tools

Throughout this book, and in particular on page 452, we stressed the close relation between conurbation areas and laggard regions. Concentration in growing conurbation areas should be limited and the growth of selected development areas must be stimulated. But according to our findings in chapter 5 further decline of large agglomerations should also be prevented.

Are there regional measures which cope with this threefold target? The combination of 'positive' and 'negative' incentives has led to positive results (see chapter 8). We do not claim to know which control system — the British or the French — offers the best chance of success; the choice may be largely influenced by a number of factors unique to each country. The differences in the real spatial problems are important. The United Kingdom and France have a pure primate-city spatial structure. Italy has a dual primate city system, and the Rimcity in the Netherlands is a polycentric agglomeration. In Germany there is no large conurbation, but there are several big cities spread all over the Federal Republic (multipolar structure). A number of legal and constitutional problems (e.g. in Germany) have also to be considered. There is reason to doubt therefore the complete transferability of regional control policies.

Control measures in the sense of administrative control systems (administrative licencing policy) are the more efficient the more they are, or can be, combined with other forms of influence such as verbal steering, package deals, warning letters (see chapter 8). The information, learning, and cooperation effects of control may be more important than its interventionist elements. Administrative control systems also guarantee selectivity and flexibility (e.g. in respect of inner city problems).

In this section we are paying attention to three new tools: (a) a regionally differentiated tax subsidy scheme, (b) a regionally differentiated credit policy, and (c) regional income transfers.

A regionally differentiated
tax subsidy scheme

Sometimes it is said that it is more appropriate to use the price mechanism than physical controls to deal with the problem of excessive urban concentration. One of the defenders of the price mechanism is B. Balassa. He proposed the introduction of a tax subsidy scheme to cope with the above mentioned threefold regional policy objective. Here we quote the essential elements of B. Balassa's Alternative Scheme of Regional Assistance.[20]

> Labor mobility, too, is on the increase although social and political factors will continue to limit its scope. Nevertheless, the spread of information on wage levels, together with nationwide collective bargaining and social pressures, tend to reduce inter-regional wage differences. Production costs in depressed regions will rise as a result, reducing the competitiveness of firms located in these regions. Now, while in intercountry relationships exchange rate devaluation or protection can be used to correct the situation, these instruments are not available to individual regions so that specialisation will be determined by absolute rather than by comparative advantage. To conform to the resource endowments of the depressed regions and to increase employment, with corresponding improvements in income distribution, an appropriate solution appears to be to subsidize the use of labor in these regions.

Under capital mobility, such a subsidy will be equivalent to a combination of an exchange rate devaluation and a transfer. It represents a devaluation as it reduces the cost of the relatively immobile factor, labor, while at the same time, it offsets the adverse effects of a devaluation on regional incomes by financing the subsidy from the general budget. It is suggested here that differential wage (or social security) taxes be used as the main instrument of regional policy in the Common Market. This would entail varying the tax rates expressed as a percentage of wages from region to region, with the highest rates applying in regions of excessive concentration. Such a scheme would alleviate the employment problem of depressed regions by providing inducement to the use of labor rather than capital in these regions and would thereby conform to the objectives of the Commission's report on regional policy that calls for job creation instead of out-migration. The tax subsidy scheme would also discourage production in regions of excessive concentration and permit dealing with the problems of the so-called grey areas to which intermediate rates would apply. At the same time, it would avoid the discrimination against existing activities in depressed regions and in favor of such activities in regions of excessive concentration, that results from the application of measures affecting only capital investment.

The proposed scheme has the advantages of flexibility, permitting variations in the rates following changes in the underlying conditions in the regions concerned. Also, just like a devaluation, it can be expected to act within a relatively short time; that will not be the case if the measures applied concern capital investment. Finally, in offsetting the adverse effects of fixed exchange rates on depressed regions, it would smooth the way towards monetary integration in the Common Market.

A. Cairncross et al. makes a similar suggestion. [21] In addition to financial incentives they plead for a fiscal system that taxes employment more heavily in some areas and less heavily in others. This system would work as a counterweight to the financial incentives which stimulate the location of the more capital intensive investments in the problem regions.

In the context of B. Balassa's ideas, we agree that under nationwide collective bargaining and social pressures, inter-regional wage differences tend to diminish. It is questionable that the abolition of wage zones is in the interest of the backward areas, which stand to lose one of their locational advantages. In view of the lower labour productivity in the laggard regions, a reduction of inter-regional wage differences may be a hindrance to the increase of employment.

G. Magnifico goes even further as he deals with the regionally differentiated payroll tax subsidy. 'The payroll subsidy would, in effect, only be available to regions that were prepared to contribute to their own growth by exercising moderation in income claims'.[22]

Our second remark concerns some drawbacks of taxation as a regional disincentive in conurbation areas (see chapter 8). Taxes can be passed on to the consumer and exported to other regions (the supply of the products of congested areas is very often price inelastic owing to their human capital intensive nature). A taxation system does not have the flexibility and selectivity of administrative control. Finally, taxes are paid after an investment has been made (no verbal steering) and the final decision whether or not to move is in the hands of the firm. Another important comment has been given by W. Fleck, M. Fritsch and R. Wettmann.

> If such a tax were limited to industrial investment only, because industrial investment is generally believed to be more mobile than tertiary or quaternary investment, it would be mainly the industrial centres and not the prosperous and dynamic tertiary and quaternary conurbations which would 'suffer' most from such a regional disincentive measure. If a tax system were applied to both industrial and tertiary sector investment, the system could still work to the detriment of the older industrial centres. Since the more modern tertiary or quaternary sector firms would be more likely to pay the tax given their higher competitiveness and lower mobility, while a higher percentage of industrial enterprises may be forced to move to a region just beyond the area covered by the tax, if they cannot pass it on. Thus a tax system applying equal tax standards to Germany's large agglomerations would probably produce highly unequal results affecting some agglomerations more heavily than others.[23]

A regionally differentiated credit policy

The consideration that (as pointed out in chapter 1), business cycles coincide spatially not with national territories but with economically homogeneous regions, and that, therefore, policies based on national aggregates alone may not be effective, has led to the suggestion of a second potential new tool, namely, a regionally differentiated credit policy. In fact, the high growth rates and inflationary pressures of the 1960s inspired the development of this tool. G. Magnifico defends it in the following terms: 'Disinflationary policies which do not discriminate between economic regions, according as to whether or not they are actually affected by excess demand, inflict an unnecessary damage to the weaker regions, where "overheating" is often the result of cyclical conditions external to them. And yet the impact of restrictive policies tends to concentrate there'.[24] The author underlines that the weaker regions have a larger share of smaller firms, and that banks as a rule find it more convenient to reduce their loans to such firms. Another argument may be added. At the same moment that laggard regions have a chance of attracting new investment, thanks to the availability of labour or the presence of other locational advantages, they are restricted in their growth by national credit restrictions. 'A differentiated credit policy should, on the one hand, make possible a more effective stand against inflation in the regions where demand for productive factors tends to exceed supply; on the other hand, it should help to shield the weaker regions from the jolts of "stop-go"'.[25] Such a policy instrument can be applied on the national and the Community level.[26] We agree with G. Magnifico that these considerations should be heeded in determining the Community's monetary policy. But he also proposes a more direct action.

> More specifically, a European credit institution endowed with large enough resources and powers might contribute to the pursuit of regionally differentiated policies. It is a matter for consideration whether this task would best be accomplished by an adequate expansion in the European Investment Bank or by the proposed European Bank adding a Development Division to function in parallel with its central banking activities. In favour of the former solution is the traditional separation of monetary activity from finance for development purposes, but the latter might be best suited to maximise results in terms of the impact which overall credit conditions throughout the Community would have on economic trends in the weaker regions.[27] [28]

Here the link with what was pointed out in chapter 6 is evident.

Regional income transfers

Given a degree of European political solidarity, real economic and monetary integration would also open prospects for the less traditional regional instrument of income transfers. Income transfers have an effect equivalent to that of depreciation of the exchange rate. We are aware that such transfers will encounter a lot of difficulties and adverse reactions from the high activity regions. This aspect is closely related to the inter-regional redistributive power of public finance. Here, we refer to the MacDougall Report.[29] In the countries studied in the latter, the net inter-regional flows of public money are to a large extent not motivated by explicit regional objectives.

The necessity of integrating tertiary and quaternary activities in the regional economic policy

There are two main reasons for paying more attention to the role of certain tertiary and quaternary sectors in regional development. First, these activities are growing fast and are mainly concentrated in the conurbations (headquarters, research and development, finance, international functions, human capital intensive activities, administration, etc.). Secondly, it must be expected that the growth of employment in manufacturing will slow down in the next decade. In all EEC countries manufacturing employment is less than half of the total. Moore and Rhodes made a similar remark:

> The UK manufacturing sector has been growing slowly in recent years — indeed in terms of employment it has actually declined since 1966. This has led some people to the view that regional policy ought to be directed more towards the rapidly growing service sector — or at least to that part of the service sector which serves a national market. In 1973 the government moved a little in this direction with the introduction of grants for private offices moving to development areas and the announcements of more dispersal of central government office jobs into assisted regions. [30]

We agree that in the 'basic — non-basic approach' tertiary and quaternary activities cannot grow unlimited without sufficient support from value added created in the primary and secondary sectors. Nevertheless some tertiary and quaternary branches belong to the basic sectors.

With the exception of France, where several large national banks as well as some ministries, have moved whole departments to provincial towns, and apart from a few minor initiatives in other countries, there is a general lack of policy to increase service mobility. K. Allen states 'Where such policy does exist it is generally weak, relative to that for industry, and usually more in the form of decentralisation policy than regional policy in the normal sense of the term'. [31]

Evidently it will be much more difficult directly to influence basic, tertiary and quaternary activities because, as service occupations, they tend to be tied firmly to existing industry and large cities. This is another argument for concentrating efforts in a few regions and selected growth poles, a policy the value of which has been stressed above. Once more we cannot generalise. The population density, the transport network, and the distance factor are different in the Benelux countries and many German Länder from those in such countries as France and Italy; that is why in the Benelux countries and Germany tertiary and quaternary activities have already started to decentralise.

The problems in stagnant
or declining large cities

On page 452 we admitted to a lack of discrimination in describing the contrast between conurbation areas and laggard regions. In chapter 3 we distinguished four types of regions: (a) prosperous regions, (b) underdeveloped regions in expansion, (c) potentially underdeveloped regions, and (d) underdeveloped regions. Of these four, only two types fit the dichotomy: certain prosperous regions and the underdeveloped ones. The potentially underdeveloped regions also deserve attention, however. They comprise, first, the regions in need of conversion, and, second, certain large agglomerations that have been giving reason for concern for a few years. The causes of agglomeration problems, which are often inner area problems, have been analysed in chapter 5, and, also, among others, by B. Nicol and G. Wehrmann in a United Kingdom setting.[32] They underline that the major trend to metropolitan decentralisation of both people and jobs has had serious repercussions on the inner areas of the British large cities. The causes are many. First, there is the age of the area's fabric; factories have become outmoded by advances in transport and production technology. Firms established in these areas have had to close down owing to their inability to adjust to trading and product cycle changes. Secondly, there is the role of physical land use planning. Thirdly, the influence of planned population dispersal has been great; its target was to cream off the expected growth of population in large cities and divert it to the new and expanded towns (NETs). The great change in the birth rates in the mid 1960s intervened as a new but very important factor; it changed in the United Kingdom the policy towards the NETs and in France that towards the new towns. It is sometimes said that regional policy in general and IDC control in particular have contributed to the decline of manufacturing employment in the inner areas. The analysis of Nicol and Wehrmann does not bring any proof of this; according to these authors, IDC policy does not appear to have been a major contributory factor. Nevertheless IDC policy has recently been relaxed to favour inner city areas, which proves that the British Government is concerned about the employment problems of the inner areas of London and Birmingham. In the framework of the recently modified IDC policy mobile projects should be steered, in order of preference, to: (a) the Assisted Areas, (b) the inner areas of London and Birmingham, and (c) the designated new and expanding towns in the non-assisted areas. In other words the inner areas of London and Birmingham get second priority after the Assisted Areas. That intention is very clearly defined in the recent document 'Policy for the inner cities'.

> . . . some of the movement of jobs and people has been facilitated by policies aimed at reducing the overcrowding of the older parts of the cities. In the post war years this was an essential part of public policy, but in most cities it has largely been achieved. It should be possible now to change the thrust of the policies which have assisted large scale decentralisation and in course of time to stem the decline, achieve a more balanced structure of jobs and population within our cities, and create healthier local economies. [33]

The problem evoked above is, of course, not only a British one; indeed, the decline in the birth rate in the mid 1960s and the expected low growth rate in the EEC during the next decade, may increase such inner city problems in most EEC countries. The consequence is twofold. First, in the above mentioned dualism between conurbation areas and laggard regions, we must make a distinction between growing conurbations and stagnant or declining ones. Secondly, in the future we shall be more and more confronted, in poor regions as well as in strong ones, with serious concentration of unemployment and industrial decline. It may be necessary, therefore, to increase the spatial selectiveness of inter-regional policy by introducing intra-regional differentiation. That will make a coherent and coordinated regional policy even harder to accomplish, and complicate the introduction of some of the new tools mentioned above.

Final considerations

There is a tremendous range of research and operational work to be done by all persons and institutions involved in regional economic development. There is little doubt that the implementation of regional policy in the EEC will be more difficult in the next decade than it was in the 1960s and 1970s. For one thing, the growth rate may be too low to give proper support. The creation of employment in manufacturing may stagnate; the location pattern for the new plants of multinational companies may change. For another, the expected enlargement of the Community is bound to affect the present EEC members, and EEC policy; indeed, a new challenge.

The regional development of the EEC represents an urgent and difficult, but also a fascinating task, for, if carried out well, it is to bring about a more just, more human European Community. Better regional policy could enhance the well being of the regions in all their variety and beauty. A policy objective of a higher order can hardly be imagined.

Notes

[1] Cairncross, A., Giersch, H., Lamfalussy, A., Petrilli, G., and Uri, P., op.cit., p.72.

[2] See 'Regional policy: the start of a new phase', *Europe Information*, no.11, 1978. The European Coal and Steel Community (ECSC) has made loans totalling nearly 5,000 million EUC to help modernise the coal and steel industries or to attract new job-creating industries in coal and steel regions. The European Investment Bank (EIB) has made available over 7,000 million EUC in loans, the bulk of it for regional development purposes. In 1977 69 per cent of the 1,500 million EUC granted in the form of loans went to regional projects. The European Social Fund (ESF) and the European Coal and Steel Community have together made grants totalling more than 1,000 million EUC for training and retraining workers otherwise unable to obtain jobs. And the Guidance Section of the European Agricultural Fund has to date spent 1,600 million EUC in the form of grants to help modernise the structure of agricultural production and distribution.

[3] Magnifico, G., op.cit., p.218.

[4] Cairncross, A. et al., op.cit., pp.75−6.

[5] EEC, 'Report on the regional problems in the enlarged Community', op.cit., p.12.

[6] Wallace, H., Wallace, W., and Webb, C., op.cit., p.158. 'As community discussion continued it became clear that the Commission was investing greater hope in the new Regional Policy Committee than in the RDF itself. It was increasingly accepted that the small Fund lacked the resources to make an immediate and quantifiable contribution to regional development, except at the margin. The Commission saw the Committee as a constructive form for concertation and for moving towards a convergence of national approaches ...'

[7] Allen, K., *European Regional Policies*, in Sant (ed.), op.cit., p.95.

[8] Cairncross, A., et al., op.cit., p.74.

[9] Ibid., p.86. See also Frey, L., op.cit., pp.145−50.

[10] Allen, K., op.cit., pp.91−2.

[11] Balassa, B., *Regional Policies and the Environment in the European Common Market*, op.cit., pp.408−9.

[12] Cairncross, A., et al., op.cit., p.73.

[13] Molle, W. and Van Holst, B., *Factors of Location in Europe. A Progress Report*, Copenhagen, 1976, pp.3—4.

[14] The FLEUR idea originated from W.T.M. Molle.

[15] Molle, W. and Van Holst, B., op.cit., p.11.

[16] Ibid., pp.13—15.

[17] Ibid., p.17.

[18] EEC, *Report on the Regional Problems in the Enlarged Community*, op.cit., p.12. See also EEC, *Community Regional Policy — new guidelines*, op.cit., p.10.

[19] Cairncross, A., et al., op.cit., p.78.

[20] Balassa, B., op.cit., pp.413—14.

[21] See also Magnifico, G., op.cit., pp.218—19.

[22] Ibid., p.219.

[23] Fleck, W., Fritsch, M. and Wettmann, R., *Transferability of Regional Control Policies*, op.cit., p.12.

[24] Magnifico, G., op.cit., pp.219—20.

[25] Ibid., p.220.

[26] Italy is a case in which territorial direction of credit has played a salient role. The Federal Republic of Germany has followed an approach similar to Italy's (see Magnifico, G., op.cit., p.27).

[27] Magnifico, G., op.cit., p.220; see also pp.29—32.

[28] As far as new financial means are concerned, G. Magnifico made a particular proposition to make use of European seigniorage gains. To a large extent this proposition is also linked to the above mentioned differentiated credit policy. He proposed that a new, additional currency should be put into circulation in the Community by a European Bank of the universal type. He calls this the Multi-role European Bank. 'The Multi-role European Bank would, among other things, issue medium- and long-term securities denominated in the new European currency. It would also be enabled to use the issues of the new currency by granting credit in a fashion that would make possible regionally differentiated demand management and contribute to balanced growth. The link that exists between the mechanism of monetary unification and the process of growth would thereby be correspondingly reflected in an institutional and instrumental arrangement, which would use the European seigniorage gains for closing regional disparities and preventing new ones.

[29] EEC, 'Report of the study group on the role of public finance in European integration', Brussels, 1977, pp.25—42.

[30] Moore, B. and Rhodes, J., 'The effects of regional economic policy in the United Kingdom', in Sant, M. (ed.), op.cit., p.50.

[31] Allen, K., 'European regional policies', op.cit., p.89.

[32] Nicol, B. and Whermann, G., op.cit., pp.16—17.

[33] HMSO, *Policy for Inner Cities*, 1977, Cmnd 6845, p.5.

Bibliography

Books and reports

Allen, K. and Hermansen, T., 'Economic growth — regional problems and growth centres', in *Regional Policy in Efta — an examination of the growth centre idea,* Edinburgh 1968.

Allen, K. and MacLennan, M.C., *Regional Problems and Policies in Italy and France,* London 1970.

Allen, K., 'Growth centres and growth centre policy', in Warne, E.J.D. (ed.), *Regional Policy in Efta,* Geneva 1971.

Allen, K., *Regional Incentives in the European Community: a comparative study,* Berlin 1978.

Anderson, A.E., 'Regional economic policy: problems, analysis and political experiments in Sweden', in Hansen, N. (ed.), *Public Finance and Regional Economic Development. The experience of nine Western countries,* Cambridge 1974.

Alonso, W., 'The question of city size and national policy', *Berkeley, Discussion Paper,* no.125, 1970.

Balassa, B., *The Theory of Economic Integration,* London, 1962.

Barlow, L., *Report of the Royal Commission on the Distribution of the Industrial Population,* London, HMSO, January 1940.

Bersani, G., 'Rapport sur la première communication de la Commission de la CEE sur la politique régionale dans la CEE', *European Parliament, Doc.,* 58, 23.5.1966.

Bersani, G., 'Rapport fait au nom de la Commission économique et financière, sur la première communication de la Commission de la CEE sur la politique régionale dans la CEE', *European Parliament, Doc.* 58, 1966—67.

Birkelbach, W., 'Rapport fait au nom de la Commission économique et financière sur la politique régional dans la CEE', *European Parliament, Doc.* 99, 1963—64.

Blake, C., 'The gains from regional policy', in Wolfe, J:N. (ed.), *Cost-benefit and Cost Effectiveness,* London 1973.

Bos. H.C., *Spatial Dispersion of Economic Activity,* Rotterdam 1964.

Boudeville, J.R., *Problems of Regional Economic Planning,* Edinburgh 1960.

Boudeville, J.R., *L'espace et les pôles de croissance,* Paris 1968.

Boudeville, J.R., 'Les notions d'espace et d'intégration', Boudeville, J.R.

463

(ed.), *L'espace et les pôles de croissance,* Paris 1968.

Boudeville, J.R., 'Les régions de villes et l'Europe', Meeting of the Association de Science régionale de langue française, Rotterdam 1974.

Bourginat, H., *Espace économique et intégration Européenne,* Paris 1962.

Brackett, J.C. and Lamale, N., 'Area differences in living costs', *American Statistical Association, Proceedings of Social Statistics Section,* 1967.

Brown, A.J. and Associates, 'Regional multiplier', in Richardson, H.W. (ed.), *Regional Economics: a reader,* London 1973.

Brown, A.J., *The Framework of Regional Economics in the United Kingdom,* Cambridge 1972.

Burchard, H.J., 'The principles determining the localisation of refineries and petro-chemical industry', in Regul (ed.), *The Future of European Ports,* Bruges 1971.

Cairncross, A., Giersch, H., Lamfalussy, A., Petrilli, G. and Uri, P., *Economic Policy for the European Community,* Kiel 1974.

Cameron, G.C., 'Regional economic policy in the United Kingdom', in Sant, M. (ed.), *Regional Policy and Planning for Europe,* London 1974.

Cameron, G.C., 'Regional economic policy in the United Kingdom', in Hansen, N. (ed.), *Public Policy and Regional Economic Development, the Experience of Nine Western Countries,* Cambridge 1974.

Cao-Pinna, V., 'Regional policy in Italy', in Hansen, N. (ed.), *Public Policy and Regional Economic Development. The Experience of Nine Western Countries,* Cambridge 1974.

Capanna, A., 'Aspects et problèmes de la sidérurgie côtière dans le monde et dans la CEE', in Regul, R. (ed.), *The Future of European Ports,* Bruges 1971.

CEE, *Documents de la Conférence sur les économies régionales,* Brussels 1961, vol.I and vol.II.

CEE, *Rapports de groupes d'experts sur la politique regionale dans la Communauté Economique Européenne,* Brussels 1964.

CEE, *Première communication de la Commission sur la politique régionale dans la CEE,* June 1965.

CEE, 'Etude pour la création d'un pôle industriel de développement en Italie Méridionale', *Série Economie et Finances,* no.5, Brussels 1966.

CEE, *L'évolution régionale dans la Communauté — Bilan analytique,* Brussels 1971.

CEE, *Le coût des concentrations urbaines et la dépopulation rurale dans la CEE,* Brussels, 1975.

CERAU, *Les coûts des infrastructures urbaines en France, 1960—67,* Paris 1970.

Chenery, H.B., *Politiche di sviluppo per l'Italia meridionale,* Rome 1962.

464

Chisholm, M. and Manners, G., *Spatial Policy Problems of the British Economy*, Cambridge 1971.

Christaller, W., *Die Zentralen Orte in Süddeutschland*, Jena 1933.

Commissariat Général Du Plan, 'Aménagement du territoire et du cadre de vie', *Préparation au 7ième Plan, Documentation française*, Paris 1976.

Commissie van Lohuizen, 'Stuwende en verzorgende bedrijven', *Rijk van het nationale plan*, no.51, 1952.

Cordon, W.M., 'Monetary integration', *Essays in International Finance*, no.93, Princeton, April 1972.

Council of Europe, *Effects of Transport Infrastructure on Regional Development. The economic impact of the Severn Bridge. A case study*, Strasbourg 1973.

Dahmen, E., 'Technology, innovation and international industrial transformation', in *Le Progrès Economique*, Leuven 1955.

Davin, L.E., Degeer, L. and Paelinck, J.H.P., *Dynamique économique de la région Liégeoise*, Liege 1959.

Davin, L.E., 'Conditions de croissance des économies régionales dans les pays développés', in *Théorie et politique de l'expansion régionale*, Bruxelles 1961.

Denison, E.F., *Why Growth Rates Differ*, Washington 1967.

Dixon, R.J. and Thirlwall, A.P., *Regional Growth and Unemployment in the United Kingdom*, London 1975.

Duncan, O.D., 'The optimum size of cities', Spengler, J.J. and Duncan, O.D. (eds), *Demographic Analysis*, 1956.

Dupont, C., 'Die europäische Investitionsbank', in Regionale Wirtschaftspolitik und Agrarstrukturpolitik in der Europäischen Wirtschaftsgemeinschaft. *Schriftenreihe des Gustav-Stresemann-Institutes e.V. für europäische Bildungs- und Informationsarbeit*, no.3, Hiltrup bei Münster.

Dziembowski, Z., *Synthetic indices of social costs of local economic infrastructure in cities of different size*, Warszawa 1976.

Easterlin, R.A., 'Long term regional income changes: some suggested factors', in *Regional Science Association, Papers and Proceedings*, vol.IV, 1958.

EEC, *Pour une politique régionale dans la Communauté*, Brussels 1969.

EEC, *Regional policy and economic and monetary union. Geographical disequilibria in the light of the implementation of fundamental economic equilibria*, Brussels 1971.

EEC, *Report on the Regional Problems in the Enlarged Community*, Brussels 1973.

EEC, *Air Sulphur Dioxyde Concentrations in the European Community*, Luxemburg 1974.

EEC, *Eight General Report on the Activities of the European Commun-*

ity in 1974, Brussels 1975.

EEC, 'General regional aid systems', *Communication of the Commission to the Council* of 26 February 1975.

EEC, 'European Regional Development Fund', Third annual report 1977.

EEC, 'Community regional policy. New guidelines', *Bulletin of the European Communities,* Supplement 2, 1977.

EEC, 'Report of the study group on the role of public finance in European integration', Brussels 1977.

Farhi, A., Lemaître, C. and Schmitges, R., *Deglomeration Policy in France. La procédure d'agrément,* Berlin 1978.

Fleck, W., Fritsch, M. and Wettmann, R., *Transferability of Regional Control Policies,* Berlin 1978.

Flockston, Ch., *Community Regional Policy,* London 1970.

Frey, L., 'Intégration économique européenne et développement regional', Petrella, R. (ed.), *Le développement regional en Europe,* The Hague, 1971.

Fuchs, V.R., *Changes in the Location of Manufacturing in the United States since 1929,* New Haven 1962.

Giersch, H., 'Marktintegration, Wechselkurs und Standortstruktur', in *Fundamentale Fragen künftiger Währungspolitik. Frankfurter Gesprach der List Gesellschaft,* 1965.

Glasson, J., *An Introduction to Regional Planning,* London 1975.

Gohman, V.M. and Karpov, L.N., 'Growth poles and growth centres', in Kuklinski, A. (ed.), *Growth Poles and Growth Centres in Regional Planning,* Paris 1972.

Gravier, J.F., *Décentralisation et progrès technique,* Paris 1954.

Gravier, J.F., *Paris et le désert français,* Paris 1958.

Gravier, J.F., *L'aménagement du territoire et l'avenir des régions françaises,* Paris 1964.

Guichard, O., *Aménager la France,* Paris 1965.

Hallett, F., 'British regional problems and policies' in Hallett, G., Randall, P. and West, E.G. (eds), *Regional Policy for Ever?,* London 1973.

Hanna, F.A., 'Analysis of interstate income differentials: theory and practice', *Regional Income, Studies in Income and Wealth,* no.21, 1957.

Hansen, N.M., *French Regional Planning,* Edinburgh 1968.

Hansen, N., *Rural Poverty and the Urban Crisis. A strategy for regional development,* Bloomington 1970.

Hansen, N., 'Efficient regional resource allocation and growth centre policy' in Paelinck, J.H.P. (ed.), *Programming for Europe's Collective Needs,* Amsterdam 1970.

Hansen, N., 'Criteria for a growth centre policy' in Kuklinski, A.R. (ed.), *Growth Poles and Growth Centres in Regional Planning,* The Hague 1972.

Hansen, N.M., *Public Policy and Regional Economic Development. The experiences of nine western countries*, Cambridge 1974.

Heijke, J.A.M., *Gastarbeid en economische structuur*, NEI, Rotterdam 1977.

Hendriks, A.J., 'Regional policy in the Netherlands' in Hansen, N. (ed.), *Public Policy and Regional Economic Development. The experience of nine western countries*, Cambridge 1974.

Hermansen, T., 'Development poles and development centres in national and regional development. Elements of a theoretical framework' in Kuklinski, A.R. (ed.), *Growth Poles and Growth Centres in Regional Planning*, Paris 1972.

Hilhorst, J.G.M., *Regional Planning. A Systems Approach*, Rotterdam 1971.

Hirschman, A.O., *The Strategy of Economic Development*, New Haven 1958.

Holland, S., *Capital versus the Regions*, London 1976.

Hoover, E.M., *The Location of Economic Activity*, New York 1948.

Jürgensen, H., 'The Regional impact of port investment and its consideration in port investment policy' in Regul, R. (ed.), *The Future of European Ports*, Bruges 1971.

Klaassen, L.H., *Regionale welvaartsverschillen en regionale politiek*, Haarlem 1959.

Klaassen, L.H., *Het regionale industrialisatiebeleid in Nederland*, Rotterdam 1962.

Klaassen, L.H., *Aménagement économique et social du territoire, Directives pour les programmes*, OCDE, Paris 1965.

Klaassen, L.H., 'Regional policy in the Benelux countries' in Meyers, F. (ed.), *Area Development Policies in Britain and the Countries of the Common Market*, Washington 1965.

Klaassen, L.H., *Méthodes de sélection d'industries pour les régions en stagnation*, OECD, Paris 1967.

Klaassen, L.H., Kroft, W.C. and Voskuil, R., 'Regional income differences in Holland' in *Papers of the Regional Science Association*, vol.X, 1963.

Klaassen, L.H., *Regionale economie en regionaal-economische politiek in Nederland*, Rotterdam 1968.

Klaassen, L.H., *Location of industries in depressed areas*, OECD, Paris 1968.

Klaassen, L.H. and Van Wickeren, A.C., 'Interindustry relations: an attraction model' in Bos, H.C. (ed.), *Towards Balanced International Growth*, Amsterdam 1969.

Klaassen, L.H. and Verster, A.C.P., *De optimale structuur van stedelijke gebieden*, Rotterdam 1970.

Klaassen, L.H., *De optimale structuur van stedelijke gebieden*, Rotterdam 1971.

467

Klaassen, L.H. and Vanhove, N., 'Macro-economic evaluation of port investments', in Regul, R. (ed.), *The Future of European Ports,* Bruges 1974.

Klaassen, L.H. and Drewe, P., *Migration Policy in Europe,* London 1973.

Klaassen, L.H., 'Urban planning and its impact on the quality of life', in Kuklinski, A. (ed.), *Social Issues in Regional Policy and Regional Planning,* The Hague, Paris 1977.

Klaassen, L.H., Paelinck, J.H.P. and Wagenaar, S., *Spatial Systems,* London 1978.

Krumme, G., 'Regional policies in West Germany', in Hansen, N. (ed.), *Public Policy and Regional Economic Development. The experience of nine western countries,* Cambridge 1974.

Kuklinski, A., *Growth Poles and Growth Centres in Regional Policies and Planning: an institutional perspective; remarks for discussion,* Geneva 1969.

Lebret, R.P., *Esquisse d'une charte a l'aménagement; L'enquête en vue de l'aménagement régional,* PUF 1958.

Lind, H., *Regional Policy in Britain and the Six,* London 1970.

Lösch, A., *Die raumliche Ordnung der Wirtschaft,* Jena 1940 (translated as *Economics of Location,* Yale University Press, 1954).

Luttrell, W.F., *Factory Location and Industrial Movement,* vol.I and vol. II, NIESR, London 1962.

Lutz, V., *Italy: a study in economic development,* Oxford 1962.

McCrone, G., *Regional Policy in Britain,* London 1966.

MacLennan, M.C., 'Regional development policies for backward regions', in *Regional Disequilibrium in Europe,* Brussels 1968.

Maillet, P., Hipp, G., Krijnse-Locker, H. and Sunnen, R., *L'économie de la Communauté,* Brussels 1968.

Menais, G.P., *La Banque Européenne d'Investissement,* Paris 1968.

Milhau, J., *Etude sur une politique des économies régionales,* PUF, Paris 1957.

Molle, W., Van Holst, B. and Smit, H., *Regional Economic Development in the European Community,* London 1979.

Moore, B. and Rhodes, J., 'The effects of regional economic policy in the United Kingdom', in Sant, M. (ed.), *Regional Policy and Planning for Europe,* London 1974.

Moore, B. and Rhodes, J., 'A quantitative analysis of the effects of the Regional Employment Premium and other regional policy instruments', in Whiting, A. (ed.), *The Economics of Industrial Subsidies,* London 1976.

Moore, B. and Rhodes, J., 'The economic and exchequer implications of British regional economic policy', in Vaizey, J. (ed.), *Economic Sovereignty and Regional Policy,* London 1976.

Mountjoy, A.B., *The Mezzogiorno,* Oxford 1973.

Mulder, E.H. and Klaassen, L.H., 'De gevolgen van de realisatie van de Euromarkt voor de intra-Europese handel', Rotterdam, NEI 1960.

Municipality of Rotterdam, *Structuurplan Rotterdam binnen de ruit*, Rotterdam 1977.

Myrdal, G., *Economic Theory and Underdeveloped Regions*, London 1957.

NEDC, *Conditions Favourable to Faster Growth*, HMSO, 1963.

NEI, *Kampen en Zwolle na tien jaar stimulering*, Rotterdam 1972.

NEI, *Population by Region and Employment by Region and Industry in the European Community, 1950, 1960, 1970*, Rotterdam 1975.

Neutze, G.M., *Economic Policy and the Size of Cities*, Camberra 1965.

Nicol, B. and Wehrmann, G., *Deglomeration Policy in Great Britain*, vol. I and II, Berlin 1978.

OCDE, *Le facteur régional dans le développement économique. Politique suivie dans quinze pays industrialisés de l'OCDE*, Paris 1970.

OCDE, *Politique de l'aménagement du territoire et du développement régional de la France*, Paris 1973.

OCDE, *Réévaluation des politiques régionales dans les pays de l'OCDE*, Paris 1974.

OCDE, *Les problèmes et les politiques de développement régionale dans les pays de l'OCDE*, vol.I and II, Paris 1976.

OCDE, *Les politiques régionales. Perspectives actuelles*, Paris 1977.

OCDE, *Les mesures restrictives de politique régionale*, Paris 1977.

OCDE, *Les politiques régionales. Perspectives régionales*, Paris 1977.

OCDE, *La politique régionale et le secteur des services*, Paris 1978.

OECD, *Salient features of regional development policy in Germany*, Paris 1968.

Ohlin, B., *Inter-regional and International Trade*, Cambridge 1933.

Olsen, E., 'Regional income differences within a Common Market', H. Richardson (ed.), *Regional Economics: a reader*, 1970.

Paelinck, J.H.P., 'Techniques of regional plan formulation. Problems of inter-regional consistency', Dundam, P. and Hilhorst, J. (eds), *Issues in Regional Planning*, The Hague 1971.

Paelinck, J.H.P., and Jaumotte, C., 'Avantages et inconvénients des régions industrielles en stagnation et des zones rurales pour l'implantation d'industries automatisées', in *Automation, Progrès Technique et Main-d'Oeuvre*, OECD, Paris 1966.

Paelinck, J.H.P., *Hoe doelmatig kan regionaal en sektorieel beleid zijn?*, *Bedrijfseconomische signalementen*, Leiden 1973.

Penouil, M.., 'Politique régionale et pôles de croissance', in Petrella, R. (ed.), *Le développement régional en Europe*, Paris 1971.

Perloff, H.S., Dunn, E.S., Lampard, E.E. and Muth, R.F., *Regions, Resources and Economic Growth*, Baltimore 1960.

Perroux, F., 'La méthode de l'économie géneralisée et l'économie de l'homme', *Science Economique et Développement*, Paris 1958.

Perroux, F., 'La coexistence pacifique', vol.II. *Pôles de développement ou nations*, Paris 1958.

Perroux, F., 'La firme motrice dans la région et la région motrice', *Théorie et Politique de l'Expansion Régionale*, Brussels 1961.

Petrella, R., 'La renaissance des cultures régionales en Europe', *Editions Entente*, Paris 1978.

Plassard, F., *Impact des investissements infrastructurels des transports sur le développement régional*, European seminar of the ministers of transport, Paris 1977.

Prud'homme, R., 'Regional economic policy in France', in Hansen, N. (ed.), *Public Policy and Regional Economic Development. The experience of nine western countries*, Cambridge 1974.

Randall, P., 'The history of British regional policy', in Hallett, G., Randall, P., and West, E.G. (eds), *Regional Policy for ever?*, London 1973.

Reilly, W.J., *The Law of Retail Gravitation*, New York 1931.

Richardson, H.W., *Regional Economics, Location Theory, Urban Structure and Regional Change*, London 1969.

Richardson, H.W., *Regional Growth Theory*, New York 1973.

River, C.A. and Associates, *The Role of Transportation on Regional Economic Development*, London 1971.

Robinson, E.A.G., 'Introduction', in Robinson, E.A.G. (ed.), *Backward Areas in Advanced Countries*, New York 1969.

Roger, Ch., *La politique de développement régional et de l'aménagement de l'espace*, Brussels 1962.

Romus, P., *L'Europe et les régions*, Brussels 1979.

Roper, B., 'Regionalpolitik für EWG-Binnengrenzgebiet, inbesondere für das Aachener Grenzgebiet', *Beitrage zur Regionalpolitik*, Berlin 1968.

Rousselot, 'L'aménagement du territoire et la régionalisation du 6ième plan', *Politique de l'aménagement du territoire et du développement régionale de la France*, OCDE, Paris 1973.

Sadler, P., Archer, B. and Owen, Ch., 'Regional income multipliers', *Bangor occasional papers in economics*, University of Wales Press 1973.

Schneider, H.K., 'Ueber die Notwendigkeit regionaler Wirtschaftspolitik', in Schneider, H.K. (ed.), *Beitrage zur Regionalpolitik*, Berlin 1968.

Scottish Development Department, *Threshold Analysis Manual*, HMSO, Edinburgh 1973.

Siebert, H., *Regional Economic Growth: theory and policy*, Scranton 1969.

Sjaastad, L.A., 'The costs and returns of human migration', Richardson, H.W., (ed.), *Regional Economics: a reader*, London 1970.

Sombart, W., *Der moderne Kapitalismus*, München 1928.

470

Stahl, H.M., *Regionalpolitische Implikationen einer EWG-Währungsunion*, Tübingen 1974.

Stilwell, F.J.B., *Regional Economic Policy*, London 1972.

Talbot, R.B., *The European Community's Regional Fund*, Oxford 1977.

The Hunt Committee, *The Intermediate Areas*, HMSO, 1969.

Theil, H., *Economics and Information Theory*, Amsterdam 1967.

Thompson, W.R., *A Preface to Urban Economics*, Baltimore 1965.

Thoss, R., 'La concentration géographique dans les pays de la Communaute européenne', *Collection Etudes, Série politique régionale*, no.4, Brussels 1977.

Thunen von, J.H., *Der isolierte Staat in Beziehung auf Landwirtschaft und Nationalökonomie*, Hamburg 1826.

Townroe, P.M., *Industrial Location and Regional Economic Policy*, Birmingham 1971.

United Nations Economic Commission for Europe, *Economic Survey of Europe since the War*, Geneva 1953.

van den Berg, C., *De structuur van de gemeentelijke uitgaven*, Leiden 1956.

van den Berg, L., Boeckhout, Sj. and Vijverberg, K., *Urban Development and Policy Response in the Netherlands*, Rotterdam 1977.

Van de Poll, E.H. and Bourdrez, J.A., 'Infrastructuur en regionale ontwikkeling' in Klaassen, L.H. (ed.), *Regionale economie*, Groningen 1972.

Van Juijn, J., *Deglomeration Policy in the Netherlands*, Berlin 1978.

Vanhove, N., *De doelmatigheid van het regionaal-ekonomisch beleid in Nederland*, Hilversum 1962.

Vanhove, N., 'Quelques considérations concernant l'efficience de la politique d'économie régionale pratiquée en Belgique et aux Pays-Bas' in *L'efficacité des mesures de politique économique régionale, Acte du 6ieme Colloque annuel de l'Association de Science Regionale de Langue Française*, 1967.

Vanhove, N., 'The development of the Flemish economy in an international perspective. Synthesis and policy options', *EEC Regional Policy Series*, Brussels, no.1, 1973.

Vanneste, O., *The Growth Pole Concept and the Regional Economic Policy*, Bruges 1971.

Vanneste, O., 'Het groeipoolconcept als strategisch element in het regionaal beleid' in *Liber Amicorum Prof. Dr. G. Eyskens*, Leuven 1975.

Vienna Center for Documentation and Coordination of Social Research, *The Costs of Urban Growth*, 1978.

Vijverberg, C., van den Berg, L. and Klaassen, L.H., 'Elements of a theory of urban development', *Foundations of Empirical Economic Research*, NEI, Rotterdam 1977.

Viner, J., *International Trade and Economic Development,* Oxford 1953.

Von der Groeben, H., 'Lignes directrices de la politique régionale de la Communauté', *European Parliament,* 6 May 1969.

Wallace, H., 'The establishment of the Regional Development Fund: common policy or park barrel', in Wallace, H., Wallace, W. and Webb, C. (eds), *Policy Making in the European Communities,* London 1977.

Weber, A., *Ueber den Standort der Industrien,* Tübingen 1909.

Wettmann, R., 'Deglomeration policy in the EEC. A comparative study', *International Institute of Management,* Berlin 1978.

Williamson, J., 'The implication of European monetary integration for the peripheral areas', in Vaizey, J. (ed.), *Economic Sovereignty and Regional Policy,* London 1976.

Yuill, D., 'A valuation of regional incentives in Great Britain', in Allen, K. (ed.), *European Regional Policy Project,* Berlin 1978.

Zangl, P., *Regionalpolitische Zielsetzungen und Strategien in Frankreich,* Köln 1974.

XXX, *Rahmenplan der Gemeinschaftsaufgabe. Verbesserung der regionalen Wirtschaftsstruktur,* Bonn 1971.

XXX, *Industrial and Regional Development,* HMSO, 1972.

XXX, 'La Banque Européenne d'Investissement', *Centre de Recherches Européennes,* Lausanne, 1977.

XXX, *European Investment Bank, 1958—78,* Brussels 1978.

XXX, *West Central Scotland Plan,* Glasgow 1974.

Periodicals and articles

Albertini, J., 'Options pour une méthode d'aménagement. Les pôles de développement', *Economie et Humanisme,* no.127, 1960.

Alonso, W. and Fajans, M., 'Cost of living and income by urban size', *Working Paper no. 128,* Center for Planning and Development Research, University of California, Berkeley 1970.

Alonso, W., 'The economics of urban size', *Papers Regional Science Association,* vol.26, 1971.

Archer, B., 'The anatomy of a multiplier', *Regional Studies,* vol.10, 1976.

Archibald, G.C., 'Regional multiplier effects in the United Kingdom', *Oxford Economic Papers,* vol.19, 1967.

Ashcroft, B. and Taylor, J., 'The movement of manufacturing industry and the effect of regional policy', *Oxford Economic Papers,* March 1977.

Atkins, H.W., 'Employment change in branch and parent manufacturing plants in the UK, 1966—71', *Trade and Industry,* 30 August 1973.

Aydalot, Ph., 'Note sur les économies externes et quelques notions connexes', *Revue économique,* no.6, 1965.

Baillargeon, 'Le rôle des pôles dans le développement', *Développement et Civilisation,* no.5, 1961.

Balassa, B., 'Regional policies and the environment in the European Common Market', *Weltwirtschaftliches Archiv,* vol.3, 1973.

Barkin, S., 'Principles for area redevelopment legislation', *Labor Law Journal,* August 1959.

Bartels, C.P.A. and Ter Walle, J., 'Een analyse van de migratie van beroepsbeoefenaren uit en naar het noorden per opleidingsniveau', *ESB,* p.3166, 1978.

Bauchet, P., 'La comptabilité économique régionale et son usage', *Economie Appliquée,* January 1961.

Beacham, A. and Osborn, W.T., 'The movement of manufacturing industry', *Regional Studies,* no.4, 1970.

Berry, B.J.L., 'Spatial organization and levels of welfare', Paper presented to the Economic Development Administration Research Conference, Washington 1967.

Biehl, D., Hussmann, E. and Schnyder, S., 'Zur regionalen Einkommensverteilung in der Europäischen Wirtschaftsgemeinschaft', *Die Weltwirtschaft,* Heft 1, 1972.

Bishop, K.C. and Simpson, C.E., 'Components of change analysis: problems of alternative approaches to industrial structure', *Regional Studies,* vol.6, 1972.

Bjork, G.C., 'Regional adjustment to economic growth: the United States, 1880–1950', *Oxford Economic Papers,* no.1, 1968.

Bloch-Laine, F., 'Justification des choix', *Urbanisme,* no.89, 1965.

Boudeville, J., 'Polarisation and urbanisation. The Canadian French examples', *Economie Appliquée,* no.1, 1975.

Bourginat, H., 'Inégalités régionales de développement et Marché Commun', *Bulletin Sedeis,* July 1962.

Brown, A.J., 'The Green Paper on the development areas', *National Institute Economic Review,* May 1967.

Buck, T.W. and Atkins, 'The impact of British regional policies on employment growth', *Oxford Economic Papers,* no.1, 1976.

Buck, T.W., 'Shift and share analysis – a guide to regional policy', *Regional Studies,* no.4, 1970.

Buck, T.W., 'Regional policy and European integration', *Journal of Common Market Studies,* June 1975.

Byé, M., 'Localisation de l'investissement et communauté économique européenne', *Revue Economique,* March 1958.

Cameron, G.C. and Clark, B.D., 'Industrial movement and the regional problem', *University of Glasgow, Social and Economic Studies,* 1966.

Cameron, G.C. and Reid, G.L., 'Scottish economic planning and the attraction of industry', *University of Glasgow, Social and Economic Studies,* 1966.

Cameron, G.C., 'Growth areas, growth centres and regional conversion', *Scottish Journal of Political Economy*, vol.21, 1970.

CEE, 'Première communication de la Commission sur la politique régionale dans la communauté européenne, 1965. Proposition d'une décision du Conseil relative à l'organisation de moyens d'action de la communauté en matière de développement régional', *Journal officiel des communautés européennes*, no. C 152, 28.11.1969.

Clark, C., 'The economic functions of a city in relation to its size', *Econometrica*, no.2, 1945.

Clark, C., 'The economic functions of a city in relation to its size', *Econometrica*, vol.13, 1954.

Clark, C., 'Industrial location and economic potential', *Lloyd's Bank Review*, no.82, 1966.

Clark, C., Wilson, F. and Bradley, J., 'Industrial location and economic potential in Western Europe', *Regional Studies*, vol.2, 1969.

Derycke, P.H., 'Les coûts de la croissance urbaine', *Revue d'Economie Politique*, no.1, 1973.

Dessant, J.W. and Smart, R., 'Evaluating the effects of regional economic policy: a critique', *Regional Studies*, vol.11, 1977.

Dischamps, J.L., 'Rôle et moyens d'action des pouvoirs publics, semi-publics et des institutions prévues dans l'amenagement du territoire en France', *Revue d'Economie Politique*, no.3 and 4, 1974.

Douglas, R., 'Selected indices of industrial characteristics for US Standard Metropolitan Statistical Areas, 1963', Discussion Paper no.20, *Regional Science Research Institute*, Philadelphia, 1967.

Dunn, E.S., 'A statistical and analytical technique for regional analysis', *Regional Science Association Paper*, vol.6, 1960.

EEC, 'Guidelines for Community regional policy', *Bulletin of European Communities*, Supplement 2/77.

Falise, M. and Lepas, A., 'Les motivations de localisation des investissements internationaux dans l'Europe du Nord-Ouest', *Revue Economique*, no.1, 1970.

Fleming, J.M., 'On exchange rate unification', *Economic Journal*, September 1971.

Giersch, H., 'Economic union between nations and the location of industries', *Review of Economic Studies*, vol.17, 1949/1950.

Girard, A. and Bastide, H., 'Les problèmes demographiques devant l'opinion', *Population*, XV, avril-mai 1960.

Goze, M. and Leymarie, D., 'Croissance des agglomerations et villes centres', *Revue juridique et économique du Sud-Ouest*, no.2, 1978.

Greenwood, M.J., 'An analysis of the determinants of geographic labour mobility in the United States', *The Review of Economics and Statistics*, no.2, 1969.

Greig, M.A., 'Regional multiplier effects in the United Kingdom, a comment', *Oxford Economic Papers*, no.2, 1977.

Hagerstrand, T., 'Aspects of the spatial structure of social communication and the diffusion of information', *PPRSA*, no.16, 1966.

Hansen, N.M., 'Development pole theory in a regional context', *Kyklos*, no.3, 1967.

Hansen, N., 'Human resources and regional development: some lessons from French experience', *The Southern Economic Journal*, July 1967.

Hansen, N., 'A Growth centre strategy for the United States', Discussion paper, Programme on the role of growth centres in regional economic development, Kentucky, 1969.

Harrison, A.J. and Whitehead, M.E., 'Is there an inner city problem?' *The Three Banks Review*, September 1978.

Harrop, J., 'The European Investment Bank', *National Westminster Bank Quarterly Review*, May 1978.

Heijke, J.A.M. and Klaassen, L.H., 'Human reactions to spatial diversity mobility in regional labour markets', *NEI/FEES*, 1977/4.

Hirsch, W.Z., 'Expenditure implications of metropolitan growth and consolidation', *Review of Economics and Statistics*, vol.41, 1959.

Holland, S.K., 'Regional under-development in a developed economy: the Italian case', *Regional Studies*, no.2, 1971.

Illeris, S., 'Funktionelle Regionen: Danmark Omkering', *Geografisk Tidskrift, LXVI*, 1960.

Isard, W. and Schooler, E.W., 'Industrial complex analysis, agglomeration economies and regional development', *Journal of Regional Science*, 1959.

Jarrett, R.J., 'Disincentives: the other side of regional development policy', *Journal of Common Market Studies*, June 1975.

Klaassen, L.H., 'Het desurbanisatieproces in de grote steden', *ESB*, 1978, no.3136.

Klemmer, P., 'Die Theorie der Entwicklungspole — strategisches Konzept für die regionale Wirtschaftspolitik?', *Raumforschung und Raumordnung*, June 1972.

Konings, M., 'La politique régionale', *Cahiers économiques de Bruxelles*, no.52, 1971.

Lemerle, P.N., 'Le Fonds Social Européen', *Reflets et perspectives de la vie économique*, no.2, 1970.

Lomax, K.S., 'Expenditure per head and size of population', *Journal of the Royal Statistical Society*, vol.106, 1943.

Marquand, 'Report on repercussions of economic and monetary union on regional development', *Consultative Assembly of the Council of Europe*, Document 3282, 1973.

Milhau, J., 'Problèmes de l'élaboration et de l'exécution des plans régionaux', *Conseil Economique et Social*, 26.4.1960.

Molle, W.T.M. and Van Holst, B., 'Factors of location in Europe, a progress report', *16th European Congress of the Regional Science*

Association, Copenhagen, August 1976.

Molle, W.T.M., 'Regional disparities in the European Community', *Association de Science Régionale de Langue Française,* Fribourg, 1978.

Monod, J., 'Région parisienne, bassin parisien et aménagement du territoire', *Revue Juridique et Economique du Sud-Ouest,* no.3, 1970.

Moore, B. and Rhodes, J., 'Evaluating the effects of British regional economic policy', *The Economic Journal,* March 1973.

Moore, B. and Rhodes, J., 'Regional economic policy and the movement of manufacturing firms to development areas', *Economica,* February 1976.

Morgan, E.V., 'Regional problems and common currencies', *Lloyd's Bank Review,* October 1973.

Moroney, J.R., and Walker, J.M., 'A regional test of the Heckscher-Ohlin hypothesis', *Journal of Political Economy,* 1966.

Needleman, L., 'What are we to do about the regional problem', *Lloyd's Bank Review,* no.75, 1965.

Nevin, E., 'Europe and the regions', *The Three Banks Review,* no.2, 1972.

Paelinck, J.H.P., 'La théorie du développement régional polarisé', *Cahiers de l'ISEA,* March 1965.

Perroux, D., 'Economic space: theory and applications', *The Quarterly Journal of Economics,* no.1, 1950.

Perroux, F., 'Note sur la notion de pôle de croissance', *Economie Appliqueé,* no.1—2, 1955.

Perroux, F., 'Les formes de concurrence dans le marché commun', *Revue d'économie politique,* no.1, 1959.

Phillips, A.W., 'The relationship between unemployment and the rate of change of money wages in the United Kingdom, 1861—1957', *Economica,* 1958.

Prud'homme, R., 'Critique de la politique d'aménagement du territoire', *Revue d'Economie Politique,* no.6, 1974.

Richardson, N.W. and West, E.G., 'Must we always take work to the workers?', *Lloyd's Bank Review,* January 1964.

Romus, P., 'Les facteurs de localisation industrielle dans le développement régional de la Communauté Européenne', *Cahiers Economiques de Bruxelles,* no.69, 1976.

Sadler, P., Archer, B. and Owen, C., 'Regional income multipliers — the Anglesey study', *Bangor Occasional Papers in Economics,* 1973.

Smith, B., 'Regional specialization and trade in the United Kingdom', *Scottish Journal of Political Economy,* February 1975.

Steele, D.B., 'Regional multipliers in Great Britain, *Oxford Economic Papers,* March 1969.

Stilwell, F.J.B., 'Regional growth and structural adaptation', *Urban*

Studies, vol.6, 1969.

Stilwell, F.J.B., 'Further thoughts on the shift and share approach', *Regional Studies,* vol.4, 1970.

Tagliacarne, G., 'Le regioni forti e le regioni deboli della Communità allargata. Indicatiori socio—economici per la politica regionale della Communità', *Note Economiche,* no.4, 1973.

Thirlwall, A.P., 'A measure of the proper distribution of industry', *Oxford Economic Papers,* March 1967.

Thomas, R.L. and Storey, P.J.M., 'Unemployment dispersal as a determinent of wage inflation in the United Kingdom, 1925—66', *Manchester School of Social and Economic Studies,* no.39, 1971.

Toothill Report, 'Report of the Committee inquiry into the Scottish economy', *Scottish Council of Development of Industry,* 1969.

Tress, R.C., 'The next stage in regional policy', *Three Banks Review,* March 1969.

Van der Auwera, G., 'Les régions frontalières et l'intégration européenne', *Revue du Marché Commun,* no.182, 1975.

Vandermotten, C., 'La politique du territoire en Belgique. Objectifs, instruments et couts', *Cahiers Economiques de Bruxelles,* no.62, 1974.

Van Ginderachter, J., 'Economic integration and regional imbalance', *Tijdschrift voor Economie en Management,* no.1, 1975.

Vanhove, N., 'De rol van een welvaartsorgaan in de regionale ekonomische expansie — Het voorbeeld van West-Vlaanderen', *De Gewesten in Europa,* Bulletin no.2, 1970.

Vaubel, R., 'Die Pläne für eine europäische Parallelwährung', *Die Weltwirtschaft,* no.2, 1972.

Vining, R., 'Location of industry and regional patterns of business-cycle behaviour', *Econometrica,* no.1, 1946.

Wäldchen, P., 'Die Studie Bari-Tarente und die Methode der industriellen Schwerpunkte', *Information,* 3.10.1966.

Weeden, R., 'Regional rates of growth of employment: an analysis of variance treatment', *National Institute of Economics and Social Research Regional Papers,* no.3, 1974.

Weiss, S. and Gooding, E., 'Estimation of differential employment multipliers in a small regional economy', *Land Economics,* vol.43, 1968.

Wilson, Th., 'The regional multiplier — a critique', *Oxford Economic Papers,* March 1966.

Wilson, T., 'The British regional policy in the European context', *The Banker,* February 1973.

Wingo, L., 'Issues in a national urban development strategy for the United States', *Urban Studies,* no.9, 1972.

Woolley, P.K., 'The European Investment Bank', *Three Banks Review,* no.1, 1975.

Zipf, G.K., 'The P_1P_2/D hypothesis on the intercity movement of persons', *American Sociological Review,* vol.11, 1946.

XXX, 'The All Saints' day manifesto for European monetary union', *The Economist,* 1—7 November 1975.

Index

ciation 86; of variation 84-6
Collective wage bargaining 234, 454, 455
Comitato Interministeriale de Programmazione Economica (CIPE) 267, 269, 321, 322
Committee for Regional Development 391, 404
Committee for Regional Policy 386, 393, 406, 407, 409, 423, 429, 430, 433, 437, 453, 461
Communication costs 124-8, 157, 158, 160, 162, 174, 211, 308
Commuting 22, 29, 78, 96, 113, 122, 184, 236, 261, 277, 281, 283, 292, 444
Complementary regions 116
Components-of-change analysis 90
Concentration areas 25-9, 50, 190, 288
Congested regions 19, 116, 271, 276, 284, 289, 292, 322, 328, 399, 404, 451, 452, 456
Congestion costs 18, 21-3, 41, 339, 340, 374, 451
Conurbation: regions 28, 102, 103, 269, 271, 285, 379, 453, 456, 459, 460; zones 273
Conversion (problem) 264, 276, 277, 459
Core: centre 144, 287; point 144; region 9, 11, 17, 21, 25, 27, 28, 43, 89, 146, 235, 249, 269, 287, 318
Cost-benefit analysis 19, 42, 45, 338-40, 347, 379
Cost-push inflation 25-8, 247
Cost rigidities 8, 12, 238

Customs union 15, 128, 227, 229-37, 242, 250, 386, 390, 395-7, 420

Decentralisation of industry 4
Decentralisation (policy) 19, 21, 181, 188, 219, 227, 264, 268, 269, 271, 285, 304, 305, 311, 321, 323, 332, 336, 357, 378, 408, 458-60
Declining regions 102, 240, 259, 404
Deconcentration 190, 284, 285, 291, 312, 422
Decongestion (policy) 262, 269, 288, 320, 323
Deflation 25, 247, 259
De-industrialisation 336
Délégation à l'Aménagement du Territoire et à l'Action Régionale (DATAR) 259, 263, 265, 321, 324, 325, 332, 333
Demand: attraction 160; elasticity of export 12; multiplier 155; oriented industries 123, 157, 159, 160; pull inflation 25, 27, 28
Depreciation 78, 413, 457
Depressed areas 8, 10, 20, 26, 102, 238, 239, 247, 271, 272, 274, 275, 286, 288, 296, 454, 455
Derelict Land Clearance Areas 280
Designated regions 30, 279-81, 284, 319, 378
Desurbanisation 180, 186, 187, 220-3
Devaluation 14, 236, 239, 248, 249, 328, 329, 340, 454, 455
Development: areas 272, 273, 276-8, 280, 281, 283, 284,